CHINESE MODERNITY
AND THE
PEASANT PATH

Kathy Le Mons Walker

Chinese Modernity and the Peasant Path

SEMICOLONIALISM IN THE NORTHERN
YANGZI DELTA

STANFORD UNIVERSITY PRESS

STANFORD, CALIFORNIA

1999

Stanford University Press
Stanford, California
© 1999 by the Board of Trustees of the
Leland Stanford Junior University

Printed in the United States of America

CIP data are at the end of the book

To my parents,
Dorothy and Joseph Le Mons

and to my son,
Brendan Matthew Walker

Preface

A DECADE AGO when I began this book on Nantong and the northern Yangzi delta, I intended to explore the social history of Chinese development in light of the often discussed but still illusive construct of underdevelopment. I soon realized, however, that the empirical data I was encountering simply could not be fitted into a framework that in the last analysis, whether in liberal or positivist Marxist form, treats capitalist development as the normalizing, universal project of the modern world. By assuming that only certain things count, implicitly using a Eurocentric yardstick for their determination, and failing to question their desirability, this framework necessarily suppresses, erases, or devalues alternative histories and concepts of the world.

In short, it became increasingly apparent to me that because the very idea of development (or underdevelopment) restrictively enforces a certain definition of modernity, it would only permit an examination of China in terms of negative analysis and residual categories. Within its framing, the modernist path of late-nineteenth- and early-twentieth-century elites could be only viewed as a failure or some form of "arrested" development, and the lives and aspirations of the majority who formed the central concern of my project would necessarily become peripheral to the main narrative. My data indicated that on both counts social reality bore little relation to this framing. What was clearly needed was an expanded understanding of modernity and concepts to account for alternative paths of economic, sociopolitical, and cultural development.

Thus to make sense of my data rather early on, I found it necessary to move outside the confines of developmentalism. The larger intellectual environment in which I was working, that is, in which standard narrative teleologies were already becoming a target of rethinking, helped me to make this shift. The book that has resulted represents my attempt to delineate the making of a distinctive modernity in the northern Yangzi delta in the late nineteenth and early twentieth centuries—one that represented not a single domain but multiple movements of history.

Many people have contributed to the development and completion of this book. I first wish to acknowledge my debt to those who assumed important roles in my graduate training at the University of California–Los Angeles, including especially Philip Huang, who chaired my dissertation committee, taught me much about China, and kindled my interests in peasant studies and the question of development; and Robert Brenner, who deepened those interests and helped me to think about them more effectively in comparative and theoretical perspective.

For the materials in both Chapters One and Nine, I am especially grateful for the work of Japanese scholars. My overview of the political economy of the southern core of the Yangzi delta during the Ming in Chapter One owes a great deal to and would not have been possible without the pioneering work of scholars such as Kobayashi Kazumi, Niida Noboro, Nishijima Sadao, Oyama Maasaki, and Tanaka Masatoshi. Their collective endeavor represents an unsurpassed moment of clarity and advancement in international China studies. Similarly, my analysis of subproletarian families in Nantong in the 1940's in Chapter Nine would not have been possible without the work of the researchers of the South Manchurian Railway Company. Their rural surveys of the late 1930's and early 1940's are among the very best ethnographic materials available for China.

I owe a debt of gratitude to the many people at various institutions in China who helped me collect materials or otherwise facilitated my research during a year's residence at Nanjing University and three field trips to Nantong. I thank the staff at Nanjing University, who arranged my first two field trips and those at the Shanghai Academy of Social Sciences, who arranged the third. Professors Cai Shaoqing of Nanjing University and Xu Xinwu of the Shanghai Academy were especially helpful; I thank them both for assistance in obtaining essential materials and taking the time to discuss various aspects of my project with me. Their research and writing and that of other Chinese scholars, including Fu Yiling, Li Wenzhi, Wu Chengming, and Yan Zhongping, and especially Qiao Qiming and Shen Shike, who made field surveys of Nantong and adjacent Haimen-Qidong in the 1920's and 1930's, have been important to this book. In Nantong Liu Daosong, Wu Huisheng, and other members of the staffs of the Nantong Library and Historical Archives Department of the No. 1 Factory were both gracious and helpful. I particularly thank Mu Xuan, vice-director of the Nantong Museum, for his instrumental role in setting up interviews and round-table meetings with former merchants in the cotton, textile, and banking trades and in helping me obtain needed materials. I thank, too, all those who participated in those interviews and round-table meetings. Finally, I am grateful to the archivists in Nantong and Nanjing who made available to me full runs of newspapers and the sets of *wenshi ziliao* (materials on culture and history) on Nantong, Rugao, and Jiangsu province.

I deeply appreciate the sustained support of Temple University and the research grants and grants-in-aid that underwrote my research in China in 1988 and made possible subsequent trips to the Harvard-Yenching and other libraries for materials. Making the notion of a community of scholars a reality, colleagues with an interest in Third World, Comparative, and Women's studies at Temple University have been an ongoing source of inspiration and intellectual engagement. I thank especially my friends and colleagues Thomas Patterson in the Anthropology Department and Peter Gran in the History Department, both of whom made valuable comments on my manuscript and in different ways helped me more than they know to think about culture and the state. Graduate students have formed an important part of the intellectual environment that helped to propel production of this book. I thank especially Jennifer Alvey and Annanth Aiyer; our shared interest in peasant political cultures, merchant capital, and gender theory created the opening for many fruitful discussions and helped me refine ideas in this book.

Many colleagues in the China field have graciously given of their time and expertise. Professor Samuel Chu's pioneering study of Zhang Jian was invaluable to me when I first began to investigate Nantong, and his subsequent sharing of materials is deeply appreciated. I thank, in particular, Arif Dirlik, Prasenjit Duara, Lynda Grove, Robert Marks, Ming Chan, Elizabeth Perry, Mark Selden, and Richard von Glahn for their support and insightful critical comments. My friend and colleague Lynda Bell has been a source of continual support throughout the project. Her parallel work on a study of silk industry development in Wuxi placed her in a unique position to both critically comment on and appreciate the evolution of my research on Nantong. The countless hours we spent debating the issues of historical process in local society in light of our research findings had a great impact on this book. I also deeply appreciate the support and patience that Muriel Bell, executive editor of Stanford University Press, has shown for this project, associate editor Nathan MacBrien's careful handling of the manuscript, and its improvement by the expert copy editing of Barbara E. Mnookin.

I have dedicated this book to my parents, Joseph and Dorothy Le Mons, and my son, Brendan Walker. They steadfastly supported me over the life of the project, and for their unending understanding, I am deeply grateful. Finally, I acknowledge the influence of the late Taijiquan Master Marshall Ho'o, who taught me about patience, perseverance, dialectics, and history.

K.L.W.

Contents

Maps and Tables

CHINESE MODERNITY
AND THE
PEASANT PATH

Modernity, the Semicolonial
Process, and Alternative Histories

IN THE LAST half century the foundations of historical knowledge have been radically altered. This alteration has come in part from challenges to the social order and from complexities of social and political reality that did not conform to, and thus called into question, standard notions of civilization, progress, and modernity.[1] In historical scholarship, it has coalesced in confrontations with paradigm and encounters between theory and history.[2] These confrontations and encounters expose the taken-for-granted assumptions and many of the silent omissions of a Eurocentric metanarrative of linear, positivist history and its role in underpinning modern forms of power. As a result, they bind us to rethink the very meaning of modernity.

Much of the rethinking emanating from and about the Third World stresses the synchronicity of colonialism and modernity. Scholarly work on various geographic regions spotlights not only the collusion of colonial and modernist discourses but also the resistance to them. This work has increasingly argued that attention to resistance should in fact occupy center stage in histories of colonialism and semicolonialism since it is central to processes that historically deflected or altered the trajectories of Western economic and nation-state expansion and continue to produce variation in contemporary societies (Chatterjee 1993, 1988, 1986; Gledhill 1994; Guha 1992, 1983, 1982; Mallon 1995).

Informed by and seeking to further this rethinking, this book, broadly speaking, attempts a social history of semicolonialism in late-nineteenth- and early-twentieth-century China. It takes the intertwining of elite constructions of modernity under global shaping and an alternate line of peasant resistance and development as its central concern. Nantong county and the northern portion of the commercially advanced Yangzi delta form its investigative focal points. Lying in the hinterland of and connected in myriad ways with the Shanghai treaty port, which in the late nineteenth century became the center of imperialist activity in China, the northern delta forms an ideal locale for examining how the acquisition, transmission, and contestation of power may have changed during the extended moment of semicolonial encounter.

As elsewhere, this activity took place not as a single shock but as an on-going series of encounters, exactions, and adjustments, and involved unevenly developed spaces organized around shifting centers and peripheries (Rose-berry 1993: 350). The process was neither homogeneous nor unidirectional. It occurred in the context of, was uniquely conditioned by, and influenced the trajectories of change within specific "local societies," which were them-selves the products of longer-term class and regional conflicts.

Unraveling the multiple strands of this semicolonial process and, thereby, the dominant and alternative histories it embodied forms the specific project of this book. In emphasizing the structural context—semicolonialism—that shaped events in the late nineteenth and early twentieth centuries, it inten-tionally opens up a pivotal silent area in the historiography of modern China.

This silence is in part the legacy of a field long dominated by a Cold War, Western-centered, modernizationist scholarship. In the decades after World War Two, modernist China scholars bypassed semicolonial power relations as a category of inquiry by presenting imperialism as a universalizing, benefi-cent modernity to which a static, traditional state had to respond so as to shed its (Orientalized) culturalist past and enter the modern world.[3] Mounting a critique of this impact-response model during the volatile years of the Viet-nam War, radical scholars catapulted imperialism onto center stage.[4] Yet that critique also steered inquiry away from the semicolonial as a category, since the ideological debate it generated continued to make capitalist development the model for evaluating modern Chinese history and, accordingly, narrowly focused on whether imperialism had impeded or stimulated this project. Chi-nese Marxist scholars exhibited these same trends. Although they adopted a semicolonial-semifeudal labeling for post–Opium War China, they limited their research to delineating how imperialism had blocked or short-circuited a presumed path of capitalist development.[5]

Subsequently, the pathbreaking analyses of critical scholars who adopted a social history approach to examine the material conditions that predated and framed the revolution began to reveal the outlines and features of semi-colonial society and economy.[6] This tenuous composite image appeared only indirectly, however, since like the earlier ones, these studies tended to main-tain a focus on imperialism as an abstract or external economic force. On the other hand, the trajectory they generated was soon partially derailed by the appearance of a so-called China-centered approach (P. Cohen 1984). In reaction to the Western-centeredness of the Cold War modernizationism, it fostered a counter turn—to the point of ignoring global shaping and domi-nance altogether (see Esherick & Rankin 1990).

The suppression of the semicolonial has become even more pronounced recently as a new narrative of modernization has gained ground. Radically revising the Cold War formulations depicting China as static and traditional, it has appeared in conjunction with an enormous amount of new empirical data; but it is often also strongly presentist in the sense of transparently creating a genealogy for postsocialist China and, indirectly, for the global capitalism that empowers it. Appearing in cross-disciplinary form, its central feature is a rearranging of available data to show a continuous line of Euro-modeled modernization from the Ming to the present.[7] In emphasizing this line and its similarity with a presumed "European" path, the new modernizationism—like most prior work, whether mainstream, radical, or Marxist—continues to take capitalist development as the central analytic model for interpreting modern Chinese history. At the same time, it is quietly erasing revolution, imperialism, and the semicolonial as factors of key significance. Within its interpretative contours, semicolonialism becomes even more of a silent area than in the past when, if problematically formulated, imperialism was a matter of debate. As a result, at the very moment scholars of other parts of the world are liberating the histories of the areas they study from the stifling constructions of a metanarrative of development and modernity (e.g., Stern 1993), modern Chinese history is being stuffed back into that flawed and ill-fitting conceptual mold.

In shifting the focus of analysis to the semicolonial, this book thus critically intervenes in China historiography. At the broadest level, in confronting the development of capitalism as a historical phenomenon and suggesting that the consequences of the commoditization of land and labor on a global scale under its expansive influence need to be worked out theoretically and historically, it forces an understanding of Chinese modernity that is specific and open-ended, rather than closed, one-dimensional, and predetermined by the constructs and categories of a Euromodeled narrative. In both its liberal and positivist Marxist variants, this narrative elevates to the level of universal truth a particularized discourse that is as problematic for its point of origination—"Europe"—as for the Third World (Brenner 1977, 1976; Kahn 1993: 29). Based on the empirical evidence for Nantong and the northern delta, this book will demonstrate that semicolonial modernity developed not out of a single trajectory but out of two intertwining trajectories, one emanating from the elite and the other from the peasantry. It was thus fashioned from multiple constructions with different and even conflicting principles and histories (Arnason 1987: 8–9; Kahn 1993: 261–63).

Recovering these trajectories and constructions exposes the suppression in modernist narratives of transformations of Chinese society and of its global context that need to be distinguished structurally (Dirlik 1996). It also draws attention to the fact that the habitual dichotomizing of conventional social science, and to some extent positivist political economy, has often rested on an obscuring of the ambiguity and contingency of the "fixed" identities underpinning it: rural/urban, worker/peasant, traditional/modern, and so on. Our examination will show that, though such ambiguity was already present in the petty commodity economy of the Ming-Qing, especially in the southern delta (Jiangnan), it became even more pronounced as a feature of semicolonialism. In Nantong the new expressions of semicolonial modernity were marked not by the separation of two distinct spheres but by their integration. Notions of "modern" cities and a "backward" countryside were in fact a myth that concealed from view real power relations and the integration of urban and rural on which those relations were based.

No less important, in recovering the different trajectories of semicolonial modernity and the politics inherent in them, this book reinserts and brings into full view the alternative histories that narrative teleologies necessarily erase. To recuperate these alternate pasts, especially those of peasants, we must finally move outside of the developmentalism that has so long dominated thinking and writing about China.

Peasants and History

Alternative pasts indicate a counter-appropriation of history that simply cannot be reduced to a logic of capitalist development or universalized modernity (Escobar 1995: 95). They must be explained on their own terms. To attempt such an explanation for the history of peasants in the Yangzi delta, we will have to discard older essentialized images of them as unchanging, immutable, and prepolitical, and begin to think instead about an independent line of development.

To a large extent those older images merely formed a foil for constructions of Western-based modernity, and thus of the traditional as something that, like peasants themselves, was destined to be displaced.[8] Positivist political economy mechanically replicated this view, the entire question of "agrarian transition" actually centering on a presumed disappearance of the peasantry as part of an assumed transition to capitalism. Overcoming such stylized conceptions necessitates discarding notions of popular culture and subaltern history as derivatives of elite-dominated society. These notions contradict history by making all occurrences appendages of existing hegemonies. In short, they negate the possibility of independent lines of development, radical discontinuities, or cleavage emanating from the subordinated.

Antonio Gramsci, among others, suggests an alternative view. As he writes:

> The history of subaltern groups is necessarily fragmented and episodic. There undoubtedly does exist a tendency toward (at least provisional stages of) unification

in the historical activity of these groups, but this tendency is continuously inter-rupted by the activity of the ruling groups; it therefore can only be demonstrated when an historical cycle is completed and this cycle culminates in a success. Sub-altern groups are always subject to the activity of ruling groups, even when they rebel and rise up; only "permanent" victory breaks their subordination, and that not immediately. . . . Every trace of independent initiative on the part of subaltern groups should therefore be of incalculable value for the integral historian. (1971: 54–55)

Gramsci thus suggests the possibility—beneath the fragmented, episodic, and spontaneous appearance of subaltern history—of a line of development toward "integral autonomy" even within a group that is subject, in myriad ways, to the ideas and interventions of the dominant classes. In seeking to un-cover an independent trajectory of this sort, as he also suggests, the specific sources of any new "tendency toward unification" must be identified. Such a tendency might involve, of course, an interweaving of historically trans-mitted sources and those arising in new conjunctural conditions, both at the material level of society and at the level of thought or consciousness.

Gramsci's approach provides a useful starting point for thinking about the way in which the emergence of tendencies toward unification and an indepen-dent line of development might be bound up with the formation of *particular peasantries*. Identifying such particular peasants, who as part of a structural whole are apt to bear cross-cultural and transhistorical traits in common, but are nevertheless historically constituted, becomes a central problem of peas-ant history. This book suggests that identifying particular peasantries must be based on an integrated analysis of the different but not fully separable economic, political, and cultural processes through which they are created and of how these processes intersect and interrelate (Kahn 1993: 30; Rose-berry 1993). For clearly, both historically and in the contemporary world, it is not just their relation to agriculture or their (partial) subordination in agrarian-based orders that characterizes peasants. "Factors broadly con-ceived as political and cultural," as Joel Kahn notes, are also "vital to the notion of a uniquely peasant mode of existence" (1993: 36).

Indeed it is precisely the duality of peasants as subordinate yet never fully "captured" or controlled that has proved so perplexing to modernists. This duality contains the grain of truth from which the analyses of peasants as "primordial," and hence never fully explicable, springs. In reality the par-tial autonomy that peasants characteristically exhibit derives not from some primordial inexplicability, but in large measure from the labor process. His-torically it has been linked to their ability to mobilize their own labor power through the household and to their access to land, which together give them a certain command over subsistence. In short the labor process has enabled peasants to shield critical resources and to find ways to combat state and ruling-class oppression.[9] That they retained their own historical memories and forms of cultural expression reinforced the autonomy derived from the labor process (Isaacman 1993: 207–8).

The growing literature of peasant studies emphasizes the importance of the concept of community within these cultures as a concomitant of both autonomy and political culture. It points to the legitimacy of this concept among many different peasantries in providing reasons and organizational forms for resistance, and through its often spiritual-like quality, in contributing to the vision of a more egalitarian, alternate, or transformed society (Chatterjee 1988; Turton & Tanabe 1984). Standing in direct contrast to state-structured power, this alternative communal vision partially explains why peasants the world over have often felt and shown themselves to be "estranged from the center, and impoverishment notwithstanding, have built up a network of defenses against the assault of the state" (Diamond 1974: 48).

On the other hand, much of the recent revisionist work in peasant studies regards community not as immutable, but as having historical determinants and historically evolved solidarities (Ranger 1987, 1985). Like peasants themselves, "community" changes with time, is imaginatively constructed, and, in the last analysis, "can only be grasped as historical process" (Chatterjee 1986; Sabean 1984: 29). Tracing changing conceptions of community, like recovering peasant history, thus becomes a process of revealing particular peasantries—peasantries that while maintaining an underlying similarity to all their kind, possess distinct, historical differences as well. Viewed in this way the culture of any class society, like its politics, appears not as a "unified corpus" but as "contested, temporal, and emergent" (Clifford & Marcus 1986: 187).

Finally, if particular kinds of peasantries have emerged under specific historical circumstances, so have particular kinds of households and household economies.[10] "Once the peasant household is taken as an historical problem," as William Roseberry has put it, "studies of gender relations move to a new plane" (1993: 357). This insight comes in large part from materialist-feminist scholars who analyze the family as a locus of unity and disunity, where gender ultimately serves as the basis for controlling and allocating labor power (Hartman 1981). Their analyses spotlight the family as the basic unit articulating gender with a given economic system, and by extension the sexual division of labor as a structural problem of both the family and larger society (Mies 1986). They also show that, historically, the development of survival, resistance, or more offensive peasant strategies has often contradictorily involved, and even depended on, the subordination of women (Feldman 1991; Mallon 1987a; Walker 1993a). Thus in seeking to delineate the key convergent processes through which particular peasantries have been created, the formation and transformation of peasant households must also be treated as historically problematic.

In sum a focus on particular peasantries enables us to move beyond conceptions of peasants based on imputed characteristics derived from historically empty sociological models or the essentialized images that sustain larger hegemonic projects (Asad 1973; Roseberry 1993). It permits analyses of peasants within the context of whole social formations, that is, within the totality of society and state. It is really only when viewed from the position of the peasant or other subalterns that such a "total history" can be grasped. The weight of a peasant history within a total history will reflect precisely the extent to which the activity of those particular peasants has been more or less decisive (Gramsci 1971: 151). This book takes the problem of the formation of particular peasants as its grounding point, both for establishing the longer-term pattern of change and for analyzing the transformations, limitations, and possibilities of the semicolonial process. It will argue that in two pivotal moments—the late Ming and the first decades of the twentieth century—peasants decisively influenced the course of change.

The So-Called Ming-Qing Impasse

Since the 1950's Chinese and Western research has gradually discredited older notions of a stagnant China in the centuries preceding the Opium War. No one now contests that vigorous commercialization began in the Ming (1368–1644), associated, principally, with the spread of cotton cultivation and textiles, or that a host of other changes took place in agrarian class relations, in international trade, and in the arts, culture, and religion.[11] Almost all scholars now agree that the magnitude of these changes marks the late Ming as a watershed in Chinese history.

As noted above, in Western scholarship, an "early modern" construct has begun to inform this research. Similarly, in China an "incipient capitalist" framing now challenges the older "feudal" model. Yet both of these constructs fail to explain the changes of the late Ming. Alike in their attempt to reimpose a linear, Eurocentric progression on Chinese history, they founder on the lack of evidence of capitalist development following the vigorous commercialization of the Ming. In fact, as Philip Huang has argued, the paradoxical problem of a lack of "further" movement along a presumed capitalist path —and thus the so-called impasse in interpreting Ming-Qing history—lies not in the historical record, but in the models themselves, specifically, the flawed taken-for-granted assumption shared by both that commercialization leads to or generates capitalist development (1990, 1991).[12] Indeed to the extent that Chinese Marxist scholars, like their Western counterparts, equate markets and trade with capitalist development, they stand closer to Smith than Marx.

Marx adamantly opposed universalist "master-key" formulations whose "supreme virtue" consisted, as he put it, "in being suprahistorical" (Shanin 1983: 136). In his abstract theorizations he did suggest that, because of the parasitic nature of merchant capital, its level of development occurs in inverse proportion to the general level of economic development (1967, 2: 328, 609). But in terms of understanding an actual situation or history, for Marx the only conceivable method was one that attempted to grasp what was socially and politically specific through concrete, historical analysis. On the role of merchants and markets in real historical settings he explicitly stated:

> To what extent it [merchant capital] brings about a dissolution of the old mode of production depends on its solidity and internal structure. And whither this process of dissolution will lead, in other words, what new mode of production will replace the old, does not depend on commerce, but on the character of the old mode of production itself. (1967, 3: 366)

A fundamental critique of the notion that market expansion generates development lies, of course, at the center of dependency, world-system, and related Third World economic analyses.[13] Moreover, even in the case of its presumed prototype—Europe—scholars have thoroughly refuted the notion of capitalist development as originating in trade and markets. This refutation began more than a half century ago as a debate with Marxism (e.g., Dobb 1946). It expanded when a new generation of liberal scholars used a neo-Malthusian critique to oppose trade-centered interpretations (Postan 1973). And it developed still further when another generation of Marxists, including most notably Robert Brenner (1976), used comparative analysis to demonstrate that neither trade nor population could adequately account for European development, since similar processes in various parts of the continent resulted in dissimilar social and economic structures. Thus, capitalism developed in England, peasant proprietorship grew in France, and in other parts of Europe serfdom either intensified or was imposed for the first time.

The importance of Brenner's analysis lies in the argument that the establishment of particular types of property relations and class structures provides the key to understanding capitalist development or the lack of it in different parts of Europe. It also drives home the point that, far from being an objective force that determines change, markets are historically and socially created, and hence a function rather than a cause of social and productive relations. Viewed in this light, the actual empirical reality of Europe becomes comprehensible, that is, that throughout the feudal epoch most often a reinforcement or expansion of feudal relations paralleled growing commercialization (Fox-Genovese & Genovese 1983: 8).

Indeed, for the Yangzi delta if one chose to make an empirically grounded rather than paradigmatically constructed comparison between the commercialization of the Ming-Qing and that of "Europe," it would have to be based not on the English model of capitalist development, but on the eastern European model of expanding serfdom (for the Ming), and on something like the French model (for the Qing). That is to say, in the delta commercialization during the Ming did not result in free wage labor in the English mode of capitalist development. Rather it formed the context for the reinforcement and greater development of a pattern extending back to the Song—an estate system of patriarchal landlord management based on serf, bondservant, servile tenant, and indentured labor. At the end of the Ming, this deep-rooted trend disintegrated, and then only because, in delta-wide local risings, bondservants, tenants, and other servile laborers demanded and, usually won, their freedom.

This book argues, in short, that these developments in agrarian class relations are key to understanding the Ming-Qing transition as a fault line in Chinese history. Where it departs from all past analyses is in spotlighting developments in peasant society as decisive, both in establishing a new tendency toward unification among peasants and, over the longer run, in shaping the pattern of change.

Peasants, the Ming-Qing Transition, and Historical Trends in the Southern Delta

At the most fundamental level, the story of the delta is the story of cotton. The growth of commercialized cotton textile production, first as a peasant-based industry and subsequently on patriarchal landlord estates, at once overshadowed and affected all the other developments during the Ming. It became bound up with the struggle of servile peasants for independence and liberation at the end of the dynasty and, in an economic sense, made those struggles possible since it enabled many peasants, for the first time, to exist independently of subsistence guarantees from patriarchal landlords (Oyama 1957-58). On the other hand, neither the late Ming rising of serfs, bondservants, and servile tenants and laborers nor the constant struggles that followed in the Qing can be viewed as simply reflections of the changing material conditions brought about by internal developments in peasant production or in the production relations of patriarchal landlordism. They also had to do with an emergent subaltern culture composed of diverse but unifying elements.

This new culture grew from the late sixteenth century on, shaped by increasingly complex networks of trade, migrations, resettlements, pilgrimages, heterodoxical religions, and the spread of martial arts. It was infused with a multifaceted spirituality, a social ethics born of an older peasant discourse of community, and new notions of absolute equality and equity gained through the influence of martial arts and millenarian religion. The evidence strongly suggests that this centerless, inherently counterhegemonic cultural movement provided the terrain for peasants to assign meaning to material changes, the means for them to rationalize the world and real life in new, anti-authoritarian terms, and the framework for practical political activity. As a "collective code" in which strategies for opposing domination and moving toward a common imagined destiny were communicated, shared, and represented ideologically, this cultural domain at once expressed a new tendency toward unification among peasants and opened up new political and ideological space for the waging of concrete struggles (Keesing 1992: 212–14). In the Yangzi delta it thus produced a distinct regional political culture. At the same time, suggesting its power as a cultural movement, similar political cultures appeared in Central and South China where servile labor also prevailed.

The other side of the Ming-Qing liberation struggles, and thus of a contradictory consciousness among peasants, was a shift to a more rigid sexual division of labor, which saw women relegated to household industry and men to farming. In effect peasant victories in the Ming-Qing struggles solidified a transformed household, one in which what has been considered the characteristic structure of Chinese peasant production, peasant patriarchy, and the subordination of peasant women were all firmly implanted.

The victories of the Ming-Qing struggles, and therewith the solidification of a particular form of "household" and "peasantry," influenced and shaped the entire subsequent history of the delta. The new structure of family production based on the combination of commercialized household industry and farming gave peasant production a stability and a certain independence from the landed classes rarely equaled in other agrarian societies. It formed the foundation for a continuing peasant powering of the commodity economy in the Qing, for the fuller and more ornate development of merchant capitalism that accompanied it, and for particular patterns in farm size and population growth.

No less important, in breaking the back of the patriarchal landlord system, the Ming-Qing struggles forced a reorganization of landlord-tenant relations. At the same time, the "structuring structures" (Bourdieu 1977) of the late Ming political culture provided the vision and "countermemory" for a sustained peasant offensive in both the southern and the northern delta during the Qing.[14] Although this sustained offensive ebbed and flowed, the relative position of peasants serving as a barometer of their gains or losses at any point in time and in any particular locality, in the southern delta it gradually eroded landlords' rights and altered the property system. Fixed rents and dual ownership became its greatest victories. As a long line of Japanese scholars and, most recently, in the Western literature, Kathryn Bernhardt (1992) have shown, the history of the Qing is in large part that of landlords and the state attempting to adjust to peasant victories so as to maintain control of peasant surpluses. The recognition of the dual-ownership system and its protection in customary law amounted to a compromise on the part of the state-elite between landlord and peasant property. Its emergence and extension reinforced the relative autonomy of delta peasants and maps the line of development among them that first coalesced in the late Ming.

Part One of this book thus suggests that the coalescence of this developmental line represented not only a profound conjunctural movement but an organic one as well. On the eve of the Opium War (1839–41), the distinctive political economy of the southern Yangzi delta represented one of the most fully articulated expressions and models of key long-term developmental dynamics in China. Balancing and interlocking with the delta's position as China's most advanced commercial region stood, on the one hand, a tense and contingent hegemony actualized through a system of landlord/state rule, in which the integration of landlordism, merchant-usury capital, and "public management" surpassed that of most other areas; and on the other hand, a peasant offensive that, in both its sustained character and its structural weakening of landlordism, formed a vanguard of peasant struggle and sociocultural bifurcation. Wedged in between them lay an exploitative and partially autonomous merchant capitalism that was at once essential to peasant reproduction and peasant struggles against landlords. This bifurcated history confronts and contradicts "early modern" formulations of the homogenization of Chinese culture and society in the Ming-Qing and the not-unrelated notions of "peaceful cores" and "troubled peripheries." It will also have to inform the history of semicolonial Jiangnan, which remains to be written.

Patterns in the Periphery: Nantong and the Northern Yangzi Delta

In the Ming-Qing period developments in Nantong—then known as Tongzhou—and the northern Yangzi delta simultaneously paralleled and diverged from those to the south, resulting in a distinctive political economy. During the first half of the Ming, owing to the spread of cotton and cotton textiles, signs of vigorous commercialization were as evident in the northern delta as in the south. Likewise, in the second half, as in the south, indications of a new cultural movement and of peasants behaving in "tough and indolent" ways were clearly present. And at the end of the dynasty, along with their southern counterparts, northern delta bondservants, serfs, and tenants fought for their freedom.

But by then differences in the patterns of agrarian class relations in the two areas were also well in evidence. These differences would deepen in the Qing as Nantong and the northern delta cotton economy came fully under the sway of a dominant Jiangnan. In fact the northern delta, its textile production increasingly overshadowed by the Songjiang-centered cotton cloth industry in the latter half of the Ming, would see its primary role within the regional economy reduced to that of supplier of raw cotton during the Qing. In short, in the Yangzi delta integrating-diffusionist economic processes were coupled with malintegration that peripheralized the north.

Antonia Finnane (1993), in her study of the Subei area,[15] which includes the northern Yangzi delta, argues that because of the dominance of the Jiangnan elite, the area was as politically and culturally peripheralized as it was economically. Similarly Emily Honig (1992, 1989) convincingly suggests that the cultural hierarchies and constructed differences embedded in the peripheralization of Subei functioned as ethnic-like divisions that operated as powerfully as race, nationality, or religion. Reinforcing these assessments of Subei, this study argues that over time the peripheralization of Nantong and the northern delta neutralized the earlier economic dynamism of the area and strengthened the cultural discrimination against it as backward and inferior.

These conditions necessarily impacted the trajectory of agrarian class conflict. To the extent that market expansion and rural-urban fluidity conditioned the development of a sustained peasant offensive in Jiangnan, the northern delta's malintegration into the delta economy limited peasant options and indirectly contributed to a pattern of peasant struggle that centered first on tenurial arrangements and later on rent resistance, rather than targeting the property system as such. The predominance of cotton cultivation in the north, in contrast to Jiangnan, where wet-rice farming was extensive, contributed to this pattern. Landlords in Jiangnan's wet-rice areas, in particular, were willing to grant peasants dual ownership (bringing permanent tenancy and reduced rents) once they could no longer call on servile labor to work their lands and maintain irrigation systems; and many hold-outs followed suit once absentee ownership became routine. In the northern delta, where wet-rice cultivation was minimal, developing on the lowlands along the edge of the Yangzi, dual ownership was more difficult to achieve than in the south and was relatively rare. Although tenure and rent struggles brought some improvement, the lack of any significant alteration in property relations placed peasants in the northern delta in a weaker class position than their counterparts in Jiangnan.

Under peripheralization and the stigma of backwardness, landlordism turned inward and became increasingly conservative. Greater landlord residence in the towns and small cities of the area from the eighteenth century on did not appreciably affect the hardening of this class pattern. Consequently, though peasants continued to chip away at landlord rule in everyday struggles, because of its relatively greater repressiveness, their line of development occasionally came to include moments of religious rebellion that more closely resembled the pattern of peasant insurgency in North China than in Jiangnan.

Following the Opium War, this distinctive embodiment of local society, and the longer-term class and regional conflicts embedded within it, profoundly influenced both the character and the course of semicolonial change. As we will see, the Shanghai treaty port created the new framework for transformative change in Nantong. It was, however, actualized by and initially dependent on a group of local men who saw in the semicolonial encounter the opportunity for Nantong to overcome its old peripheral status and, simultaneously, to redress their own positions as outsiders and adjuncts to the inner circle of local landed elite power.

Their ability to do so reflected the different outcomes of longer-term class struggles in the delta. Most importantly, to the extent that their modernist project centered on a regearing of the rural economy to urban-based capital, the lack of a secure base in property made peasants vulnerable to this new urban elite and later, to modern landlordism. The associated changes of that regearing stripped peasants of many of their gains and undermined their stability. Yet reflecting and inseparable from a much older pattern, these same changes formed the crucible for an escalation of class conflict and renewed militancy in the semicolonial struggles of peasants in the first decades of the twentieth century.

Conceptualizing Semicolonialism

Semicolonialism can be viewed both as a historical moment—specified in relation to European and more generally international capitalist political, economic, and cultural projects in the modern era—and as a trope for domination, violation, and resistance (Dirks 1992: 5). Dominance in semicolonial China was doubly articulated. It stood, on the one hand, for imperialism's power to limit the sovereignty of the Chinese state and, thereby, advance its own interests; and on the other hand, for the power exercised by the indigenous elite over the productive classes. Violation was inherent in both of these forms of dominance since, in the late nineteenth and early twentieth centuries, both came to be articulated along similar ideological lines: a discourse of progress and modernity that lent an "aura of power" to a certain model of development and excluded others from consideration (Cooper 1993: 196). Because this developmental model was antithetical to the trajectory and vision of an older peasant path, it met with intense popular resistance and could not establish its legitimacy. Thus also common to both forms of domination was a lack—a lack of hegemony (Guha 1992: 69).

This lack of hegemony is most obvious and understandable in the case of imperialism, since its formal power was limited and partial. Indeed semicolonialism has usually been treated as a political concept denoting a constellation of interventions, practices, institutions, and policies through which foreign imperialists established positions of advantage and semiautonomous operation—but not rule—for economic exploitation. In the specific case of China, these ranged from aggression and unequal treaties to spheres of influence and semicolonial agencies like the customs bureau. The result was something more than a mere advantageous position, particularly in certain sectors of the economy. By 1920 foreigners controlled 99 percent of China's iron ore and pig iron, 93 percent of the railways, 76 percent of the coal, 83 percent of the steam tonnage cleared through maritime customs, and 73 percent of the steam tonnage on the Yangzi (Stavrianos 1981: 326).

The treaty ports formed the nerve centers of these operations. They served both as the sites of foreign industry, banks, and commercial businesses in China and as the nodal points of the trading networks through which foreign businesses disseminated manufactured goods and procured agricultural and other commodities from the hinterland. In the delta the rise of Shanghai as a center of semicolonial power entailed a fundamental restructuring of the regional economy. Although this commercial restructuring is only just beginning to be systematically explored, it is apparent that in the delta as a whole it entailed, on the one hand, the decline or disappearance of forms of rural production, market towns, and older core cities, such as Suzhou, and on the other, the growing importance of new commercial areas and forms of production tied to the Shanghai port (P. Huang 1990: 117–19). Wuxi in the southern delta and Nantong in the north are the two leading examples of the latter.

As bastions of foreign capital, power, and restructuring, Shanghai and the other treaty ports thus stood as open symbols of imperialist dominance in China. At the same time, however, both practically and symbolically, they represented the limitations on that dominance. For it was precisely by restricting foreigners to the ports that the Chinese state, though forced into compliant dependency in other ways, continued to assert its autonomy. In research on the Third World, economic processes such as the penetration of foreign capital, imperialist-induced commercialization, and world market linkage have often figured prominently in analyses of underdevelopment, dependency, and world-system expansion. In colonial settings, more often than not, foreign merchant capitalists controlled and reaped the lion's share of benefits from these processes and, thereby, compounded the difficulties and displacement of indigenous merchants. But in China, thanks to the treaty port system, this was only partially true. If this system created a special arena for imperialist penetration, exploitation, and benefit, it simultaneously made those operations dependent on and established new opportunities for indigenous merchants and elites.

Understanding the general configuration of semicolonial power thus requires a detailed empirical examination of how over time globally framed economic processes took root and played out in local contexts, that is, in changes within the elite, in new modes of power, and ultimately in alterations in the ways work was organized and society replicated. Attention to the last should illuminate how changes in labor processes may have merged with rural struggles and alliances, both intra- and interclass. Understanding semicolonial process and power also requires an analysis of the sources of resistance, to foreign and hybridized semicolonial domination and in both its elite and its peasant form. Yet neither elite nor peasant was a homogeneous social category, and thus shifting alliances and contradictions within both groups also at once reflected and shaped semicolonialism. Our examination will demonstrate that in Nantong and the northern delta, social reproduction in the late nineteenth and early twentieth centuries simply cannot be understood apart from the semicolonial context.

The effect on local society was of course not merely economic, but political and cultural as well. It was in the cultural realm that imperialist dominance came closest to achieving a certain form of hegemony, at least among the Chinese elite. Along with creating new opportunities for trade and profit, through a discourse of modernity, progress, and civilization, imperialism aligned itself with "inexorable and universal forces" that to a considerable degree undercut and neutralized the opposition of the Chinese elite. That is to say, as various segments of elite Chinese came to buy into the imperialist argument, "consent was less the issue than the reality of power itself" (Dirks 1992: 7–8).

Spawned by semicolonialism, the elite nationalism that appeared in the late nineteenth century was in large part a derivative discourse—one that was less than and could never be fully autonomous. Like the source that gave rise to it, it was increasingly embedded within a Western-oriented, modernist, and antipeasant view of the world. In the words of Partha Chatterjee:

> Nationalism sought to demonstrate the falsity of the colonial claim that the backward peoples were culturally incapable of ruling themselves in the conditions of the modern world. Nationalism denied the alleged inferiority of the colonized people; it also asserted that a backward nation could "modernize" itself while retaining its cultural identity. It thus produced a discourse in which, even as it challenged the colonial claim to political domination, it also accepted the very intellectual premises of "modernity" on which colonial domination was based. . . . There is, consequently, an inherent contradictoriness in nationalist thinking, because it reasons within a framework of knowledge whose representational structure corresponds to the very structure of power nationalist thought seeks to repudiate. (1986: 30, 38)

Thus a capitalist universalization, in which the dominant ideologies and cultural artifacts produced in the West were copied and reproduced by members of the Chinese elite, became an integral part of the semicolonial process. It functioned as an aspect of imperialist domination and paved the way for the emergence of new forms of indigenous power that, more often than not, served the needs of imperialism. Like their foreign counterparts, different segments of the Chinese elite soon came to understand the extent to which, as an "intimidating claim to write and speak for the world" (Asad 1992: 345), the imperialist discourse of progress and modernity was a regime of power. It became the conscious articulation of a project through which a "modern" elite identified its destiny and that of China as a whole with development and, simultaneously, used this project to build new modes of local power. The nationalist variant of this project created even greater maneuverability by providing "a defense against slurs of acculturation and legitimat[ing] all economic activities pursued in the name of overriding national interests" (Bergère 1989: 46–47).

Building new modes of local power necessarily had a political as well as an economic side. The particular role of local elites in spearheading political and economic change brings into sharp relief a key difference between developments in China and in colonial states. Near the turn of the century, pressured by nationalist elites and foreigners, and eager to expand its commercial revenues, the Qing state began to exhibit most of the features of modernizing colonial regimes in the same period, especially those in South and Southeast Asia (Kahn 1993). In effect it took on the attributes of a semicolonial state. But rather than developing its new focus by expanding the bureaucracy, as was the case in most colonial regimes, the Qing acted through the informal bureaucracy of local merchants and landlord-gentry. In other words the state provided the framework for the elite to bring about political and economic change.

In much of the recent work on modernization in China, the Qing state is depicted as resistant to the activities of nationalist and modern-minded elites (e.g., Rankin 1986). The record for Nantong contradicts this image. The Qing government played an instrumental role in initiating modernization; and it was only with its continuing encouragement, support, and financial assistance that Nantong's most famous nationalist, Zhang Jian, was able to inaugurate a program of Westernizing development in the area. With state support the imperialist discourse of modernity and progress provided a ready-made ideology for Zhang and other members of an emerging modern elite to construct a new mode of local sociopolitical and economic power. At first grafted onto and then gradually replacing older hegemonic notions of elite "concern for local society," it justified their borrowing from the West and validated their actions.

As in other parts of the delta and the country, their actions reveal the contradictory path of the modern nationalist elite: by extending Western narratives of modernity, their nationalism furthered imperialist dominance at the same moment it opposed it. The practical effect was that whereas some elite projects were specifically aimed at thwarting foreign dominance, many others became the indigenous arms of foreign-controlled semicolonial operations.

Class Formation Within the Elite

In Nantong and the northern delta, a heterogeneous merchant-entrepre-neurial-industrial elite, urban-based and urban-oriented, emerged to challenge the once firmly entrenched landed elite. Ideologically and increasingly culturally, the Westernizing discourse of modernity and development formed a central unifying commonality among the members of this new class. That alignment, as past scholarship argues, alienated them from the peasantry and caused them to turn their backs on rural problems (Esherick 1976). Yet contradicting their apparent separation from the countryside, their modernist project contained another fundamental commonality: a particular class strategy based on controlling and exacting surpluses from peasants, as well as from urban workers. Materially, then, their class nature is best defined by their project (R. Joseph 1980). For that reason, we will have to put aside standard notions of a separation of city and countryside as lying at the core of a universal modernist path and come to understand that the elite path in Nantong instead interlocked urban and rural, and indeed specifically aimed at reordering the rural economy to the needs of urban-based capital.

Although this project represented a continuation of the older pattern of rule and a line of development in which, especially in Jiangnan, merchant capital was already challenging landlordism as "master of the countryside," what accelerated and revolutionized it was semicolonialism: as expressed in Nantong's integration into the Shanghai treaty port economy; in new political and economic prerogatives; and in forms of labor and production that did not grow organically out of existing society but rather were quickly grafted onto it. These conditions formed the crucible for the coalescence of a new heterogeneous ruling bloc. Despite internal contradictions and varying degrees of competition within it, its members stood as one in the sense that they pursued a class strategy based, in the last analysis, on a mode of power that combined growing political prerogatives, the exploitation of peasants, and the interlinking of city and countryside in a local economic system.

In the short run this mode of power fostered significant economic growth. But to the extent that, as Colin Leys (1978) argues, (Euromodeled) economic development is really about whether entrenched extractors of absolute surplus value can be supplanted by classes capable of developing the forces of production and accumulating relative surplus value, the development project of Nantong's modern elite assumed a different trajectory from the start. Rooted in rural-urban interlocking, its chief characteristic was a process of uneven accumulation based on *both* absolute and relative surplus value. Apparent by the 1920's, the outcome of this process—an outcome that reflected semicolonial politics as much as economics—was an overdevelopment of social inequities and an underdevelopment of development.[16]

The Semicolonial Process

A major focus of our examination will be to detail the multiple processes and structures of semicolonialism in the northern delta. Economically, developments in the local cotton textile industry and in cotton farming and marketing lie at the heart of our story. Following the Opium War, peasant-based cotton textile production became the axis of the semicolonial process and elite transformation. Initially the most important stimulus for change was the introduction of foreign machine-spun yarn in the production of cotton cloth, a development that led to a rapid expansion of the textile industry. Rather quickly as well, and increasingly so in the twentieth century, the cotton trade became a second axis. Viewed in global context, the disruptions of the American Civil War and then the boll weevil epidemic "unleashed an obsession with cotton that occupied the British Empire for decades"—an obsession that became more generalized in the centers of capitalist production as competition for cotton supplies accelerated (Cooper 1993: 119–20; Isaacman et al. 1980; Pearse 1929; Warren 1980). In many parts of the colonial world, this obsession led to the forced planting of cotton and to harsh labor regimes to step up production, with the result that cotton came to be known as "the mother of poverty." The northern delta was no exception. But there cotton cultivators so intensely resisted and even subverted the new regimes that cotton also could be said to have been "the mother of rural radicalism." In this respect as well, developments in the northern delta reinforced the colonial pattern.

THE ASCENDANCY OF THE
CLOTH MERCHANT ELITE

As played out in cotton and textile developments engineered and directed by modernist elites, the semicolonial process in Nantong and the northern delta encompassed three overlapping yet distinct moments. The first, the focus of Chapter Four, covered the last decades of the nineteenth century but was most pronounced after 1884, the year foreign yarn entered Nantong. That innovation brought Nantong into a new Shanghai-based, foreign-controlled commercial-financial network that dominated the import-export trade. Representing a "commercialization from above" that gave a new group of cloth merchants greater prerogatives over peasant production, the replacement of homespun by foreign yarn as warping in the production of handwoven cloth instantly splintered the unity of cotton-yarn-cloth as an integrated peasant enterprise. The upshot was to increase the cash needs of peasants and bring them into new forms of market dependency. In this moment the emergent cloth merchant elite assumed growing social importance in the Nantong area. Concurrently, this moment accentuated and deepened differences in the emerging northern subregion of the Shanghai-centered delta economy, replicating in new form older spatial relations of dominance and subordination in the area by favoring Nantong.

ZHANG JIAN AND THE NATIONALIST ALTERNATIVE

The double-edged process through which semicolonization and a new mode of local elite power took shape deepened at the end of the nineteenth century, when in a second moment of semicolonial process the renowned scholar Zhang Jian began to spearhead local development in Nantong. Zhang epitomizes the degree-holding Yangzi delta urban elite who both advocated the modernist path and were courted by the Qing state to direct economic and political change. Their close association with the state gave these men prerogatives and privileges that were crucial to the new trajectory of change. At the same time, that association conferred legitimacy on the new self-government organizations and local autonomy projects mandated by the state in its so-called New Policies of 1902–8.

As Chapter Five details, Zhang Jian, in alliance with the local cloth merchant elite, attempted to construct a nationalist alternative to semicolonial development. It centered on establishing modern spinning mills in the greater Nantong area and monopolistically interlocking them with peasant farming and textile production. In reality the nationalist pretensions of the project as a "self-reliant" alternative were only partially justified. The new system still depended on the marketing of peasant-produced cloth through the Shanghai-based comprador network that formed the axis of the treaty-port trade. And its monopolistic contours were aimed as much at Chinese as at foreign competitors. These facts notwithstanding, in combination with a cluster of other modernizing local projects, the interlocking of city and countryside in a monopolistic system enabled Zhang Jian to establish an independent base of local power of an unprecedented nature.

Through the development of this system, early industrial development in Nantong attained unusual strength. Zhang's Dasheng mills became the most successful Chinese-owned factories in the pre–World War One period, and the expansion of peasant weaving effected through the mills made Nantong the most important center of rural cotton weaving in China. Paralleling these developments, Zhang's opening of vast new areas of tenant-based cotton farming by land development companies connected to the Dasheng mills rapidly expanded local cotton output. In elite eyes these developments made Nantong a model of the modernist route and Zhang Jian the example par excellence of a modern gentry-entrepreneur.

Yet these "successes" masked a central characteristic of the elite-led modernist path: an overdevelopment of social inequities as the benefits of economic growth came to be concentrated in the hands of Nantong's modern urban elite. Moreover, Zhang's breakthrough did not endure. By the early 1920's the self-reliant contours of the local system had disintegrated. Banking consortia were managing the mills, most of the subsidiary industries had failed or were failing, the land development companies that supported Zhang's monopolistic cotton collection system were falling into private hands, and other features of the collection system had already disappeared. In short an underdevelopment of development also became a key characteristic of the local modernist path. To explain this turn of events, we must move to the third moment of the semicolonial process.

MERCHANTS, LANDLORDS, AND PEASANTS

What brought Zhang Jian and the Dasheng group to grief was the fact that, despite a marriage of convenience between them and the modern merchant elite at the start, the interests of the two were not identical. Thanks to older tendencies in the local economy, and their acceleration in the late nineteenth century with the expansion of rural weaving, merchants had an independent center of gravity, what we might term a second modernist path. The interlocked rural-urban system reinforced this center of gravity by providing the framework for the rapid accumulation and concentration of merchant capital in a new financial-commercial complex in Nantong city. In this respect, as Chapter Six details, the sources of the system's early strength also contained the seeds of weakness.

In a third moment of semicolonial process, the local cotton trade became the arena in which Nantong's merchant elite challenged Dasheng's hegemony. In the 1910's and 1920's, the large merchant firms, pressured by a decline in the northeastern cloth market with the growth of Japanese competition, established new prerogatives over the local cotton trade that undermined Dasheng's collection system and irreparably weakened its mills. In the 1930's these firms extended their prerogatives through alliances with new bureaucratic-capitalist forces that were gaining control of the national commodities market, a development that enabled the largest firms to strengthen their position at the expense of local competitors. In the process Nantong's modern merchants more fully assumed the traits of a semicolonial elite.

Modern Landlordism and Subproletarianization

The merchant path formed only one dimension of the multifaceted process through which local self-reliance disintegrated and the rural economy increasingly functioned in support of local urban-based capital and along semicolonial lines. Viewed in terms of this differentiating rural economy, developments in the northern delta contradict both recent revisionist analyses contending that sustained development was improving conditions in the countryside (Brandt 1989; Rawski 1989) and those explicitly arguing that accelerating commercialization contributed to the stability of the small peasant family economy in the Yangzi delta (P. Huang 1990).[17]

Disputing both of these views, the evidence for the northern delta shows two broad trends. The first was the emergence of *modern landlordism*. Although some studies of local elites have hypothesized a rupture between modern urban business and rural landlord elites (e.g., Esherick & Rankin 1990: 305–45), landlords in the northern delta, especially after 1911, allied themselves with the modern Nantong elite. The urban entrepreneurial-merchant class continued to direct the modernist drive, but conservative rural landlords, including those who relinquished urban for rural residence, acquiesced to and became involved in the modernist project, politically and economically.

As detailed in Chapter Seven, northern delta landlords, like the new urban elite, came over to the side of the 1911 revolution in order to control it, and then "jumped on the bandwagon" of reform so as to also "grasp the power to lead" (Mao Zedong 1990: 199). Their involvement in various self-government and functional "worlds" (*jie*)—such as school circles and militia building—intertwined with a new offensive to regain control of an increasingly recalcitrant peasantry. That offensive exposes the hidden underside of the new expressions of modernity: the military character of the evolving mode of power. It reveals the antipeasant stance of the modernizers and the fundamental rejection of their project by peasants, who viewed their activities as illegitimate and whose protestations and resistance formed the only truly autonomous nationalist discourse of the period. Thus unlike studies that pin the decline of the elite's authority to later decades (e.g., Duara 1988), this book emphasizes the degree to which the modern elite failed to establish hegemony from the outset.

Chapter Eight turns to look at the economic side of modern landlordism, and more specifically, the development of capitalist-style managerial farming among medium and larger landlords. This change had a marked impact on rural society, further disadvantaging poorer peasants and contributing to the simultaneous expansion of semilandlord–rich peasant farming. Though the new breed of landlords was clearly concerned with maximizing their profits, few were improving landlords of the standard capitalist variety. For most the route to riches lay not in productive innovations, but in the control of cotton and labor. These concerns are most strikingly evidenced by their use of various forms of disguised wage labor, acquired through labor rents, debt labor, sharecropping, female bondage, and in other ways. Involving new juridical constraints on peasant-workers, these labor forms were not simply precapitalist holdovers in an otherwise modernizing economy. Their proliferation characteristically interconnected with a modern landlordism that became the economic ally of urban capital and a historically specific semicolonial modernity in which the vast majority of peasants were transformed.

This transformative *repeasantization* stands as the second broad developmental trend in the rural political economy. It resulted in the creation of what, in effect, was a historically new class of subproletarian peasants, who much more fully than in the past functioned as poor, petty commodity producers on their own farms and as a disadvantaged wage labor force. Chapters Eight and Nine chart how, as a specific process of class formation, this trend played out differently in the agriculturally specialized districts of the countryside and in the rural centers of household industry, but culminated in both types of communities in a modern peasantry whose economic options and stability were more severely constrained and precarious than before. They also show that even as their commodity production intensified, overexploited subproletarian families retreated more deeply into the "natural" or second subsistence economy, both as a means of survival and as a historical alternative to growing market dependency.

Hill Gates (1996) has referred to the petty commodity economy, that is, as she defines it, one in which the continued reproduction of producers depends on engagement with the market, as a petty capitalist mode of production. She argues for its persistence as a motor of Chinese development from Song times until the present. Yet her kin-centered formulation fails to note important distinctions between peasant and fully proletarianized urban production.[18] Moreover, because it does not take into account structural changes in the forms of commodity production or in the historically specific social relations through which it was constituted, it fails to illuminate historical process and, by extension, moments of discontinuity.

My evidence indicates that in both the agricultural and the rural industrial districts in the early twentieth century, the expansion of the commercial economy was effected through a weakening or dissolving of the older structure of peasant production. Viewed in this light, though there was a certain continuity and even intensification of both petty commodity and subsistence production, the semicolonial moment was one of radical disjuncture. Along with elite class formation and a new economic system based on the collusion and competition of the many "capitalisms" of the semicolonial mode, it is precisely in this discontinuity—expressed structurally in repeasantization and subproletarianization—that the real meaning of semicolonialism lies and that, as a category, it becomes analytically significant. In the northern delta, as much as new forms of urban industry and business, the growing instability of the vast majority of peasant producers and the simultaneous strengthening of subsistence and petty commodity production defined the semicolonial. To fully understand these changes, we must put aside any notion of them as evidence of Nantong's "failure" to effectively advance along some universalist path of modernity. On the contrary, Nantong stands as the embodiment of a particular modernity constituted in semicolonial form—just as the impoverished and marginalized subproletarian peasants who lived the changes of the period stand as a stark reminder of the inequities, destructiveness, and assault on the human spirit it involved.

The Peasant Path

In the last analysis, the class formation that for a brief historical moment reconstituted peasants as a rural labor force underpinning the many "capitalisms" of the semicolonial mode—and the means by which profits could be extracted—depended on how peasant labor could be controlled. Stated differently, the intensifying commoditization of land, labor, and production that structurally transformed peasants were contested changes that brought various forms of capital (and the state) into confrontation with peasants. Thus from the outset peasants' resistance and vision of an alternative modernity formed a constituent element and characteristic feature of the semicolonial process.

This resistance cannot be understood as the simple reflection of abstract semicolonizing, imperialist, or commercializing forces. It must be considered in its specific context, especially in terms of the impact of the new mode of elite power in its urban and rural forms on peasant politics and consciousness. Similarly, that resistance, though clearly informed by an older line of development based on antistatist imaginings of universal rights and an equal and equitable community, did not merely continue or replicate those imaginings.

Students of popular movements and revolution like Craig Calhoun (1982) and Douglas Kincaid (1987) argue for the centrality of community over class in the process of political radicalization. The evidence for the northern delta confirms the significance of residence, of notions of community, over class-occupation in a strict structural sense, and of earlier practices and patterns of action in shaping twentieth-century peasant politics. But it also calls into question their view that community is dependent on tradition or "recreated" solidarities based on "residual" social bonds, so that new ideas and practices must be fit into "traditional structures of thought and action" (Calhoun 1983: 898). The situation in our area appears much more like that described by Jeffrey Gould (1990) and Carol Smith (1987), who argue that class and community are not analytically separate and emphasize the relation between changing politico-economic fields of power and ideological transformations among peasants. Simply stated, in the northern delta community formation and peasant politics at once reflected and contributed to the transformation of peasants into subproletarians.

To the extent that class struggle is "a struggle about class before it is a struggle among classes" (Przeworsky 1977: 374), from the late nineteenth century to the late 1920's, subproletarianization came to be expressed in two phases or formulations of peasant politics. In the first most peasants opposed the making of a new mode of power by the modern elite, the roles they were being assigned, and the array of exploitative practices that were disadvantaging and changing them. Viewed broadly, to a large extent the struggles growing out of this opposition were *about class*. They bear some resemblance to the class struggle in England described so well by E. P. Thompson (1963), which in fact was mostly a struggle of artisans, tenants, and many others against becoming a working class.

This political movement, as Chapter Seven shows, developed rapidly in the last decade of the Qing, and reached a high point at the time of and immediately following the 1911 revolution. It was more than just the work of poor peasants; rich peasants and even small semilandlords, concerned to protect what gains they had made, often assumed leading roles in individual risings and protests. In its village coalitions and communal discourses different groups thus not only advanced their particular class interests but came to more clearly understand and reject as illegitimate the modernist elite project. At the same time, by giving new meanings to older forms of struggle and the notions informing them, the movement simultaneously reinvented the older line of peasant development and moved into uncharted, radical political terrain—terrain on which the ideas of community and nation began to merge.

Following the crescendo of 1911–12, collective resistance subsided, largely because of a brutal military crackdown launched by the modern elite. Downward processes among the majority of peasants also accelerated, and the unity that had marked the multiclass pre-1912 movement dissolved. By the late teens–early 1920's, however, when the landlord offensive against peasants moved into full gear, a new wave of resistance began. As Chapter Nine examines, it revolved around more explicit class-based struggles by the poor peasant-subproletarian majority.

Recent studies in labor history emphasize the degree to which strikes and other forms of collective action are more the precondition than the outcome of working-class formation (Perry 1993; Marshall 1983). In this respect, both structurally and politically, the struggles of the 1920's became a pivotal moment of subproletarian peasant history. Born of the previous genres of struggle and the shared experience of subproletarian life and work, this second phase of peasant politics at once expressed the contradictions of a tense and contingent semicolonial process and the reconfiguring of notions of community more closely along poor peasant–subproletarian lines. As such, it re-flected what perhaps can only be described as a distinctly modern, alternative nationalist consciousness of the oppressed (see Comaroff 1985; Jewsiewicki 1980). To the extent, as Odoric Wou (1994: 13) stresses, that the disintegra-tion of elite hegemony is a precondition for revolution, this second phase of subproletarian peasant politics, like the early-twentieth-century struggles that preceded it, provides as well a crucial vantage point for understanding the meaning and significance of semicolonialism as a conceptual category.

Part One

SIGNPOSTS: THE MING-QING
TRANSITION AND BEYOND

1 Agrarian Class Relations and Peasant History in the Southern Yangzi Delta During the Ming

GEOLOGICALLY SPEAKING, the Yangzi delta (Map 1) is a large basin in the lower Yangzi rice-wheat region, bordered in the north by the New Tongyang Canal and in the south by Hangzhou Bay. It slopes from north to south and east to west toward Lake Tai (Taihu). Economically speaking, it encompassed, in the Ming-Qing period, parts of Jiangsu province (Tongzhou on the northern bank of the Yangzi, and Suzhou, Changzhou, and Songjiang prefectures and Taicang department to the south) and Zhejiang province (Huzhou and Jiaxing).[1] This chapter sets the stage for our study of the peripheralized northern delta by focusing on the area that dominated it, politically and culturally, as well as economically. The chapter outlines the important changes in the southern delta in the course of the Ming-Qing period, with special attention to how the changes in the sphere of production, and in gender, cultural, and class relations, splintered late imperial society.[2] It spotlights peasant politics and a new line of development among peasants as decisively shaping longer-term patterns.

The Spread of Cotton and Cotton Textiles

The spread of cotton farming and the commercialization of cotton cloth production lie at the heart of our story. In 1350, few people in China wore cotton clothes; by 1750, as Philip Huang has emphasized, almost everyone did. In the Yangzi delta, the dramatic spread of cotton powered a host of other changes and dwarfed in importance the history of other crops and industries (P. Huang 1990).

Cotton was introduced into China during the Han (202 B.C.–220 A.D.) along Western trade routes. After passing through a long gestation period in the border regions of Yunnan and Xinjiang, it gradually spread northward from Yunnan. By the thirteenth century, peasants in Guangdong, Fujian, and

MAP 1. The Yangzi Delta in the Qing

Hainan Island were planting cotton. It reached the southern Yangzi delta by the end of the Song, made its way to the Huai River in the Yuan (1279–1368), and spread to various other areas of the country in the Ming (Chao Kang 1977: 4–16; Nishijima 1948–49).

In the Yangzi delta, cotton acreage expanded rapidly during the Ming, propelled by the spread of cotton textile techniques and the mounting popularity of cotton cloth. Because of its superior qualities compared with ramie—it was lighter, yet warmer in winter and cooler in summer—cotton quickly outstripped that fabric as the basic clothing material of the non-elite classes. This change was stimulated, on the technical level, by the ease with which the weaving techniques of silk and ramie were transferred to cotton, and the facility with which spinning techniques were developed. Another important factor was the Ming state's policy of requiring certain amounts of taxes to be paid in cotton and cotton cloth (Chao Kang 1977: 19; Nishijima 1948–49; Sun Jingzhi 1959: 27).[3]

On the supply side, the opportunity costs of cotton were low compared with crops such as rice, since it could be cultivated on sandy, non-irrigated soils. Thus when the crop first reached the southern delta, it was grown only in the higher parts of eastern Songjiang prefecture along a coastal ridge stretching from Shanghai county to the borders of Taicang department, where irrigation was too difficult for rice and the soil too saline for most other crops (Nishijima 1984: 33). After the introduction of spinning and weaving techniques in the area in the late thirteenth century (Chu Hua n.d.: 12; Lin Jubai 1984), cultivation spread eastward toward the sea and westward along the high-lying ground of the outer basin. Cotton acreage eventually formed a belt that rimmed the rice-mulberry fields of the lower-lying inner coastal basin (P. Huang 1990: 22, 44-45). By the beginning of the Qing, most of the total arable land in the two cotton-belt counties of Shanghai and Jiading was devoted to the crop (70 percent and 90 percent, respectively; Nishijima 1966: 822–23). Once cotton reached the northern delta, coming first to Haimen and then Nantong, it developed over a much wider area than in Jiangnan, thanks to the higher elevation of the land, the prevalence of dry farming, and cotton's tolerance for the region's highly alkaline soil. By the early twentieth century, it commanded at least 70 percent of the total cropland in the Nantong-Haimen area (Lin Jubai 1984: 5-28; TZZ, 1754, 1: 309-12).

More than state policies or other factors, it was the suitability of cotton textile production to peasant household management that crucially influenced its rapid development after the introduction of spinning and weaving techniques in the thirteenth century. Cloth production required little capital investment and technical skill; the single spinning wheel and wooden handloom were cheap and simple tools that could be operated by one person; and production could be pursued as time allowed (Chao Kang 1977: 33). In short, the activity was ideally suited to household industry carried out, as in ramie production, by female family members (often with the help of children and the aged), while the men farmed the fields.

At first, peasant families mostly produced cloth to clothe themselves. But because of cotton's popularity as a clothing material, especially in the Yangzi delta, where strong commercial foundations dated back to the Song, market production quickly outpaced home production. Peasants powered much of this early commercial growth. Even so important an outlet as the Shanghai cloth market still revolved around peasant traders conducting transactions among themselves in the late Ming (H. Lu 1992: 487–88).

Past scholarship has often emphasized this early association of cotton textiles with peasant production and deplored its persistence into the nineteenth and twentieth centuries.[4] But even in the Ming, in fact, other, larger-scale producers flourished in the countryside.[5] In other words, the long-term association of cotton textiles with peasant production was neither a singular linear development nor a foregone conclusion. It was intimately bound up with the dynamics of agrarian class conflict and the reorganization of landlord-tenant relations in the Ming-Qing period. To understand this historical outcome, we must turn our attention to the servile labor relations that predominated in the Ming.

Bondservantry, Managerial Landlordism, and Commercialization

During the Ming the peasantry was by and large a dependent and servile class. Whether as bondservants (*nupu*), tenant-serfs (*dianpu*), tenants (*dianhu*), or hired laborers (*gunu*), they were tied to landlords in ways that limited their personal and economic freedom (Fu Yiling 1981–82, 1975, 1961; Li Wenzhi et al. 1983; McDermott 1981; Niida 1962a; Oyama 1957–58, 1974; J. W. Tong 1991).[6] Though hereditary bondservantry tracing back to the Song and Yuan periods still existed in the Ming, in the delta most of these relationships were new to that dynasty.[7] The extension of bondservantry and other forms of servile labor over the course of the Ming intertwined, on the one hand, with sociopolitical change and on the other, with the growth of the commercial economy.

The sociopolitical developments concerned, most importantly, the rise in the first half of the dynasty of a new breed of gentry-landlords (*xiangshen*) who had ties to the state and, increasingly, commercial interests. State linkage enabled these landholders to avoid and/or pass tax and corvée obligations on to others (Mori 1980; Shigeta 1984). Further helped by several changes in state policy, the *xiangshen* gained prominence over the older wealthy landed elite, men who had served as local tax chiefs (*liangzhang*) but generally did not hold examination degrees or enjoy official status. At the same time, once the tax burden was shifted to those who were least able to pay, more and more land came to be concentrated in the hands of this rising elite and more and more peasants fell into tenancy, or worse, on their expanding estates. Both developments undercut early Ming efforts to establish an independent peasantry and, through fiscal reforms, discourage tax abuse (Hamashima 1980; Oyama 1969: 25–40; Shigeta 1984; Wada 1978; Wakeman 1985: 604–9; Zurndorfer 1989: 115–16).[8]

To avoid rising tax obligations, numbers of beleaguered peasants took flight. Some became vagabonds, but many indentured or sold themselves (*maishen*) to landowners who would feed and clothe them (Hosono 1967: 18; Nishimura 1979: 25; Wakeman 1985: 622). Others entered bondservantry or servile tenancy by commending themselves (*toukao*) or their land (*touxian*) to gentry-landlords and other tax-exempt families.[9] Since the Ming state prohibited commoners having bondservants, these new relations were often hidden under the guise of kinship, with the bondservant taking the name of his or her master (Hosono 1967: 18; Nishimura 1979: 24–28). The well-used phrase "begging to be adopted" denotes this practice. Marriage, coercion, and outright purchase in an expanding bondservant market were also common means of acquiring servile labor (Fu Yiling 1961: 68–153, 1963: 66–68; Nishimura 1979: 28–29; Oyama 1957–58, 1: 7, 9–10).[10]

That bondservantry became most pronounced in the areas of greatest market development plainly shows how the expansion of servile labor interlinked with new commercial processes, especially those associated with cotton and silk, and the growing market orientation of landholders (Oyama 1957–58; Sudō 1954: 116–21). One of the most important factors in this expansion was the spread of managerial farming operations within the upper strata of the landed classes. Contemporary sources contain numerous references to gentry-landlords and other wealthy landholders who personally "led their serfs and slaves in agricultural production" (Fu Yiling 1981–82: 75; see also Oyama 1957–58; 1974). As one official records of his father, "He bought a large number of bondservants for his rich and splendid agricultural properties. Depending on the season of the year, he would supervise plowing, sowing, [and] weeding. . . . A program of work was laid out for each of the bondservants he organized" (cited in Fu Yiling 1956: 33).

Such personal management appears to have become the norm on the largest estates, where bondservants and servile tenants often numbered in the hundreds or even thousands (Fu Yiling 1981–82: 76, 1961: 69–71; Oyama 1957–58, 1974; M. Wiens 1979: 57). Any lands an owner could not effectively supervise himself were typically assigned to indentured tenants or rented out (Oyama 1957–58). But after the mid-Ming, when absentee landlordism increased, the urban owners of large estates often delegated supervisory powers to bondservant overseers. Forming, according to contemporary sources, a haughty and oppressive upper stratum, these overseers frequently tyrannized the tenants and bondservants of their masters.[11]

Songjiang prefecture provides a clear illustration of these trends. We have already referred to Songjiang as the area where cotton cultivation first developed in the delta. By the late Ming, over half its two million mu had been converted to cotton (P. Huang 1990: 45). Correlatively, whereas 86 percent of Songjiang's land had been held by the state and worked by state tenants at the start of the dynasty, private landholding and bondservant/servile tenant labor now predominated. According to a gazetteer for Shanghai, located in the prefecture, "the gentry had acquired numerous bondservants whom they held in hereditary subjection," with the result that "there were almost no free commoners [left] in the county" (cited in Elvin 1973: 241). As an account from 1546 notes: "It has been the custom in Songjiang for the great families to own land they cannot farm themselves and to use dependent tenants. The tenants desire to do the farmwork but do not have enough food, so they must rely for it upon the great households" (cited in ibid., p. 458).

By now too Songjiang had become the country's most important center of cotton cloth production. In the sixteenth century, its output rose dramatically, from 175,000 bolts in 1503 to 365,000 in 1579 (Nishijima 1948–49, 2: 29). By the beginning of the seventeenth century, reaching northern, southern, and inland markets, Songjiang was said to have "clothed the empire" (Nishijima 1947: 125).

At the same time, the Songjiang-centered cotton economy powered commercialization in other regions (Fu Yiling 1981–82: 63; P. Huang 1990; Wu Chengming 1983). Once committed to cotton, for instance, the delta was faced with annual food deficits. Consequently, a grain import trade developed in tandem with the cotton economy. Cotton itself became a major item of trade as well, for Songjiang could only "clothe the empire" by purchasing large quantities of the crop from other producing regions (Nishijima 1947: 125). Apart from encouraging the turn to cotton elsewhere, these imports became a source of supply for production in neighboring areas where little or no cotton was grown (Nishijima 1948–49).

A seventeenth-century gazetteer from Jiading county, located in Songjiang, suggests the large volume and importance of this cotton trade: "Every part of Henan and Huguang [Hubei and Hunan] knows how to grow it. They [merchants] load their bales of it on an unending line of boats and come down to Jiangnan to sell it" (cited in Nishijima 1947: 126). And, as a late Ming gazetteer for Yanzhou (Shandong) indicates, "The land here is suited to cotton. Merchants sell it in Jiangnan where they set up shops. It is more than twice as profitable as growing grain" (ibid.).

In sum, cotton textile commercialization in the delta had far-reaching effects. To the extent that it stimulated economic growth in other regions, it propelled movement toward the formation of a national market structured on the exchange of grain for cotton cloth (and also salt) by petty producers (Terada 1958: 59; Wu Chengming 1983). And to the extent that it stimulated demand for and the international flow of silver as a commodity, it also drove the formation of a global monetary system.[12]

Cotton, the State, and Merchant-Landlordism

The shift of textiles from family-oriented to commodity production was intimately connected to the spread of silver exchange in the delta and to the development of commercial institutions accompanying this monetization of the economy (Nishijima 1984: 31). The state played an important role in these processes, particularly through its general unification of tax collection methods in the Single Whip reform of 1486 (on which more below). In the southern delta, these developments brought a significant portion of the managerial landlord–gentry to become urban dwellers and key organizers of marketing relationships.

Even before this, between rents in kind and estate supervision of textile manufacture, landlords in the cotton districts had been well involved in marketing activity. Especially during the late Ming, they played a key role in the rapid proliferation of markets, towns, and cities in the lower delta, either founding new markets or accelerating the development of the existing peasant cotton markets on the outskirts of towns and cities (Fu Yiling 1963: 84, 103–4, 1961: 68–70; Nishijima 1947: 132, 1966: 835, 874, 884; P. Yang 1988: 149).

Attracted by this growing marketing infrastructure, more and more members of "well-connected families" took up urban residence and a mercantile life. Concentrated as brokers or wholesalers in the cotton and cotton cloth trades, they were pivotal figures in the interregional traffic, acting as intermediaries between local sellers and long-distance buyers from Shanxi, Shaanxi, and other areas. By the late Ming, when long-distance merchants were handling shipments of cloth worth hundreds of thousands of taels (Nishijima 1947: 134–38), the profit potential for well-positioned brokers was enormous. As Chu Hua noted in his late-eighteenth-century account of the exploits of a Ming-period ancestor in the Shanghai cloth market: "[He was] a man who was proficient in the skills of commerce. Very often tens of cotton merchants from Shanxi and Shaanxi provinces resided in his house. He established a firm to purchase cotton cloth for these merchants. . . .Since it was a profitable business, he became the wealthiest man in the county" (n.d.: 10).

Such mercantile operations gave the new landlord-gentry brokers and independent merchants a growing say in marketing structures and the pricing system, and extended their power in local society. Susan Mann has argued that, in North China, the state helped the gentry to climb to power when it authorized them to collect commercial taxes. Because of that assignment, (merchant-gentry) elites were able to "win control over the terms of trade" in local markets (1987: 72–93). In the delta from the late fifteenth century, the state also played an influential role. But in this case what counted most were the policy changes surrounding the collection of the land tax.

In the Single Whip reform of 1486, the state urged that silver be substituted for the portion of the land tax obligated in cotton. Moreover, cotton wholesale merchants replaced the old *lijia* tax captains as tax collectors. As the Songjiang prefect Fan Ying memorialized:

> Excluding the portion of the grain tax that has for a long time been delivered in kind, the remainder should be converted and collected in silver. . . . This should reduce infringements by tax captains. The cloth wholesalers will replace the [tax captains] as those responsible for forwarding cloth, and when there are deficits, they should use their private stocks to fill the quota. (Quoted in Nishijima 1984: 31)

As a result, approximately 40 percent of the cotton tax payment was converted to silver. By 1620, all cotton taxes had been converted (Nishijima 1984: 32).

With the Single Whip reform, the state furthered both the monetization of the Jiangnan economy and the transfer of power from the old established tax-captain families to the landlord-gentry that was already taking place in the countryside. In so doing, it not only opened the door for an even greater manipulation of the market by the landlord-gentry but deepened their hold over those in rural society who stood outside their direct control—namely, other local landlords and freeholder peasants (Mann 1987: 258; see also Bix 1986: 69).

Not surprisingly, as gentry-landlords set themselves to amassing "new" wealth, the distinctions between landlord and merchant began to blur (Fu Yiling 1963: 31–32, 1956; Li Wenzhi et al. 1983: 37; Shigeta 1984: 363–64; Tanaka Masatoshi 1984b). Contemporary sources contain numerous references to the increasing importance of business and profits within this landed elite. According to He Liangjun (1503–76), a native of Songjiang:

> Prior to the reigns of Xuanzong and Xiaozong [latter half of the fifteenth century], scholar officials still did not amass wealth. . . . The property of higher standing officials was only of medium size. . . . By the Zhengde period [first quarter of the sixteenth century], they all competed in running businesses to seek profit. (Cited in Shigeta 1984: 364–65)

He further noted that once the Songjiang gentry-landlords received their metropolitan (*jinshi*) degrees, they quickly tired of associating with those who "talk of literature and discuss morals." Instead they sought out "profit-seeking fellows" like themselves, whose topic of conversation was "how much profit can be made each year from estate land [or from] lending several hundred taels" (ibid., p. 365).

It was precisely among the profit-seeking landlord-gentry, then, that the commercial influences of the Ming most clearly crystallized. Through their growing involvement in an expanding commodity economy driven by peasant production and their ability to both benefit from and avoid the exactions of the state, gentry-landlords rapidly amassed extensive landholdings, large numbers of bondservants, and considerable amounts of new wealth, which they spent lavishly on luxuries and hobbies and the further accumulation of both moveable and immovable assets (Mori 1980: 47).

In the eyes of "righteous" literati, as the above and many other late Ming accounts suggest, despite their Confucian education, these profit-seeking gentrymen were abandoning established mores and morality. By "indulging in luxury without worrying about anything else," as Mori Masao puts it, they were abandoning "any regard whatsoever for the interests of local society" (1980: 46–48; see also Li Wenzhi 1981: 68–69; and Meskill 1994: 43–44). Growing outcries from the righteous gentry about the "daily weakening" of "guiding principles" reveal a mounting alarm about the disintegration of hegemony—not just at the bottom of society, where a new wave of peasant opposition was gaining momentum, but at the top as well.

Female Bondservant Labor, Cotton Textiles, and Patriarchal Landlord Operations

Along with managerial farming, centralized textile management developed on patriarchal landlord estates in various areas of the delta. It thus intertwined with agriculture as a cause and consequence of the expanding servile labor system (Fu Yiling 1981–82: 74; Nishimura 1979: 30–31; Oyama 1957–58: 5–9; Wakeman 1985: 610–11; M. Wiens 1979: 57).

"In Songjiang," as a literati-scholar of the Jiajing reign (1522–66) noted, "[even if] the great households do not themselves [weave cloth], they do supervise women workers, so we cannot say that they are not working" (Xu Xianzhong 1564, 12: 10a. Frequently, estate mistresses not only directed the operations but took part in them as well. That fact suggests that as the commodity economy developed, within the managerial landlord class the role of women, if more subtly than that of men, also changed. Consider, for example, this epitaph for a woman "who came from an old lineage" in Qingpu, Jiading county:

> Her family employed women who worked diligently as women textile laborers, and she continued to work with them. Then her husband died. After this, she often ate only vegetables and refused to wear silk garments and cosmetics. Even in the bitterest cold, she led the bondservant women in spinning. (Nishijima 1984: 62)

Indeed, even the aristocratic Lady née Yang, a noblewoman of the fourth class and wife of a governor-general, supervised the textile work of the female bondservants on the family's estate (ibid.).

The reference in the epitaph to spinning alone, rather than both spinning and weaving, is interesting. It suggests that some estates combined centralized spinning—as a form of "upper-class home industry"—with peasant household weaving. Precedent for such a combined operation can be found in the ramie industry of the Song. Using improved spinning technology, such as the multispindled water-powered frame, Song estates centralized spinning in workshops but delegated weaving to servile tenant households (A. Sheng 1990: 43–49, 160–61; Wang Zhen 1313, 20: 424–25). In the Ming, as in the Song, members of bondservant and tenant households were forced to provide various types of services to their landlord masters. Women seem to have been especially targeted for these duties, as evidenced by a statutory change in the Qing legal code prohibiting landlords from forcing a tenant's wife or daughter to perform labor service or become a concubine (Xue Yunsheng 1970, 4: 912–13). Accordingly, on some Ming estates, in what amounted to a forced putting-out system, wives of bondservants and tenants may have been required to weave estate cloth from yarn produced under more centralized management. Joseph McDermott has suggested the likelihood of a similar combined operation for silk (1981: 686).[13]

The reliance on female labor for centralized spinning, and probably for weaving as well, brought increasing numbers of women into bondservantry. In general during the Ming, they were not reduced to this condition by direct sale. As a gazetteer from Xiangshan county in Zhejiang notes: "Even if [families] suffer from extreme poverty, they are not willing to sell their sons and daughters. . . .Sometimes, however, there are years of bad harvests, and they do sell their sons. The rich families may bring them up as adopted sons" (cited in Hosono 1967: 26). And as Dong Hongdu's poem "Complaint of a Weaving Wife" says, hard-pressed peasants, to remain afloat (and probably prevent the slide into servile relations for the entire household), first sold their loom "and finally had to sell their son" (Nishijima 1984: 59–60).

But in fact the estate owners' control over their bondservants, including especially their control of marriage, at once made a commodity market in women unnecessary and created a steady supply of female bondservants (Fu Yiling 1961: 6–7; Hosono 1967: 18; Oyama 1974: 90). Male bondservants who were purchased outright or "adopted" were normally given wives selected for them by the landlord-master. These women were usually of bondservant status. Children of these unions became hereditary bondservants (Hosono 1967: 26–27) and thus constituted an expanding pool of both male and female labor. Hereditary female bondservants, if not given out as wives to the landlord's male servants, were offered in marriage—as "inducements" to long-term contractual laborers. In this kind of transaction, a laborer bonded himself to a landlord for a specified period of time—often extending over one or two decades—in exchange for a wife and support. Children of the couple automatically became bonded laborers themselves. Most got their freedom on the termination of the contract, but the laborer was forced to give up a daughter, who stayed with the master as a permanent bondservant in "compensation" for the wife he originally supplied (Fu Yiling 1961: 6–7; McDermott 1981: 681–82).

Consequently, beneath the surface of male-centered labor transactions, women became invisible links through which the entire bondservant system was expanded. At the same time, owing to landlord control of both marriage and the age when it might occur, this system created a self-perpetuating female labor force for cotton textile and other forms of production/service that could be expanded or contracted according to the wishes of the master. There are in fact strong indications that as textile production increased on the estates, landlords began delaying the marriage of female workers. The *Family Rules of the Jiang Lineage*, for example, imply as much in the stricture that "female bondservants should be married off before they are nineteen years of age. Sometimes they are given to male bondservants; sometimes one selects a [free] husband for them to marry. One should not be greedy for profit [and delay their marriage]" (cited in Hosono 1967: 18). More telling is the remark by Yao Yongji, who served as magistrate in Dongyang county (Zhejiang), that in the latter half of the Ming it became customary in some localities "for the hair of female bondservants of the powerful households to grow white without their being able to marry" (ibid.).

In sum, in the course of the Ming, both agriculture and industry managerial operations expanded on the great delta estates. The result was a broadening of patriarchal landlordism, and of its attendant effects: rural class differentiation and the economic and personal subordination of much of the peasantry. These trends accelerated with the imposition of tax payments in silver in the later Ming as more and more peasants found themselves strapped for cash. Driven by estate management and signs of growing peasant disobedience, they were pushed further still by new efforts on the part of the elite both to extend hereditary bondservantry and impose servile status on tenants and hired workers who were legally free (McDermott 1981: 680; Oyama 1974: 89; Tanaka Masatoshi 1984b: 196; P. Yang 1988: 20). In short, the internal relations of the delta were already implicitly creating conditions in which the landlord-merchant-gentry might have opted to move in decidedly new and uncharted directions.

We need not speculate, however, about what that developmental trajectory might have been for peasants, landlords, or the state. For in deepening the contradictions between peasants and their overlords, coupled with the continuing development of the commodity economy, those relations also created the general conditions out of which social institutions, economic trends, and patterns of peasant cultural politics of greater permanency would emerge. These began to appear near the end of the Ming, when a new peasant offensive fundamentally weakened patriarchal landlordism and, in containing and restricting elite options, altered the parameters of agrarian change.

Making New Terrain: Economy, Culture, and Political Community

The first signs of a new line of development surfaced in the Jiajing period (1522–66), when peasants became increasingly disobedient and rebellious. They became even more so in the Wanli reign (1573–1619), which saw tenants in various delta localities "even [going] so far as to make agreements with each other. . . not to pay their rent" (Fu Yiling 1961: 172) and increasing instances of religious insurgency (Y. Chu 1967: 109; Hamashima 1982). The momentum continued to build through the 1630's. A temporary but dislocating economic depression produced by drops in silver imports, declining foreign trade, and a drastic fall in cotton cloth prices, followed by a series of natural disasters, almost certainly contributed to this acceleration (Wakeman 1985: 632–33). With it, in any event, peasant organization improved. In 1638, 30 Suzhou villages organized a league for rent resistance in which all participants were registered and each village elected a league leader. As was common in the period, this collective resistance eventually developed into a uprising (Fu Yiling 1961: 130–37; Tanigawa & Mori 1983, 4: 271–77).

In the 1640's, as elsewhere in China with unfree labor systems, violent serf, bondservant, and servile tenant revolts erupted throughout the southern and northern Yangzi delta (Fu Yiling 1975, 1961; Oyama 1984; TZZ 1875). The almost simultaneous occurrence of these revolts in different parts of the country, and the radicalized discourse of freedom and equality they advanced, unambiguously mark not only a new line of cultural development among peasants, but a new tendency toward unification and what appears as a profound shift in peasant thought. The sources and formation of this common line of development in the late Ming warrant consideration.

THE MATERIAL BASIS

At the material level, in the delta and possibly other regions as well, the point of gestation—in the sense of creating new possibilities—unquestionably lay in the expansion of commodity production, especially of cotton textiles. Oyama Masaaki has argued this point well (see especially his seminal articles of 1957–58 and 1974). In Oyama's view, by potentially making it possible for servile bondservants and tenants, who were often dependent on patriarchal landlords for food, clothing, and other subsistence guarantees, to subsist on their own, the development of cotton spinning and weaving as a commercial household industry created a new material basis for peasants to struggle against landlords for their freedom and other gains. In short, this internal development in peasant production undermined the structural foundations of patriarchal landlordism.

Oyama's work remains controversial because of his description of the patriarchal landlord-bondservant relations as a slave system. Nevertheless, many scholars share his view that commercialized home industry, including silk and other products as well as cotton textiles, assumed new importance in the late Ming, by creating new possibilities for subsistence-level incomes among poorer, servile peasants and for the production of a surplus among the more economically stable peasant strata (Fu Yiling 1981–82; 1980; Li Wenzhi 1981; Li Wenzhi et al. 1983; M. Wiens 1974: 522–29).

On the other hand, these possibilities could not be fully realized as long as patriarchal landlords controlled peasant labor, especially that of women, the primary producers of textiles. As we have already seen, landlords required unmarried female bondservants and the women of bondservant tenant families to produce textiles in estate workshops and perhaps in their homes as well, thus robbing them of precious time for their own spinning and weaving. Moreover, they also compelled female bondservants and tenants, like their male counterparts, to participate in the work of irrigation maintenance and water control. Frequently, the bulk of this work took place in the slack agricultural season after the autumn harvest, that is, precisely when most spinning and weaving were done.

Late Ming writers were quite aware of the degree to which the unremunerated and time-consuming work of dike repair and creek dredging robbed peasants of time for and income from home industry. In the words of a Songjiang resident: "At this very moment tens and hundred of people are engaged in collective pumping. Men have to leave their tilling and women cease their weaving" (cited in Hamashima 1980: 88–89). And further: "[They] devote themselves, together with their whole family, to draining water and building dikes. The situation being thus, how can they spare time for spinning and weaving? And if they have no time for spinning and weaving, how can they obtain rice?" (ibid., p. 88).

Viewed in this light, it becomes clear that in creating new possibilities for peasants to subsist independently on their own, the expansion of commodity production simultaneously intensified the contradictions between patriarchal landlordism and peasant production. In the last analysis, those contradictions could be resolved in favor of peasants only by limiting or thwarting entirely landlords' control over peasant labor. Consequently, as we will see, along with the issues of freedom and equality in a general sense, the late Ming struggles of peasants were, strictly speaking, also struggles to establish the autonomy of peasant production.

THE CULTURAL AND POLITICAL BASIS

If thanks to Oyama and his successors, we are able to identify, with some confidence, the economic points of gestation of the late Ming risings, the circumstances of thought that gave rise to them, that is, their ideological and cultural underpinnings, are still at best dimly perceived. No one, for example, has made a systematic study of, or formulated a theory to explain, the possible connections between the emergence in the late Ming of a sustained peasant offensive and such simultaneous developments in the domain of popular thought and culture in the sixteenth and seventeenth centuries as the appearance of a radical new millenarian religion—usually termed the New White Lotus teaching (*bailianjiao*). Yet in many localities these trends intersected or overlapped. In the space permitted here, let me spotlight several elements that, I suggest, interacted with economic changes to fuel and express the new line of development among peasants.

The discourse about community and local society.   We earlier noted that, in the late Ming, "righteous" literati—many of whom were of the lesser landlord elite—mounted a critique of the "powerful and rapacious," "profit-seeking" landlord-gentry. In this critique, framed in a discourse about "concern for local society," they not only expressed real fears about the decline of established morals and values, but sought to define community in such a way as to enlarge their own role in local affairs (Mizoguchi 1978; Mori 1980). As Chen Longzheng, an urban landlord who lived near the end of the Ming, stated:

> Insofar as one lives in his own county (*xiang*), he must pay attention to the common interests of the county. . . . Problems of the empire can only be dealt with by high officials and no one is allowed to meddle in them unless he is given authority. It is only in affairs related with one's local society (*xiangbang*) that anyone regardless of whether they have official status or not can have a free say. (cited in Mori 1980: 50)

Past scholarship has dwelled largely on the importance of a dialectical "spiritual link" between this elite discourse and the growing social power of popular urban forces in the late Ming, as evidenced in urban riots and risings. Mori Masao has extended this analysis to the countryside, arguing that the ties that discourse generated created a community based on a common interest in and critical discussion of local problems, or a *xiangping* community (1980: 36–38).[14] From the Wanli period, the same period in which the wave of peasant resistance began to gain momentum, there are examples from various parts of the empire of urban risings (*minbian*) in which "the people" joined with students and lower landlord elite to purify the fiction of official action—that is, to demand that the state live up to its professed ideals by eliminating tax abuses, punishing corrupt officials, and so forth (Liu Yan 1957; Miyazaki 1954; Wakeman 1985: 105–10). But though the suggestion that such united action was based in a spiritual linkage or a community of shared concerns may give insight into the mechanisms of hegemony, especially in urban areas, it ignores the domination inherent in the class relations of the late Ming, privileges the role of the elites, and obscures the fact that in both city and countryside an altogether different—class-based—dynamic was operating.[15] Peasants became its most radical voice.

Given the evidence of that voice and other associated developments, I argue that it was not so much a matter of a single "critical community" with shared values, a common understanding, or integrated interests as a matter of members of different groups and classes engaging in the same argument, the same discourse. In this discourse, alternative strategies and conflicting goals and values were threshed out (Sabean 1984: 29). In short, though at times the discourse about community may have formed the springboard for elite-popular alliances, as a broad social initiative produced by various, essentially opposed classes, it was grounded in contested terrain. Through it, peasants, vagrants, and propertyless urban poor transformed older notions and developed their own ideas about what community meant.

It is of course quite possible to argue that, at the level of ideology, the agrarian class system had long been marked, on the one hand, by peasants' acquiescence to the dominant order; but on the other, by a unified world-view in which peasants maintained a conception of social authority based on community, and by extension, defined themselves in opposition to the hierarchical landlord-state. In earlier times the notion of community had been based on the village collectivity and an ethic, as Chinese historians have often termed it, of "land equalizationism." By the late Ming, however, as the bondservant risings revealed, the notion of community came to encompass a much broader arena, superseding village and even market town boundaries, and involving multiclassed subaltern constituencies.

Markets and itinerant intellectuals.   In historical studies of China the connection between commercial development and the highly sophisticated elite culture of the delta—as well as the large numbers of upper degree-holders and officials who congregated there—is taken as almost axiomatic.[16] The local righteous elites' discourse about community was of course shaped by these socioeconomic conditions. Similarly, although the point has often been overlooked, rapid commercialization and urban-rural linkage at once influenced, facilitated the transmission of, and provided new social space for the development of subaltern culture—among peasants as well as subordinate urban dwellers. In particular:

> The spread of intermediate market towns presented the rural poor with a freer urban environment, where they could begin to acquire a new identity of their own as the "marketplace" (*shijing*) mobs of gentry texts. . . . Many texts noted the way in which "unreliables" (*wulai*) gathered in urban marketplaces, often to gamble at night together with the *shipu* of great households and yamen lictors. There seems to have been a discernible increase in the amount of gambling that was observed in market towns in the early 1600s. (Wakeman 1985: 624–25)

Market towns not only became the nodal points for the proliferation of new pastimes and the spread of "deviant religions," but also became transmission points for the circulation of new ideas among the populace.

Teachers of radical sectarian religions, who often emerged from the ranks of the déclassé, but whose outlook was sympathetic to and resonated with that of peasants and poor urban workers, played a special role in advancing these ideas. Traveling as healers, martial arts instructors, geomancers, fortune-tellers, hawkers, food vendors, or drifters, these itinerant intellectuals established and maintained ties with students and disciples over hundreds and even thousands of miles (Naquin 1985, 1982; Walker 1993b).

I use the term "itinerant intellectual" to denote the place that such people, beyond their specific role as religious teachers, occupied in the unfolding social process—that is, as individuals engaged in organizational, directive, and educative activities (Feierman 1990: 20). Gramsci emphasizes the potential role of "organic intellectuals" of this type in developing cultural movements aimed at replacing old conceptions of the world, especially in periods when new conceptions have not yet won full acceptance. They are in a position to foster, in his words, "the condition which really modifies the ideological panorama of an age" (1971: 340).

It is in this sense that the itinerant religious intellectuals of the late Ming assume such special significance. They extended the vision of the downtrodden and propertyless, giving glimpses of "worlds unknown to the common people."

> Acting not out of private interest but out of a belief in their own absolute spiritual value, they practiced asceticism and believed themselves to be messiahs. . . . They were a stratum that stood outside or at the bottom of the already existing social hierarchy, so that in a sense they were standing at the Archimedean fulcrum in relation to the customs of their society. In other words, they had to a certain degree fallen out of their society's nominal order and customary attitudes. Because they were not fettered by these customs, they were in a position to adopt a radically different idea of the world and to promote a fervent moral religious vision unobstructed by material concerns. (Kobayashi 1984: 233, 236)

Acting as conduits of the impulses, sufferings, and desires of a subaltern world that was already in flux, itinerant intellectuals developed and transmitted a sacralized vision of a new horizontal collectivity, in which an urban-rural alliance of the poor, dispossessed, and servile would transform society. The congregations they nurtured became concrete embodiments of this vision, while in the villages, market towns, and cities, both personally and through their disciples, they advanced the ideas of radical egalitarianism to a much broader constituency.

Sectarian religion.   The most important of the radical religions was the White Lotus. Although it had much older antecedents, the White Lotus tradition coalesced as a new religious teaching in the sixteenth century, when a female-based cosmology and a millenarian eschatology were combined with written scriptures and sectarian organization (Naquin 1985: 255; 1976). The female deity it revolved around was the Eternal Mother (*wusheng laomu*), who was credited with being both the creator of humankind and the source of personal salvation for her disciples. Despite a variety of female deities in popular religious practice, there was no direct precedent for the Eternal Mother. She seems to have been a creation of the sixteenth-century sects themselves (Chesneaux 1971: 67; Overmyer 1976: 138–40). As such, her very appearance suggests that a shift in the peasants' worldview was already occurring. She stood as a symbolic beacon of communitarian ideals of absolute equality and absolute equity.

The dissemination by her teacher-disciples of an implicitly insurgent, radical discourse contributed to the decline of older certainties and ways of thought; and to the emergence of a new religiopolitical identity and conception of the world in which the notion of community transcended local and even regional boundaries. From the mid-sixteenth century, despite state prohibition and persecution, White Lotus networks steadily expanded. By the end of the century, officials stated with alarm that the White Lotus was "active everywhere." Thereafter, regenerating and intensifying its older insurgent role, the White Lotus religion increasingly became associated with violence, peasant risings, and eschatological warfare aimed at bringing about a new order or preparing the way for it (Overmyer 1976).

In the Yangzi delta, the new wave of peasant activism that began in the Jiajing reign coincided with a proliferation of White Lotus and other sectarian networks. As a literati resident of Songjiang, chagrined at the "widespread esteem" for the White Lotus and the Nonaction Sects, complained:

> The White Lotus followers burned incense and invoked Buddha like Buddhist monks praying everywhere. The Nonaction followers dispensed with Buddhist images and incense offerings alike and did not even offer sacrifices to mourn a father or mother. Actually I do not know where these teachings came from. Once they had come, simple people, men and women, were aroused and drawn to them as if mad. Males and females mixed indiscriminately and had reckless sexual relations. Then the doctrine was proclaimed of rubbing navels to direct the vital breath. (Cited in Meskill 1994: 105)

The rapid mid-century spread of heterodox religious teachings was flanked in 1557 by an abortive millenarian rebellion.[17] Moreover, in the years 1555–58, rumors of miracle-working magicians and magical flying objects rapidly spread to virtually every delta community, and then along the entire coastal region from the Yangzi to Canton (Ter Haar 1992: 172–95).[18]

Increasing resistance in the early seventeenth century was interspersed with religiously inspired actions, including an aborted attempt to link White

Lotus sects in a delta-wide rebellion (Hamashima 1982). Although they did not take a religious form, many of the bondservant risings at the end of the Ming and in the early Qing had religious or secret society ties. And such insurgencies as the Black Dragon Society rising of 1645, waged by rural bondservants and urban hired laborers, reflected the urban-rural groupings common to White Lotus communities (Tanaka Masatoshi 1984b: 197).

The key point here is that by the late Ming, the radically egalitarian and communal ideas of White Lotus and affiliated teachings were becoming deeply embedded in local society. To the extent that, in certain circumstances, religion can become a means of rationalizing the world and real life, and provide a general framework for practical activity, the proliferation of these religious networks concretely expressed "the will of the people." As such, it clearly contributed to the changing ideological and cultural environment in which peasants and their allies became so bold as to fight for equality and liberation and thereby radically altered the contours of the discourse about community.

Martial arts.   Like the heterodox religions, martial arts training rose in popularity and spread among the peasantry in the late sixteenth and early seventeenth centuries to serve as another wellspring of new modes of thought and action. By forming the medium for the militarization of peasant society, both psychologically and strategically, martial arts began to alter the balance of forces and dynamics of class struggle, and thus also became a point of crystallization of a more independent popular will.

The practice carried other significant implications as well, for martial arts training did not simply concentrate on developing physical-martial prowess. It emphasized spiritual enlightenment as well. In fact, until its incorporation into the White Lotus organizational structure near the turn of the eighteenth century, martial arts created an arena for independent action and offered practitioners the prospect of determining their destiny in this life—something that was unavailable to White Lotus adherents, who could only expect to make contact with the Eternal Mother at death (Naquin 1985: 275).

In short, martial arts created the ideological possibility for producers and the dispossessed to move beyond the world of the village or market town and "set out on the long task" to become the political and religious "true" person (Kobayashi 1984: 239). Its political and spiritual concerns blended with those of sectarian religion, and like the latter, it worked to expand older notions of community. Both not only became forms of expression of a popular consciousness, but functioned as key integrative elements of a new historical configuration—an emerging subaltern culture of multiregional, even national, proportion. At the same time changes in White Lotus and in peasant culture interpenetrated—the martial arts tradition of the peasantry forming the foundation for the transformation of religious groups into armed factions, and the

White Lotus network becoming the vehicle for actualizing a shared vision of an unbounded horizontal community that was expanding in peasant society.

Other integrating elements undoubtedly contributed to this emergent culture of the oppressed, including new conduits of transmission like the great interprovincial pilgrimages (Naquin & Yu 1992; see also Walthall 1986). Our identification and understanding of such elements must await future research. In any case, there is little doubt that this era of social, economic, and cultural change saw a profound shift in peasant thought.

Actualizing Community: The Ming-Qing Risings

In this time of enormous change, peasants lost faith in their old ideologies—that is to say, stopped believing what they used to believe. This is not to suggest a complete break with the past, merely that new conceptions began intermingling with and transforming the old ones in "bizarre . . . combinations" (Gramsci 1971: 341). The most visible sign of this ideological shift was the new tack that peasants and other subalterns began to take toward the system of domination. Exposure to a sociopolitical discourse permeated with moral, ethical, and spiritual concerns opened up new possibilities for loosening the suffocating grip of Confucian fatalism and for transforming individual resistance into communal initiative.

The bondservant-serf risings in the Yangzi delta in the 1640's and 1650's provide incontrovertible evidence of this political impulse. Their "eruption" throughout the delta (as in other areas) can only be understood in light of the larger cultural movement that framed their appearance and, relatedly, the radical regional political culture that had already begun to coalesce in antirent and religious struggles.[19] This passage from relative passivity to militant offensive brought to the surface a crisis in ruling-class hegemony and, by extension, a general crisis of the state.[20]

This is not to deny, of course, any connection between the rather sudden appearance of these revolts and the fall of the Ming state. Plainly, Song Qi, who commanded 12 legions of armed bondservants in Anhui, recognized the tactical advantages created by the new power vacuum: "When our grandfather was made a bondservant," he said, "his descendants were automatically categorized in that fashion. Now we are endowed by Heaven with a special opportunity, for our masters are all weak and feeble and are not able to take up arms. We can take advantage of their crisis. Even if they want to suppress us, they do not have time" (cited in M. Wiens 1979: 59). Nevertheless, it is clear that what drove peasants and their urban allies to avail themselves of this "special opportunity" was an entirely new discourse of freedom, equality, and liberation. In the words of one participant: "The emperor has changed, so the masters should be made into servants; master and servants should address each other as brothers." Consequently, as an account from Shanghai illustrates, the destruction of deeds of servitude, coupled with a demand for freedom, became the hallmark of the risings:

> The farmers of the city are all or almost all slaves of the retired officials and literati of high standing and cultivate their lands with a share for their sustenance. . . . Now seeing that there was no king, since the one of Nanking was not yet acclaimed, they made a body of many thousands, and asked their lords for papers of bondage because [with the fall] of the Chinese government they already were free. (Cited in Wakeman 1985: 634)

Another text elaborates:

> The bondservants of Chu Shengyao seized knives and butchered their master and his son, after which they burnt them to ashes. The trouble spread to the great households in other village communities, all of which were burned and pillaged. In addition, Lu and others led a band of bondservants from various families into the county capital. They first went to the homes of the gentry to seek out the bonds recording their sale. Once the gentry's houses had been razed and the masters beaten and insulted, the owners hastily wrote out deeds of manumission. (Cited in Fu Yiling 1961: 95)

The risings, as noted, were the work of various groups and classes. Armed bondservant bands and legions allied and combined with "tenant armies" (Wakeman 1985: 636). Multiclassed-occupational solidarities were also common (Mori 1977; M. Wiens 1979: 60). A rising in Runing (Henan) in 1658, for example, brought together bondservant-serfs demanding their freedom; hired laborers who, on the termination of their contracts, had tried to leave but had been pursued by their masters as "renegade bondservants"; and tenants who, though legally free, had found themselves and their families being treated as bondservants (Tanaka Masatoshi 1984b: 196). The unity of these groups reveals a merging of class interests in a political movement aimed at overturning the existing social order and establishing a new principle of equality in local society. The Ming-Qing struggles, in short, reinforced and began to actualize the imaginings of the emergent political culture by projecting a sense of community to a wider collectivity—to all those who shared an antagonism to the agrarian elite. In practice and in terms of their worldview, peasants thus moved beyond the boundedness of locality and the differences in legal status among them.

Although some risings met with defeat, the movement as a whole succeeded. Large numbers of peasants immediately gained their freedom, which effectively broke the back of the patriarchal landlord system. The Qing government eventually recognized and sealed this victory. In a series of decrees (1727–1825), it emancipated bondservants and other hereditarily inferior groups by legally recognizing them as commoners rather than "base people" (1727-38); and it declared it illegal for any landlord to justify reducing tenants to bondservantry on the grounds that he provided "land, burial-ground, or housing" for them (M. Wiens 1979: 60; Ye Xianen 1981: 117; 1979).[21]

The Ming-Qing risings, moreover, involved more than the issues of servitude, freedom, and independence. Since large numbers, if not the majority, of bondservants worked the land as servile tenants rather than as fieldhands under the direct supervision of managerial landlords or their overseers, many of the risings also became struggles for new terms of tenure and even property rights of a sort. In this respect, they built on and extended the resistance of servile and free tenants during the preceding decades. They played a major role in bringing about fixed rents, the abolition of extra labor services and customary donations to landholders, and permanent cultivating rights that amounted, for all practical purposes, to dual ownership (Fu Yiling 1961; Hamashima 1974; Li Wenzhi 1981: 75-78; Oyama 1984; M. Wiens 1980). With dual ownership, or the "one field, two owners" (*yitian liangzhu*) system as it is commonly known, landlords retained legal ownership of and paid taxes on the subsoil, and tenants paid fixed rent on and gained permanent cultivating rights to the topsoil. Rents were usually lower than in nonpermanent tenures (Fujii 1984, 1979-80, 1975; Kusano 1975, 1970).

The overall impact of the combined bondservant-tenant risings also served to further landlord acceptance of dual ownership. Most important, in forcing the disintegration of the servile labor system, the risings brought about the rather rapid demise of estate-based managerial farming and accelerated urban residence among landlords. In a situation made worse by population depletion during the Ming-Qing transition, some urban landlords willingly accepted permanent tenures and fixed rents or dual ownership (or both) in order to ensure a continuous labor force on their rural property. This was particularly the case in areas of wet-rice farming, presumably because landlords were thereby relieved of part of the expense of maintaining irrigation systems (Bernhardt 1992: 24-27; Shiraishi 1960; P. Yang 1988: 205, 232-55).[22] Previously, as noted, patriarchal landlords did not have to hire labor for this work since they could order bondservants and tenants to perform it. It was, in fact, precisely because such unremunerated work consumed time and energy that tenants otherwise could have devoted to their own plots and textile production that the abolition of extra labor services became a key issue in the risings. On the other hand, the evidence indicates that prior to the risings in some localities where landlords (presumably because of absenteeism) had begun to neglect or even disregard water control responsibilities, tenants had already assumed that authority themselves, giving them further justification for demanding permanent tenure and topsoil rights.[23]

Viewed in longer-term perspective, along with peasants' winning their freedom, the change in the property system embodied in the new institution of dual ownership stands as a milestone in the agrarian class struggle in the Yangzi delta and in a new line of development among peasants. It at once gave peasants greater stability and independence and created a new foundation for further rent resistance in the Qing.

The Other Side of Peasant Liberation Struggles: Reestablishing Patriarchy at Home

The egalitarian impulses of the late Ming peasant struggles were paradoxically constrained and undercut by a central contradiction: the very developments in production that undergirded the new activism also deepened sexual inequality.

We earlier noted the pathbreaking analyses of Oyama Masaaki and other scholars who spotlight the critical role played by household commodity production in providing new material terrain for peasant struggles. Nevertheless, they fail to draw attention to the important fact that, whether working on their family's account or for a master, women still formed the primary workforce in cotton textiles. For this reason, the peasants' success in wresting patriarchal controls from landlords had very different consequences for women than for men. Simply put, it not only established the greater autonomy of peasant production, but in a very real sense relocated patriarchal relations to the peasant family and thus gave new strength to the sexual division of labor on which production was based. Whereas earlier in the delta peasant women had shared in much of the productive work, including farming, with the expansion of the commodity economy, spinning and weaving increasingly became their central productive activity (Nishijima 1984: 26, 33, 59–60, 63).

Signifying the importance of these activities to the family economy, a chronicler from Songjiang tersely noted: "When weaving supplements farming, weaving females are profitable" (cited in M. Wiens 1974: 527). And as Xu Guangqi indicated in his late Ming agricultural handbook, in many localities women's "profitability" became more than a mere supplement to agriculture. In Songjiang, he noted, where the total tax assessment was ten times the Song assessment,

> the people all depend on the shuttle and the loom. This situation is not peculiar to Songjiang. The same applies to the cloth and silk floss produced in Suzhou, Hangzhou, Changzhou, and Zhenjiang, and to the silk produced in Jiaxing and Huzhou. All depend on women's skills. [By relying on them] it is possible to pay all of the [assessed] taxes and also provide for a daily livelihood. If [people] had to rely on the income from the land, there would be no way to manage. (Cited in Nishijima 1984: 33)

Yet as I have discussed elsewhere (Walker 1993a), women did not improve their position as a result of their growing commercial importance in the family and rural economies. On the contrary, within the family the redefining of the sexual division of labor to accommodate household commodity production reinforced male control of female labor and created a new arena for the intensification of patriarchal relations. The income they generated was controlled not by the women themselves, but by the family head. Moreover, as women became more closely confined to the household and to labor within it—thereby also establishing in peasant society new material conditions for the spread of Confucian norms—along with farming, they lost marketing and other activities that had been common in the delta earlier (Elvin 1973: 273–74; Nishijima 1984: 55; A. Sheng 1990).

Thus, the common saying, "The men till and the women weave" (*nangong nuzhi*), which is usually taken as expressing the traditional sexual division of labor in China, really only became fully applicable with the spread of the commercial cotton economy in the Ming. It summarizes the fundamental features of a structure of production based on unequal relations between the sexes and formed by a unity of small-scale farming and commercial home industry. As such, it also exposes the underside of peasants' liberation struggles: an intensification of peasant patriarchy achieved in large part through the systematic control of women for commodity production in a rigid sexual division of labor.

The result was a contradictory mind-set that led peasants to at once struggle against and acquiesce to an oppressive social system capped by a despotic state. By simultaneously undermining patriarchal landlordism and strengthening the power of peasant men as independent patriarchs of their own households, the Ming-Qing risings produced a crisis of ruling-class hegemony. At the same time, however, they acted as a powerful dissolvant of the state-landlord contradiction over the peasantry inherent in the servile labor system and, in effect, deepened the peasantry's ties to the state by making patriarchal peasant households mediums for the extension of its power and a force of its ideology.[24] In this sense, like the landlord-gentry they opposed, peasant families were "not separate from state power" but became its basic unit.[25] As one scholar has put it, the notions of peasant patriarchy (or literally of the small peasant patriarchal system, *xiaonong jiazhang zhi*) had a way of extending themselves, making it easier for hierarchical authority, and thus monarchial despotism, to be accepted (Mao Jiaqi 1979: 47–50).[26]

2 *The View from the Periphery:*
Tongzhou and the Northern Delta

RECENT STUDIES OF "early modern" China, transparently recreating the narrative teleologies of capitalism and the nation state, have broadly supported a view of increasing social, economic, and cultural integration during the last centuries of imperial rule. They suggest that factors such as the growth of commerce, towns, and interregional trade, spreading literacy, and the state's promotion of cultural orthodoxy reduced the importance of regional differences and fueled Chinese *cultural homogenization* (D. Johnson et al. 1985; Rowe 1984; J. Watson & Rawski 1988). In stressing the development of a distinctly subaltern culture and a new unifying tendency in oppositional peasant politics during the late Ming, the preceding chapter has already called these notions into question. This chapter further problematizes them by considering the position of Tongzhou and the northern delta within the larger regional economy during that period.

It argues that during the Ming, stimulated by the spread of cotton cultivation and the commercializing cotton economy, many of the dynamics characterizing the elite and peasant paths in Jiangnan also appeared in the northern delta. Over the course of the dynasty, however, cultural diffusion and economic integration were counterbalanced by tendencies that simultaneously increased Jiangnan's dominance and worked to peripheralize the north. Complementing and extending the commercial economic trajectory, state actions and agencies in the northern delta, as in Subei more generally, contributed to the construction of Tongzhou and its environs as a periphery.

The Origins of Cotton Textile Production in Tongzhou

The story of cotton textile transmission from the southern delta to Tongzhou is intimately bound up with that of migrants and the dramatic changes in land structure that occurred along the northern banks of the Yangzi after the Song. Most sources agree that migrants from Songjiang, specifically the Pudong district east of Shanghai, first transmitted knowledge of cotton farming and cotton textile techniques to Chongming, Haimen, and then Nantong.

In the late Yuan or early Ming, Song-Pu residents had begun to migrate to sparsely inhabited Chongming, an island north of Chuansha that formed during the Tang dynasty when shifting currents caused alluvium deposits to build up at the mouth of the Yangzi (You Qing 1936: 57). Earlier settlers had made their living primarily from fishing and salt collection. In the Yuan-Ming they and the Song-Pu migrants took up cotton cultivation, converting the reed-covered marsh and salt flats to cotton fields (Lin Jubai 1984: 6–8).

Some of the Song-Pu migrants settled to the northwest of Chongming in Haimen, an area that also originally formed as an alluvial island but later connected with the northern land mass (Lin Jubai 1984: 23). Designated as a county in the tenth century, Haimen was placed under the administrative jurisdiction of Tongzhou (Zhu Zhangmin & Cheng Yun 1984: 7).[1] In contrast to Tongzhou, however, where population density reflected much older settlement patterns, Haimen was still relatively unpopulated (TZZ, 1: 1, 5: 2–5). Thus like Chongming, it attracted migrant settlers. Its popular name in the Ming, "eastern cloth domain" (dongbuzhou), suggests the importance of cotton weaving by that time (Lin Jubai 1984: 23).

Large numbers of these migrants or their descendants were subsequently pressed to move to eastern Nantong by natural disasters. A major land collapse on Chongming in the reign of Hongwu (1368–99) saw a wholesale exodus to the mainland, and the waisha (outer sand flats and islands) areas of Haimen collapsed several times during the Yuan and Ming. Because of these disasters, the Haimen county government changed its location four times in a 300-year period (Lin Jubai 1984: 23; You Qing 1936: 57; Zhu Zhangmin & Cheng Yun 1984: 7). In one of the most disastrous floods in Haimen, in 1528, 30,000 people were said to have lost their lives, 30 percent of the total land area collapsed, and half the population was forced to relocate (Lu Jubai 1984: 12; TZZ, 4: 8).[2] Tongzhou authorities permitted many of the destitute to relocate in the new land areas on the edge of the Yangzi near the Nantong-Haimen border, where the town of Xingren later emerged. These lands had gradually been built up from alluvial soil and sand eroded away in Haimen and Chongming (Cihai 1979: 2: 2152; You Qing 1936: 57; Zhu Zhangmin & Cheng Yun 1984: 8).

By the mid-Ming, as a result of the original migrations and resettlements, Jiangnan settlers constituted a distinct group in Haimen and southeastern Nantong, their language (belonging to the Wu dialect, as opposed to the Huai dialect of Nantong-Rugao), customs, and production skills differing from those of the indigenous residents (Guan Jincheng 1956: 3; 43; Lin Jubai 1984: 7). Their settlements spurred the development of cotton cultivation and the dissemination of cotton textile production throughout the Nantong-Haimen area (Lin Jubai 1984).

Commercial Development

Cotton acreage spread rapidly in Nantong-Haimen during the Ming (Zou Qiang 1984: 31). By the Qianlong period (1736–95), a Qing official who toured Tongzhou, Taicang, and Songjiang estimated that in all three localities eight of every ten peasants devoted some land to cotton (Li Wenzhi 1957, 1: 83). The rapid expansion of cotton acreage reflected not only soil and climatic conditions, but factors favoring commercialization as well. Tongzhou's location on the Yangzi made it easily accessible by water. At the same time, it lay near the terminal point of the overland trade route extending from Shandong southward to Rugao. Internal water transport was also convenient. The Yuyan canal that crossed the department, a second river, the Quanchang, and a dense network of creeks and small canals connected the two major towns, Jinsha and Nantong, with outlying districts (MMT 1941: 2; Shiyebu 1933, 4: 41; *Tongzhou zhi* 1577). Finally, Nantong cotton was of the highest quality. It possessed fine, long fibers, superior texture, and an unusual whiteness. Given these attributes, "Tongzhou cotton" gradually gained a wide reputation, creating significant demand for it in the Ming-Qing and enabling it to take premier position on the Shanghai cotton exchange in the twentieth century ("Diaocha Tongchonghai" 1918: 65; *Shina* 1920: 448–49).

Commercialized production and marketing emerged during the first half of the Ming, carried on by peasants and petty traders, principally from Haimen and Chongming, who crossed the river to sell their surplus cotton in the Taicang-Songjiang areas (*Songjiang fuzhi* 1631, 8: 16–17; Walker 1986). There is little evidence of local merchant involvement in cotton trading in this period (ZSZ n.d., 1: 25). Merchants in marketing towns such as Jinsha confined themselves chiefly to the grain trade that accompanied the expansion of cotton acreage and local sales of handwoven cloth (Jin Zhihuai 1984: 1).

By the mid-Ming, however, stimulated by textile expansion in the south and the quality of northern delta cotton, Jiangnan cloth merchants had developed a preference for yarn spun from or including Tongzhou and Chongming cotton. Moreover, cotton prices in Tongzhou-Haimen were consistently lower than in the southern delta. Consequently, southern delta merchants regularly purchased large supplies of cotton in Nantong for Jiangnan producers (Lin Jubai 1984: 8). Large merchant firms from Anhui purchased Tongzhou cotton for marketing in Jiangnan as well. Traders from Shandong and northern Jiangsu cities such as Xuzhou and Haiying also became regular customers but on a much smaller scale. They drove donkey and horse trains carrying items of trade down the overland route to Rugao, then made the return trip home, their pack animals laden with 60-*jin* bags of cotton purchased in Nantong (Lin Jubai 1984: 7–8). In the early Qing merchants from Canton and Fujian also came to Tongzhou to buy cotton for use in their home areas, where sugarcane and tea were displacing cotton farming (Chao Kang 1977: 23; Lin Jubai 1984: 8).

Wang Yunchao's *A Glimpse of Tongzhou*, written in the Qianlong period, indicates that by then the Guangdong-Fujian merchants who arrived in the delta each fall with hundreds of sugar-laden boats had begun to purchase cloth instead of cotton, reflecting the almost total demise of weaving in their home areas (Chu Hua n.d.: 11; Lin Jubai 1984: 8). In addition to cotton, the Shandong traders were purchasing cloth for shipment to Manchuria, which in the late nineteenth century became the principal marketing area for Nantong *tubu* (local handwoven cloth). This trade in fact first developed through the Shandong traders' acquaintance with the handwoven cloth sacks used for packing raw cotton (Lin Jubai 1984: 7–8). Migrants from Chongming-Haimen who settled in Xingren and other new land areas initially produced much of this cloth, locally called *shabu* (sand cloth) or *xibu* (loosely woven cloth; Lin Jubai 1984: 24).

By the mid-Qing commercial cloth production was an important source of supplemental income for many peasant families in Xingren, Jinsha, and other eastern districts. In the oldest production districts where population density was greatest, it may have been the principal source of income for some families. A Qianlong gazetteer records that, in Xingren, income from one textile worker could support three people, and the labor of three was sufficient for the support of eight people (*[Qianlong] Zhili Tongzhou zhi* 1775, 11: 9).

Centered in Jinsha, new commercial and entrepreneurial operations paralleled the growth of the cloth trade. The first group of firms involved with nonlocal trade were collectively known as the "county firms" (*xianzhuang*), an appellation reflecting their local brokerage character. These firms originally acted as brokers who selected cloth and managed transactions for traveling merchants, charging a fee for their services. But by the late Qing they had turned to buying quantities of cloth from peasant-weavers at local markets for sale to merchants from other areas. Even so, their "commission" was still based on the old method of discounting, that is, they received a small fee for each bolt of cloth sold. Eventually these firms developed a limited number of regular credit customers who sent in orders by post and made prepayment through native banking networks (Lin Jubai 1984: 140–64; Peng Zeyi et al. 1957, 3: 715; Wang Zunwu 1980).

Sometime after the emergence of the county firms, a second group of Nantong brokers, the "Nanjing firms" (*jingzhuang*), began arranging shipments of goods to merchants in the vicinity of Nanjing. By the late Qing those firms too were selling directly from their personal stocks (Da Shiji 1980; Lin Jubai 1984: 165–72).

In the Ming-Qing period, then, revolving around cotton, cloth, native banking, and imports of grain, commercialization gradually expanded and became more complex. Yet despite the popularity of Nantong cotton, and hence the potential for local textile development that might have rivaled the Songjiang industry, raw cotton rather than cloth remained the dominant item of trade. Indeed, Tongzhou-Haimen's annual cloth output never surpassed the production levels reached in Songjiang in the sixteenth century (Nishijima 1948–49, 1: 29; Zhu Zhangmin & Cheng Yun 1984: 8).[3]

The commercial structure presents another apparent anomaly. Although specialized cloth brokerages and wholesalers developed in the cloth trade, no comparable structure appeared to handle the large volume of cotton exports. Even by the late nineteenth century, though relatively numerous, cotton firms were extremely small, their operations usually involving only tiny amounts of capital and one- or two-person staffs (*Shina* 1920: 453–63).

When viewed in isolation, the pattern of commercialization in Tongzhou-Haimen thus appears paradoxical. If considered in the context of the larger delta economy, however, and especially from the perspective of Jiangnan's earlier start, these contradictions dissolve. In this context, as Antonia Finnane argues for the Subei area as a whole, the analytic insights of internal colonial models are especially useful. These models draw attention to the ways in which core areas at once seek to exploit an internal periphery materially so as to stabilize and augment their own advantages by exerting influence on that periphery's production, infrastructure, and finance (Finnane 1993: 215). Michael Hechter, whose study of Celtic ethnicity in Great Britain informs Finnane's analysis, argues that such situations, and the division of labor that springs from them, become possible precisely because core areas are able to maintain their initial advantages as they enter into closer relations with a periphery (Finnane 1993: 216; Hechter 1977). Over time, of course, since core areas are the principal beneficiaries, relations of this type tend to widen the gap between the two.

The operation of a similar dynamic in the delta in the Ming-Qing period became a key factor creating the apparent contradictions in the developmental path of Nantong and the cotton-producing areas of the northern delta. Jiangnan's merchant elites, privileged by older commercial foundations and a well-established cotton textile industry in their own region, were able to keep the north a mere supplier of raw materials. To a large extent their activities, and those of the large, well-connected merchant firms that serviced the Jiangnan area, short-circuited the development of local merchant capital in the northern delta. Viewed from the perspective of commodity and merchant capitalist development, outside rather than local merchants became key beneficiaries of cotton commercialization in Nantong.

Although as discussed above long-distance trade did develop through merchants from Shandong, Nanjing, and Guangdong-Fujian, only in the last case did cloth sales ever reach a sizable proportion. Even more significant in the long run, Nantong's cloth merchants were never able to break into the interregional trade in the south's products. Consequently, as the delta economy grew, the northern delta increasingly became a structurally subordinate partner of Jiangnan, and Nantong's merchant-entrepreneurs were forced to carve out marketing spheres that did not fundamentally challenge Songjiang's established position as clothier of the empire.

The State and Subei as Periphery

Finnane highlights the role of the state in peripheralizing Subei in general. She emphasizes the "ambivalent, arguably regressive, effects" of its control over salt collection; the additional layers beyond the usual bureaucratic structures of "outsider" salt and water-control administrations in the area; and the way in which Jiangnan's cultural dominance developed in tandem with its economic and political domination of Subei.[4]

In the Ming-Qing period coastal portions of Nantong-Haimen lay within the Huainan Salt Yards, which traversed the entire coastal region of Jiangsu province from the Yangzi to the Huai rivers and constituted China's major salt-producing area. There were six salterns in Tongzhou alone (ZSZ n.d., I: 49). A government monopoly, the Lianghuai Salt Administration, supervised production in both the Huainan yards and the less productive Huaibei salterns, situated north of the Huai River. As a commodity of enormous commercial value, salt might have compensated for the poor state of agriculture in much of Subei stemming from a lack of diversity and an inadequate waterway system (Finanne 1993: 218–20). Instead, the structural inequalities created by the Lianghuai monopoly worked against economic change in the area. As Finnane states:

> First, the monopoly placed the control of and profits from the trade in the hands of a relatively small number of licensed merchants, mostly . . . from the southern Anhui prefecture of Huizhou. Second, the salt merchants mostly congregated in Yangzhou, the administrative center of the monopoly. . . . Third, from the beginning of the Qing dynasty, ownership of the salterns was devolving into the hands of salt merchants, giving them increasing control over production. This meant that outsiders, rather than natives of the region, increasingly enjoyed the profits of both the retail and the wholesale trades. . . . Finally, the restrictions on types of land use within the salt production zone, much as they were often honoured in the breach, . . . prevented diversified economic activities in this area. . . . Despite the reform of the monopoly in the nineteenth century, the power of the salt merchants and salt officials remained entrenched and was pitched against efforts to broaden the economic base in Subei. (1993: 220–21)

Finnane further argues that political subordination, in a complex layering of state administration, also bore powerfully against economic growth in Subei. She emphasizes that this was not so much a consequence of intentional discriminatory treatment by the state as the fact that in China

> a necessary premise for the concept of metropole . . . is that the regional cores through which power was dispersed were harnessed to the machine of the centralized state. . . . This is not to cede too much authority to the state but to describe the total system of power achieved through the bureaucratic organization of China, a system which yielded internal peripheries which can be described as more than purely economic in nature. (1993: 224)

Accordingly, most of the centers of official power for Subei lay outside the region. These included, besides the imperial government in Beijing, the Liangjiang governor-general in Nanjing and the governor of Jiangsu in Suzhou. Moreover, the salt administration and Jiangnan branch of the river administration, "both of which had enormous power in Subei," were centered in Yangzhou and Qingjiangpu, that is, in cities located on the edge of Subei. Yangzhou especially was "like a colonial port city." It was also the only Subei city considered to be of any consequence by the Jiangnan elite. But in large part it owed its reputation and prosperity to its housing of powerful southern salt merchants and salt administrators. In a major exception to the rule, even the local gentry played only a marginal role in the city until the salt merchants' power began to decline near the turn of the nineteenth century (Finnane 1993: 224–25, 228).

The presence of large numbers of state officials, functionaries, and military forces used in the administration of water control and the salt trade lent unusual strength to the state apparatus in Subei—a situation that inevitably created clashes with local officials and elites. This was nowhere more obvious than in the matter of irrigation and water control. The state's interests in maintaining salt transport routes and the Grand Canal for tax grain shipments meant that salt and river administrators had the final say in water control. The consequence was policies on water levels and drainage that appear not only to have often conflicted with the desires of local officials charged with protecting farmland and dwellings, but to have contributed to frequent flooding in Subei (Finnane 1993: 225–26).

The major protection against coastal flooding in the Tongzhou-Haimen area was a 350-km sea wall known as Fan's Dike (*Fan di*). The first segment of the dike, extending southward 70 km from Taizhou, was constructed in the eleventh century under the supervision of Fan Zhongyan, the salt commissioner of Xixi in Taizhou department. Working continuously for three years, some 40,000 state-recruited laborers completed construction of this segment, which measured 10 m wide at its base and 6.7 m high. Gradual extensions brought the wall all the way to Nantong-Haimen (Lu Mei 1984: 9–11).

Although the dike provided needed protection to salters and coastal residents, over time salt administrators and other outside officials gave little priority to its maintenance. When they did make periodic repairs, it was usually only following a major disaster or in response to repeated pressure from local residents. Consequently, within a hundred years of its construction, parts of the wall frequently gave way, leaving houses and fields deep in water and residents homeless. In a major collapse during the early Ming, thousands of peasants perished. By the mid-Ming high tides were regularly breaching the wall in 72 places, and by the late Ming some sections had disappeared entirely (Lu Mei 1984: 11–12).[5] The neglect of coastal protection by state agents concerned primarily with extracting the resources of the area contributed to Subei's peripheralization and often entailed disastrous consequences for local residents.

The presence of influential outsiders in the Tongzhou area and their affiliation with the centers of power also affected the development of landlordism. In the last chapter we saw that in the southern delta through most of the Ming water control had fallen largely to the patriarchal landlords. Similarly, the next chapter will show that, in the Qing, though the state assumed a greater regulatory role, irrigation and water control became key arenas of gentry management in the evolving structure of landlord rule in the south. But in Subei, the larger state presence continued to deter this type of landlord involvement. The result was new forms of rentier ownership in which the local gentry lost out as "powerful and crafty military officers and salt merchants [were able to] occupy the good land" (ZSZ n.d., 1: 46). Bureaucratic connections also enabled members of the powerful Jiangnan elite to become rentier landlords in Tongzhou, especially in cases of land reclamation.

After the Qianlong emperor's famous inspection tour of Jiangnan, for example, officials and gentry in Changshu and Taicang used the emperor's remarks about the need to reclaim a large alluvial oasis that had formed along the Yangzi near Nantong city as their entry into gaining control of a large portion of the new land. With a director sent by the imperial government and workers (who later became tenant-settlers) recruited from Chongming, Changshu, and Taicang, they embarked on a huge reclamation project, earning themselves paddy areas ranging in size from several hundred to 2,000 mu (Xu Chaoming 1985: 1–2).[6] Dominance and state connections thus favored the Jiangnan elite in land acquisition as well as mercantile activity in the north.

Cultural Peripheralization

Throughout the Ming and most of the Qing Tongzhou, like Subei, was culturally defined by the Jiangnan elite as a backward, unchanging, and inferior area. By reinforcing notions of its material weakness, this cultural construction contributed to the south's dominance and subordination of the north. In point of fact, however, the evidence strongly suggests that, until the late Ming, under the stimulus of the commercializing cotton economy, social and economic change was as dramatic in the northern as the southern delta. Thereafter, as the gap between north and south developed and continued to widen, peripheralization took its toll. It not only sapped the economic energy of the earlier dynamism, but necessarily affected the character both of the elite and agrarian class relations.

To the extent that local gazetteers and other contemporary accounts for the Tongzhou-Haimen area are reliable and not merely rearticulations of texts and ideas produced at higher, more prestigious levels of the cultural hierarchy, they suggest an astonishing cultural fluidity until the mid-sixteenth century in which older standards, mores, and practices were decomposing among all classes. The interpenetrating effects of commercial growth, new wealth, and cultural flow were already becoming evident within the elite by the end of the fifteenth century. According to one account:

> The written history of Tongzhou [in 1410] said that people respected each other. They were not engaged in trade . . . and used only 10 percent of their wealth to build their houses. They believed in living sincerely and honestly and hated obscene things. Their marriages maintained [familial] status and prestige. . . . When they worshipped Heaven, they adopted traditional etiquette and customs and did not [turn to] Buddhism. They paid taxes and performed corvée services promptly. In the city, there were no vagabonds, prostitutes, or gamblers. Women were confined to the inner rooms of their homes and were not allowed to attend banquets. Although we are now only seventy or eighty years away [from that time] nothing remains as before. (ZSZ n.d., 1: 25)

The author goes on to deplore the new extravagance that was beginning to replace the austerity of former times. This tendency deepened in myriad ways in the sixteenth century, especially during the Jiajing reign (1522–66; TZZ 1875, 1: 57). Not only did weddings and funerals become much more expensive and elaborate (ZSZ n.d., 1: 38), but members of the elite had taken to aping the fashions and coveting the products of Jiangnan and other centers. In the words of a sixteenth-century writer:

> Young people today are not satisfied with locally made luxury products but instead want the well-known brands of silk and satin produced elsewhere. They do not care about price and only pay attention to beauty and fashion. It has become standard to treat a person according to his dress. [Even] if you attend a rural gathering dressed in simple clothing, the local people will look down on you and offer you an insignificant seat. Consequently, simple cloth disappeared from the markets quite some time ago because no one wanted to wear it. (TZZ 1875, 1: 57)

Extravagance and conspicuous consumption became even more notable with the rise of a more characteristically urban culture in Tongzhou town:

"Today, from the rich to the poor, everyone enjoys drinking in tea and wine houses with their prostitutes and lovers, playing chess, and chatting about everything. . . . They do not mind spending all the money their ancestors accumulated to enjoy themselves" (ZSZ n.d., 1: 37). Even in the countryside food and entertaining became more sumptuous in the sixteenth century:

[Now even] rural [elites] tend to hold feasts many times a month for no explicit purpose. There must be a special table for guests and fine fruits brought in from afar are served. No inexpensive food can be included in the meal. . . . Singing and dancing are added to please the guests. Some dandies are almost illiterate but indulge themselves in strolling about admiring the mountains and water. They try to imitate celebrated [literary] figures, but they are actually only worthless people in imposing attire. Our forefathers did not slaughter livestock unless for some significant event, and they held feasts according to social status and rites. Today people simply pursue luxury and do not care about order. (TZZ 1875, 1: 57)

As these moralistic accounts suggest, the new wealth of the commercializing economy was bringing social divisions within the elite into flux. As in Jiangnan, these changes were compounded by and often intertwined with the growing local importance of landlord-gentry, who, stimulated by state policies, were assuming prerogatives previously exercised only by officials and prominent Tongzhou lineages.

The older group of landlord-magnate (*haojia*) families held large amounts of land and numerous bondservant-serfs. They formed the counterpart to the semiofficial landed elite in Jiangnan who had served as tax captains before the rise of the gentry-landlords.[7] At the outset of the Ming, as nonbureaucratic literati of neo-Confucian training, they reportedly maintained the austere lifestyles and values that were so idealized in later gazetteer accounts. But exemplary as these families may have been as Confucian practitioners who followed rules of social propriety, attended to local problems, and served as functionaries of the state, they were dominant and virtually autonomous in their own districts. As such, they could and did easily run roughshod over local populations. Various accounts suggest that their bondservant overseers and sons tyrannized local communities, and that they themselves were not beyond acquiring new servants and land through coercion and forcible seizure. Commercialization and the instability of land and labor as a result of flooding and land collapse added to the latter tendency, both among *haojia* and emergent landed gentry (Wakeman 1985, 1: 629; ZSZ n.d., 1: 39).[8]

During the fifteenth and sixteenth centuries, relations between these magnates and families on the rise were at times clearly antagonistic. But as in some districts of Jiangnan, the established lineages used intermarriage with nouveau-riche and/or bureaucratically connected families as a strategy for maintaining their wealth and influence. Like notable lineages in the Jiaxing district of Jiangnan, they carefully planned marriages, especially for their daughters, with ascendant families as a means of renewing talent and economic resources (Wakeman 1985, 1: 96–97). Merchant and gentry families, on their side, appear to have been quite willing to improve their status through marriage. By the turn of the sixteenth century, strategic unions of this type had become common enough for moralistic observers to complain that marriage, like other facets of society, was becoming commercialized. Furthermore, in such unions prominent lineages seem to have reinforced the control of their wealth, daughters, and sons-in-law by requiring uxorilocal rather than patrilocal residence.[9] According to a sixteenth-century account:

> Marriage in Tongzhou began to be determined by both status and wealth. The status of literati and officials [*shidafu*] is higher than that of others. Admiring their influence and desiring their social status, some [gentry] began spending large amounts of money to develop marriage linkages with them. Learning from the gentry, the common people followed suit. [Now] before a man marries a woman, his family asks how much dowry she has; and before a daughter marries, her parents ask how many betrothal gifts they will receive. Is this any different from traders selling servants and slaves? Once a marriage takes place, whether it has been of longer or shorter duration, if anything happens to the wife, her parents and brothers beat up the son-in-law and take back all her dowry. Often they file a lawsuit against the son-in-law as well, with the aim of preventing his family from complaining. If a wife is not satisfied with her husband, her parents and uncles force the son-in-law to leave. This has become convention. . . . What can we do? (ZSZ n.d., 1: 26)

Emulating and extending the activities of their Jiangnan counterparts, officials and wealthy elites also entered into a new range of cultural activities, including the establishment of schools, such as the Tongzhou Academy; the building of palatial homes, exemplified by the locally famous Cuijing mansion on Lang Mountain; and the construction, embellishment, or repair of temples (ZSZ n.d., 1: 25); Lu Mei 1985: 5). The last activity was often connected with the celebration of local gods, notable persons, or such ubiquitous deities as the City God. But it reflected another significant social trend: the spread of Buddhism.

As indicated in the first quote above, Buddhism had not enjoyed a strong following among the landed elite before the Ming. The Hongwu emperor as part of his program of reinforcing and encouraging wider adherence to Confucian norms, attempted to limit Buddhism's influence by decreeing that subprefectures and counties were to have only one major Buddhist temple. But by the late Ming, over 800 "Buddhist" temples, ranging in size from large to small and housing "no fewer than several ten thousands" of monks were said to have "prevailed all over" Tongzhou (ZSZ n.d., 1: 35).

Although this institutional development was on the whole a popular movement, elites had also clearly begun developing close associations with prominent Buddhist temples. The most famous of these were the Beishan and Nanshan temples near Jinsha, which included numerous structures and were noted for their beautiful settings. One of the buildings in this complex, the Chuiwei Hall, became well-known as a place where "local gentry and scholars" gathered for conversation and poetic inspiration; "watching rain in Chuiwei" was considered one of the grand moments of the time (Chen Ji 1984: 14–15; Jin Zhihuai 1984: 2). In the mid-Ming informal activities like this, or the more formal "Chuiwei Poetry Society" (*Chuiwei shishe*) later organized by the brothers Zhang Keqi and Zhang Keqian (Lu Mei 1985: 5), as well as philosophical societies, lecture-discussions, and coteries based on the "pursuit of urban pleasures," became media of elite cohesiveness (Wakeman 1985, 1: 99, 100–103). Such practices and mentalities culturally linked members of the local dominant classes with their more powerful and opulent southern counterparts.

Yet despite this commonality, a deep division based on the cultural dominance of the south persisted. In effect, the one area ignored and denied the changes in the other. Through much of the sixteenth century, despite at least 150 years of dramatic social change, commercial growth, and cultural diffusion in the northern delta, the southern elites continued to view Tongzhou as a backward "frontier" area (ZSZ n.d., 1: 19). Yangzhou prefectural records near the turn of the seventeenth century painted Tongzhou, like Subei, as a remote and inferior area of little interest or attraction. It was simply a place where "people [made] their living from fishing and salt production," and thus "unattractive to officials" (TZZ 1875, 1: 58). This image reinforced the parallel conception of Yangzhou as the only true outpost of culture and civilization in Subei. As the late-eighteenth-century bureaucrat Shen Fu tersely noted, his four years of official service as a government clerk in Subei were "entirely lacking in any enjoyable travel worth recording" (Finnane 1993: 217–18).

In short, by disregarding sociocultural developments in Tongzhou and culturally defining it as an area bearing the characteristic traits of Subei, the categorizations of Jiangnan elites actually furthered and became essential to the construction of the northern delta as a periphery. In assuming an ethnic-like dimension (Honig 1992), their discriminatory constructs and the cultural subordination inherent in them bear some resemblance to the requisite racism of colonial projects. They also illustrate well, as theories of internal colonization suggest, that assertions of cultural superiority by a core area are inextricably linked to perceptions of a periphery's material weakness (Barrera 1979; Finnane 1993: 231; Hechter 1977).

The longer-term effects of the northern delta's peripheralization served only to reinforce those discriminatory constructs. Over time, for instance, the poor record of examination-bureaucratic success among the Tongzhou elites, especially at the upper levels, deepened the north-south divide and the advanced-backward dichotomy underlying it. Tongzhou did not produce even one great official in the Ming-Qing.[10] And, as in other parts of Subei, with the notable exception of Yangzhou, whose salt merchant families achieved high success rates, both its higher-level degree-holders and first-class honors men were few in number. Only four Tongzhou men attained first-class honor status during the Qing, compared with 42 and 20 in Suzhou and Changzhou, respectively (Bastid 1988: 32–33; P.-t. Ho 1964: 250).

The accumulated evidence suggests that, from the late Ming, in both direct and indirect ways, the combined force of cultural, economic, and political peripheralization profoundly affected the character of landlord rule in the northern delta. Not only did the Tongzhou landed elite lack the crucial linkages to the state possessed by the Jiangnan gentry, but owing to the northern delta's malintegration into the delta economy, their involvement in mercantile activity fell well below that of Jiangnan landlords. Of course there was overlap, with some merchant-landlords eventually constituting among the largest landholders. Nevertheless, generally speaking, as the economic dynamism of the Ming subsided, even urban-dwelling landlord-gentry formed a separate and distinct group from the merchants who specialized in the native banking, grain, and cotton-cloth trades. Their commercial activities rarely went beyond moneylending and pawnbroking. In moments of crisis the landed elite could count on assistance from armed forces of the various state agencies positioned in and around Tongzhou, but these same agencies limited their power and freedom of initiative.

Circumscribed and discriminated against by the state and their powerful counterparts to the south, the northern landed elite turned inward. In this respect peripheralization bred a deeply rooted social conservatism among them, at once intransigent and reactionary. It formed the prism for their retreat into Confucian platitudes in the Qing and, especially after the Ming-Qing bondservant risings, to their repression of peasant discourse. To a striking degree their growing conservatism resembles that of the European colonialists of a later period who made their permanent homes among their subject populations. Always consciously aware that their privileged position rested on the continuing subordination—at all costs—of the colonized, they were inalterably opposed to any radical change in the colonial policies of their home countries and on the whole more deeply conservative than their class counterparts back home in the centers of power.[11] Similarly, the conservatism of the northern delta elite in the Qing highlights both the processes of peripheralization in which it was partially rooted and the subtle ways in which these very processes—despite the commonalities and diffusion of elite culture that modernists have so emphasized—hierarchically split and divided the dominant classes in the delta.

Peasant Culture and Politics

In Tongzhou, as in Jiangnan, social and economic change in the Ming stimulated new forms of cultural politics among the subordinate classes. In the late Ming the resonance of northern peasant politics with the peasant path in the south reinforces the notion, developed in Chapter One, of the embryonic formation of a centerless, geographically dispersed, and relatively autonomous cultural movement among the oppressed. While subalterns on the southern side of the Yangzi were undoubtedly affected by the views of their society, the unifying tendencies embedded in this new line of peasant development appear to have worked against, and in crucial moments negated, the north-south divide so prevalent within the elite. The fact that many northern delta peasants were originally migrants from the south also worked against political fragmentation.[12]

These new political currents among peasants interconnected with a rising religious radicalism. A sizable number of the more than 800 Buddhist temples in existence by the end of the Ming appear to have been affiliated with the new White Lotus or other heterodox religions (ZSZ n.d., 1: 36). Like immigrant communities in other parts of China, the migrant communities in the new land areas along the Yangzi in Nantong-Haimen and further west formed natural constituencies for the development of syncretic religions. At the same time, as the floating population swelled, the relatively untamed, sparsely populated, and poorly patrolled coastal salt flats attracted vagrants, refugees, and outlaw-bandits. Their communities formed another locus of radical religious practice. By the mid-Ming, officials were expressing growing concern about the "refugee problem" in the coastal areas. This concern reflected not only their dismay at the illicit salt production and smuggling often carried out by refugees, but their fears about the absence of conventional norms—and thus the threat to the social order—in refugee communities as well. In fact the fluid social arrangements and outcast position of the makeshift refugee communities made them fertile ground for the growth of the egalitarian doctrines of the White Lotus religion and other heterodox teachings (ZSZ n.d., 1: 34).

The intertwining of illicit activity, insurgent doctrines, and religious heterodoxy was not confined to the coastal or river districts. As Buddhist, folk Buddhist, and radical millenarian beliefs mushroomed throughout Tongzhou-Haimen, the activities of monks in various districts also took on an insurgent character. Local histories report numerous instances of monks who were armed and adept at martial arts banding together and in the style typical of social bandits, robbing and even confiscating the homes and property of the wealthy. They also suggest that such men only shaved their heads and pretended to be monks because of the excellent cover this identity provided for criminal and/or sectarian activities. In the words of one source: "As soon as several dozen commoners gather together, the authorities are aware of it. But hundreds of monks can congregate and even if detected, the government [authorities] simply think they are chanting scriptures and practicing Buddhism" (ZSZ n.d., 1: 35). The activities of armed monk bands and other "unscrupulous" clergy added to the growing sense of lawlessness produced by the land seizures of the ruling classes and, increasingly in the late-fifteenth and sixteenth centuries, by the forays of Japanese and Chinese pirates, who terrorized entire communities (*Tongzhou zhi* 1577, 8: 27; TZZ 1875, 1: 31; ZSZ n.d., 1: 35–36, 39).[13]

By the mid-sixteenth century the signs of rebelliousness and outlaw activity were becoming more widespread. In the late 1540's, corresponding in time to the spread of White Lotus networks in Jiangnan, a new group known as the Heavenly Stars Society (Tiangangdang) appeared. Virtually "ignoring local authorities," its members began bullying and initiating terrorist attacks against members of the dominant classes in various parts of Tongzhou. In 1551 the group laid plans to launch a rising simultaneously at several local markets. Before the set date, however, officials learned of the plans, arrested 36 of the society members, and squelched the incipient rebellion (ZSZ n.d., 1: 27).

Marketing networks and contacts, especially those established by peasant traders who traveled to Jiangnan to sell cotton, provided one medium for the spread and cross-fertilization of insurgent thought and planning on both sides of the Yangzi. The kin and native-place contacts of migrant tenants and petty proprietors who settled the new land areas also facilitated communication and linkage, both with the south and within the northern delta. Some of these new settlements were populated wholly or nearly so by migrants from a single locality (Walker 1993b). But in many cases their residents came from "the four corners and eight directions." Yongan, located near the Rugao-Nantong border, for example, was settled by squatters from no fewer than 18 different localities in Rugao-Nantong and at least six other counties, including Chongming Island and Changshu and Jiangyin in the southern delta (Hu Xianru 1981: 87).[14] Tongzhou was also well situated to transmit cultural currents to the north and west. The temples of Lang Mountain, which became a regional site for religious pilgrims from as far away as Anhui, played a particularly pivotal role in such transmissions.

Signs of disobedience and a more brazen attitude within the larger peasant population paralleled the increasing insurgent activity. This was particularly so among bondservants and serfs, who became "tough" and "impolite." Trying to appease them, masters first resorted to kindness. Yet in elite eyes the situation only worsened:

> If their masters are powerful, they bully people by flaunting their masters' influence. . . . If their masters punish them with family law, they rise up against

them. . . . If a servant dies, his relatives ask the master to pay for the burial. Timid masters cannot handle the situation. There are even bondservants, both among the older and the more recently acquired, who lure bandits to rob their masters' properties. (ZSZ n.d., 1: 26–27)

By the last decades of the dynasty, foreshadowing the delta-wide bond-servant-serf rebellions,

latent turmoil began to surface and gradually spread. In 1614 an upheaval . . . exploded. In the rising the gentry in several villages were burned and robbed. . . . The survivors of the rising—probably 140 or 150 of them—still remain in Tongzhou. They are in contact with each other, sometimes separated into groups, sometimes acting as one to make trouble and poison people's minds. They have stricter discipline than anyone else, and they are very strong. . . . A terrible trend is prevailing here. . . . A crisis is rising and demons are everywhere. (Ibid., p. 27)

Demons, mounting popular audacity, and the hint of rebellion permeated local festivals as well. By custom in Tongzhou and other localities, when a god's birthday occurred, local elites organized a commemorative festival. In the second half of the Ming, events of this type became quite extravagant, reflecting growing wealth and, probably, given the instability of the times, the elite's uneasiness and desire to placate the masses. During Tongzhou's City God festival of 1616, uneasiness turned to fright when costumed ghosts and demons suddenly appeared and began parading through the city "just as if [they were] replacing the present world by a ghost world" (ZSZ n.d., 1: 36–37). Apparently on the allegation that the intruders from the underworld intended to steal the valuable items set out for the god, the chief constable, Gong Shangwen, arrested the demon leaders, who were subsequently sentenced to hard labor; and no demons appeared at the fair the next year. But at the festival a few years later, with Constable Gong now dead, ghosts and demons resurfaced in greater numbers, and they made regular appearances thereafter. Sensing the subversive implications of this innovation in cultural warfare but fearful of attempting further arrests, local officials lamely resorted to posting public messages to the demons asking them to desist. Not only did they ignore the request, but by the 1630's, to the delight of the crowds, they surfaced at other festivals as well, including the state-supported Jade Emperor festival (ibid., pp. 37–38).

The appearance of ghosts and demons walking about in broad daylight might simply be viewed as a symbolic inversion, or an instance of the type of liminal behavior described by Victor Turner, who suggests that in such moments peasants simultaneously reaffirm their belief in an unstructured, homogeneous *communitas* and escape from the structured hierarchies of their normal, everyday lives (1969: 131–32, 167). But in the case of late Ming China, the intrusion into an elite-sponsored event of figures from another world cannot be interpreted as merely a moment of liminality. As Sidney Mintz argues, new role-playing—and with it the possibility of engineering new social arrangements according to new rules—can occur only when older categories of status are thrown into doubt by open acts (1982: 187). Viewed in this light, the demons' appearance was a political act. Like the bondservants and subaltern sectarians who had begun to discard the culture of deference, ghosts and demons became signifying markers of a new cultural movement. To be sure, that movement contained culture-specific traits, but it also produced decidedly new elements through which the subordinated denied the power of past practice to govern social relations in the present and future. Blowing trumpets and waving flags, the demons in Tongzhou appropriated sacred symbols and thus at once sanctified popular will and ominously announced to the ruling classes that the coming of a different social order was close if not already at hand.[15]

3 Historical Trends
During the Qing

THE CONTRADICTORY interplay of state, class, and gender relations that first took shape in and then altered the course of late Ming history also profoundly affected historical trends in the Qing. To conclude this section, this chapter briefly spotlights important trends in rural political economy that were grounded in these relations.

The Southern Delta

By strengthening peasant production and household autonomy—and thereby solidifying a historically new "particular peasantry"—the victories of the late Ming peasant risings ensured that small-scale, peasant-based management forms would exert a powerful influence on the trajectory of change in the Qing. After the risings some managing landlords tried to maintain production by hiring former bondservants, servile tenants, and indentured laborers as wage laborers. But the low fixed rents that many peasant families had gained, combined with the income from home industry, appear to have made them economically stable enough to avoid hiring-out. Their victories in the late Ming struggles thus not only limited the supply of local labor available for landlord and rich peasant farming, but apparently also drove up its price.

As *Mr. Shen's Agricultural Treatise,* a mid-seventeenth-century text documenting conditions in Huzhou prefecture, indicates: "The hired people now are arrogant and lazy as a matter of course. They can only be motivated by wine and food, and are much different from a hundred years ago" (*Shenshi nongshu* 1936: 13). Under such conditions, for many landlords hiring labor simply did not pay (P. Huang 1990: 58–59; *Shenshi nongshu* 1936: 13–16; see also Liu Yongcheng 1980; and Li Wenzhi 1981). The gradual spread of the "one-field, two-owners" system became an added impediment to large-scale landlord farming.[1] Consequently, in the delta, through most of the Qing, instead of the large-scale management operations common in the Ming, in both agriculture and rural industry the peasant family powered economic growth.[2]

In textile production this pattern held sway well into the nineteenth century, when the production of cotton cloth still constituted the largest single rural industry. Even at mid-century, the 45 percent of peasant families responsible for cloth output produced sufficient quantities of cloth to satisfy their own and the consumption needs of the 55 percent of the population that did not weave (Xu Xinwu 1988: 41–42).

The deepening of this pattern reinforced rigidity in the sexual division of labor, matched perhaps by further decline in women's status (Bernhardt 1996; R. Watson & Ebrey 1991). Over time some variation in the division did occur. Pictorial representations of the phases of cotton farming show, for example, that by the mid-eighteenth century, to meet the crop's intense labor requirements, specialized tasks, such as weeding, had become part of women's work in some delta localities. The evidence strongly suggests, however, that the rigid division of labor in textile production prevailed. It was only in the latter half of the nineteenth century—under the emerging social relations of semicolonialism—that changes in the division of labor accelerated and, in the twentieth century, became pronounced.[3] Through much of the Qing, then, a relatively stable peasant production, and the subordination of women that so inextricably interconnected with it, underpinned continuing economic growth. To a considerable degree, it formed as well the essential foundation for and determinant of other key trends of the period, namely, structural changes in landlordism, new elaborations of merchant capital, and a "routinization" of rent resistance among peasants.

THE CHANGING STRUCTURE OF LANDLORD RULE

In the perspective of landlords, the breakdown of the estate system at the end of the Ming necessitated the creation of new forces to guarantee their continuing domination of peasants and the appropriation of peasant surpluses. The strengthening of peasant production through the expansion of commercialized home industry indirectly aided them in this goal, in the sense that it at once prompted rapid population growth and enabled peasants to live on smaller plots of land than under conditions where farming was the sole source of subsistence. This situation, combined with the fact that cultivators could no longer count on patriarchal estate owners to supply part of subsistence or to assist them in bad years, created new openings for both usury and merchant capital. In effect the expansion and deepening of merchant-usurious operations became a significant new arena through which landlords gained control of peasant surpluses.

Hence the phenomenal growth, especially in the eighteenth century, of pawnshops and other usurious institutions (Elvin 1973: 249; Shigeta 1984: 364). An eighteenth-century account illustrates the resultant complexity of peasant subsistence in the fertile Wuxi-Jinkui area:

> Local people only live off their land for the three winter months. After paying the rent, they pound the husks off the rice that is left and deposit it in the granaries of the pawnshops, retrieving the clothes they had there in pawn. In the spring months, they lock themselves in their houses to spin and weave, exchanging their cloth for rice to eat. There is no surplus grain in their households. In the fifth month when the demands of field work become pressing, they once again retrieve the rice they pawned by returning their winter clothes. . . . In autumn when the rains come, the sound of the loom is heard again in all of the villages. (*Xi Jin* 1753, 1: 6b–7a)[4]

To circumvent the barrier imposed by fixed rent and combat escalating rent resistance, landlords introduced changes in their arrangements with tenants. The most important of these was the widespread adoption of rent deposits (*dingshou yin*) (*Qingdai* 1982, 2: 349–63, 413–15; Shiraishi 1960).[5] Often totaling over half the annual rent or more, deposits were designed to protect landlords from rent default or reduced payments. Furthermore, deposits at once increased the total amount of capital available to landlords for usury operations and stimulated those operations, since peasants frequently had to borrow to obtain the deposit amount. In combination with the deepening of usury capital, structural adjustments of this type enabled landlord-merchants to neutralize some of the economic gains won by peasants in struggle.

CONSTITUTING SOCIOPOLITICAL DOMINANCE

From the perspective of the Qing state, especially in the face of the breakdown of "feudal mores" (Li Wenzhi 1981: 68–69), the class consolidation of gentry-landlordism was essential to the control of the peasantry and the restoration of Confucian hegemony. By standardizing a combined land and poll tax (*diding yin*), it effectively designated landlordism as the social form of organization through which it would rule the peasantry. It also wrote penalties into imperial law for tenants who refused to pay rent. But the new enactments made it clear that, though the state was prepared to serve landlord interests, it alone had the right to punish tenants. Seeking to ensure its own collection of taxes from landlords—and in the process giving new force to the idea that "taxes come out of rents"—the state thus reinforced landlord rule at the same time that it brought landlords more firmly under its authority (Bernhardt 1992: 31; Shigeta 1984: 365, 375, 377–78).

The disruptions in the countryside also compelled the Qing state to wade into cultural waters. Many scholars have suggested that the Qing's vigorous promotion of cultural orthodoxy was grounded in its need as an alien dynasty to legitimize its rule, that is, to become more orthodox than the orthodox. Equally, if not more importantly, the Qing state/elite appears to have understood only too well that, though the wave of peasant rebellions had receded, the cultural movement underlying them was continuing and intensifying. The cries of alarm of various officials, noted previously, that White Lotus groups were "active everywhere" only serves to illustrate the point. Indeed, Qing attempts at prohibition provide a precise refractory view of the various integrating elements of this movement that we earlier discussed. Thus in the Yongzheng (1723–35) and Qianlong (1736–95) reigns the state broadened the Ming provisions against heterodox religion and outlawed martial arts practice and interprovincial pilgrimages (Hsiao Kung-chuan 1960: 23; Kobayashi 1984: 238; Overmyer 1976: 102).

Reinstituting public order under a centralized authority pushed the state to assume a more active role in molding the ruling elite as well—particularly the upstart, profit-seeking gentry, who in myriad ways were failing to conform to and even undermining established ideological norms. In some respects this task became easier because the crisis produced by Ming-Qing liberation risings pushed the upstart gentry, as it were, back into the fold. Factions within the elite, especially the influential "righteous" gentry, also indirectly facilitated it. Functioning as state intellectuals in the Gramscian sense, they published "morality books" (*shanshu*), in an effort to reinvigorate moral precepts within the elite (Okuzaki 1978; Sakai 1960). At the same time their advocacy of an expanded "local activism" for landlord-gentry provided the framework, under conditions of growing absenteeism, for continuing landlord management of local affairs. With the triple intent, then, of reestablishing control over the peasantry, rectifying the "excesses and malpractices" of the upstart gentry, and bringing under state guidance and control the kinds of voluntary activities that could make the landlord elite too powerful (Mori 1980: 52), in the eighteenth century the Qing inaugurated or sanctioned a cluster of practical programs and policies for the management of local society. Eventually these covered an array of diverse functions, including water control, famine relief, education, welfare, and philanthropic activities.

The appearance in official literature of the new term "gentry-director" or "gentry-manager" (*shendong*) signified the shift in the style of local rule from a system based on personal control and responsibility for one's own estates/laborers to a system of "public management" by groups of local elites. Functioning as an extrabureaucratic force, but in such a way that it, like tax-farming, was actually elevated and absorbed into the structure of state rule, the new system resonated with and gave impetus to the discourse and idealized Confucian notion of "community" as an arena of interest in which decisions were articulated and services managed by local elite "leaders" (Elvin

1977: 463; Rankin 1986: 15; Shigeta 1984: 377). As such, it both served and became a key construct of Qing ideology, while its institutions acted as a veil concealing landlord domination of the peasantry from view (see Ooms 1985; and Turton 1984).

Through the landlord-gentry's domination of "local management," "social welfare," and "public order" (Takahashi 1977), their performance of a host of state-associated ideological and cultural functions (Hsiao Kung-chuan 1960; Watson 1985), and their refinement of an evolving gentry culture centered organizationally on overlapping, horizontal networks (Wakeman 1985: 92), both their own conception of themselves as a ruling elite and the varied dimensions of their sociopolitical power took firm root. By the eighteenth century the class that in the late Ming had displayed "no concern whatsoever for the needs of local society" had become a pillar of hegemonic rule.[6] This gave the Qing the appearance of being one of China's most stable political regimes.

Beneath the veneer of stability and reinstitution of control, however, the discourse of the oppressed indicated that the ruling bloc was only partially leading. That is to say, the crisis of authority of the late Ming period that had laid bare fundamental fissures of Chinese society and produced a new line of development among peasants, had been averted but not fully resolved, resulting in what was at best only a tense and incomplete hegemony. Though landlord-gentry were able to regain control of some community functions, such as irrigation and state-approved rituals, their overall efforts to destroy the social organization of peasants and the sources of communal autonomy among them were only superficially realized.

PEASANT PRODUCTION AND MERCHANT CAPITAL

Tanaka Masatoshi has argued that, by the end of the Ming, peasant agriculture was already tied up in a set of relationships that pointed to two lines of development: a "greater dependence on merchant capital" and "a sharpening of the contradictions and peasant rebellion, with the potential to split the existing system" (1984a: 92). In fact in the Qing there was movement along both of these developmental lines. What needs to be considered is how they interrelated.

First, we must restate a point emphasized earlier, namely, that in weakening the power of a patriarchal landlordism rooted in direct personal rule, the victories of peasants at the end of the Ming set the framework for further commercial development. In the core Jiangnan region, both the elaboration of merchant-landlordism and the growing dependence of peasants on merchant capital reflected this specificity of agrarian class conflict. In other locally concentrated areas of cotton textile production, including the northern delta, where raw material and cloth production largely remained an integrated process within the peasant family, the penetration of capital into the cycle of peasant reproduction was limited, and producers maintained relative independence vis-à-vis merchants.

In the southern delta, however, although many families continued to integrate cotton farming, spinning, and weaving, greater specialization and a sharper division of labor developed in tandem with the development of usury capital. The example cited earlier of peasants in Wuxi-Jinkui who pawned rice for the return of winter clothes they had previously pawned, and for cash with which to purchase raw cotton for spinning and weaving is a case in point. Many peasant families in rice-producing areas also supplemented their incomes with both cotton spinning-weaving and silkworm raising–silk reeling, a development that reflected and furthered the rapid commercialization of silk as well as cotton. In such cases they sold raw silk for cash in the spring and then bought cotton or silk yarn in the fall to weave (Tanaka 1984a: 86, 97). In other localities peasants simply purchased cotton or yarn for spinning and/or weaving (Nishijima 1984: 57–58).

The widespread adoption of these various household strategies indicates the extent to which in both the cotton districts and areas where little cotton was grown, in place of an integrated system the entire production process came to be mediated by commodity exchange. Among peasant families the need for the rapid circulation of small amounts of capital—for purchasing food and meeting obligations—introduced increasing opportunities for exchange and usury to enter the internal processes of peasant farming and industry (Fu Yiling 1961; Tanaka 1984a: 86; 1972).

Developmentalist economic analyses often associate the rapid growth of commodity production with incipient capitalist development. Similarly, because of the role of putting-out systems in the protoindustrialization of some parts of Europe, they too have often been regarded as "normal" accompaniments to the expansion of commodity production. But in the lower Yangzi delta, despite the amazing expansion of a commodity economy, neither capitalist development nor significant putting-out systems appeared. Indeed, to the extent that putting-out systems drive a wedge between and break up agriculture and industry and thus can promote proletarianization, they were inimical to the evolving economic organization and structure of power in the delta—that is, to the operation of rural merchant capital not as in opposition to but as a key component of and complement to landlordism. In the villages and small towns of the countryside there were, of course, innumerable merchants and peddlers specializing in various aspects of the cotton and silk trades.[7] But the involvement of many small merchants with limited capital was in large part also a corollary to the division of the production process into many parts, as well as to the small scale of production itself. In other words, they supported and became integral to the preservation of the larger structures of landlord rule and the commodity economy.

In a descriptive sense, Mark Elvin asserts accurately (1973) that putting-out systems were unnecessary because of the dense marketing networks in the southern delta. But in contending that these networks *explain* the lack of such systems (and by extension, Eurocentrically, the "failure" of merchant capital to lead China along a western-patterned developmental path), Elvin's analysis suppresses consideration of how the politics and economics of class relations in the delta influenced both the developmental trajectory and the complex structure of market relations.

On the other hand, as Elvin correctly notes, the large-scale merchant operations of urban areas were even further removed from production than those of the countryside. They centered on the finishing processes, such as calendaring and dyeing, which were concentrated in urban workshops (Chu Hua n.d.; Xu Xinwu 1981; Yokohama 1960–61).[8] Or they principally focused on long-distance trade. Increasingly in the Qing, the large firms involved in long-distance trade displaced local (merchant and merchant-landlord) whole-salers by establishing their own retail cotton and cotton/cloth procurement shops (Chu Hua n.d.: 11; Lu Hanchao 1992: 489; Terada 1958; Ye Mengzhu 1936). At the same time they constructed large warehouses for storing and packing cloth before it was loaded onto junks for shipment (Fortune 1847: 272–73).

In the latter case, to some extent independent merchant capital competed with landlordism for peasant surpluses. And as the directive role of merchant capital in rural society increased, in certain respects merchants, like peasants, eroded landlords' prerogatives and power. Yet generally speaking, even the large-scale long-distance merchants did not pose a *significant* threat to landlord rule. Many were in fact landlords in their home districts. Hence both in the delta and in other commercial areas, from the late sixteenth century on, what had been a landlord class was increasingly transformed into a landlord-merchant class (Tanaka 1984b: 209). The notable exception was in the largest entrepots of trade where, as William Rowe (1984) has shown for Hankou, independent merchant capital assumed significant influence in urban life. But even there, in the last analysis, it remained subservient, socio-politically and culturally, to the landlord gentry (Bergère 1989: 46).

Consequently, well into the nineteenth century, when new conditions emerged, independent merchant capital chiefly confined itself to the spheres of circulation and usury, and thus generally complemented the transformation of landlordism into merchant-landlordism so as to exploit the existing forms of production "ever anew." In contrast, then, to modernist-positivist views of the market as automatically generating development, market expansion and the expansion of merchant capital became integral to social reproduction along increasingly petty commoditized but distinctly noncapitalist lines.

MERCHANT CAPITAL, LANDLORDISM,
AND PEASANT POLITICS

In peasant society the elaboration of merchant capital carried political as well as economic implications. Most important, it gave peasants greater independence from and leverage in their relations with landlords. They used their deepening relations with merchants as a vehicle to attack and undermine landlordism (Tanaka 1984a: 93–95).

This strategic avenue seems to have first appeared in tandem with the new wave of tenant struggles in the late Ming. As a 1596 gazetteer from Xiushui county, a silk-producing center in northern Zhejiang, noted:

> the rich merchants [were at this point operating] rice pawnshops. The tenants pawn their high quality rice for silver and use middle or inferior quality rice to pay their rent. Even in years of good harvest they claim a poor harvest and demand another extension of payment. Recently, cheating peasants along the shores of the Tiao creek joined together in cliques and pledged not to transfer rent to the rich. Although this particular situation has eased a little now, this kind of practice is gradually spreading. (Tanaka 1984a: 100)

In other words, new forms of rent resistance accompanied and became possible precisely because of the social relations created by the development of commodity production and merchant capital. This is not to suggest that peasants thought any more highly of the merchants and merchant-usurers they dealt with than they did of their landlords. Phrases such as "death merchants," denoting the low prices offered by cloth merchants, and "silk devils," a euphemism for silk wholesalers, expressed both the bitterness of these relations and their exploitative character in peasants' eyes (Nishijima 1984: 63; Tanaka 1984a: 93).

Yet as a seventeenth-century observer concluded: "Tenants would rather default on their landlord's rent than dare not to pay back their debt to the grain-lender, for fear that in the latter case they might be unable to borrow again the following year" (cited in Elvin 1973: 249–50).[9] In short, though the peasants' dependence on merchant capital gave merchants a measure of protection, paradoxically, it enabled tenants to independently establish new terrain in their struggles with landlords.

In the eighteenth and nineteenth centuries offensive actions by "cheating" and "stubborn" tenants became a normal phenomenon as rent resistance and more profound challenges to the property system reached "an altogether unprecedented scale" (Bernhardt 1992: 27). This "routinized struggle of the peasantry" (Hamashima 1982) as the new pattern of social conflict in China's most advanced commercial region stands as a hallmark of Qing history. Throughout the Jiangnan region "regular failures to pay rent" by peasants organized in multi-village and territorial alliances emerged. According to a 1760 account from Wuqing county:

> They [tenants] secretly discuss and decide the amount of rent they should pay, strengthen their solidarity by showing plays, and make contracts and pacts. If they discover anyone paying rent over and above the amount they have decided among themselves, sly members of the group form a band to go to make a din at the offender's home, reproaching him for going against the group's wishes and secretly bringing disaster against him if he remains disobedient. (Oyama 1984: 143)

Eroding landlord property even more, peasant struggles for topsoil rights in the expanding "one field, two owners" system, paralleled and interpenetrated with the rent resistance offensive. The (1827) *Treatise on Rent Collection in Shanyang County* provides a clear illustration of how, in Suzhou, peasants at once reacted to landlords' imposition of rent deposits and, proactively, combined rent resistance with the struggle for topsoil rights. According to the *Treatise,* once rent deposits became a standard institution, tenants began paying reduced rents as they saw fit. When landlords demanded that they surrender their tenures because of these rent defaults, the tenants refused on the grounds that they had paid deposits. In so doing they both subverted the intended protective function of deposits for landlords and established their own claims to the land.

Even when tenants had not paid deposits, they still rebuffed landlords' attempts to replace them. Some justified their actions by claiming that they could not be evicted until they were fully compensated for their labor and capital investments, especially fertilizer. Others insisted on maintaining cultivating rights until their landlords reimbursed them for *dingshou* money they claimed they had paid to former tenants (P. Yang 1988: 153–54). The *dingshou* practice (*dingshou* being the same term used for deposits to landlords), which was really a forerunner to full topsoil rights, allowed a tenant who relinquished a tenure to receive a payment from the person who assumed it. In most cases landlords had no knowledge of these arrangements. During cases of prolonged dispute over such issues, the land in question sometimes went untilled, but in the end landlords were generally helpless because the increasing force of customary law favored peasants.

Put most simply, then, as the results of peasant struggle were institutionalized, landlords were forced to make concessions regarding landownership (Liu Kwang-ching 1981: 312). By the nineteenth century many of the peasants in Suzhou had acquired topsoil rights (P. Yang 1988: 153–54). To the extent that law, as recent scholarship in legal studies argues, "must be recognized as an aspect of the total culture of a people" (Chiba 1986: 1), these trends in class relations–customary law give us a glimpse not only of culture as contested terrain, but, in their furthering of peasant rights in the established structure, of what appears as another dynamic in a line of development set by peasants.[10]

Ironically, after the mid-nineteenth century, expansion of dual ownership accelerated as an indirect result of the enormous destruction and loss of human life brought about by the state's offensive against the Taiping rebellion. In the immediate post-Taiping years, landlords willingly offered topsoil rights and the lower fixed rents that accompanied them in an effort to attract new tenants to their depopulated holdings.

Muramatsu Yuji's work on Jiangnan suggests the transformative effect of these twin processes on the economic structure. He estimates that, by the early twentieth century, southern-delta tenants held permanent tenure rights on from one-third to two-fifths of cultivated land (1949: 318). In the most commercialized districts, the figure was even higher—to the point where, by the early 1930's fully 90 percent of the rented land in Suzhou, Wuxi, and Changshu was occupied by tenants with topsoil rights (He Menglei 1977: 45). Fueled by the growth of usury capital, a developing market in topsoil rights paralleled the expansion of dual ownership. It worked principally to the advantage of merchants, since they, rather than landlords, usually accepted these rights as security on loans. Prices in this market rose much more rapidly than in the land (subsoil) market, sometimes fetching several times the subsoil price (Fujii 1979–80; M. Wiens 1980: 30; P. Yang 1988).

The protracted peasant offensive during the Qing naturally produced a reaction among both landlords and the state. At various points the government attempted to ameliorate the worst abuses of landlord-tenant relations and, thereby, neutralize peasant dissatisfaction. But endemic, routine resistance eventually forced it into more active support of landlord rule. By the mid-Qing county government offices were assuming responsibility for the collection of rent in arrears (Oyama 1984: 150). This trend deepened in the latter half of the dynasty (Bernhardt 1992). The effect was to sharpen peasant antagonism toward the state.

THE SOUTHERN DELTA PATTERN

Thus at the time of the Opium War, when the semicolonial encounter began, the broad social, political, and economic changes of the Ming had produced, in varying degrees throughout the southern delta, two interlinked trends. First was a mode of elite rule that continued to be based on landownership, but in which merchant-usury capital had come to assume a position of unusual importance. Constituting a more profitable and secure source of income than landownership, while underwriting and extracting the profits of peasant production in myriad ways, trade and usury capital were in fact essential to peasant society in the localities of greatest market development. In this respect, foreshadowing future developments, merchants were already assuming a directive role in the contemporary countryside. Any analysis of landlordism, and thus of the relations among peasants, landlords, merchants, and the state, must take this central fact into consideration.

Various extra-bureaucratic public management functions serving and constituting part of the state formed a third pillar of landlord rule. Gentry-directors filled the leadership gap created in the early Qing as increasing urban residence by landlords signaled a decline in the estate system based on direct, personal rule. Public management interconnected with the new trend from the mid-Qing for absentee landlords to rely on county government offices to enforce their claims against rent-resisting tenants. State involvement in rent relations thus at once underpinned public management as an aspect of landlord rule and reflected the mutually supporting relations between landlords and the state on which that rule depended. Yet precisely because the institutions of gentry-management combined dominance with considerable autonomy, they also created a spatial arena in which alternative or oppositional ideas might develop. In the late nineteenth century, when new pressures and opportunities converged, such was to be the case.

Although other factors contributed to this tripartite form of landlord rule, to a significant degree it was the result of specific political processes that originated among peasants. Constituting the second major trend in the delta, this alternative peasant history at once deepened and added new dimensions to the radical political culture that first coalesced in the late Ming. By simultaneously routinizing rent resistance and pushing for a tenure system that in effect gave them new rights to property, peasants increasingly challenged and rejected landlords' ownership claims.

Kobayashi Kazumi and other scholars have argued that in the Qing the more the ideologies of rent resistance and topsoil rights developed, the more peasants questioned the very existence of the landlord-tenant relationship, and by extension, the concepts and principles of the imperial system (Koybayashi 1984: 226–27; see also Kojima 1978; and Tanaka 1984a: 94; 1984b: 205). If this was indeed the case, then politically the really significant import of the Qing peasant offensive lay in its deepening of the organic crisis. On the other hand, viewed in a socioeconomic light, the relative stability and independence that peasants gained from the phenomenal spread of rent resistance and, especially, topsoil rights stand unarguably as crucial pivotal factors shaping the particular pattern of development in the southern delta.

The Northern Delta

As in the south, the bondservant risings in the northern delta at the end of the Ming dealt a serious blow to the existing social order. During the Qing points of congruence between the northern and southern delta peasant paths continued. Yet shaped by peripheralization, as well as by the particular agricultural regime of the area, peasant struggles in Tongzhou and developments in agrarian class relations also differed in significant ways from those in Jiangnan.

AGRARIAN CLASS RELATIONS

In the northern delta lower levels of urban-rural integration and merchant capitalist development prevented peasants from gaining the kind of independence from landlords attained by Jiangnan peasants. At the same time peripheralized growth indirectly impeded their ability to win permanent tenancy and dual ownership, a second structural feature heightening the power of southern peasants. In Jiangnan, as we have seen, after the bondservant risings landlords made various adjustments to compensate for the loss of servile labor and the growing class strength of peasants, a development that also made many willing to accept the dual-ownership system. The landlords of the northern delta, lacking the economic options of the southern elite, instead pursued a course of repression and control. This policy, as well as the greater preponderance of cotton cultivation than in the south, conditioned and limited the spread of dual ownership. In general peasants succeeded in gaining permanent tenancy/topsoil rights on a wide scale only in Haimen, where much of the land had to be reclaimed; it developed on a much smaller scale in areas along the Yangzi and coast that also required reclamation before farming could take place (Hu Xianru 1981; Huang Xiaoxian 1927; Shen Shike 1934; Zhan Ran 1934; Zhang Renren 1915–16; Zhu Fucheng 1977).

The economic circumstances of the northern delta appear to account as well for the fact that after the bondservant risings, landlords there seldom attempted to turn to managerial farming based on hired labor. Conditions in Tongzhou were actually more conducive to this type of farming than in the south, since few Tongzhou peasants enjoyed the rights of dual ownership and the lack of economic options blocked the same sort of developmental course for landlordism. But in the northern delta, as in Jiangnan, after the demise of servile labor, although some labor hiring did occur, there is no indication of managerial farming as a significant trend (ZSZ n.d., 1: 57).

This situation stands in sharp contrast to the cotton belt of the North China plain where, as Jing Su and Luo Lun (1959) and Philip Huang (1985) document, managerial farming became a pronounced trend in the eighteenth and nineteenth centuries. It developed in North China under the impact of intense regional economic growth of the sort that had occurred in the delta 200–300 years earlier (Li Wenzhi et al. 1983: 56–61). In that period, as we have seen, managerial farming had rapidly expanded in the delta as well, but of a different stripe—patriarchal and reliant on bondservant, serf, and indentured labor rather than hired labor. By the eighteenth century, when the new tendencies were taking strong root in North China, class relations in Tongzhou had already long been conditioned by the dynamics of peripheralization. In the aftermath of the bondservant rebellions, repression and rentier landlordism rather than greater mercantile activity or managerial farming formed the specific terrain of agrarian class conflict.

Yet neither the organized power of landlords nor their conservative reaction to the Ming-Qing rebellions could destroy or even completely neutralize the new peasant militancy. While southern peasants challenged landlords' ownership rights, peasants in the northern delta pursued the more limited aim of further eroding the social status of landlords and securing in customary practice long-term tenures with fixed rents. Although we cannot reconstruct a detailed picture of the structure of rents and tenures over time, fragmentary data suggest that sharecropping for 40 percent of the harvest predominated in Tongzhou in the early Qing (*Qingdai nongmin* 1984; TZZ 1875, 1: 56) but increasingly gave way to fixed rents from the mid-Qing on. As in other areas greater urban residence among larger landlords during the eighteenth century may have facilitated the shift to fixed rents (Liu Daosong 1980; *Qingdai dizu boxue* 1982; Zhang Renren 1915-16).

From a purely economic point of view, the shift to fixed rents in no way compared with the gains made by the southern delta peasants. But the northerners were the better off for it, in the sense that landlords no longer had the right to inspect, comment on, and generally intervene in their tenants' activities, as they could in a sharecropping arrangement. Accordingly, landlords lost one of the subtle mechanisms that undergirded their extraeconomic compulsory powers. In effect the transition from a percentage draw to a fixed rent gave the tenants greater independence. Thus, during the Qing, this and other developments in the peasant path that challenged tenacious landlord prerogatives, such as the right of land redemption and first right of land purchase for kin, combined to further weaken patriarchal landlordism and improve the peasant's lot and status (Li Wenzhi 1981: 77-78).

Like their southern counterparts, landlords attempted to offset these gains by imposing measures such as rent deposits, but peasants countered and continued their offensive by the ploys of rent default and/or partial payment (Liu Daosong 1980; Qiao Qiming 1926; Zhang Renren 1915-16). They also resisted, although not always successfully, the forcible attempts of landlords to gain control of land they had reclaimed (Liu Daosong 1980; Walker 1993a). The surge in litigation near the end of the Ming and in the first half of the Qing suggests that, as in Jiangnan, the courts surfaced as a key arena in which these developing struggles in agrarian class relations played out.

Gazetteer entries for Tongzhou, Rugao, and Taixing insist that, before the mid-Jiaqing period (1522-66), "ethics prevailed" and "people seldom became involved in lawsuits to settle disputes" (TZZ 1875, 1: 58–59). What such references actually denote, of course, is that in a system of rule lacking a clear basis for a strict hierarchical structure in land rights, the ethical concepts of superior-inferior and senior-junior functioned as aspects of hegemony. In other words they became mechanisms for gaining peasants' consent to their own domination. As such, these concepts became a necessary supplement to and played an important role in consolidating and perpetuating patriarchal landlordism (Li Wenzhi 1981: 69).

In the late Ming–early Qing, however, according to literati texts, "ethics were lost and litigation became prevalent." This situation, as we have already seen in the case of tenant struggles in Suzhou, reflected simultaneous changes in the militancy of peasants, in the nature of land transactions, and in the status of landlords. By the Kangxi (1662–1722) reign cases of "gentry going to court to defend their position" had become commonplace. Although part of this activity clearly involved contentious relations among elites, much of it centered on conflicts over rents. Moreover, peasants, as well as landlords, brought charges. Indeed, moralistic commentators found this audacity by subordinates most distressing of all. In their view it had much to do with the educated plaint writers who filed for peasants. According to one contemporary account, these professional advocates, whose "nature [was] low and sinister but who were good at making written complaints," were key culprits in "abetting the people to file charges" (TZZ 1875, 1: 57). Yet as Richard von Glahn has so superbly illustrated for the late Ming popular reform movement in Hangzhou, many of those "abettors" were degreeholders who crystallized and spearheaded the sentiments of the people (von Glahn 1991; see also Fuma 1993).

Ample evidence suggests further that if, over time, rent resistance and the use of the courts as a new arena of struggle brought some improvement in the class position of peasants, for individual peasants, especially women and children, the consequences were often devastating. As one gazetteer states, "Some cases last for years without final judgment. If a person is at large, his wife and children are put in jail. The prisons are full of people and some even die there. As a result, [peasant] men quit farming and women stop weaving. . . . The general social mood turns evil—for which lawsuits are surely responsible" (TZZ 1875, 1: 57). Commentaries like this suggest the intensity of the effort among members of the dominant classes to maintain their status, position, and rights.

LONGER-TERM IMPLICATIONS

In sum, at the end of the Ming, Tongzhou peasants, pursuing their own line of independent development and inspired morally and ideologically by a cultural movement of regional and even national proportions, decisively shaped the course of change. As in the southern delta, the victories of their liberation struggles brought new stability and independence to their families and production. Over the course of the Qing, through rent resistance and the development of fixed rents, they further improved their economic position. Even the slow growth of textile production in the Qing added to peasant stability, since it occurred mostly as part of an integrated process in which peasant families not only produced cloth as a commodity but grew their own supplies of raw cotton as well. Accordingly, merchant capital's penetration of peasant household industry was much more limited than in Jiangnan.

On the other hand, if this general situation gave northern delta peasants greater control over subsistence, it simultaneously made them more dependent on landlords than in the south, placed certain restrictions on their resistance, and prevented them from making significant inroads into the landlords' hold on property. On the eve of the Opium War, despite the gains and relative stability they achieved, the outcome of the agrarian struggles in the northern delta left peasants in a weaker class position than in Jiangnan.

Northern landlords likewise both won and lost ground. So far as local society was concerned, they remained relatively strong. But the deep-rooted conservatism and cultural inbreeding that solidified them as a class and helped them to maintain their status were born precisely in their subordinate position in a hierarchy of power in which the state and members of the dominant Jiangnan elite viewed them and the terrain they so zealously guarded as of little count. Their deeply entrenched conservatism continued well into the late Qing. It infected state officials assigned to the Tongzhou area, a sharing of attitudes that became eminently clear near the turn of the twentieth century, when the two joined forces against the efforts of Zhang Jian, a local scholar of national renown, to bring Western-style modernization to Nantong. In the late 1890's, for instance, fiercely opposing Zhang's construction of a mechanized cotton mill, a group of more than 300 students and landlord-gentry banded together and signed petitions in an attempt to sabotage the enterprise (JS [3] 1919: 4). In 1904 the Lianghuai salt commissioner tried to short-circuit Zhang's efforts to improve the flow of raw materials and supplies to the mill by prohibiting his newly organized transport company from using salt transport canals (S. Chu 1965: 39). And in 1908, in opposition to both Zhang's Tonghai Land Development Company and his plans to organize additional companies in the old coastal salt beds, an alliance of salt merchants and officials succeeded in persuading the salt administration to prohibit the formation of any other land company (ibid., pp. 123–27).

To mention the conservative local reaction to Zhang Jian's modernizing activities, however, is to already draw attention to the semicolonial process and a new class grouping within the elite. Reflecting the longer-term pattern of change, that urban grouping was initially composed principally of merchants and men like Zhang, who together lacked the credentials for inclusion in the closed social world of the Tongzhou landed elite. In the late nineteenth and early twentieth centuries, these men would seize the semi-colonial moment to break the landlord-gentry's stranglehold on power and carve out a sphere of dominance for themselves. Around them they gathered other outsiders and those who were disenchanted, including especially, as was common, men who had repeatedly failed to pass the higher-level examinations and were thus quick to show interest in finding some different avenue to prestige and power (Shao Qin 1994: 87–88). The confrontation between the old and new elites, then, was not a mere clash between the traditional and the modern, as is still often assumed, but in fact a struggle for power in local society, a struggle that at once reflected and was the legacy of a much older history of a periphery.

During the semicolonial moment this history, and the class conflicts embedded within it, expressed itself in other significant ways. To a certain extent, the prevailing cultural construct of the area as inferior and its resultant neglect by the state (outside of its own narrow interests) gave men like Zhang Jian the latitude to make rapid changes and subsequently assume what was in fact dictatorial-like authority to which even the county magistrates had to bow. Older state institutions, particularly the Huainan Salt Yard, that had contributed to peripheralization also worked to the advantage of the new power brokers. The drying up of the salterns left an immense expanse of sparsely inhabited land along the Jiangsu coast. Despite the early roadblocks noted above, Zhang Jian's privileged relations with the state allowed him to acquire the rights to a sizable portion of this land and interweave them into his modernist project of power.

As important, in leaving northern delta peasants in a weaker class position than peasants in Jiangnan, the class struggles during the Qing crucially conditioned the specific constructions of semicolonial modernity in the northern delta. In the first instance, the regearing of the rural economy to the needs of urban capital that was so fundamental to the project of the new urban elite did not have to confront a peasantry with well-established claims to property, as was the case in Jiangnan. That circumstance, combined with new forms of commercialization generated by imperialism that gave them additional leverage over peasants, permitted a rapid transformation of the area in ways that were devastating to many peasants. Similarly, by the second decade of the twentieth century, when the conservative landlord-gentry abruptly changed course, their ability to transform themselves into modern landlords depended on initiatives that would not have been possible without their full control of the land. On the other hand, in eroding earlier peasant gains and effecting changes in the labor process that undermined peasants' stability and autonomy, the modernist project of the urban-rural elite became the terrain for a reconstituting of the older peasant path in new form.

Part Two

THE SEMICOLONIAL PROCESS

4 *Shanghai, Cotton Cloth, and the Shaping of Nantong's Modern Merchant Elite*

IN NANTONG, as in other parts of the Yangzi delta, the forcible opening of China to imperialism conditioned the course of economic and social change. The signing of the Treaty of Nanjing (1842), which formally concluded the Opium War, ended the state's hundred-year-old policy of restricting foreigners' economic activities to the single port of Canton.[1] But the treaty did far more than just give foreigners access to a wider geographic area by opening Shanghai and four other ports to foreign trade.[2] In granting them special privileges and limiting China's sovereignty, it laid the foundation for semicolonial development.

Armed with large amounts of capital, inexpensive machine-made cloth and yarn, and a growing desire for raw cotton, foreign economic penetration worked a radical transformation in the Chinese cotton textile industry. In the southern delta, especially in key producing areas like Songjiang that were situated close to the new Shanghai treaty port, the influx of cheap foreign cloth and the demand for cotton simultaneously undermined the old structure of production and the existing economic hierarchy. These changes formed part of and reflected a more general restructuring and commercial realignment of the delta economy, in which old towns disappeared, new ones emerged, and "core" cities such as Suzhou gave way to Shanghai's dominance. Emanating from the treaty port, a new comprador-banking-merchant network became the axis of foreign-controlled commercial activity and power.

In the northern delta the restructuring undercut the elements that had restricted Nantong's growth as a textile center. Except for a brief period of decline in the 1880's, it became the springboard for increasing productivity, market expansion, and a strengthening of local merchant capital. The last development, in particular, formed one of the key features of the emergent semicolonial economy.

Broadly speaking, the process was one that occurred in all parts of the

Third World where international capitalism expanded in the late nineteenth and early twentieth centuries. Merchants were quick to seize the opportunities that the outgoing flow of raw materials and the incoming flow of industrial products presented.[3] Especially in colonial settings, foreign merchants dominated these activities, frequently displacing indigenous merchants in the process. But in China, where foreigners, though allowed to travel in the interior, had to confine their business activities to designated ports, indigenous merchants assumed a more prominent and pivotal role. The transfer of commodities and raw materials between the ports and the interior had to be conducted through compradors and successive layers of Chinese merchants. Structurally, therefore, with the growth of foreign trade, Chinese merchant capital also expanded, became an indirect agent of capitalist accumulation, and succeeded in retaining a certain autonomy that, in colonial states, often passed to foreigners (Chen Shiqi 1979: 978; McElderry 1976: 71–75; Nie Baozhang 1979: 146–49). In short, merchant capital both limited and became a conduit of semicolonization.

In Nantong textile expansion was the key to the new merchant elite's climb to power. How these merchants forged a link between dispersed peasant family labor in the countryside, machine-spun yarn produced abroad, and a marketing outlet in distant Manchuria; how they extended their prerogatives in local society vis-à-vis both peasants and landlord-gentry; and how all this was done at the price of bringing the local textile industry into the foreign-dominated commercial network are the subjects of this chapter. It spotlights the rise of a class that, culturally and economically, acted as an agent of imperialist expansion, yet at the same time established its own centers of economic gravity. The chapter also highlights the monopsonistic nature of the Shanghai-centered commercial network. Based on native place and on monopolistic arrangements with powerful operatives within the comprador-banking-merchant community, especially the agents of Shanghai's "Ningbo *bang*" (group), ties of this sort were a cornerstone of the new elite's power. The *overdevelopment* of these traditional forms as merchant capital proliferated and merchant control of peasant production grew also appears as a prominent feature in the changing and unstable socioeconomic landscape of an emergent semicolonial modernity.

The Rise of the Guanzhuang Merchants

Despite the achievements of later years, in the wake of the Opium War Nantong, like Jiangnan, was hard hit by foreign textile competition. By the early 1870's foreign goods were competing with Jiangnan products in both local and distant markets (Oyama 1960; *Shanghai shi mianbu shangye* 1979:

2–13). In 1871 cotton goods, predominantly cloth but also including small amounts of yarn, already made up one-third of China's imports by value. A steady decline in the price of machine-made cloth from the 1870's until the mid-1880's sharpened the competitive edge of foreign products (Feuerwerker 1969: 21–23).

By 1880 foreign competition was pushing the price of handwoven cloth in Nantong down too. Yet despite a steady fall in prices in the next few years, local cloth became increasingly unmarketable. Conditions reached a crisis point by the winter of 1883–84, when the industry came to a virtual standstill. Many cloth firms closed as the price dropped to five–six fen per piece, an amount insufficient to cover even production costs. With no alternative but to suspend production, countless destitute peasants took to the road, wandering throughout the area in search of food and employment. By the spring of 1884, thousands began leaving Nantong for Shanghai in search of employment (*Shenbao*, March 6, 1884).

As it turned out, this was the bottom. Foreign cloth prices reached a low in 1884, and then trended sharply upward, with a doubling of price between 1885 and 1900 (Feuerwerker 1969: 22–23). More important from the long-term point of view, as in other districts that were initially outcompeted, Nantong merchants took steps to repair the situation.

The first adjustment they made—turning production to a cloth of higher quality than the old-style narrow cloth—was in fact well in train already before the 1884 crisis (Lin Jubai 1984: 28–29). The new cloth, called *chitaobu*, was both longer and wider than the prevailing form, *xibu*.[4] Its production became possible with technical improvements in the wooden loom, the width and length of *xibu* having been the maximum allowed by the old-style loom (Da Shiji 1980).

Changes in marketing patterns after the Opium War compelled another adjustment. The opening of Shanghai and its growing importance as a commercial port deepened a trend among Chinese merchants to abandon the north-south overland trade in favor of sea transport.[5] Nantong's merchants joined this trend, with the result that the cloth trade with Shandong merchants declined, and exports began moving to Shanghai for transshipment to the northeast by sea (Li Wenzhi: 297; Lin Jubai 1984: 29, 42). With the opening of the northeastern city of Yingkou as a treaty port in 1858, it became the destination of choice. Northern merchants purchased Nantong cloth in Shanghai from brokers, rented ships from Shanghai companies to transport it and other goods to Yingkou, and then shipped cooking oil, soybean cakes, and other local products back to Shanghai to sell. The switch to *chitao* cloth was a direct response to the expansion of the Yingkou trade, engineered by the northern delta merchants to hold on to Manchurian buyers, who had traditionally preferred Nantong cotton for its warmth but might be tempted away by the new choices now available to them (Chen Zengyu 1986: 158; Da Shiji 1980; Lin Jubai 1984).[6]

A group of merchant firms known as the *guanzhuang* stood at the center of these changes.[7] Commanding larger amounts of capital than the county or Nanjing firms, the *guanzhuang* merchants gradually took over the purchase of most of the cloth destined for Shanghai. They also made arrangements with brokers there for its sale to northern (and later Shanghai-based) wholesalers (Lin Jubai 1984: 63–73; NT [8] 1930: 2, 6). The first of these firms began operating during the 1850's in Haimen in the vicinity of Jinsha (earlier a part of Haimen county) and older cloth production areas such as Maozhen. Others rather quickly appeared. Under their guidance production of *chitaobu* moved west and southwest toward Baochang and Liujia, that is, in the direction of Nantong city, as the point of departure for cloth shipments to Shanghai (Chen Zhengyu 1986: 159; Lin Jubai 1984: 29). The twofold result was that Nantong city eventually replaced Jinsha-Haimen as the cloth industry's commercial center of gravity and a raft of new producing districts cropped up in the surrounding areas.

By the turn of the century a majority of the *guanzhuang* firms, including the largest and most influential, made their base in Nantong (Lin Jubai 1984: 59–61). Table 4.1, which breaks them down by area, shows that fully 18 of the 24 that survived into or were founded in the twentieth century were Nantong-based. With one exception, this *tongbang*, or Nantong group, eventually handled only superior or middle grades of cloth. The six Haimen-centered firms continued to handle mostly lower grades (Lin Jubai 1984: 61).

A handful of the *guanzhuang* firms were joint or family ventures, but most were established by individual men as independent enterprises. At least four of these men were owners of native banks (*qianzhuang*; Table 4.1). The rest appear to have been successful merchants engaged in a range of other commercial activities, especially the grain trade (Da Shiji 1980; Yu Yikong 1982: 28). The same was true in other rural weaving centers that developed under foreign stimulus. Merchants who had prospered in banking, the grain trade, and other ventures were the one group with the capital and connections to play a central role in activating textile development when new conditions appeared (H. Fong 1936: 702–6; Wu Zhi 1935).

The fact that none of the county or Nanjing merchant firms moved into the *guanzhuang* trade suggests their low levels of capitalization, relatively small-scale operations, and inability to handle shipping operations to Shanghai. It also suggests the connection between Shanghai's rise as the entrepôt for much of the foreign and central-northeastern China trade and the emergence of a new commercial hierarchy with strong merchant-gentry affiliations in Nantong's textile industry. Although the *guanzhuang* firms remained rather few in number—never surpassing 20 at any one time, as compared with over

TABLE 4.1
Guanzhuang *Cloth Firms in Haimen and Nantong, ca. 1850–1930*

Firm name	Location	Owner
Haimen firms		
Gongdachang	Tianbu	—
Taoyuanchang	—	He Tianlin
Taiji	Menmao	San family
Wangzhengda[a]	Mao (township)	Wang Ziqing
Wangzhengyuan	Menmao	—
Zhonghexing	Menmao	Joint venture
Nantong firms		
Bigongda	Nantong city (east gate)	Bi family[b]
Dashengkui	Nantong city (east gate)	Gao Anjiu
Deji	Nantong city (west gate)	Deji Native Bank (owner, Zhang Jingpu)
Gulongchang	Xiaohai	Gu Baiyan
Hengfenghe	Nantong city	Chen Ziyu
Hengji	Jianzaogang	Joint venture (Shen Jing, Xi Zhongping, Zhang Weishan)[c]
Hengshengfuji	Chuangang	Xi Zhongping[c]
Linji	Nantong city (east gate)	Yongchanglin Native Bank (owner, Liu Xuchu)
Liuzhengda	Chuangang	Liu Yishan
Mingji	Nantong city (west gate)	Wu Didu
Renyuanxin	Xiehongjian	Joint venture[d]
Shengkang	Nantong city (west gate)	Shengkang Native Bank (owner, Ma Yunxi)
Shenji	Xiting	—
Tongyuanxin	—	Wu Dounan[d]
Weigonghe[e]	Sanyutou	Wei Zhongxuan
Xiangji	Yuanzaogang	Wang Shaolan
Xingyongshu[f]	Xingjiayuan	Xing Yingchu
Zhangyuanda	Jianzaogang	Zhang Weishan[c]

SOURCE: Lin Jubai 1984: 58–62.

[a] The first *guanzhuang* firm.

[b] The family later leased the firm to other merchants.

[c] The Hengji firm closed in 1908 or 1909, and Xi Zhongping and Zhang Weishan then established their own firms.

[d] Renyuanxin went bankrupt near the end of the Qing dynasty and was sold to the Yongchanglin Native Bank. Later the bank also took over Tongyuanxin.

[e] Closed in 1904.

[f] Closed in the early 20th century.

100 county and Nanjing firms—their scale of operation and volume of business overshadowed the older firms. By the early 1900's they controlled over 80 percent of the total cloth trade (Lin Jubai 1984; NT [8] 1930: 7–11).

In sum, well before the crisis of 1884, Nantong's textile industry had entered a new, expansionist phase. With the growing importance of the Shanghai treaty port and the astute promotion by a new group of cloth merchants of a product geared to the northeastern market, the older pattern of peripheralized textile development began to dissolve. Nevertheless, both capital shortages among merchants and the constraints on peasant production, namely, the handspinning of yarn, which required four times more labor time than weaving, continued to limit cloth output. In the mid-1880's, thanks to a second radical adjustment in the industry—the adoption of foreign machine-spun yarn—Nantong's weaving industry weathered the crisis, and the *guanzhuang* merchants expanded the scope of their activities and gained greater control of the productive process.

The Comprador-Banking-Merchant Network

Most foreign commodities flowed into the Chinese market via the native banks in Shanghai. Through their comprador agents, foreign banks made deposits in the Chinese banks, which in turn extended loans to Chinese merchants for the purchase of foreign goods. In effect foreign firms via foreign banks guaranteed these loans (McElderry 1976). The native banks owned by members of the Ningbo clique (*Ningbobang*), also known as the Zhejiang financial clique,[8] played a central role in these operations. As the name indicates, Ningbo was the native place of the merchants in this group, but Shanghai became the center of their financial-commercial operations. From roughly 1800 to the 1920's, the "control of the organization of Shanghai finance" lay primarily in their hands (Jones 1974: 73).

Before 1842 the *bang*'s financial preeminence had rested in large part on a network of native-place associations, local business relations, and enterprises Ningbo merchants had created along internal trade routes, particularly in the lower Yangzi and in the north around Tianjin (Jones 1974: 74). In Nantong, for example, Ningbo merchants had regularly purchased small quantities of local cloth and had been, after Anhui merchants, the second largest group of nonnative retail storeowners (with concentrations in the tea and herb businesses; Wang Xiangwu 1982: 2; Yu Yikong 1982: 29). With the opening of Shanghai as a treaty port, this network of personal business ties, combined with the clique's domination of Shanghai finance, placed its members in a position to become key operatives in a foreign-controlled comprador-banking-merchant network.

In the latter decades of the century, these men and other native bankers who received the deposits of foreign capital expanded and strengthened this network along particularistic and monopsonistic lines. To effect this, they and/or their commodity-firm offshoots, which were often established by *bang* members for these very purposes, "tended to develop a specialized clientele and a well-defined sphere of operations" (Jones 1974: 85). As Jones elucidates:

The Ankang Native Bank, founded in 1870, conducted exchange transactions between Shanghai and Ningbo, Hangzhou, Jiaxing, Huzhou, Jinjiang, Yangzhou, Tongzhou, and Nanking, its main clientele being drawn from the cotton industry. The Anyu Native Bank, founded in 1879, catered primarily to silk merchants. The Chengyu, founded in 1892, had a diversified clientele drawn from the silk and tea trades and the trade in metals and imported goods. (Ibid.)

Thus, rather than indicating the tenacious persistence of older, well-established Chinese business practices in the face of otherwise modernizing influences in the treaty ports, the elaboration and strengthening of particularistic ties in a new structural context became an integral part of the semicolonial project. Contrary to the assumptions of modernizationist scholars about the displacement of traditional forms by universalizing processes, developments in China reinforce the view that Third World modernities emerging within the framework of imperialism and colonialism have often entailed the extension, hardening, and even the resurrection of preexisting forms (Chatterjee 1986; Goodman & Redclift 1982; Hart 1986; Kahn 1993; Patterson & Gailey 1987).

In an important study, Nie Baozhang (1979) convincingly argues that the influence of the comprador-banking operation on the Chinese economy was not limited simply to expanding the export-import trade; rather, it increasingly enabled foreign firms to control successive layers of Chinese merchant capital. In the rapidly changing business climate of the 1870's–90's, Chinese merchants were eager to take advantage of the opportunities for profits and power offered by that foreign-controlled network (Xu Gengqi 1982: 49). They were attracted especially by the new sources of capital and credit now open to them.

Participation in this network, however, quickly led to a pattern of forced buying and selling among Chinese merchants, due in part to the nature of the arrangements compradors made with the Chinese banks. What they often got in the way of foreign funds was the infamous "chop-loan" (*chepiao*), which normally fell due after only two to seven days. At the same time, because of growing competition, merchants increasingly relied on ever-larger loans to expand their volume of trade. As a result the original autonomy of the Chinese banking system was compromised, and both native banks and their merchant-clients "became increasingly dependent on loans from foreign banks to ensure their solvency" (Jones 1974: 83).

Nie further argues that the prosperous appearance of the treaty-port economies in the late nineteenth century concealed the real fragility of the comprador-banking-merchant network. It disguised the fact that trade had come to have a direct bearing on the financial market and the price of money, so that failure in any one segment could lead to failure in all segments. According to Nie, this fragility underlay the tendency toward perpetual crisis in the treaty ports, especially Shanghai. Although she examines these conditions from a different perspective, Andrea McElderry's (1976) findings reinforce Nie's analysis.

Nie's work contributes to the body of literature suggesting that once industrial capital penetrated the Third World, merchant capital both lost and retained its independence. The ability of established financial-commercial groups in Shanghai, such as the Ningbo *bang*, to maintain and extend their power, as well as the hierarchical reordering and rise of merchant groups in myriad and often distant local areas, exemplified by the *guanzhuang* merchants in Nantong, intertwined to function as a key mechanism of semicolonization (Nie 1979: 100–149).

A textile industry increasingly reliant on foreign yarn proved to be particularly susceptible to this dual development in the sphere of merchant capital, especially since that innovation tended to erode the old divide between marketing and production (Fei Hsiao-tung & Chang Chih-i 1945; H. Fong 1935, 1936; Wu Zhi 1935). The foreign yarn trade became a propelling force in the expansion of old rural handweaving centers and the emergence of new ones in various areas of China. The phenomenal rise in annual yarn imports reflects these developments, increasing 24 times—from an average of 97,451 piculs in the 1871–80 period to 2,363,000 in 1901–10 (Feuerwerker 1969: 21).[9]

Foreign Yarn and Textile Expansion in Nantong

For Nantong's cloth merchants foreign yarn provided not only a means of recovering from the crisis of 1884 but an avenue to new wealth. Merchants first introduced machine-spun yarn in Haimen and then Nantong in 1884, that is, at the time of the marketing crisis. The first shipments were brought on mail ships, which also carried small quantities of goods on which no customs (*waituo*) were declared. Though merchants like Chen Yugang, who imported furs from Jiangnan and was knowledgeable about sales in Shanghai, handled these initial shipments, the *guanzhuang* cloth merchants very quickly began dealing in 10- and 12-count yarns (Yu Yikong 1982: 31). Some of the larger firms, such as the Yongchangling Native Bank, also established business representatives in Shanghai to handle the yarn trade (Lin Jubai 1984: 31). In addition independent yarn firms emerged, reaching a total of 27 or 28 in 1890 (Yu Yikong 1982: 31).

Weaving families quickly adopted the new product. As prices fell in the 1880's–90's, yarn came to cost little more than raw cotton, and it was of more even quality with less broken ends than homespun.[10] Usually weavers adopted machine-spun yarn for warping and continued to use handspun for weft, hence the nickname "*yangjing benwei*" (foreign warp, homespun weft).

Merchants established a standard width and length (1.2 *chi* by 4.5 *zhang*) for what came to be variously known as *dachibu* (big *chi* cloth, indicating cloth of a larger size than *chitaobu*), *baidabu* (big white cloth), or simply, *guanzhuangbu* (*guanzhuang* cloth) (Lin Jubai 1984: 33; Yu Yikong 1982: 35).

The elimination of part of the time-consuming work of spinning was very quickly reflected in a remarkable expansion in the cloth industry. For example, contemporary estimates indicated that, by 1895, sales of foreign yarn in the Tonghai area reached 20 jian a day, or the equivalent of the output of 10,000 mechanized spindles, with a market value of over 400,000 taels (Peng Zeyi et al. 1957, 2: 211; TZ 1910, 1: 5). The total cloth output for that year was about 1,000,000 bolts, as against just 20,000 to 30,000 in 1884. *Guanzhuang* cloth constituted the lion's share of the 1895 total (Da Shiji 1980; Lin Jubai 1984: 31).

Since, contrary to common assumption, weaving families did not fully shift to foreign yarns but continued to use homespun for weft, as output increased a market for handspun yarn also developed, leading to a greater specialization and division of labor by peasant producers and the handling of both products by cloth-yarn merchants. The new cotton firms (*huahang*) that sprang up in the 1880's and 1890's in producing districts such as Jinsha, Yuxi, Pingchao, Liuqiao, and Shian also frequently handled homespun yarn (Yu Yikong 1982: 33). In this respect production divisions in Nantong began to more closely resemble those that had characterized the cotton districts of Jiangnan in the late Ming and Qing. As we will examine in detail in Chapter Nine, in the long run this division contributed to the marginalization of the poorest producers in the weaving districts. Suffice it to say here that viewed from a structural perspective, their inability to bear the costs of weaving ensured a continuous supply of yarn for the production of *guanzhuang* cloth.

After the turn of the century *guanzhuang* production shifted entirely to machine-spun yarn. Nevertheless, because peasants continued to weave small white, *chitao*, *dachi*, and other forms of cloth made in part or in whole of homespun, a small market in homespun yarn persisted. So did the market for homespun cloth, especially among the many peasant producers in the rural industrial districts, whose deepening involvement in market relations, growing need for cash, and poverty prevented them from keeping or wearing the superior and more durable forms of cloth they produced (MMT 1941).

The Guanzhuang Cloth Trade and
the Modern Merchant Elite

At the other end of the social spectrum, the dramatic increase in *guanzhuang* cloth production, coupled with growing demand in the northeast, lent new complexity and sophistication to merchant operations. As the market expanded *guanzhuang* merchants developed a wide variety of specific brand names for their products, and thus an elaborate system of cloth grading and brand ranking appeared (Lin Jubai 1984: 31–40). Marketing relations in Shanghai also became more complex.

As early as the 1870's Shanghai brokers who regularly handled cloth transactions for *guanzhuang* firms had established a lodging house called "Tonghaiyuan" as a convenient boarding place for *guangzhuang* merchants on their trips to the city and a way to attract their business. The Nantong cloth merchants Li Boyan, Jiang Chunping, and others established a second lodging house in the 1880's, when because of the expanding cloth and yarn business, the accommodations at the Tonghai became insufficient (Lin Jubai 1984: 63).

Over the next decade several of the largest Nantong-Haimen firms set up branch offices in Shanghai (*shenzhuang* or *zuozhuang*) as a means of establishing closer personal relations with the owners or directors of Shanghai native banks, compradors, and cloth brokers (Chen Zengyu 1986: 161).[11] In almost all cases, the firm's owner or highest-ranking functionary was the principal representative in the Shanghai branch. Liu Yishan, the merchant founder of one of the major *guanzhuang* firms, was one of the first to establish a branch office. Other Tonghai owners quickly followed Liu's lead (Lin Jubai 1984: 63–64). Consequently the most important *guanzhuang* merchants also became regular participants in the culture of the center par excellence of treaty-port modernity in China.

This development deepened the hierarchical restructuring among cloth merchants already under way in Nantong, as the native bank–owned *guanzhuang* firms began to dominate the cloth trade and its center shifted from Jinsha-Haimen to Nantong city (Yu Yikong 1982: 31). At the same time it gave those firms new leverage over smaller cloth dealers who, unable to support a Shanghai office of their own, selected a branch firm to do business for them on a commission basis (*daizhuang*). The activities of Chen Ziyu, owner-manager of the Hengfenghe *buzhuang*, typify the new arrangements. Through his Shanghai office Chen represented the Xiangji cloth firm and sold cloth on the side for Shenji and Yongchanglin. He had dealings in the cotton business as well (Lin Jubai 1984: 60, 70).

Heads of the Shanghai offices formalized the new hierarchy in 1898, with Li Yishan's organization of the Cotton Cloth Guild (Shabu gongsuo). Trade/occupational organizations of this type were standard among late-nineteenth-century Chinese merchants; part of the Ningbo clique's power, for example, rested in its control of Shanghai's Native Bank Guild (Jones 1974). Similarly, although the cloth guild was open to all members of the trade, with the heads of the Shanghai branch offices sitting on the board of directors, the largest *guanzhuang* firms monopolized the new organization (Lin Jubai 1984: 66–67).

The chief function of the guild, or more precisely its directors, was to set prices for the various grades and brands of Nantong cloth sold on the Shanghai market (Yu Yikong 1982: 35).[12] Ostensibly the aim of this collective price-setting was to maximize Nantong's position in the Shanghai market. In practice it became a means for the larger businesses to dominate the market by imposing checks and balances on smaller firms (NT [3] 1987: 6; Yu Yikong 1982: 35, 44–45).

Moreover, from the outset, the board authorized only eight Shanghai brokerage firms to act as commissioned agents for Nantong products (Lin Jubai 1984: 66, 73), thereby integrating the Nantong cloth and yarn trade still more tightly into the personalized, supraregional comprador-banking-merchant network. The brokers' (*qianke*) privileged position not only gave them the opportunity for large profits but invited abuses. Conducting negotiations between buyers and sellers (as well as making loans and handling the delivery of goods and loading of ships), the brokers made large sales commissions up front and, in a business where speculation was rampant, secret profits by manipulating the prices of the more than 200 brands of *guanzhuang* cloth (ibid., p. 77).

The four most important of the authorized brokers, Renyuanhao, Shunji, Yuanguoji, and Zhengdahe, were all affiliates of the Ningbo *bang* and in turn dealt exclusively with Ningbo banking and cloth-shipping firms. The latter were known collectively as the *chuanhaobang* or, simply, *haobang* (shipping merchants). The owners of the three largest *haobang* firms, Jiuda, Xinji, and Zhenkang, headed the Shipping Merchants Guild and possessed at least 15 oceangoing ships (Lin Jubai 1984: 74–76, 79). The Ningbo *haobang* were the major purchasers of *guanzhuang* cloth. They were always the first large-scale buyers in the four periods of the year when the wholesale market for *guanzhuang* cloth opened,[13] and, in fact, all of the full-commissioned brokers "came and went through the doors of the *haobang*" (ibid., pp. 77–78).

Among the four Ningbo brokers, Renyuanhao occupied premier position. Having, according to Lin Jubai, "the majority of the brokers under its control" and "unimaginable financial power" (1984: 79), it was an arm of Jiuda, the leading and most famous of the Ningbo *haobang*. Owned jointly by local merchants and bankers, Jiuda had originally run shiploads of various commodities. But after the opening of Yingkou, many Shandong merchants became its regular customers as it moved into and then concentrated on the cloth and cotton trade (ibid., pp. 78, 105–8). Jiuda's financial strength enabled it to become the principal purchaser of *guanzhuang* cloth, and to maintain and expand this position by offering the Shanghai branch offices, through its Renyuanhao brokerage, funds for advance purchase when current supplies of cloth ran out (ibid., p. 74).[14] Those offices in turn funneled the funds on to Nantong merchants as money orders (*huipiao*) and 10- to 20-day notes (*shenpiao*). In this way Ningbo banking money at once permitted the large *guan-*

zhuang firms to strengthen their position and underpinned a sizable portion of the *guanzhuang* business, which in the first years of the twentieth century reached an annual volume of 15,000,000 yuan (Chen Zengyu 1986: 162).

The four brokerage firms that were not Ningbo affiliates specialized in transactions with three other merchant groups, the *kebang*, the *Andongbang*, and the *sanbang*. The *kebang* (guest merchant group) was composed of Shandong firms, a number of which had originally engaged in the overland trade. They controlled important businesses in Yingkou and frequently rented sailing ships from the *haobang* to transport cloth to the port and bring back soybeans and cooking oil to Shanghai (Lin Jubai 1984: 79–80). The 20 merchants of the *Andongbang* were also from Shandong; they possessed their own ships and, as the name indicates, specialized in shipments to Andong, the point of entry for the Yalu River area. The volume of sales in that port was only a tenth of that in Yingkou (ibid., p. 80). The eight merchants of the *sanbang* ("loose" or "unaffiliated" group, a name that suggests a lack of guild organization), were from the Lusi, Yudong, and Yuxi areas of Nantong. All but one, who was a cloth merchant, were from families that had been bookkeepers on *haobang* ships and had accumulated enough capital to buy their own ships, which eventually totaled about a dozen. Their operations were similar to those of the *haobang*, although on a much smaller scale. They often acted as auxiliary agents for the *haobang* (ibid., pp. 81–83).[15]

Another of the board's early steps illustrates as well as anything the growing sophistication of the Nantong cloth industry and a recognition of where its future lay. To cement the cotton merchants' ties with their major outlet, the directors established a permanent guild representative in Yingkou. His primary responsibilities were to investigate and report the market situation to the board (Lin Jubai 1984: 67).

Finally, immediately after its founding, the cloth guild decided to impose a fee on each bolt of cloth sold by its members to maintain a permanent headquarters and place of residence for visiting Nantong merchants. In December 1898, it purchased (on mortgage) a house and adjacent building totaling 20 rooms on Maojian Lane in Shanghai. Lin Jubai, author of the most authoritative history of the Nantong cloth industry to date, momentarily digresses from his otherwise straightforward account to describe in meticulous detail the main house of the guild's new complex:

> There was a narrow courtyard leading to a tall wall with a door that opened in the middle. On the door were two thick knockers with animal faces. It looked like a big residential building for government officials. . . . The ground was covered with slabstones, all tidy and smooth. . . . Three spacious halls led out from the entrance. The two halls on both sides had walls whose lower parts were built with ground bricks and had delicate window frames. In the middle, there were six long casement windows. On the right and left walls in the [main] hall were four screens with Zhang Jian's calligraphy and Yang Yi's landscape painting. In the center of the hall

there was a conference table with chairs around it. Along the side wall, there were six high armchairs and four tea tables. . . . There was a long corridor leading to a pavilion. . . . The three side walls of this building had five-colored glass fixed in exquisite carved window frames. In the center of the room there were sacrificial tables, [and] a portrait of the Empress of Heaven hung on the wall facing the entrance. This portrait was done by a famous artist from Shanghai. (1984: 64–65) [16]

Lin's nostalgic account seems to capture the pride and importance that Nantong's cloth merchants attached to their guild complex. Although hardly comparable to the opulent quarters of the Ningbo clique's native-place association on the outskirts of Shanghai, it nevertheless stood as a symbol of the county's shedding of its peripheral status and the *guanzhuang* merchants' rise as a new elite. Situated in the dynamic center of Westernizing trends and imperialist operations in China, the guild complex also starkly symbolized the growing distance between that elite and the rural peasant weavers who formed the lifeblood of Nantong's textile business.

Merchant Capital and Rural Industrial Expansion

With the shift to machine-spun yarn, the unified management system that had characterized peasant family textile production in the northern delta since the Ming began to disintegrate. Cotton, yarn, and cloth production were no longer fully integrated into a single process under the control of peasant households. Weaving families could now sell the cotton they had previously reserved for handspinning, and indeed had to sell it to raise the cash for yarn. Although the merchants who supplied them with the new raw material did not directly control production, they did so indirectly.

This assumption of new prerogatives in the spheres of circulation and production by merchant capital, and the new market dependence of peasant weavers that it entailed, formed the *specifica differentia* between earlier textile development and expansion under foreign penetration. Whereas in the Ming internal developments in peasant production powered the expansion of the commodity economy, nineteenth-century semicolonialism fostered commercialization from above.

In short, with the introduction of foreign yarn, merchants' prerogatives and the commercialization of both agriculture and rural household industry developed further. Not only were yarn sales tied to foreign trade, but the elaborate, overdeveloped structures through which the commercial and marketing networks functioned stripped peasant producers of potential profits and distributed them instead to a long line of beneficiaries. Local merchants and native banks; Shanghai brokers, bankers, cloth dealers, and shipping merchants; compradors, foreign banks, foreign businessmen, and foreign industry; and merchant wholesalers and retailers in the northeast all took their bite. The cotton they grew was also increasingly bought up by foreign cloth companies to be blended with their American and Indian stocks (Li Wenzhi 1957: 397). From 1885 to 1895 exports of raw cotton rose from 61,850 piculs to 895,096 piculs (Chen Shiqi 1979: 985). Foreign purchases increased after 1895 with the establishment of foreign factories in China and the rapid expansion of the Japanese textile industry. As a result, near the end of the century, Nantong's new commercial elite began branching out into the cotton trade.

Paradoxically, then, the new economic processes in Nantong fostered a modern merchant class that was at once stronger and weaker than local merchant capitalists in the past. Through its promotion of textile production, that emergent class strengthened its position in local society and linked its interests to the development of a transregional internal trade, that is, to a Chinese center of gravity. But what appear to be its autonomous operations were, strictly speaking, not autonomous at all since in large part those operations—and certainly the rapidity with which they occurred—became possible only because the new class also acted as an indirect agent of foreign capital. Local merchant capital was made increasingly dependent on international economic forces.

The Janus-face of this modern merchant capitalism highlights the kind of contradictory interaction that Steve Stern sees as the key to understanding the structures, changes, and driving forces of colonial economic life (1988: 871). In his provocative critique of Immanuel Wallerstein's world-system theory, Stern argues that a developing international capitalism constituted only one of three "great motor forces" shaping labor and the economy in the colonized world. In his view, "laborers' resistance and assertion of 'rights' " formed a second motor, while "the rise . . . of regional and inter-regional markets and elites whose 'logic' and interests did not always coincide" with those of an expanding global capitalism acted as a third of equal and independent weight (p. 857). It was precisely in the interplay of forces of this type, and the internal divisions and contradictions in each of them, that Nantong's semicolonial economic and sociopolitical life took shape and assumed new form.

5 Remaking Local Power:
Zhang Jian's Self-Reliant Path

IN THE HISTORY of Chinese industrial development, the scholar-bureaucrat, "nationalist" leader, and domestic industrialist Zhang Jian (1853–1926) stands as a key figure. Zhang's pioneering efforts in founding the Dasheng Spinning Factory and instituting other Westernizing projects in Nantong placed him at the forefront of elite-sponsored modernization in China. The success of these projects conclusively dislodged all remaining notions of Nantong as an inferior backwater.

Like other early modernizers, Zhang viewed the "promotion of industry" as an economic solution to China's semicolonial predicament. Seeking to short-circuit the drain of profits and raw materials through the foreign-centered Shanghai commercial network, he engineered a program of "local production, local sales" (*tuchan tuxiao*), in which the Dasheng mill used locally grown cotton as its raw material and marketed its output to peasant producers of *guanzhuang* cloth. From the perspective of short-term economic growth, this self-reliant "nationalist" alternative proved to be remarkably effective. Dasheng became the most successful Chinese-owned mill in the pre–World War One period, its success paralleled by Nantong's rise as the major rural handweaving center in China. Expanding cotton acreage accompanied these developments.

Past studies of this early modernization emphasize Zhang's entrepreneurship, Dasheng's volume cotton purchasing policy, and local conditions, especially the availability of raw materials and a ready-made handweaving industry, as central factors in the mill's unusual success (S. Chu 1965; Nakai 1980; Yan Zhongping 1963). Clearly each of these was important. But to emphasize them alone or in combination is to mask the real foundation of Dasheng's success and the most important characteristic of modern industry in Nantong: its monopolistic interlinking with the peasant economy and merchant capital. Realized in large part through Zhang's bureaucratic prerogatives, this interlocked rural-urban system concentrated the benefits of growth in the hands of modern, urban-based elites and fundamentally altered the contours of agrarian conflict and change.

This chapter considers the implications of Zhang's elite-centered alternative to semicolonized growth. It emphasizes how the changes he worked in the economic system constituted a new cultural strategy and mode of modern elite power. It thus expands the term modern elite to denote industrialists, such as Zhang Jian, as well as the merchants and gentry businessmen who participated in the foreign-centered commercial network and/or Western-inspired economic ventures. In the late Qing–early Republican period, these three groups came to rather clearly coalesce as a commercial-entrepreneurial capitalist class, within which, for a time, close cooperation and alliance concealed and minimized significant internal contradictions.

My definition of the modern elite roughly corresponds to Marie-Claire Bergère's use of the term (1989). It also overlaps with the "urban reformist elite" that Joseph Esherick speaks of in his pioneering study of the 1911 revolution (1976). Esherick identifies that elite as a group in the upper layers of the landlord-merchant-gentry class that, through the sponsorship of Western education, industrial development, resistance to foreign economic encroachment, and new movements to limit governmental interference in the rights of private citizens, dominated provincial politics at the end of the Qing (1976: 66).

In characterizing this new elite as urban, Esherick stresses both residence and orientation—an orientation that, tainted by the West, alienated it, and, in his view, severed it from the countryside. Here, as the following pages will demonstrate, my view of the modern elite departs from Esherick's. To be sure, as he argues, because of its physical and cultural separation from the countryside, the urban elite increasingly turned its back on rural problems— even while wrapping its discourse in the older rhetoric of "concern for local society." I contend, however, that its ascendancy rested to a significant degree precisely on its links to and growing control of rural labor. Thus in Nantong, as in other localities where modernization became a formula for actualizing power,[1] development was structured in an older, culturally prescribed framework.

In short the exploitation of the peasantry—in old and new forms—was a cornerstone of the modern elite's power. In the end, the elite achieved a hybridized modernity based not only on the semicolonial conditions that aided its emergence, but to a large extent on the intensification of the trends through which, in the most highly commercialized areas, urban-based merchant capital had set out to establish itself as the real master of the countryside.

The Setting: Westernization and Local Elite Power

The diverse social composition of the elite "nationalist" movement in China reflected the changing social context in which it was born. Beginning as an expression of the collective sociopolitical and economic aspirations of those who were forming a modern, partially Westernized commercial elite, it drew support from compradors, bankers, and various strata of merchants. Especially in the treaty ports, members of this group, like the *guanzhuang* merchants encountered in the last chapter, internalized China's growing humiliation at the hands of foreigners, yet were also attracted by the business opportunities of foreign trade and the legitimacy the imperialist discourse of progress and modernity conferred on nonbureaucratic economic activity. Beyond and often linked with these commercial circles, many if not the bulk of the movement's activists—and unquestionably its leadership—came from the established landlord-gentry official elite. Though desirous of reestablishing national prestige, these members of the establishment also began to embrace the Western discourse. Increasingly, as well, they viewed Westernizing change as an avenue for developing new forms of independent power, especially at the local level (Esherick 1976).

In the 1870's and 1880's, these groups supported the limited self-strengthening (*ziqiang*) sponsored by the Qing state, as exemplified in *guandu shangban* (government-supervised, merchant-managed) enterprises. Representing a continuation in new form of the state policy of closely supervising and restricting merchant activity, these enterprises afforded the only legitimate arena for private capital investment in modern industry. Although they ostensibly offered new, if limited, opportunities for industrial development, the state's control of them stripped private investors of both power and profits. In the 1880's the urban elite's support for them began to wane, and dissatisfaction over the state's supervisory policies reached new levels (Feuerwerker 1958).

The watershed came with China's devastating defeat in the Sino-Japanese War of 1894–95. In the eyes of the urban elite, that humiliation definitively exposed the inadequacies of the Qing's limited effort. Following the war, as nationalist sentiments deepened, activists began calling for thoroughgoing change in various areas, from political structure and economics to education and philosophy. It was in this context of expanding activism that a new leadership group appeared in the treaty ports and larger commercial centers. Viewing the state as increasingly incapable of protecting local economic interests from foreign encroachment, members of the upper layers of the landlord-merchant-gentry set out, with new vigor, to provide that protection themselves (Bastid 1976; Bergère 1968: 248–49). Denouncing China's semicolonial status as the chief source of its ills, they made "recovering lost rights" and "saving the country by developing industry" two of their central themes (Feuerwerker 1958: 35–36; Li Shiyue 1979: 1295).

They pursued these goals, first, by encouraging the establishment of non-bureaucratic associational networks, thinly disguised political societies, educational projects, and organizational groups promoting economic change in their home areas (Fei Fanjiu 1981a; see also, for full treatments, Esherick 1976; and Rankin 1986). They also vigorously promoted industrial development, not only as a path of national regeneration but also, as Zhang Jian put it, in familiar ruling-class rhetoric, as a means of "improving the welfare of the people" (*minsheng*; Bergère 1968: 285). To the degree that the state had granted these groups taxing privileges toward militia building during the massive peasant rebellions of the 1860's and extended commercial tax-farming among them, it strengthened the fiscal power, extrabureaucratic roles, and local autonomist trends among them (Bastid-Bruguiere 1980).

Under the pressure of this expanding activism, and with its own evolving agenda, the Qing state began to make concessions. In the economic realm, most importantly, it relinquished some of its control over industrial development. In 1895 it instructed provincial officials to establish business bureaus for the purpose of encouraging merchant-gentry to found private industrial projects. This was a considerable concession, for though these projects still required state approval, the state claimed no supervisory powers over them after their organization (TZ 1910, 1: 1).

Although the failure of the Hundred Days program of 1897–98 resulted in the suspension of government concessions,[2] the Boxer Rebellion in 1900 brought a new discrediting of the court and mounting pressure for elitist-led or more revolutionary change. The Qing responded by launching what is known as the New Policies (*xinzheng*) program (1902–8), which implemented, or promised to implement, the full range of measures for business and industry put forth in the Hundred Days edict. Among other things the state established a Ministry of Commerce; set out commercial laws and regulations governing company registration and investment requirements for banks, railroad, mines, and other forms of modern enterprise; and developed guidelines for the organizing of local chambers of commerce (Fan Baichuan 1983: 12).

These concessions, effectively sanctioning private industry as a legal form of production and providing a more favorable political climate for its growth, represented an important breakthrough. If, for the Qing, the New Policies program was a means of gaining back lost ground by recentralizing, its posture created new maneuvering space in which modern elites expanded their initiative and built a new mode of power. Indeed in the years between 1895, when the ban on private industry was lifted, and 1898 alone more than 80 industries were established, the bulk of which were private ventures (Li Shiyue 1979: 1296–1302).

In this new political and economic climate, the pace of local change quickened. With the sanction of the New Policies and the backing of fellow members of the urban elite who had both bureaucratic connections and prestige, the increasingly Western-oriented fractions of the local elite charged head-on into modernization. Aiming their sights as much on the public as on the private sector, they knit an institutional network in which industrial-commercial enterprises, private policing-military forces, and politically oriented business associations interplayed with Western-style schools, taxing and tax dispensation agencies, and other "self-governing" (*zizhi*) offices to produce a new form of local power and rule (Bergère 1968; Chauncey 1992; Duara 1988; Fei Fanjiu 1981a, b; Kuhn 1978–79; NT [2] n.d.).

These developments hastened both class fissure and class formation. In the most highly commercialized areas, the result was a shift in the balance of power within the landlord-gentry-merchant class in favor of the modern commercial elite (Bastid-Bruguiere 1980: 563; Bergère 1983: 727; 1989; Walker 1986). On the other hand, as we will see, the result was disastrous for the urban poor and even more so for the peasants, now subjected to new types of rural exploitation emanating from the cities. In illustration of both patterns, let me turn now to the activities of Zhang Jian, the central figure of Nantong's modernizing elite.

Zhang Jian and the Urban Elite

In many respects Zhang Jian exemplified the urban elite leadership. Like its other members, he had good state credentials, having attained a degree and served as an official in his home county of Nantong and in Haimen, his birthplace (Bastid 1988: 169; Zhang Jian 1931, 6: 17; Zhang Xiaoruo 1930: 50–52). But unlike almost all those men, Zhang did not come from a family of landed wealth, a fact that undoubtedly became an added motivation in his adoption of the modernist path to wealth and power.

In 1894 Zhang became the epitome of success for those whose lives revolved around the bureaucracy and the examination system. Culminating almost 40 years of study, he placed first in the metropolitan examinations, receiving the prestigious title of *zhuangyuan* for his achievement. He was subsequently appointed to the Han Lin Academy and seemed assured of a high-level governmental career. Within a year, however, he abandoned the idea of governmental service. Sensing a new urgency in the task of self-strengthening because of China's defeat by Japan, he announced his decision to return to Nantong to devote his energies to modernization.

Zhang's decision reflected a long association with moderate officials such as Zhang Zhidong and members of the urban elite. Principally in Shanghai — the point of convergence in the delta of modernist circles and trends — Zhang maintained close personal contact with other rising urban leaders such as Li Houyou, Xu Shulan, and Tang Shouqian who shared his growing concern about China's weakness in the face of imperialism.[3] His published writings from the 1880's and early 1890's pinpoint industrial and educational development as twin pillars of Western strength. In them, we also find his clear perception of the semicolonial thrust in China. He observes that, like other victimized countries, China was simultaneously contributing to the economic development of the capitalist West and its own decline. Using sales of Nantong cotton to foreigners and purchases of foreign yarn as examples, he equates the process of "giving away" local resources to foreigners and then repurchasing them in the form of finished products with offering one's blood and flesh to a tiger. Writing, in 1895, for the new Shanghai branch of the Self-Strengthening Society that he organized at the behest of Zhang Zhidong, Zhang further suggests that China's defeat by Japan could only exacerbate the problem: the Western powers would take China's weakness as a signal to intensify their aggression, and Japan itself would gradually extend its economic penetration until it was in a position to "devour" the country (Zhang Jian 1931, 1: 20).

Through their writings, personal relationships, and associations, Zhang and the urban elite gained greater definition and became more clearly bound together by common institutional ties, material interests, and political aspirations (Bastid-Bruguiere 1980: 558). In this context Zhang's move to short-circuit the semicolonizing process by returning to Nantong to establish a spinning mill and other projects was a logical step. It also marked a new stage in the development of the urban elite, for he was only one of many men who retired from official life to promote economic development in their home localities.

Zhang's decision to found a spinning mill was also astute and practical. He was intimately aware of the rapid expansion of cloth production in Nantong through close associates in the industry, such as Shen Xiejun, a native of Haimen and cloth-firm owner who later invested in and became a Dasheng administrator (Bastid 1988: 169; Ji Bin et al. 1985; Lin Jubai 1984: 60). Zhang understood that with the local cloth industry as its foundation and his own bureaucratic connections as its protective shield, he would be able to develop a monopolistic system of local production of unusual strength.

Finally, personal considerations were no less important. Despite his scholarly fame and close association with modernist urban gentry throughout the delta, Zhang was in key respects treated as an outsider in his home county. Because of his peasant background he had never been fully accepted in the narrow circles of landed elite society. His outside connections and associations with merchants only distanced him further from the conservative gentry of Nantong. The discourse and praxis of modernity became a means for Zhang and his colleagues to challenge and finally reformulate local dominance.

The Modern Elite and the State

Reference to Zhang's bureaucratic connections highlights the close co-operative relations that persisted between the urban elite and the Qing state until the 1911 revolution and, not infrequently, allowed men like Zhang to pursue their modernizing projects. Though the urban elite's growing involvement in constitutional politics and other forms of overt political activity in the first decade of the century can properly be viewed as one of the centrifugal forces that pulled the Qing regime apart,[4] neither this involvement nor the growing exercise of local power ruptured that relationship. To be sure, the strategic aims and economic agendas of the modern local elites often deviated from those of the state. This was evident in their conflicts over taxes, especially with provincial governments (Bell 1985; Jones 1978–79; Walker 1986). Nevertheless, until the final days of the dynasty, urban leaders like Zhang Jian exercised the prerogative of meeting with top-level central government officials to gain support for their projects. More significant over time were the close associations Zhang and his colleagues nurtured with important provincial and regional officials such as Yuan Shikai and Liu Kunyi, who succeeded Zhang Zhidong as governor of Zhejiang-Jiangsu. Zhang Jian and Tang Shouqian in fact became part of a small group of trusted advisers whom Liu regularly consulted on regional and national matters (S. Chu 1965: 57).

These relations underscore the elitist, antidemocratic conception of change that these modernists shared with the state—a class perspective rooted in the rule of the peasantry. Their growing orientation toward the West deepened their disdain for the peasant, who in the developmentalist discourse of modernity was the antithesis of what one should be. This shared class perspective made the threat of revolution and social disruption from below as inimical to the elite as it was to the state. That was quite clearly true of Zhang Jian. Although he was one of the founders of the constitutionalist movement and a leader in the drive for local autonomy, his fear of radical social impulses kept him firmly attached to the central regime. He fundamentally opposed the growing revolutionary movement and had little contact with its adherents (S. Chu 1965: 71; Fujioka 1985). When things came to a head on October 10, 1911, he urged the regional military commander to send troops to Wuchang to squelch the insurrection and to suggest to the Qing court that it immediately declare a constitutional government to undercut the revolution's momentum (Zhang 1931, 8: 21). Over the next month Zhang continued his constitutionalist efforts to "prop up the tottering Qing regime" (S. Chu 1965).

In the end what led him, like other members of the provincial and urban elites, to abandon the imperial state was not merely the Qing's demonstrated weakness in 1911 but its failure to deal with the mounting peasant insurrections of its last decade. And like many of them, he joined the revolution only so as to capture it and restore "order and stability" in the countryside. As gentry in Huizhou candidly stated, they would choose independence if the revolutionaries assisted them in suppressing the peasant "bandits" (Yangzhou shifan xueyuan 1963: 370).

In locality after locality, as well as in upper administrative levels, the pattern was the same: after joining the revolution, the urban elite displaced the revolutionaries, assumed leading positions in the provisional administrations, and then moved swiftly to wipe out the peasant rebels in their areas and deradicalize the revolutionary program (Guan Jincheng 1991; NT [9] 1981–87, vol. 1; Y.-t. Wong 1977; Yangzhou shifan xueyuan 1963). Zhang Jian himself, for example, became the military governor of Nantong. Although he and other urban elite leaders subsequently accepted cabinet positions in the central provisional government, they were even then planning a new party to counteract the radical Tongmenghui. Almost immediately as well, they began drifting toward the counterrevolutionary military-centralizer Yuan Shikai (S. Chu 1965: 73–85; Esherick 1976; Y.-t. Wong 1977). Plainly, they continued to view a strong national state apparatus with solid coercive power as the desirable and necessary counterpart to their own local autonomous rule.

Local Power and Semicolonial State Formation

In the circumstances, analyses pinpointing an expansion of local elite activism and power, but not necessarily at the expense of the central state — and even overlapping with a simultaneous expansion of central state power — seem to most closely capture the complex social reality of the late Qing period (e.g., Duara 1988, 1987; Kuhn & Jones 1979; Liu Kwang-ching 1978; MacKinnon 1980; Mann 1987).[5] Giving the merchant-gentry a free hand in their local communities could serve state ends in terms of both governance and revenue generation.

Indeed in some part the Qing's New Policies resemble the response of colonial states to a changing revenue base, especially their promotion of export-oriented growth (Kahn 1993: 196). The difference is that the Qing state's interests were served by encouraging commercial-industrial growth, whether externally oriented or not. In the late nineteenth century, as imperialist aggression progressively drained the financial reserves of the Qing government and produced a staggering burden of debt, the court sought to enlarge its revenues by tapping the surpluses of the expanding commodity economy. It abandoned its older trade control and imposed a variety of new commercial taxes (Jones 1978–79). These taxes became an increasingly important part of governmental income. As Wang Yeh-chien notes, where land taxes had yielded three of every four tax dollars in 1753, they yielded only one in three in 1908; commercial taxes accounted for the remainder (1973: 80). The colonial analogy also breaks down in the matter of tax collection. Whereas in modernizing colonial states expanding bureaucracies assumed responsibility for the collection of new forms of taxation, the Qing state, as we have seen, appointed private merchants as tax-farmers and thus enlarged the fiscal power of modern merchant elites.

This changing revenue source almost certainly explains why the Qing state increasingly facilitated private investments and, after 1900, acquiesced to the entire range of business measures put forth in the Hundred Days. In so doing, although business circles continually pressed for tax exemptions and reductions, the state at once stimulated further development of the commercial sector, enlarged the arena for cooperation and collaboration with the modern elite, and, as Fan Baichuan puts it, paved the way for "the first liberation of Chinese capitalism" (1983: 12). As we will see, this liberation came to include special privileges for Chinese industry. At the same time, however, along with the larger cluster of special privileges forcibly won by foreigners, many of the state's general economic measures also benefited and even opened the door to greater foreign penetration and control.

Thus the Qing state, emerging at the interstices of imperialist dominance, its own centralizing aims, and modern elite strategies for local power, in effect assumed semicolonial form.[6] One of the chief points of difference between the constituent processes of this semicolonial state and modern colonial state formation in the same period, especially in South and Southeast Asia, was the interweaving of centralizing tendencies with the "involutional" (Duara 1987) overdevelopment of private, nonbureaucratic economic and administrative structures in local society.[7] It was as part of this emergent complex, that, in 1895, in compliance with the Qing rulers' instructions to promote private industry among local merchants and gentry, the then-governor of Jiangsu-Zhejiang, Zhang Zhidong, met with Zhang Jian to discuss the idea of establishing a spinning factory in Nantong (TZ 1910, 1: 1–2, 111). The founding of that factory illustrates the pivotal role of the state in economic development, as well as the dialectical interaction of modern elite, old-style privilege, and government in that process.

The Founding of Dasheng

From the outset Zhang Jian exploited the state's need to neutralize the emerging social groups that potentially threatened it, and played on his bureaucratic connections to obtain government aid for his project. Without that backing his enterprise would never have gotten off the ground. His four-year struggle to found the Dasheng factory (1895–99) ended in success only through an extraordinary combination of bureaucratic prerogative and government investment (TZ 1910, 1: 11–122). In important respects Zhang's difficulties during those four years typified the problems of late-nineteenth-century Chinese capital formation. By the close of the century, sparked by growing nationalist sentiments, many members of the modern elite accepted the proposition that China must oppose foreign aggression by industrializing. Yet in practice they displayed extreme caution. This was not principally because of a shortage of capital, since as we have seen, this group as a whole had profited royally from foreign-linked commercialization. Rather, aware of the competitive advantages held by better capitalized, better financed, and more leniently taxed foreign firms, as well as the precarious record of success among fledgling Chinese enterprises, many potential investors held back. They either refrained from investing at all or invested only small sums, preferring to devote the bulk of their capital to investments in land, to money-lending, and, increasingly, to the expanding treaty port trade.

The general problems of capital formation were compounded in the Da-sheng case. From the point of view of attracting investors, Zhang, the project's central organizer and most diligent supporter, actually became one of its greatest liabilities. Zhang originally conceived of the venture as a private joint stock company. In late 1895 he found six backers: three merchant-gentrymen from Nantong; and three Shanghai residents, a Cantonese comprador, a Fujianese comprador, and a wealthy member of the Ningbo clique. The start-up goal was 600,000 taels with a stock issue of 6,000 shares at 100 taels each. The Shanghai group agreed to raise 400,000, the Nantong group the remainder (TZ 1910, 1: 1–2). But because private investors had not fared well in the semiofficial government-sponsored enterprises, potential purchasers, especially in Shanghai, apparently distrusted Zhang's close association with the state. Fearing that despite the founders' guarantees to the contrary, Da-sheng would become a semiofficial enterprise, they shunned the project. In any case the Shanghai business community was not much attracted by an industrial project in Nantong.

After almost a year less than 60,000 taels had been raised, none of this amount by the Shanghai group. At that point Zhang persuaded the government to sign a contract for a joint venture, the government investment consisting of 20,400 spindles originally purchased by Zhang Zhidong for a spinning factory that never materialized. Zhang's acquisition of the machinery—an adroit entrepreneurial maneuver under the circumstances—only heightened the fears of potential investors of government involvement, making it even more difficult to obtain private funding. By mid-1897, without having raised a single tael, all of the Shanghai backers had withdrawn from the project. By the end of 1899, when the mill finally opened—and on a smaller scale than originally planned—only 195,000 taels all told had been raised.

To make matters worse, a portion of this sum had already been paid out in guaranteed dividends (*guanli*). Such payments were standard among Chinese industries until the 1930's–1940's. They usually offered investors a guaranteed annual dividend of 8 percent before start-up and after, in good times and bad. In years of profit extra dividends were also paid (NJ 1959a: 4). Because of the financial burden this practice created, especially in a company's founding stages, it is generally regarded as having weakened Chinese industry (Sun Yutang 1957: 1011–1012). Yet new enterprises were forced to adopt it. Given the growing strength of the foreign establishment in China, the uncertainties of new domestic ventures, and especially the extremely high rates of return — normally 20–50 percent — to be made in things like loansharking, investors were simply unwilling to divert funds from traditional investments without some guarantee. Usury capital in fact continued to control the investment market, and industrial capital became "subservient" to it (Yan Zhongping 1963: 123, 144–45). In Dasheng's case, during the 1895–99 founding period, when the lack of investment capital almost wrecked the project, the company paid out over 17,000 taels in guaranteed dividends (NT [2] n.d.: 24–25; Zhang Jian 1931, 5: 8).

The main beneficiaries were merchants from the northern delta, who accounted for the bulk of the company's private funding. The intense hostility of conservative local landlords to the project is reflected in the fact that only 800 of the 195,000 taels raised came from that group (DSXT 1990: 18). In the end the biggest investor of all was the government. With a value of 250,000 taels, its initial investment of 20,400 spindles well outstripped the 195,000 taels in private investments. Moreover, it contributed a crucial 60,000 taels in loans as operations were about to begin. This final 60,000 came only after Zhang Jian made a desperate plea to Governor-General Liu Kunyi, who in turn urged various county governments and bureaus to loan funds to the Dasheng group. Thus in terms of machinery and capital, it was official, not private, sources that saw the Dasheng project through to completion (ibid., pp. 10–24).[8]

All these difficulties notwithstanding, Dasheng began showing a profit after the first year of operations, and its investment difficulties largely disappeared thereafter. Because government investment did not lead to official interference in the company's internal affairs and because, along with its early showing of a profit, Dasheng never defaulted on its guaranteed payments (unlike earlier government-affiliated firms), confidence in the new venture increased. Table 5.1 indicates the rapid growth in net profits and private investments during its first five years. State investment doubled in 1903, when the government contributed an additional 20,400 spindles valued at 250,000 taels. By that point, however, private investments were well above the total government figure of 500,000 taels, and they continued to rise in

TABLE 5.1

Dasheng Textile Company, Annual Summary of Accounts, 1899–1903

(Taels)

Category	1899	1900	1901	1902	1903
Government investment	250,000[a]	250,000[a]	250,000[a]	250,000[a]	500,000[b]
Private investment	195,000	269,400	319,500	537,500	630,000
Net profits	−23,852	52,369	105,978	187,002	255,134
Accumulated reserves	—	10,000	25,600	57,136	141,494
Cotton inventory	—	173,831	427,974	520,990	1,024,498
Debts	60,000	163,619	596,513	207,500	594,230

SOURCES: TZ 1910, 1: 56–70, 118–21; DSXT 1990: 126.

[a] Value of 20,400 contributed spindles.

[b] Reflects a contribution of 20,400 additional spindles.

the following years. Growing investor faith in Dasheng allowed it to flourish after its precarious beginnings. But the real sources of its success lay in its development of a monopolistic, interlocked rural-urban system.

Dasheng's Privileged Position

The state not only rescued the Dasheng mill initially, but by granting it special privileges and exemptions, favored its development. One of these, a prohibition against the establishment of other local spinning mills, set the stage for Zhang's monopolistic "local production, local sales" system.

Precedent for such a monopoly right (*zhuanli*) dated back to 1880, when the Qing government bestowed it on the semiofficial Shanghai Machine Weaving Mill, one of the first Chinese factories (Bergère 1968: 247). Thereafter the Qing often complied with requests for monopoly status from well-connected investors, usually granting it for five- or ten-year periods, and occasionally, for 20 years (Li Shiyue 1979: 1304). Though the government undoubtedly viewed this as a mechanism for supervising industrial growth, a function it actually served, officials, as well as potential beneficiaries and recipients, justified the right as a means of protecting infant industries by limiting the founding of new enterprises to specified groups or individuals. Given the competitive advantages of foreign industry and the precarious record of success among undercapitalized and interest-burdened Chinese enterprises, survival of the few through monopoly was deemed essential to long-term industrializing goals.

In his request for monopoly status, Zhang Jian ardently supported this position, arguing that only this would ensure Dasheng's local preeminence and future expansion (TZ 1910, 1: 3). The result was a territorial enclave that grew immensely over the years. Initially the government granted Zhang au-

thority to establish mills only in the Nantong-Haimen area. But in 1904 he
learned that a group of Shanghai investors was planning to establish a textile
mill on Chongming Island, a location he considered to be within Nantong's
sphere of influence and where he eventually planned to open a branch factory
(Zhang Jian 1931, 2: 19–21). To block the Shanghai group, he at once accelerated his plans for the branch and moved to secure government permission
to do so. In negotiations with the government, he argued that Chongming
should be considered part of "the greater Nantong area" (NT [2] n.d.: 23).
The state agreed, and in 1907, the year the Chongming mill opened, Zhang
was given a new 20-year monopoly right in the Nantong-Haimen area and
on Chongming. By 1914 Zhang was ready to exercise his prerogatives in Haimen, where he began construction on a second branch mill (NT [4] 1987).[9]
Thanks to Zhang's zealous protection of Dasheng's interests, the company
enjoyed free rein in Nantong-Haimen-Chongming for over two decades.

Dasheng's Cotton Collection System:
Benzhuang *Operations*

For Zhang Jian, protecting Dasheng's interests meant more than just
establishing a territorial sanctuary. It also meant ensuring that the mill got all
the cotton it needed at the lowest possible cost. The instrument he used was
the *benzhuang* (primary agency), an internal organ that the directors established as the mill was about to begin operations to supervise cotton purchase.
This was the start of a monopolistic procurement system (*shouhua xitong*)
that ultimately chained local peasant growers to the Dasheng market. From
then on, all the mill's cotton purchases were handled by the *benzhuang* and
its branch units.[10]

At the time the agency set up shop, competition in the cotton trade had
not yet reached the intense proportions that characterized it a decade or so
later. Although, as we earlier saw, new cotton firms (*huahang*) with relatively large operations were then emerging, and the Shanghai offices of some
guanzhuang firms were also beginning to trade in cotton, most local dealers
still operated on a small scale. The bulk of the firms were run by individual
families that could afford to purchase no more than 20–30 piculs at a time
(*Shina* 1920: 63; Wu Huisheng 1980a). At this stage the pattern of outsider
buying we discussed in connection with Nantong's peripheralization had not
changed. Even with the opening of the Shanghai treaty port, representatives
of the southern mills and foreign firms, especially Japanese firms, were still
making most of the large-scale purchases (Zhang Jian 1931, 1: 20; Zou Qiang
1984: 33).

In these circumstances Dasheng found it relatively easy to corner the local market. Through the *benzhuang* it was able to bypass local merchants and purchase cotton directly from peasant growers. Reflecting Zhang's personal ties in his place of birth, and probably because he considered it a convenient means of avoiding conflicts with Nantong cotton firms, the agency was staffed with personnel who, from director Yang Xiuqing to the lowliest collection agent, were all from Haimen (-Qidong). With the influence of Zhang and Dasheng behind it, the *benzhuang* quickly established hegemony in the districts where it regularly operated (Wu Huisheng 1980a). Surrounding and extending outward from the mill, located in a northwestern suburb of Nantong city, those districts included some of the best cotton-producing areas in the county.

De facto control allowed Dasheng to set its own prices (Wu Huisheng 1980a). To that end the *benzhuang* skillfully manipulated popular opinion, cultivating the perception of Zhang Jian as a powerful official, emphasizing the degree-holding status of staff members, and above all, aligning itself with state authority. By endowing its main office at the mill with an official aura and sending officially clad agents to rural districts to make purchases, it created the illusion that its operations were state sanctioned and its nonnegotiable, below-market prices the "officially" quoted ones (ibid.).[11] The use of these tactics may say more about the Dasheng leadership's perception of the peasantry than about its power to deceive its clients. Peasants, after all, as demonstrated by sophisticated everyday forms of resistance, were long accustomed to dealing with the tactical exploits of the state and the elite. In the face of forced sales at noncompetitive prices, peasants now took to adding water to their cotton and extra starch to their cloth so as to increase the weight. Despite the repeated efforts of the Nantong Chamber of Commerce and the Tongruhai Cotton Association to put an end to weight inflation, it was still "a chronic problem" in the 1920's, according to the chamber (Lin Zuobo 1931: 3; Liu Jiawang 1920: 4; *Tonghai xinbao*, Oct. 20, 1920: 3, Mar. 15, 1922: 3, Sept. 18, 1923: 6; *Tongruhai mianye nianbo*, 1923–24).

As was typical of Chinese factories until the 1930's, Dasheng retained little of its earnings for working capital, relying instead on loans to maintain operations, including the purchase of raw materials (Chao Kang 1977: 146–47; Table 5.1). Local native banks became the primary lending agencies. More reluctant on the whole than cloth and cloth-banking firms to invest in the unproven Dasheng project, local banks quickly became converts, and after the mill's first year, regularly financed its cotton purchases. At the beginning of the season, as soon as Dasheng started buying, it used the store of cotton in its warehouse as collateral for further purchases. The next round of purchases secured additional loans, so that in any one year the company needed to use only a relatively small amount of its own capital to keep its supplies coming (Wu Huisheng 1980a; Yin Yuepu 1980). Underwritten by

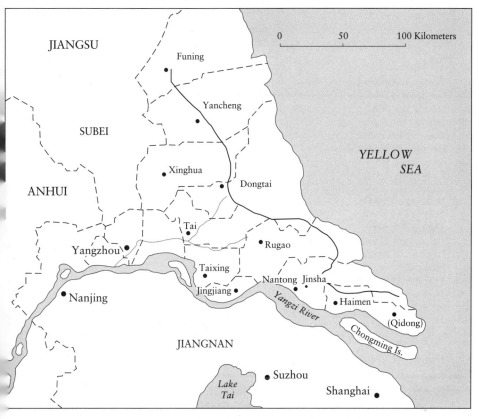

MAP 2. The Northern Yangzi Delta and Subei in the Early Republican Period

local bank funding, it was free to carry out volume purchasing at noncompetitive prices in the areas under *benzhuang* control.

Ensuring Cotton Supplies Through Land Development

Rising profits and investments after 1900 gave Zhang Jian the funds to push his modernizing project much further. Exercising his loosely defined authority as policy maker for Dasheng and regulator of its profits, he used perhaps as much as 400,000 yuan of the company's capital to establish more than 30 smaller industrial and commercial ventures in the next 20 years (NJ 1959b, 2: 10–14).[12] What is more, he maintained close supervision over each and every one of them, personally managing many himself and putting trusted associates and relatives in charge of the rest.[13] Table 5.2 lists the most important of the enterprises he founded in the first decade of Dasheng's operation.

TABLE 5.2
Zhang Jian's First Enterprises, 1901–1909

Name	Year founded	Capitalization (in thousands of yuan)
Tonghai Land Development Co.	1901	308
Guangsheng Oil Co.	1901	70
Daxing Flour Co.	1901	20
Dalong Soap Co.	1902	20
Zesheng Waterways Co.	1903	50
Dada Inland Navigation Co.	1903	50
Tongrengtai Salt Co.	1903	140
Fusheng Silk Co.	1903	20
Hanmulin Publishing House	1903	14
Dada Steamship Co.	1904	186.2
Zisheng Iron Factory	1905	70
Yisheng Brewery	1905	70
Datong Navigation & Transport Co.	1906	13.5
Daxian Salt Warehouse	1906	20
Dazhong Transport Co.	1906	20
Yuansheng Native Bank	1907	?
Dachang Paper Co.	1908	20
Fuxin Flour Co.	1909	140

SOURCES: Wang Jingyu & Sun Yutang 1957: 1069; Zhang Jian 1931, 2: 17.

Known collectively as the Dasheng Capital Group, most of these firms either used Dasheng's waste products or serviced the company. The Dada Inland Navigation Company, for example, was founded specifically to ship cotton supplies to the main and branch mills (DSXT 1990: 165–209; NJ 1959b, 2: 12–22).[14]

Of all the subsidiaries, land reclamation companies played the most significant role in Zhang's consolidation of a new economy system. These companies converted the 200-mile strip of saline marshalnds that had once been part of the Huainan Salt Yard to productive cotton land (Hu Huangyong 1947: 60; Shiyebu 1933: 220). By the twentieth century, as we noted in Chapter Two, the buildup of silt deposits had pushed the coastline almost 40 miles east of the old salt beds, and the area was now only sparsely populated, inhabited principally by permanent tenants of large landlords who, often illegally, had seized sections of land for reclamation, by former salters who had reclaimed small plots to cultivate cotton and other crops, and by bandits (Hu Huanyong 1947: 60; Shiyebu 1933: 229; Zhu Fucheng 1977). It was in fact Zhang's concern for Dasheng's future raw material needs that first attracted him to the idea of reclaiming this area. As he stated: "If I had studied only matters of industry and commerce relating to the spinning factory and had not paid attention to agriculture, then an adequate foundation could not have been laid. Consequently, I resolutely set about opening up the wasteland in order to improve cotton production and favor the development of the factory" (Zhang Jian 1931, 4: 30).

Zhang made his first move in this direction with the founding of the Tonghai Development Company, on the Nantong-Haimen coast in 1901, just two years after Dasheng opened its doors. That action, as we earlier noted, brought the Salt Administration under pressure from entrenched interests to prohibit any further reclamation. But this was only a temporary setback. When Zhang became Minister of Agriculture and Commerce in the Yuan Shi-kai government (a post he held from 1913 to 1915), one of his first official acts was to remove the ban on reclamation (S. Chu 1965: 82–83, 126–27; Zhang Jian 1931, 8: 13). With that obstacle removed, Zhang, along with his brother Zhang Cha, his son Xiaoruo, and members of the Dasheng board of directors, organized 15 additional companies in the seven years between 1914 and 1920 (Table 5.3). All were tied into the mills in one way or another. Collectively, these companies laid claim to roughly 6,000,000 mu of "wasteland."

The bulk of the companies' capital came from Dasheng staff members and merchants and landlord gentry from Nantong-Haimen and surrounding counties. Investors in the Tonghai company, for example, included Zhang Jian (86 shares), Zhang Cha (99), Liu Yishan, mentioned previously as a

TABLE 5.3
Dasheng Capital Group Land Development Companies, 1901–1920

Company	Year founded	Capitalization (Thousands of taels)	Acreage (Thousands of mu)		Founder
			Amount claimed	Amount developed	
Tonghai	1901	308	120	90	Zhang Jian
Dayoujin	1914	500	2,360	276+	Zhang Cha
Dayu	1916	1,500	480	150	Zhang Xuyan
Dalai	1917	800	130	50	Zhang Xuyan, Zhang Cha
Dafeng	1918	2,000	850	180	Zhang Cha, Zhang Xuyan
Dagang	1918	—	240	—	Zhang Cha
Huacheng	1919	1,200	700	80	Zhang Jian
Xintong	1919	120	150	20	Zhang Jian, Zhang Xiaoruo
Dayou	1919	750	200	40	Zhang Xiaoruo
Foyu	1919	170?	60	20	Zhang Jingxuan
Hede	1919	—	60	30	—
Xinnan	1920	200	200	20	Zhang Jian
Dafo	1920	—	—	—	Zhang Xiaoruo
Zhongfu	1920	—	520	—	Zhang Cha
Tongsui	1920	350	400	—	Zhang Jian
Suiji	1920	—	50	—	Zhang Xuyan, Zhang Xiaoruo

SOURCE: *Ershinianlai zhi Nantong* 1930, 2: 38–50; Zhang Youyi 1957, 2: 343, 348–49.
NOTE: As can be seen, Zhang Jian entrusted this activity to just four others, including most prominently his brother Zhang Cha and son Xiaoruo. Zhang Xuyan, involved in the Dayu, Dalai, Dafeng, and Suiji companies, was a member of the Dasheng mill's board of directors. Zhang Jingxuan, founder of the Foyu Company, was a Nantong cloth merchant and vice-director of the Nantong Chamber of Commerce.

guanzhuang cloth merchant and director of the cloth guild (79), and Liu Housheng, a Nantong merchant and Dasheng board member (143). But their holdings together did not compare with the 400–500 blocks held by some wealthy merchants and landlords (DSXT 1990: 47). Unlike other capital group enterprises, the land development companies tended to limit the number of stocks issued. Thus, as in the Tonghai case, it became possible for a few individual shareholders to acquire the lion's share of stock. The obvious effect was to make the companies a vehicle for land concentration. The Dayoujin company (1914) is a case in point: 76 percent of its investors, each possessing a share worth 100 mu, owned only 7.17 percent of the land to which it staked claim; and 1 percent of its investors, some with holdings entitling them to tracts as large as 50,000 mu, owned fully 56.86 percent of that claim (Chen Hongjin 1939: 39–40).

All of the companies faced the initial problem of gaining clear title to the land. Tonghai's experience was typical. As Zhang Jian later recounted of his inspection tour of the Nantong-Haimen coast: "I did not see a single human being the whole day. [The area] seemed like a lonely wasteland belonging to no one, so that we could do what we wanted to develop it. But when I decided to make sure of our ownership, I found that . . . every centimeter of the land was claimed by someone" (Zhang Jian 1931, 4: 30–31). In all, it took Tonghai over eight years to gain title to the 120,000 mu it claimed. In this case and in later cases as well, title disputes seem to have been exacerbated by the companies' attempts to incorporate as much cultivated land as possible. In these disputes smallholders were generally no match for Zhang's well-financed and bureaucratically backed companies. If they were not dispossessed outright, they were often arm-twisted into turning over their titles with no more recompense than two years' free rent (Chen Hongjin 1939: 41).

To put it bluntly, the Dasheng companies and their imitators simply grabbed millions of mu at minimal cost.[15] Studies across the five counties of Nantong, Rugao, Dongtai, Foning, and Yancheng—where with the exception of Tonghai, all the Dasheng group's companies were located—revealed that they paid at most one yuan a mu for land that could be reclaimed for two yuan or less to give a market value of between 20 and 50 yuan, depending on the quality (*Ershinianlai zhi Nantong* 1930, 2: 41–42; Zhang Renren 1915–16, 2.5: 17; Zhang Youyi 1957, 2: 371). Furthermore, Zhang's position and connections enabled the companies to begin reclamation before many of the title disputes had been resolved. Tonghai began dike and canal construction just one year after it was founded and recruited its first tenants a year later (DSXT 1990: 48; Li Wenzhi 1957: 703).

Eventually the Dasheng group and other companies reclaimed more than 2,000,000 mu of coastal land. The job, which sometimes took several years, was carried out by hired workers, usually local salters and peasants. The

Tonghai company employed over 7,000 workers for dike and canal construction alone. Once this phase was completed, in places where the soil was saturated with brine, reeds had to be grown for one or more years before cotton cultivation could begin. During this period many companies engaged in salt production to compensate for the lack of agricultural income. Since only low yields could be expected in the first year, many also used hired labor for the initial crop (DSXT 1990: 49–51; Zhang Jian 1931, 2: 30).

Thereafter, preserving the basic features of the landlord economy, they rented out uniform 20- to 25-mu plots to peasant tenants for 30–40 percent of the cotton harvest. Tenants were also required to pay a rent deposit, usually 120 yuan per plot, and a small spring rent in cash, normally 10–15 cents a mu. Some companies required them to submit six piculs of straw annually as well (Li Wenzhi 1957: 705–6; Shiyebu 1933: 264–65). Tenants were responsible for providing their own implements and building their own dwellings. Although to attract tenants and make it possible for them to begin cultivation, companies would occasionally provide them with houses and tools and allow them to pay these off over a set period of years, most relied on advance loans for deposits and fees as inducements (Hu Huanyong 1947: 64; Shiyebu 1933: 264).

The relatively large tracts of land, attractive rents, company loans, and what were in effect permanent cultivating rights (since tenants could be evicted only if they failed to pay rent or committed a crime) all worked to create a stable peasantry in the new land areas and, thereby, ensure a continuity of production. In a manner reminiscent of the company towns of early American capitalism, however, this company management also involved new forms of control, supervision, and coercion. Companies limited the accumulation potential of tenants by restricting their holdings to two plots (*Ershinianlai zhi Nantong* 1930, 2: 39; Zhang Renren 1915–16, 2.5: 18). They imposed what peasants viewed as unreasonable and arbitrary regulations, such as prohibiting fishing on company land, and thus in the brooks, streams, and canals of their new communities (Mu Xuan 1980: 8). Not least they brought the self-government bureaus that ran the local law tribunals, jails, and schools to their beck and call (DSXT 1990: 60).

Tonghai, for example, garrisoned units of the Dasheng Industrial Police Guard in all of its dike areas as backups for the self-government district offices that supervised rent and tax payments. In cases of late payments, the offices relied on guardsmen to bring in offenders, who were sometimes chained outside the office for a day to serve as examples of unacceptable behavior. Tenants who violated company regulations (such as fishing) were not only arrested and fined, but as a deterrent against repeated offense, publicly humiliated by guard members, who paraded them through the streets before releasing them from custody (Mu Xuan 1980: 8). Dasheng's other affiliates operated in the same way, combining relatively lenient rental policies with restrictions on the size of holdings, surveillance, and coercion to create and maintain a small producer cotton economy favoring the expansion of Dasheng.

All the cotton rents in these Capital Group companies were channeled to the Dasheng mills. So was all the cotton the tenants marketed, because company regulations routinely stated that it could only be sold to the land company's agents. In actuality those agents were Dasheng functionaries (DSXT 1990: 111; Li Wenzhi 1957: 767; Wu Huisheng 1980a, b). Since peasants normally sold much of their share of the cotton harvest, by purchase or by rent payment, Dasheng obtained virtually all the cotton produced in the reclaimed land areas each year.

To collect and ship these stocks, Dasheng established auxiliary units called *fenzhuang*. Those units worked side by side with the *benzhuang* and eventually totaled 23 in number; each was staffed by 15–20 persons (DSXT 1990: 111; Wu Huisheng 1980a). Because of their monopolistic position in the new land areas, like the primary agency, they set their own prices. In fact, those prices were always exactly the same as the *benzhuang*'s (Wu Huisheng 1980b). In shipping their collections to the Dasheng plants, *fenzhuang* agents relied principally on boats belonging to the Dasheng-affiliated Dada Inland Navigation Company (NJ 1959b, 2: 13–14; Sun Yutang 1957: 1069; Wu Huisheng 1980b). Accordingly, Dasheng minimized transport as well as raw material costs.

In sum, early on, Zhang set up a monopoly in Nantong's cotton districts and the reclaimed land areas that form a cornerstone of a new local system combining various forms of labor and labor relations into a single optimal package. By vertically integrating peasant cotton farming into the Dasheng mill's operations and, thereby, ensuring it a continuous supply of raw materials at noncompetitive prices, that system led the company to new heights of success in the succeeding years.

Dasheng and Rural Cloth Production

In Zhang's self-reliant development model, Dasheng's privileged position rested on integrating peasant cotton farming, mechanized spinning, and peasant household weaving into a single economic system. To do that, the mill had to corner the local yarn market. This required supplementing, and later replacing, the use of foreign yarn in *guanzhuang* cloth production. Monopolizing the local yarn market formed Dasheng's second point of interlinkage with the peasant economy and tied its development to the growth or decline of cloth production in peasant households.

That dependence on peasant industry in turn necessitated close relations with *guanzhuang* merchants. Since their marketing of both yarn to peasant weavers and *guanzhuang* cloth in Shanghai and the northeast affected Dasheng's entire capital accumulation process, Zhang could not afford to bypass them as he did local cotton dealers. Consequently, from the time Dasheng opened, Zhang worked with local native banks to provide special credit arrangements for the *guanzhuang* merchants who controlled the Manchurian cloth trade (Zhang Zhiqing 1980).

The *guanzhuang* firms, a number of which had already invested in the Dasheng venture, quickly responded to Zhang's initiatives (Da Shiji 1980; Lin Jubai 1984: 145–47). In effect, they gained the best of both worlds from his local economic system. By eliminating the fees of compradors and brokers who handled the foreign yarn trade, the new credit arrangements and supply of local yarn worked to their advantage. At the same time locally manufactured yarn gave them significant new opportunities to expand cloth output. Even though handspun yarn placed limits on production, *guanzhuang* merchants had till now advocated its retention for warping because it was made from the premium local cotton preferred by northeastern buyers. Machine-spun yarn produced from local cotton created the possibility of eliminating handspun altogether and improving the market appeal of the product. After 1905 most *guanzhuang* cloth did not contain any homespun yarn (Lin Jubai 1984). On the other hand, the new Dasheng-centered system in no way jeopardized the *guanzhuang* merchants' relations with Shanghai brokers, banks, and merchants—the comprador-commercial network on which they still relied for the bulk of their marketing transactions. Thus though Zhang's "nationalist" model created a closed local system for yarn production and sales, it did not disturb Nantong's linkage to the Shanghai-based structures of the developing semicolonial economy.

Growth figures for the cloth industry illustrate Dasheng's significant local impact. In 1895 peasants produced roughly 1,500,000 pieces of *guanzhuang* cloth (TZ 1910, 1: 2). By 1910, just two years after the mill opened, the quantity had almost tripled, to 4,000,000; and in 1907, after Dasheng started up its Chongming factory, the figure reached 6,000,000. Combined with the continuing production of large quantities of older types of cloth, this output established Nantong as China's premier handweaving center, a position it maintained for more than a decade (Da Shiji 1980; NT [8] 1930: 2; Peng Zeyi et al. 1957, 3: 398). As Table 5.4 indicates, though *guanzhuang* cloth would continue to be outstripped by the older cloths, it accounted for 70 percent of the total value.

In the first few years Dasheng was able to supply only about a third of the yarn required by an industry that was climbing to 4,000,000 pieces of cloth (Da Shiji 1980). Doubling its capacity in 1904, it increased its market share to over half, and with the addition of the Chongming branch in 1907, it was more than able to cover all the needs of local producers (Zhang Jian 1931, 5:

TABLE 5.4

Average Annual Output and Value of Nantong Handwoven Cloth at the Height of Guanzhuang *Cloth Production,* 1908–1917

(All figures in thousands)

Type of cloth	Pieces	Value (Yuan)
Guanzhuangbu	6,000	14,400
Other cloths	7,700	6,370
Xiaobu	4,000	2,800
Ersitibu	1,500	1,200
Sidabu	700	1,400
Sanerbu	500	500
Shuangtibu	500	200
Hongbianbu	100	90
Taobu	100	40
Zhangliaobu	100	40
Miscellaneous	200	100
TOTAL	13,700	20,770

SOURCE: Peng Zeyi et al. 1957, 3: 459.
NOTE: Production began to decline in the 1920's; only about 3,000,000 pieces were produced in 1931.

11, 6: 2). Once this level was reached, Zhang Jian and the commercial elite moved to restrict the importation of foreign yarn.

The Nantong Chamber of Commerce

The Nantong Chamber of Commerce played a crucial role in Zhang Jian's drive for local autonomy. It was the second organization of its type established in Jiangsu province. The first was organized in 1902 in Shanghai by Sheng Xuanhuai on government initiative. Authorized as part of the New Policies, it and others of its kind were envisioned by the state as a means of maintaining political and administrative control over local business communities. With their tax collection privileges, administrative functions, and paramilitary duties, they were clearly part of an informal state apparatus. This fact notwithstanding, the larger chambers in major treaty ports and in cities like Nantong where commercial power developed rapidly achieved a considerable degree of independence (Bergère 1968: 241, 249; Feuerwerker 1958: 70–71). They at once advanced and protected local interests and became part of the organizational nexus through which the modern elite extended its control over local society. In short they were the political expression of modern urban elite power.[16]

Some months after Sheng Xuanhuai founded the Shanghai chamber, Zhang

Cha and other members of Nantong's merchant elite founded their own organization, formally named the General Chamber of Commerce of Southern
Tongzhou (NanTongzhou zongshanghui).[17] From its start in 1902 until the
1920's, it reflected the close alliance between Dasheng and the *guanzhuang*
merchants. Either Zhang Cha, its first director, or Liu Guixin, a merchant
and member of the Dasheng board, the first vice-director, usually held the
post of general director (elected every three years); and the leading cloth
merchants who sat in the second chair were all Dasheng board members. By
the early 1920's the chamber had branches or affiliates in Nantong, Haimen,
Chongming, Rugao, Tai, and Taixing counties, with a reported membership
in the tens of thousands (*Ershinianlai zhi Nantong* 1930, 2: 52; NT [2] n.d.:
71–72; *Tonghai xinbao*, Dec. 26, 1921: 3, Aug. 17, 1923: 3; Yu Yikong 1982:
46–47).

From its inception the chamber was involved in three overlapping arenas
of activity: first, participating in the construction, especially through its taxing and militia powers, of organs of local self-government; second, reinforcing and extending Nantong's economic dominance in the northern delta; and
third, shaking off the old ways of doing business that had allowed outside
economic interests to operate freely in and disadvantage the local economy.
As such, the chamber was part and parcel of the Dasheng-modern elite's
drive for local autonomy.

The chamber policies that are of concern in this connection fall into three
broad categories: ensuring Dasheng's hegemony in the yarn market; protecting its monopoly over cotton collection in the areas of *benzhuang* operation;
and prohibiting outside firms—whether Chinese or foreign—from buying
directly from peasant growers in other cotton-producing districts (*Tongruhai mianye nianbo* 1923–24: 2; Walker 1986: 308–16; Wu Huisheng 1980b).[18]
The chamber moved quickly to establish its authority. Nonmembers who
violated its ordinances could be reported to the police for official action; and
members who did so were directly penalized, usually by fines (*Tonghai xinbao*, Oct. 11, 1923: 3, Oct. 29, 1923: 3). No less importantly, the hierarchical
relations and interpersonal ties characterizing Nantong's commercial sector
pressured the entire merchant community to comply with the wishes of, or
the regulations that in effect were set by, Zhang Jian and the cloth industry
elite (Yu Yikong 1981).

Consequently, the chamber had little trouble limiting the sale of foreign
yarn in the county. In the early 1900's, when the local yarn market became
sluggish, it voted to temporarily prohibit the importation of machine-spun
yarn from Shanghai. And when, in 1907, the Dasheng mills achieved the capacity to cover the needs of the local market, the chamber's leadership easily
persuaded its members to switch entirely to the local product. As a result,
except for very small quantities of the finer count yarns that were used for

specialty fabrics (and initially composed only 5 percent of Dasheng's output), foreign yarn sales in the county dwindled into insignificance (Lin Jubai 1984: 32–33).

Spatial Dimensions of New Growth Patterns: Reconstituting a Northern Delta Periphery

Spatially, within the northern delta Nantong city was the primary beneficiary of the new patterns of economic growth. Besides the imposing Dasheng mill, other tangible, visible symbols of the modernizing road dotted its landscape—new schools and roads, a public library, a museum, a prison, a home for the aged, and an opera house with Western-style seats. Awed by these achievements—and by an area that seemed to have chosen the right route for achieving sustained development—contemporary observers designated Nantong as a "model district" of modernization (*Ershinianlai zhi Nantong* 1930).

What these symbols did not and could not convey was that Nantong city had become the central hub of an important new commercial-banking complex, and that along with the Dasheng elite, the real beneficiaries of the expanding economy were the city merchants who played a key organizational role in Zhang's integrated urban-rural system. Standing at the helm of the new complex, these merchants underwrote Dasheng's cotton collection system, and (as we will discuss more fully in the next chapter) through their dealings in cloth, yarn, and later cotton, they linked concentric layers of smaller merchants, peasants, and landlords together as parts of a single structural whole. To be sure, middle and lower-level merchants and petty traders in smaller towns and markets also benefited. But increasingly, they functioned as auxiliary agents to the Nantong complex, and those who could not be subordinated were displaced. The concentration of capital and the benefits of economic growth in Nantong city restricted and precluded similar development in other parts of the system. Thus, in effect, Nantong's hegemony in the new economic system, and the power relations and class forces it embodied, required and created a new periphery. Reconstituting much of the old northern delta periphery in new form, this reordering contradicted popular perceptions of Nantong's path as the springboard for sustained development in the area as a whole.

The coalescence of the Dasheng-commercial-banking complex in Nantong city accelerated the trend that had begun with the cloth industry's shift away from Haimen in the late nineteenth century. Weaving came to be even more concentrated in the city's environs, that is, in a core weaving area that extended out from Nantong city westward to Jinsha and southwest Haimen. Although weaving families within this crowded, roughly 500-square-mile

area continued to exist on the land, the portion of total family income supplied by agriculture fell far below the amount they earned from spinning and
weaving (Peng Zeyi 1957, 4: 120; Yu Yikong 1982: 31–32). In contrast to the
past, household industry outside this core area gradually diminished or disappeared altogether. What production there was tended to be confined to the
most primitive forms of cloth, which at best had only a limited local market.
In any case the best-quality cotton and the products of the No. 1 mill were
reserved for the Nantong-area producers of *guanzhuang* cloth.

Structurally, then, under new patterns of interlocked rural-urban growth,
both commercial realignment and productive specialization in rural areas
rapidly accelerated. Yet as orchestrated by the Nantong merchant-industry
elite who concentrated the benefits of economic growth in their own hands,
these changes did little to benefit the smaller towns or the bulk of rural residents in the countryside. By the 1920's the rural residents of the core weaving
areas were among the most destitute in the countryside. At the same time,
their labor and the surpluses they generated provided the wherewithal for
a development scheme in which the rest of the northern delta countryside
came to function principally as a peripheralized supplier of cotton and cheap
casual labor. Land development companies like Tonghai and Dayoujin actually enlarged this periphery. Rather quickly as well, along with the other
companies they added to the growing economic power of the Nantong elite
by becoming vehicles of land concentration.

The Nantong chamber's initial choice of name, the General Chamber of
Commerce of Southern Tongzhou, was thus not arbitrary. By then in fact
there was a very real divide between the peripheralized agricultural districts
and the industrial-commercial nexus in southern Nantong. That this divide
persisted or has perhaps been recently renewed, was unwittingly suggested
by Fei Xiaotong following his early 1980's tour of Subei. After remarking that
Nantong is usually considered part of Jiangnan, since the two areas "have
something identical in their economic development," Fei goes on to say: "if
the matter is given more thought, it can be seen that the northern part of
the Nantong Municipality . . . is not very much influenced economically by
Shanghai." Consequently, he proposes that only southern Nantong should be
included in a southern administrative region (Fei Hsiao-tung et al. 1986: 88–
89). As Emily Honig notes, Subei is thus conceptually reconstructed as that
which is poor, though wealthier places north of the river, such as southern
Nantong or Yangzhou, are paradoxically "economically Jiangnan" (1992:
33–34).

Haimen well exemplifies the effects of peripheralization. Its southwestern
districts were part of the textile industry's core area. In the late 1910's, using
yarn manufactured in the branch mills for the lower-*guanzhuang* grades, they
produced all or most of the *guanzhuang* cloth that the county turned out in

a year: an average of 1,000,000 *pi*, worth 1,300,000 yuan, or about one-sixth the total *guanzhuang* output (Shen Qixi 1920b: 4). But the financing, shipping, and marketing of this cloth were all handled through the Nantong-Shanghai network. Similarly, other parts of the county failed to experience the small town–urban expansion often posited in models of economic growth. As late as 1920 all five of Haimen's small towns still catered principally to the local market and carried on only a small export trade in beans, sesame, peanuts, eggs, and primitive cloth. The only two urban industries were a small stocking workshop with 17 workers and a brewery with 24. Because both the trade and the financing of the most important agricultural commodity, cotton, continued to be dominated by the large Nantong firms (and the modern Haimen landlords who functioned as their economic allies), there was just one small native bank in the whole of the county in 1920. Capitalized at 30,000 yuan, it had been in operation less than a year (Shen Qixi 1920b: 4).

Chongming, with its predominantly agricultural economy, provides an even more extreme example. From 1907, when Dasheng established its branch factory there, the county served chiefly as a hinterland for cotton collection. As in Haimen after the establishment of the No. 3 mill, the presence of modern factory production did little to stimulate the local economy. Indeed the Dasheng mill appears to have acted instead as a repressive new force that at once exploited the countryside and reinforced large-scale landlordism.

In 1920 Chongming had only one small town, Jiulong, site of the No. 2 mill, and two small weaving and dyeing workshops.[19] Outside of cotton, what commerce there was centered on food imports and a tiny export trade based on such agricultural products as sesame and gaoliang. Essentially all the local (noncotton) trade was conducted in cash, since Chongming had neither modern nor native banks. In fact the only commercial institutions showing any development of note were pawnshops, of which there were 16 (Shen Qixi 1920a: 3).

This was an unusually large number of pawnshops for a locality of Chongming's size, and in a period when the change to a semicolonial economy had sharply reduced their role. Their numbers declined drastically, from some 25,000 at the beginning of the nineteenth century to just 4,500 by the mid-1930's, 75 percent of which were in rural areas (Geisert 1979: 244; Whelan 1979: 10, 13). But in Chongming the vitality of an operation that was backed almost entirely by landlord capital and represented the area's only commercial achievement clearly expressed the continuing power of trade-usury-landlordism (Institute of Pacific Relations 1939: 139).[20] In fact, as the 1920 investigator put it, the local economy turned on regularized pawning, mortgaging, and borrowing for the maintenance of daily life (Shen Qixi 1920a: 3). Among Chongming's impoverished, debt-ridden, and marginalized tenants, there could hardly have been much enthusiasm for Nantong's chosen path of modernity.

As the locales of most of the Capital Group land development companies, portions of Rugao, Dongtai, Yancheng, and Funing and counties such as Taixing were also clearly part of this periphery. Nantong's growing influence over commercial circles in Taixing, a supplier of food for grain-deficient Nantong, was clearly expressed in 1910, when the Nantong chamber incorporated Taixing and revised its organizational structure. Unlike the earlier structure in which Chongming, Haimen, and Nantong each maintained a separate county organization, the expanded organization worked on a trusteeship system with only one directing body, that situated in Nantong. As previously, either Zhang Cha or Liu Guixin continued to act as director (Fei Fanjiu 1981a: 140; NT [2] n.d.: 71–72; Yu Yikong 1982: 46–47).[21]

Rugao was drawn into Nantong's sphere of influence in the same period with the formation of the Tongruhai Cotton Association, an auxiliary of the chamber that was also headed by Zhang Cha. A huge county, with the largest population in Jiangsu by the late 1920's,[22] and site of two Dasheng Capital Group land companies, Rugao was an important producer of cotton. In fact, its total cotton acreage (roughly 750,000 mu in the mid-1930's) outstripped Haimen's (567,000 mu) and totaled more than Chongming's (380,000 mu) and Qidong's (300,000 mu) combined (Lin Jubai 1984: 20; *Tongruhai mianye gonghui* 1923).

Under other circumstances Rugao, like Taixing, would probably have been incorporated into the Nantong chamber in 1910. Instead, in 1911, the local magnate Sha Yuanbing established a separate Rugao chamber. With little independent commercial development, Rugao hardly needed such a body. It was simply that Sha was of the same modernizing bent as Zhang Jian. He was in fact an ardent supporter and close friend of Zhang's, an investor in many of the Dasheng Capital Group enterprises, and one of the largest landlords in Rugao (He Binghua 1981: 43; Sha Yangao 1981: 67). Using capital gained from landholding and his Dasheng investments, he set a number of modest projects in train in Rugao city, organizing, in addition to the chamber, several small factories (all of which failed in the 1920's) and an educational association (Barkan 1990: 201–5; Bastid 1988: 168–69; Sha Yangao 1981).

These activities placed Sha in the limelight and within the camp of the urban elite. But they did little to reverse Rugao's decline as a trading center following the displacement of the north-south overland route by sea transport. Instead, like Chongming, it became increasingly tied to Nantong. In 1913, only two years after Sha's Rugao chamber was founded, it became part of the Nantong organization. And, as in Chongming, pawnshops remained firmly embedded in the local rural economy as institutional aspects of landlordism. In 1933, 80 percent of the county's 11 pawnshops were

TABLE 5.5
Pawnshops and Native Banks in Nantong and Rugao Counties, 1875–1936

Institution	Nantong	Rugao	Institution	Nantong	Rugao
Pawnshops			Native banks		
1875	40+		1890		20+
1890		10	1900		10
1905	24		1910		3
1933		11	1912	20	
1936	14		1927		5
			1930	30+	

SOURCES: Chen Shouhua & Du Wenqing 1980: 52; Institute of Pacific Relations 1939: 192; JS [8] 1913: 61; Xu Genqi 1982: 56; Yu Yikong 1982: 42; Zhu Huchen 1980: 91.

owned and controlled by landlords (Institute of Pacific Relations 1939: 192). In these respects, patterns in Rugao (just as in Haimen and Chongming) ran directly counter to the more general trends of pawnshop decline and merchant ownership of the remaining businesses. Indeed in the case of Nantong, that ownership extended to what few numbers of pawnshops were left. The merchant-controlled Dongyan Native Bank, for example, owned five or six large pawnshops (Chen Zengyu 1986: 162). The comparative figures for the two localities in Table 5.5 tell this story in skeletal form.

Still, the persistence of landlord-controlled pawnshops in Nantong's new hinterland must not be taken as evidence that landlord-peasant relations also remained pretty much unchanged. On the contrary, those institutions were a facet of a rapacious, modernizing landlordism that, in alliance with the Nantong-based complex, collided with and actively worked to undermine prior gains peasants had made. As we will see, modern landlordism in its varied forms in different localities played an integral role in regearing the rural economy to the needs of urban capital. The peasants, as we will also see, did not sit idly by. It is hardly accidental that, in the late 1920's, the Communists were able to establish one of their first base areas in the outlying rural districts along the borders of Nantong, Haimen-Qidong, Rugao, and Taixing.

Zhang Jian, the Rural-Urban System, and Semicolonial Modernity

Zhang Jian's program of local development for Nantong provides a striking example of semicolonial modernity as envisioned and constructed by "nationalist" urban elites at the turn of the twentieth century. Wrapped in a discourse of progress and development, it replicated in new form older Confucian justifications for rule centered in ideas about "the proper role of the gentry in local society" and "concern for local society." From the first half of the Qing, these notions had legitimated landlord-gentry management as a form of rule of the peasantry and a (largely unsuccessful) attempt to crush its social organization. Aided by like-minded men in the business community, Zhang and other leaders of the urban elite cast modernization as an urgent nationalist task to be directed by "men of ability" like themselves. The Qing's inability to halt the slide into semicolonialism added fuel to their fire for change. But for all these nationalist trappings, the modernizers followed a road that brought them and the state to increasingly identify with the very forces they wished to repel, and that, in creating the space for new modes of local domination, in fact furthered the imperialist project in China.

Achieved through a combination of state support, bureaucratic access and privilege, and monopoly structures, Zhang's self-reliant "nationalist" model for textile industry development turned out to be a new form of elite-induced growth from above. That initially he was remarkably successful in his ventures is unarguable. Yet his interlocking of peasant production with modern industry in a local economic system did not generate rural improvement. On the contrary, this combined and uneven system led to pronounced spatial variation based on a growing gap between, on the one hand, Nantong city, and, on the other, discrete areas of rural industry and an expanding agricultural periphery. Nor were these spatial-structural characteristics a matter simply, as some historians have posited, of core areas being in a better position than peripheries to exploit new economic opportunities. Rather, the making of this local economic system required the suppression and demise of the older centers of the cloth industry and the remodeling of an older agricultural periphery along new lines.

That double-sided project lay at the heart of class formation within the elite and the development of a new mode of modernist power emanating from Nantong city. As it happened, it also provided the contours for the first and last stand of modern gentry rule, a form of rule that for a brief moment enabled men like Zhang Jian to turn their home communities into what Marie-Claire Bergère (1983) once referred to as "private kingdoms."

6 Extending the Sway of Commercial Capital

IN THE YEARS 1915–19, when the imperialist powers' preoccupation with world war gave Chinese industry new breathing space, the Dasheng mills generated such large profits that shareholders joked they had to take carts to the factory to collect their dividend payments. By the mid-1920's, however, the mills had fallen prey to a consortium of modern banks and, deprived of their monopoly position in cotton collection, were scrambling to purchase supplies when and where they could. Zhang Jian had abandoned plans for additional Dasheng branches, and most of the subsidiary enterprises had failed or were failing. Meanwhile the land development companies were distributing their lands to shareholders. In short, although the urban-rural nexus discussed in the last chapter remained as a fundamental feature of the local economic system, Zhang's self-reliant program was disintegrating.

Viewed from this perspective, though remarkable, the industrial achievements of Zhang Jian in the first two decades of the twentieth century—and his particular brand of modern gentry rule—appear as a brief transitional moment in a larger story of semicolonial restructuring and changing power relations, both at the local level and at higher levels. To understand this turn of events, and thus the broader pattern, we must examine at this point the growing tension and conflict between Dasheng and the merchant community.

On one level, the surfacing of this conflict can be viewed as a contradiction between industrial capital, which grafted itself onto the existing socioeconomic structure in monopolistic form, and a centralizing merchant capital that also had an inherent tendency toward monopoly. As a distinct form of capital, by its very nature the greater market control merchant capital exercised, the greater its rate of profit. Simply put, then, the strengthening of merchant capital in the economic formation brought the monopolizing tendencies of merchants into conflict with the monopolistic prerogatives of Dasheng.

As a multidimensional phenomenon, the contradictions between Dasheng and merchants also reflected Nantong's shaping by larger economic and political forces, including the global capitalist economy, state-bureaucratic capitalists, and Japanese imperialism in Manchuria. In the late nineteenth and early twentieth centuries, as we earlier saw, Nantong's cloth merchant elite geared their economic activities to the Manchurian market, that is, to a "national" center of gravity. This thrust formed the principal foundation for the interlocking of merchants, peasants, and industry in Zhang Jian's Dasheng-centered system. But as time wore on and international and domestic demand heightened the competition for cotton supplies, Nantong's leading merchant firms also became deeply involved in the cotton trade. In doing so they made choices that tied them to the world market and larger forces of monopoly emerging within the domestic economy and that, conversely, irreparably weakened Zhang Jian's self-reliant system and industrial capital in Nantong.

In this respect the activities of Nantong's modern merchants seem to substantiate Marie Bergère's contention that the "defining characteristic of the Chinese commercial bourgeoisie was that it belonged to the system of imperialist exploitation, and any attempt to protest this system was bound to be self-destructive" (1968: 253). On the other hand, its new alliances also reflected and were formed in the context of a declining *guanzhuang* cloth trade as Japanese economic activity in Manchuria intensified.

The relations between merchants and Dasheng are thus crucial to our story, for they decisively influenced the course of local change. At the same time these relations clearly demonstrate how the evolving contours of the semicolonial economy both influenced and were affected by the dynamics and wider functions of local economic systems. Examining these developments, this chapter concentrates on the strengthening of merchant capitalism, first within the Dasheng-centered nexus, and subsequently in conjunction with the growth of the cotton trade, the principal arena in which conflictive relations between Dasheng and merchants surfaced.

The Expansion of the Guanzhuang Firms

In stimulating the local handweaving industry, first imperialism and then the Dasheng mill paved the way for the concentration and centralization of commercial capital in Nantong. As we have seen, the *guanzhuang* merchants occupied center stage in this process. By the 1920's all of the *guanzhuang* firms had capital of at least 40,000–50,000 yuan. The largest had capital of over 100,000 yuan and an annual volume of business of over 1,000,000 yuan (Chen Zengyu 1986; Cheng Zengchong 1980; Peng Zeyi et al. 1957, 4: 119). Increasing complexity in the commercial structure and rising cloth output formed the local context for this growth; the special relations among *guangzhuang* firms, local banking institutions, and Dasheng propelled it.

In their earliest period, the *guanzhuang* firms had purchased the bulk of their goods directly from (male) members of producing families, who brought their cloth to collecting offices in the nearest market center. The Nantong city firms' offices, at the west gate, were open each day from sunrise till noon and attracted peasant sellers from as far as 20 miles away. The companies all followed basically the same operating procedures. When a weaver accepted the offered price, the firm's agent either paid him on the spot or issued a certificate of payment redeemable at its main office. Since there was no putting-out system, sellers were free to reject an offer. In reality, however, there was little reason to do so (other than mismanagement during the course of a transaction), because firm managers met together over tea each morning to determine the daily price. Only peasants who succeeded in placing their cloth on the first or second stacks in line each morning faced the possibility of a slightly lower price, but to obtain such a favorable position, they normally had to arrive at the market by at least midnight (Da Shiji 1980; Lin Jubai 1984: 42–46; NT [8] 1930: 3–4; Peng Zeyi et al. 1957, 3: 785; Yu Yikong 1982: 37).

For buying cloth, no firm could do without an experienced evaluator. Lin Jubai provides an excellent description of the typical marketing transaction between peasant and cloth evaluator:

> [The evaluator] unfolded the already folded cloth of 32 folds and made it into 16 folds, then measured the cloth with the ruler carved out on the counter and folded it again to measure its width. After that, he dangled the cloth in the air by his fingers to try the weight. . . . Then he held one of the corners of 3 or 5 layers in his right hand to evaluate the density of the warp and woof and the smoothness of texture. Meanwhile, he had been mumbling out unclear numerals called "*ma*" and jotting them down in red chalk on the second layer of the cloth. Finally, he threw the cloth . . . onto the shelf. This was the complete process of the deal. Peasants who were familiar with the process could roughly figure out the price by hearing the numerals, but those who were not, were usually confused. They tried to memorize how many bolts of cloth they had, as well as the numerals, and then waited until they were called by number to receive payment. They had the right to ask about or contest the price. If they were underpaid, they could only blame themselves for having a bad day. (1984: 42)

Although the market operated year-round, the heaviest buying periods were in the slack agricultural seasons between August and December and March and April. This was so even when, as production expanded, firms began working more through branch agents and wholesale dealers. The wholesalers were for the most part itinerant peddlers with only small amounts of capital. They traveled in producing areas in the periods of greatest supply purchasing small quantities of cloth from peasant families, then typically transported it on carts to the *guanzhuang* firms. In heavily industrialized districts and in a few new land areas, however, a stratum of intermediate wholesale firms emerged. They often made cash advances to peddlers to collect cloth for them (Cheng Zengchong 1980; Lin Jubai 1984: 46–49).

In Nantong city, the cloth firms reserved the hours from 2:00 P.M. to 5:00 P.M. for wholesale purchases. The prices in this afternoon market tended to correspond more closely to the prevailing cost of yarn than the ones the peasants got in the morning. Even so, there was considerable room for manipulation on the part of the *guanzhuang* agents. For this reason, according to Lin Jubai, resale merchants stand out as the most blatant exploiters in the system. When they suffered from a "market price" that did not allow any profit, they recouped their loss by lowering the price they offered peasant sellers in the next round of buying (1984: 45, 48; Yu Yikong 1982: 37).

As the cloth industry expanded, then, the *guanzhuang* firms continued to profit from their earlier capital advantages and especially their domination of cloth transport to Shanghai. The local proliferation of merchant capital within a more elaborate commercial structure as wholesalers came to play an important role, far from jeopardizing their control or preventing them from enlarging their scale of operations, worked to increase both since, in practice, the smaller merchants acted as their agents (Cheng Zengchong 1980).

The Rise of Integrated Cloth and Native Banking Firms

By the 1920's all the *guanzhuang* firms were engaged in other fields of commercial activity. Many had separate cloth-yarn, banking, and cotton sections, each with its own name and financial resources (Cheng Zengchong 1980; Wu Huisheng 1980b). For them, clearly, the partnership they had entered into with Dasheng at the turn of the century had paid off handsomely. But the key third parties in that partnership, as we earlier saw, were the local native banks. Viewed in terms of the concentration and centralization of commercial capital, this association stimulated the expansion of both cloth and native banking firms, and produced a joining of the two.

The native banks had played a pivotal role from the start, issuing collateral-free short-term loans to reliable merchants in the form of *zhuangpiao*, or guaranteed promissory notes, payable to the bearer. Notes of this type had become a standard credit mechanism in the treaty port–merchant network during the late nineteenth century as a way to facilitate dealings between Chinese and foreign firms (McElderry 1976: 39). In Nantong's case they facilitated the dealings between Chinese entrepreneurs. To procure these notes, the cloth merchants paid the banks a fee, which in effect amounted to a discounted interest payment, since the charges (usually 12 percent) were lower than on standard longer-term commercial loans. Generally the note was only good for 10 to 15 days. When it fell due, Dasheng exchanged it at the issuing bank for its value, minus a transaction fee. On the same date the merchant repaid the loan. Thus on the due date, even if a merchant defaulted, the bank still made payment to the bearer of the note (in this case Dasheng; Xu Gengqi 1982: 50–51; Zhang Jintao 1980). Theoretically when a merchant firm failed to pay, the bank could confiscate its goods to cover the loss. But most banks simply renewed the loan at a higher rate of interest (Zhang Jintao 1980).

This system benefited and linked all three parties in a mutually dependent financial relationship. Dasheng benefited because it was able to market its product locally at a relatively low cost. The banks benefited because, with the Shanghai banks now largely out of the yarn picture, their volume of business grew mightily. Serving as the backbone of the new local system through their dual role in financing cotton collection and yarn marketing, native banks became the central connecting link between the modern industrial and rural sectors. Finally, the *guanzhuang firms* expanded their working capital by gaining a new source of funding at low interest.

Furthermore the new triangular relationship deepened the tendency for *guanzhuang* firms to add banking to their list of operations, thus assuring themselves of interest-free working capital for the purchase of Dasheng yarn. In practice no money at all had to exchange hands in this arrangement. The firm's banking section could simply issue a *zhuangpiao* to the cloth section, and that section would quickly sell the Dasheng yarn it purchased and repay the "loan" within the required period from the profits. Frequently, as well, firms had time enough to use those profits to purchase cloth and sell it in Shanghai before the note fell due. By this resort, a joint cloth-banking firm could complete the entire marketing cycle at no cost to itself (Zhang Jintao 1980; Zhang Zhiqing 1980).

Because of the obvious advantages of these commercial arrangements, joint firms became more and more the rule from the 1910's on. A large number of the 22–25 banks that operated in Nantong through most of the 1920's were actually parts of *guanzhuang* firms (or vice versa); and most of the others had at least a cloth and yarn section. (Wu Huisheng 1980b; Yu Yikong 1982: 31; Zhang Jintao 1980; Zhang Zhiqing 1980). For all practical purposes, then, there was little distinction between banking capital and commercial capital. Organizationally, they were integrated or very closely related.

The number of Nantong banks, compared with other localities, serves as a barometer of this situation. By 1912, with 20 banks, Nantong was second only to Shanghai among the cities of Jiangsu province. Wuxi placed third, with 18 (JS [8] 1913: 61; *Shina* 1920: 1115–1123). Detailed data on the capitalization and volume of business of those banks in the early years are unavailable, but a 1932 Ministry of Industry survey provides some insight.

It found that of 27 native banks in Nantong, 14 were capitalized at 10,000 to 50,000 yuan; three at 50,000 to 100,000; nine at 100,000 to 500,000; and one at 500,000 to 1,000,000 (Shiyebu 1933: 57). These amounts far exceeded the norm for native banks in other interior areas of Jiangsu, where only the largest ever commanded as much as 100,000 yuan.

There were, of course, always limits to the total amount of funding banks could supply, a problem that was exacerbated by the peculiarities of both the Yingkou trade, which limited the rate of capital turnover, and the buying cycles, which required enormous expenditures in two relatively short spans of time. To overcome this problem, the banks followed the long-established custom of issuing a large amount of credit on a small amount of specie. Emphasizing the firm's (and owner's) reputation rather than the balance sheet of the business, which by convention was never made public, native banks operated on close margins with no set reserves and depended on a quick turnover of funds to make profits. By Western standards these business practices were extremely unsound. Nevertheless they yielded rich profits to successful banks and at the same time made the greatest possible amount of credit available (McElderry 1976: 146, 187–90).

In sum, the same system that accounted for the remarkable strength of early industrial development in Nantong also created extraordinary opportunities for the accumulation and concentration of commercial capital. Built on a foundation of late-nineteenth-century textile growth, a commercial-financial complex dominated by an oligopoly of the modern merchant elite was well in place by the early Republican period. Serving as the point of convergence of the interlocked rural-urban economy, this complex formed the material basis for Dasheng and merchants to pursue common economic goals and unite politically whenever outside forces threatened their preeminence in the local system.

Yet common goals did not mean a coincidence of interest. From the outset the dual nature of modern merchants as both intermediaries of capitalist production and autonomous agents with their own logic created a cleavage with the industrial sector. In the early self-reliant period, the marriage of convenience between the two, the relative weakness of merchants vis-à-vis Zhang Jian and his empire, and the leading merchants' assumption of positions as directors and staff members of Dasheng masked this contradiction in interests. But as the merchant elites deepened their control in the countryside and consolidated their economic power in the urban-based commercial-financial complex, the tendency to concentrate and centralize inevitably drew them to the expanding, increasingly competitive, and lucrative cotton trade. In so doing, their contradictions with Dasheng moved closer to the surface.

The Growth of the Cotton Trade

Exports of Chinese cotton continued on the spectacular climb that had started in 1888. By 1920 more than 1,000,000 piculs were being exported annually (Chen Shiqi 1979: 985; Liu Jiawang 1920: 2). What was different now was that Japan, with the ninth-largest spinning industry in the world, was absorbing the bulk of these exports (70 percent in 1917; "Zhongguo mianye" 1917: 2). Domestic demand also increased rapidly after 1895. In 1920 the foreign- and native-owned mills in China between them consumed about 2,000,000 piculs of the 4,300,000 grown annually in China, or about one-half of the total, as against 1,300,000 for foreign exports, or slightly over a fourth (Liu Jiawang 1920: 2; JS [3] 1919).

Nantong growers kept pace with this rising demand. In 1920 they produced nearly 1,000,000 piculs of cotton, or almost a quarter of all the country's production. Of this amount, roughly 200,000 piculs were consumed by Dasheng, 400,000 were sold to Shanghai exporters and factories; and 70,000 went to factories in Jiangnan and Shandong. The rest was used locally for handspinning and padding and wadding (Liu Jiawang 1920: 2).

The local cotton trade also expanded rapidly—and not just in the areas of Dasheng's control. As early as 1912 at least 78 independent dealers (*huahang*) operated in Nantong, Haimen, and Chongming (*Shina* 1920: 453–63). The next decade saw such an intensification that, by 1923, there were over 100 independents in Nantong alone (*Tongruhai mianye gongui* 1924).

The expanding number of firms brought a reorganization in which what had once been a mass of small, individually operated enterprises became differentiated by size, with a three-tiered structure of small, medium, and large firms similar to the structure of the cloth industry (Cheng Zengchong 1980; Wu Huisheng 1980a). Most of the larger firms maintained their main offices in the market towns of the producing districts, including especially Jinsha, Yuxi, Pingchao, Liuqiao, and Shian (Yu Yikong 1982: 33). Some of the largest monopolized entire districts. The Santaihe company's branches, for example, controlled sales in the Liujiazhen area and other important producing districts (*Shina* 1920: 463; Wu Huisheng 1980a).

Initially most large firms purchased cotton in volume at harvest time and then either sold it themselves in Shanghai or sent it to Nantong for spot purchase by the representatives of Shanghai cotton brokerage firms and factories (Yin Yuepu 1980; Zhang Jintao 1980; Zou Qiang 1984: 33). By 1910 or so many had shifted to contract buying, committing themselves to supplying particular spinning factories. Contracts were normally made before the harvest season, stipulated the quantity, price, and date of delivery, and required the factory to advance the firms the money for their purchases. Jiangnan factories were apparently the first to turn to contracts as a means of both avoiding the growing competitiveness of the Shanghai market and meeting their raw material needs (Wu Huisheng 1980a). As competition increased, Shanghai mills and foreign firms adopted the practice (Yu Yikong 1982: 33–34). Because of advance payments, contract buying provided a new source of capital for Nantong cotton firms, stimulating their expansion in the teens and influencing the growth of large trading companies in the 1920's (Cheng Zengchong 1980; Wu Huisheng 1980a).

Advance payment contracts also led the largest firms to develop a system of preharvest buying. To ensure that they could both fill their contracts and take advantage of peasants' preharvest cash shortages, their employees surveyed crops during the growing season, then contracted for a specified amount or all of the harvest. They made partial advance payment at the time of transaction, the remainder at harvest. The price paid at both times was that quoted at the time of transaction. It was always below the market price, usually 30–40 percent below (Wang Nanping 1936: 619–20).

Extending usury capital in the countryside, preharvest buying allowed the largest firms to increase surplus appropriation and gain control over cotton supplies. As many scholars have noted, an increase in "exploitation space" like this narrowed the peasants' range of choices, since entry into the preharvest market reduced their options in other markets (Bharadwaj 1979; Srivastava 1989). For cotton merchants, however, the risk of subsequent weather damage to the crop notwithstanding, predetermined prices with both peasant cultivators and factory representatives provided the opportunity for extraordinary profits of as much as 500 percent (Shiyebu 1933: 341; Wang Nanping 1936: 620). Moreover, that system put them in a position to still further challenge landlords' prerogatives in the countryside.

The larger firms also began purchasing in bulk from middle-size firms commanding comparatively small amounts of capital. In turn those firms, along with their own direct purchases, bought up cotton collected by small *huahang* of only one or two persons. Concentrated in small towns and villages, these small operators typically acted as agents for medium-sized or large firms, fanning out into the countryside with loans that were advanced and repayable in cotton on the same day (Cheng Zengchong 1980).

This thriving trade came under threat as the century wore on, when, owing to intensifying competition for cotton supplies, factories in Jiangnan and Shanghai, as well as operatives of foreign firms, began running their own collecting stations in cotton-producing districts during the harvest season (JS [8] 1913: 71–72; Lin Jubai 1984: 9; Yu Yikong 1982: 33–34; Zhang Youyi 1957, 2: 504). The most potent of these challengers were the Japanese firms and mills. Although British as well as American and other European firms did assume direct control of some commercial transactions, into the 1920's they continued to rely principally on compradors and the Chinese merchant network for their export-import trade (Odell 1916: 119). Not so the Japanese firms, and particularly the three major cotton trading Toyo Menka, Nihon Menka, and Gosho, whose procurement agents, often clandestinely, established offices in the cotton districts to deal directly with peasants and local merchants. These three firms operated with huge capital reserves as they purchased cotton in China and India for the Japanese Cotton Mills Association (Boseki Rengokai), which oversaw procurement and marketing for its members (Seki 1956: 12). Other Japanese firms were backed by Japanese banks.

Such funding allowed the Japanese to establish an extensive network of marketing and purchasing offices in China. In contrast to British and American firms, which continued to deal on a cash basis, it also enabled their firms to advance credit to peasant growers and local merchants (Seki 1956: 125; Zhang Youyi 1957, 2: 504). Because of the substantial savings involved, these local marketing arrangements became a significant factor in Japan's capture of the Chinese textile market between 1909 and 1919, and in its position as the major foreign purchaser of Chinese cotton (Chao Kang 1977: 99–102).

Fortunately for the Nantong traders, the Chamber of Commerce aggressively beat back such threats in their area. In the early teens, when a British firm tried to establish a buying station on Chongming, the chamber vehemently opposed direct foreign purchase as a violation of treaty agreements (JS [8] 1913: 71–72). Several years later, when the Guangqin and Liyong mills in Wuxi and Jiangyin established stations in Liuhaisha, where some of Nantong's finest cotton grew, the chamber moved again. In 1920, led by Santaihe and other leading firms, it prohibited direct purchase by all outside companies and mills, Chinese and foreign alike (Cheng Zengchong 1980; *Tonghai xinbao*, Oct. 18, 1920: 3; *Tongruhai mianye gonghui*, 1924: 2).

The prohibition appears to have been effective. There is little evidence of direct buying by nonlocal cotton firms in the county after 1920. In fact the only major attempt to thwart the regulation surfaced in 1927, when the chamber learned that the large Japanese trading company Mitsui was using the Yuandachang Company, a medium-sized local cotton firm, as a front for its operations. According to the chamber's findings, Mitsui had established collecting stations in 18 districts of the greater Nantong area. Although these stations used the Yuandachang name, Mitsui supplied all of the capital, and all of the cotton they purchased was shipped to Japan via Shanghai. Citing this as "the first instance of direct purchase by foreign capital in the greater Nantong area," the chamber condemned Zhang Mozhe, owner of Yuandachang, for his covert operations, and in an obvious effort to publicize the case, published the details in Shanghai in the *Banker's Weekly* (Zhang Youyi 1957, 2: 504).

Although the incident assumed nationalistic overtones, from the chamber's perspective, the central issue was not Zhang's having entered into dealings with the Japanese; by then a number of local cotton dealers had advance-payment agreements with Japanese firms (Lin Jubai 1984: 9; Yu Yi-kong 1982: 33–34). The main objection was Zhang's circumvention of the Nantong marketing network. His operations allowed Japanese capital to by-pass the large firms that were beginning to dominate the county's cotton trade. As later developments reveal, the large firms that led the attack against Zhang were quite willing to enter into similar covert operations when out-side funding meant establishing their own hegemony over the market.

Cotton Firm Growth in Dasheng's Chaozhuang Period

Not surprisingly, just as in the case of the *guanzhuang* firms, the close asso-ciation between local banks and cotton firms stimulated an integration of the two. Faced with rising capital requirements, some cotton firms opened their own banks in order to draw on the funds of individual depositors.[1] More frequently, however, the large cloth-yarn-banking firms expanded into the cotton business. Consequently, the lines separating these enterprises began to blur, and capital came to be even more concentrated and centralized in the commercial-banking complex. Leading cloth merchant–bankers such as Lin Zuobo opened and managed their own cotton firms (Wu Huisheng 1980b). Others were content to leave the management to someone else. Though Zhang Jingpu, owner of Deji, one of the oldest and largest *guanzhuang*-banking firms (it was reputedly capitalized at over 2,000,000 yuan), did not open a cotton business himself, by the 1920's he had investments or joint ownership in several large cotton firms (NT [4] 1987; Wu Huisheng 1980b). Again, it is impossible to pinpoint from the sketchy records how many cloth merchant–bankers eventually entered the trade. It is clear, however, that by the teens at least half the *guanzhuang* firms in Nantong and two in Haimen were directly operating or had investments in a cotton firm, and that others joined them in the 1920's (Cheng Zengchong 1980; Wu Huisheng 1980b).

Dasheng was the victim of this development. As the cotton firms grew larger, stronger, and ever more competitive, Dasheng found it increasingly difficult to maintain its monopoly system. In the years after the establishment of the Chongming mill and the expansion of the No. 1 mill, it was unable to meet its growing demand for raw materials on its own and began sup-plementing its supplies with purchases from cotton dealers. Zhang Jian and company really had no other choice, since Dasheng was now hemmed in by dealers in districts outside its control. At first it simply purchased what it needed from various merchants, some of whom acted as its agents. But to ensure adequate supplies, it soon regularized all its purchases in a system known as *chaozhuang* (duplicate or supplemental agency; DSXT 1990: 111; Wu Huisheng 1980a).

Under this system Dasheng negotiated regular contracts with select Nantong cotton firms for a guaranteed amount of cotton each year. Like outside
factories, it advanced them most of the capital for these purchases and paid
them a fixed commission for their services (DSXT 1990: 111–12; Wu Huisheng 1980a). In effect the *chaozhuang* policy spelled the beginning of the
end for Zhang's policy of self-reliance. Conversely, it allowed local cotton
merchants, who had previously been excluded from Dasheng's operations,
to achieve even greater control over cotton supplies.

The *chaozhuang* policy was a boon for the firms that obtained Dasheng
contracts. Since the mill often advanced 70–80 percent of the money they
needed to carry out their contracts, they, and the native banks to which they
were usually linked, had decided advantages over their competitors. Not
surprisingly, the firms that profited from the contracts were owned or part-
owned by Dasheng staff members and their relatives or, through cloth or
banking, were closely affiliated with the company. Thanks to his contract,
for example, Ni Yanyang, a Dasheng staff member and future director of
the board, was able to expand his business to the point where he eventually
owned one of the largest cotton trading companies. Other beneficiaries were
Dasheng's collection officer, Zhang Yaotang, owner of the Ximen cotton
firm, and Du Sengguo, who as the director of Dasheng's business department was well positioned to channel contracts to his already large cotton
company. Zhang Jingpu, whom we have met several times as the owner of
a cloth-banking firm and an investor in several cotton businesses, provides a
final example. Zhang had extremely close relations with Dasheng. Not only
did his firm regularly float loans to the mill for cotton collection and make
sizable purchases of yarn, Zhang himself served as a Dasheng board member
for several years, and one of his sons was a Dasheng staff officer. These close
personal and professional ties enabled him to secure *chaozhuang* contracts
for his cotton firm interests (Wu Huisheng 1980b).

Though Dasheng's *chaozhuang* policy compounded the blending of commercial interests in Nantong, they became still more interlocked as single
proprietorships gave way to joint ownership, particularly among bank and
cotton firms. The trend paralleled that in other highly commercialized areas,
where increasing volumes of business, as well as competition from modern
banks and foreign interests, prompted the owners of native banks and commercial firms to reorganize and enlarge their capital by entering into partner-
ships (McElderry 1976: 33; Shiyebu 1933: 915). In Nantong joint ownership
served as an added stimulus to the concentration and centralization of capital in the upper echelons of the merchant elite during the 1920's.

By then, most of their competitors had been edged out. Some firms that
lacked the right connections with Dasheng were able to remedy the situation
by offering staff members stock in their firms and yearly dividends in return

for *chaozhuang* contracts. But those who could obtain no special position found it increasingly difficult to compete and were eventually forced out of business or into auxiliary roles (Wu Huisheng 1980b).

The Decline of the Land Development Companies

In one sense the *chaozhuang* period represented a transitional phase during which the interests of the merchant–banking elite and Dasheng balanced. Nevertheless, it saw torn loyalties even then within Dasheng itself. Dasheng's merchant managers used their positions in the mill to promote their private interests in the commercial sector. They formulated the *chaozhuang* policy as a solution to Dasheng's cotton shortages, but at the same time pursued a route that helped block the mill from expanding its internal system.

Other changes in the *chaozhuang* period, notably in the policies of the land development companies, provide further evidence of the divergence of interests between Dasheng and the commercial elite. Beginning in 1915 those companies were forced into periodic divisions of their lands, a process that badly damaged Dasheng's cotton collection system and strengthened the economic interests of private investors, many of whom were merchants.

Tonghai set the precedent for this process. Article 13 of its charter provided for a complicated system of division among shareholders after cultivation had begun. At the first stockholders' meeting, in 1907, investors were already pressing for division. Protecting Dasheng's cotton system and the company's long-term interests, Zhang Jian opposed the move and succeeded in having a new "nondivision" clause written into the charter. Eight years later, however, shareholders not only reinstated the division principle but voted two to one for an immediate division. Some 40,000 mu of the company's 97,000 mu were pared off that year, at a rate of 10 mu per share. In a second division in 1928, 12 mu were issued for each share. In 1934, most of the remaining company land was parceled out with the allotting of 22 mu per share (Chen Hongjin 1939: 34–38; DSXT 1990; Hu Huanyong 1947: 65).

All of the development companies established after 1914 followed Tonghai's lead. Company charters indicated that division should proceed rapidly, so that "as soon as all land . . . is cultivated, all land is divided" (Chen Hongjin 1939: 38). Practice was quick to follow principle. The Dayoujin Company began dividing its land in 1916, two years after its founding. That division involved fully 80 percent of the 32,425 mu then under cultivation.[2]

No company could thrive under such circumstances. Dayoujin and the others had no way to accumulate capital and so continue reclaiming the land they had acquired, let alone buy more (Xu Gengqi 1982: 53–54). With the rent deposits and rents they had counted on to supplement their investment capital removed to shareholders, additional reclamation could often only be accomplished through loans. Between that and the many setbacks caused by flooding and dike destruction, most companies were heavily indebted by the 1920's. By the 1930's many had been taken over by their creditors (Shiyebu 1933: 266–72; *Tonghai xinbao*, Oct. 18: 1923: 1; Zhang Youyi 1957, 3: 840). Meanwhile the pace of reclamation had slowed almost to the vanishing point. As late as the mid-1930's only 2,000,000–3,000,000 of the approximately 10,000,000 mu originally owned by the Capital Group companies had actually been reclaimed.

The push for division among shareholders makes it clear that from the outset investors were primarily concerned with their own enrichment and cared little about the long-term interests of Dasheng or the development companies. Cotton merchants, in particular, saw investment and division as a way to expand control over cotton supplies. Their gain was Dasheng's loss.

But if the steady and continuous expansion of cotton supplies Zhang Jian had envisioned was no longer possible, he did his best to preserve what he could. Although he could not forestall the division of almost 40 percent of Tonghai's cultivated acreage in 1915, he did succeed in having the company retain the management of that land. Acting as agent for the shareholders, the company continued to collect rents and pay taxes on them. For him, obviously, cotton collection was the key issue, since by retaining the right of rent collection, Dasheng continued to monopolize the cotton crop. Shareholders were paid a cash equivalent for their portion of the collected rent (Chen Hongjin 1939: 39).

In this way Dasheng was able to minimize the effects of division on its collection system for several years. In the 1920's, however, Tonghai's shareholders began to collect their own rents, and after the division of 1928, independent and separate management became general practice on all divided land. Company efforts to forestall this trend proved ineffective. By 1935 only 9.3 percent of the 97,000-odd mu brought to a cultivable state remained as company property, and the company continued to manage only 22.7 percent of the divided land (Chen Hongjin 1939: 39). Like Tonghai, some of the other companies succeeded in retaining management privileges for a time, but by the 1930's most handled only a small proportion of the total land they had reclaimed (Shiyebu 1933: 234–36, 266–72).

The Effects of Competition on the Chinese Textile Industry and the Nantong Cotton Firms

For a time after World War One, the rapid expansion of Chinese-owned industry that had marked the war years continued, although at a slower rate

TABLE 6.1

Profits and Losses of Chinese Spinning Mills, 1914–1922

(Prices in yuan for 16-count yarn)

Year	Cotton price (per picul)	Production cost (per bale)	Yarn price (per bale)	Profit/loss (per bale of yarn)
1914	21.00	85.50	99.50	14.00
1915	23.00	93.63	90.50	−3.13
1916	24.10	97.56	103.00	5.45
1917	31.25	125.60	152.00	26.40
1918	37.00	143.18	158.50	15.33
1919	34.25	149.55	200.00	50.55
1920	33.75	147.75	194.20	46.45
1921	32.50	143.20	150.50	7.30
1922	35.85	155.25	140.50	−14.75

SOURCE: Yan Zhongping 1963: 172.
NOTE: Production costs include the cost of cotton. Pearse 1929 bases his estimates for 1923–29 (given in Table 6.2) on a rate of 3.5 piculs per bale (400 lbs.). Yan Zhongping, the source of these earlier data, does not give a breakout on production costs.

of perhaps 8–9 percent annually (J. Chang 1969: 70–74). What reversed this trend was renewed foreign investment and activity and especially the entrance of Japanese competitors. The new Japanese-owned mills improved their share of spindles and looms year after year during the 1920's. By the early 1930's they commanded the greatest working capital and reserves of all mills in China (*Nankai Weekly Statistical Service*, Dec. 11, 1933: 231). They and other foreign mills between them owned 45.5 percent of the country's yarn spindles, 67.2 percent of the thread spindles, and 54.4 percent of the looms (Yan Zhongping 1963: 136).[3]

The rising internal demand for cotton, coupled with outside demand from the textile industries that had sprung up in Asian countries during the war and a rapidly recovered Western industry, pushed prices to a record high in the early 1920's. At the same time yarn prices dropped precipitously. The result was a worldwide crisis in textiles. In China it exacerbated the problems of the Chinese-owned mills and exposed the degree to which the domestic economy had come to be globally shaped. Tables 6.1 and 6.2, charting the yarn and cotton prices from 1914 to 1929, show the adverse effects of the "expensive cotton–cheap yarn" syndrome on profit margins after 1920.

By 1922 the plight of the Chinese-owned mills was so serious that the Chinese Spinning Mill Owners Association attempted to set a floor of 135 yuan per bale for yarn. Nevertheless by August of that year the price had dropped below that, to 124 yuan (Yan Zhongping 1963: 173). Some mills were forced to reduce their output, and as the crisis deepened, the association called on all member mills to follow suit. Again its efforts proved to be fruitless. Many members would not abide by its suggestions because foreign factories, taking

TABLE 6.2

Estimated Profits and Losses of Chinese Spinning Mills, 1923–1929

(Prices in taels for 16-count yarn)

Year	Cotton price (per picul)	Production cost (per bale)	Yarn price (per bale)	Profit/loss (per bale of yarn)
1923	39.25	162.37	150.15	−12.22
1924	41.67	170.87	166.55	−4.32
1925	39.65	163.77	165.07	1.30
1926	31.77	136.22	143.75	7.53
1927	33.45	142.07	140.17	−1.90
1928	36.75	153.67	157.55	3.88
1929	34.31	145.11	162.96	17.85

SOURCE: Pearse 1929: 157.

NOTE: Pearse notes that he arbitrarily assigned the price of 3.5 piculs of cotton plus 25 taels in labor and overhead to the cost of production for a bale of yarn (400 lbs.), so that his profit and loss data are not exact. Nevertheless he believes that they can be taken as a close guide to the financial state of the trade over the period.

TABLE 6.3

Price Index of Cotton Yarn in China, 1932–1934

(1931 high = 100)

Year	10-count yarn		16-count yarn		20-count yarn	
	High	Low	High	Low	High	Low
1932	81	94	74	98	75	98
1933	72	82	68	78	67	80
1934	68	70	66	69	66	69

SOURCE: "Huashang shachang lianhehui nianhui baogaoshu" 1934: 18.

advantage of the problems in the Chinese industry, had deliberately begun to expand output (Chao Kang 1977: 121).

The mills' situation improved a little in 1925, when bumper harvests began to reverse the rise in cotton prices. Through the rest of the decade most were able to make a profit (except for 1927), though at a level substantially below that of 1920. But in 1932, as Table 6.3 indicates, yarn prices once again began to plummet, caused in part by a drop in demand as inflation threw the countryside into depression. Meanwhile the price of both domestic and imported cotton remained high.[4] By 1933 yarn prices had again fallen below production costs for many mills, forcing them to reduce output (Liu Dajun 1940: 21). The value of production of Chinese yarn mills in central China, for example, dropped 45 percent ("Huashang shachang lianhehui nianhui baogaoshu" 1934: 189). In 1935, 25 of the surviving 92 Chinese-owned mills collapsed, and 14 others reduced their production schedules, leaving a third of Chinese spindles and looms idle (Wang Jingyu & Sun Yutang 1957: 22).

Thus despite an overall expansion of the textile industry, Chinese mills steadily lost ground. Between 1923 and 1931 (which is to say, well before the collapse of 1935), 19 were reorganized, five were taken over by creditors, 11 went bankrupt, and 17 were sold (Yan Zhongping 1963: 173–74). Inefficient plants simply could not survive the narrowing margin between yarn prices and cotton costs. Competitors, especially the Japanese firms, quickly took advantage of the situation; the buying out of marginal and bankrupt mills became one of the chief means through which the Japanese increased their share of the textile establishment.[5]

As one might guess, the most obvious winners in this game were the large cotton trading companies (*huahao*) of Nantong. Under intensifying competition and high cotton prices, they came to hold a position of relative advantage vis-à-vis both Dasheng and other purchasers of Nantong-area cotton. And then, as the competition continued to mount, they tightened their terms.

By the mid-1920's some of the largest companies had already constructed their own warehouses, where they amassed huge supplies of cotton for periodic release and speculative activities on the Shanghai market. That marked a total change of character for them, from companies that acted merely as commission agents or brokers for outside trading companies and factories, including Dasheng, to companies that traded on their own account. Abandoning the practice of preseason contracts, they turned to open competitive bidding for supplies whose release time they alone determined. Some chose, in addition, to play the Shanghai cotton exchange, where speculation ran rampant (Xu Gengqi 1982: 55–57; Yu Yikong 1982: 34).

Within the county as a consequence, many competing firms, both medium-size and large, were either forced to scale back or give up business entirely (Wu Huisheng 1980a, b). At the same time, functioning as agents for the large firms, small firms continued to proliferate. In the same period, then, that a handful of large companies gained virtual domination of the cotton trade in the county, the total number of firms increased, rising from slightly over 100 in the early 1920's to more than 200 in the early 1930's (*Tongruhai mianye gonghui*, 1924; Zhang Jintao 1980). At least two-thirds of the 200 firms were probably just one- or two-person *hang*; and medium and large firms together probably numbered no more than 50 (Cheng Zengchong 1980; Shiyebu 1933, 4: 52; *Tongruhai mianye gonghui*, 1924).

Modern Banks and the Cotton Trade

The 1920's saw important changes as well in Nantong's banking circles that at once hardened local merchant capital in monopoly structures and created new linkages between it, a fast-developing commodities market controlled by state capitalists, and the world economy. As a result, in the northern delta the imprint of the semicolonial economy became more distinct.

By the early 1920's four leading modern Chinese banks, the Bank of

China and the Shanghai, Jiangsu, and Communications banks, had established branches in Nantong. In the early 1930's they were joined by five others (Shiyebu 1933, 10: 52; Xu Gengqi 1982). The local appearance of these banks made good the threat to the preeminence of native institutions in commercial banking posed by the rise of modern banks after 1911. In 1912 there were only nine modern Chinese banks in the country; by 1921 there were 123 (and including branches, 343; McElderry 1976: 142–43). ·

These banks had had a substantial edge over native banks since 1912 as the primary underwriters of the state's borrowing. Most centered their operations on, and royally profited from, floating government bonds at huge discounts. From 1927 to 1931, for example, the state issued bonds in the amount of 1,006,000,000 yuan but received only 538,700,717 for them, or 54 percent of their face value (L. Wu 1935: 43). The large capital amounts accrued through this association enabled the modern banks to challenge native banks in commercial financing.

The Guomindang state's currency reforms in the years 1928–35 further weakened the native banks. Two measures, in particular, worked against them. The first, in 1932, was the abolition of the tael and the adoption of a standard silver dollar. That measure took away one lucrative source of their profits, a charge on exchanging dollars into taels. The second and more important blow came three years later, when the government banned privately held silver and made the bank notes of the Bank of China, the Bank of Communications, and the Central Bank the only legal tender. Removing the native banks' right to issue their own notes struck at the very heart of their institutional power; it sharply limited their ability to create credit and engage in speculative operations (McElderry 1976: 161–76). Thereafter, as one author puts it, native banks essentially became "street-runners for modern banks" (Zhang Yulan 1957: 122).

But this is to jump ahead of our story. In the 1920's, in fact, though the modern banks gradually made inroads, native bank notes (*zhuangpiao*) remained the preferred instrument of credit.[6] Because they made possible greater volumes of business, merchants continued to prefer the unsecured loans offered by native banks to the low-interest collateralized loans of the modern banks. Indeed, at this stage native banks were more benefited than hurt by the growth of these competitors. Modern banks made short-term loans to them, and until those banks established their own clearing house in 1933, also kept deposits in them. Native banks paid the modern banks a modest rate of interest for these deposits, then loaned the funds out at higher interest (*Shanghai qianzhuang shiliao* 1960: 167). Thus through most of the 1920's, native banks not only continued to dominate commercial banking,[7] but profited from their relations with modern banks.

Nevertheless it was the four major modern banks on which Nantong's large integrated commercial-banking firms, as well as Dasheng and the Capital Group enterprises relied. With respect to the Dasheng enterprises, they staked out separate areas of concentration. The Shanghai Bank specialized in loans to the land reclamation companies and through foreclosures came to acquire substantial land interests (Xu Gengqi 1982: 53–54; Yin Yuepu 1980). The Communications Bank lent mainly to Dasheng subsidiaries, and the Bank of China established a close relationship with Dasheng itself, supplying loans to both the No. 1 and the Chongming mill (Yin Yuepu 1980).

The banks were more competitive when it came to other business. All four extended credit to the native bank-commercial firms engaged in the cloth, and especially, the cotton trade. Both the Jiangsu and the Shanghai bank constructed large warehouses for the stocks of cotton, cloth, and yarn they received as collateral (Cheng Zengchong 1980). The other banks were content to secure their loans with the stocks the borrowers held in their own or rented warehouses. All the banks also had the right to issue their own notes, and since they made their loans in that form, rather than in silver, the standard currency of the time, the circulation of paper expanded enormously. The native banks passed these notes on in their loans to merchants, and the merchants used them to pay peasant weavers and cotton growers for their cloth and cotton (Cheng Zengchong 1980; Xu Gengqi 1982: 60).

Initially peasants were reluctant to accept this form of payment and immediately cashed the notes in for silver. One of the men I interviewed, a former Bank of China official, recalled, for example, that as a trainee in the Nantong branch in 1922, his first assignment each day between 6:00 and 7:00 A.M. was to convert notes to silver for peasants who had just sold their cloth in the morning market. Since the banks always made these conversions, the stigma against the notes gradually disappeared (Yin Yuepu 1980). Indeed because of their convenience, local residents came to prefer the notes and often exchanged silver for them. The banks succeeded in taking in large amounts of silver in this way. At the same time, through their loans to commercial firms and native banks, they substantially increased the amount of money in circulation, as well as their local influence.

In focusing almost exclusively on commercial loans, especially to cotton firms, these modern banks were catering to the sophisticated commodities market that emerged in the postwar years with the growing foreign demand for agricultural products. From the 1920's they played a central role in that market, an involvement that went beyond merely financing the commercial activities of others to include direct investment in rural areas as well. Because of world market demand and steady price increases, the cotton trade became a focal point of this activity (Coble 1980: 223–28; Shiyebu 1933, 5: 264; Zhang Youyi 1957, 3: 179–85).

During the Nanjing decade (1927–37) especially, when the symbiotic relationship among government, bureaucrats, and banks that formed the backbone of what has been variously termed bureaucratic or state capitalism reached new heights, the banking thrust into the cotton and textile trades became more aggressive (Coble 1980: 224). In so doing, it at once reflected and contributed to bureaucratic capitalist development. Led by the Bank of China, the most powerful financial institution in China, banks expanded their interests in both industry and agriculture, taking over directorships and the management of a large number of textile mills and carving out spheres of influence in cotton-producing regions (Zhang Youyi 1957, 3: 182–84; Zhang Yulan 1957: 120).[8] At the same time they supported the formation of huge trading companies that specialized in commodity trading and speculation and underpinned the new-style commodities market tied to the world market (Coble 1980: 228).

One leading example is the China Cotton Company, organized in 1936 by T. V. Soong with a capital of 10,000,000 yen, subscribed largely by Shanghai banks. It became one of the largest commodity firms in China. In its first year of operation alone, the total volume of business surpassed 20,000,000 yen. Of this amount, trade in raw cotton accounted for 13,000,000 yen, and trade in textiles 5,000,000 (Wang Jingyu & Sun Yutang 1957: 1041–1042).

Modern Banks and Nantong's Merchant Elite

It is in the context of this interconnection among modern banks, the commodities market, and the world market that modern banking activity in cotton and textile centers such as Nantong takes on special significance. Over time this activity clearly revolved around establishing access to the products of peasant cultivators, especially cotton, to strengthen the hand of powerful, bureaucratically connected firms like Soong's China Cotton Company in the commodities market. Paradoxically, in Nantong and other localities, modern banks worked to accomplish this by fueling the drive of the leading commercial firms to establish monopoly control over local cotton supplies. Significantly also, as creditors to Dasheng and the Capital Group enterprises, banks made inroads into modern industry in Nantong.

That cotton rather than textile financing became primary was not solely a matter of banking preference. It also reflected developments within the *guanzhuang* cloth trade, namely the fact that during the first decade of the century the rapid expansion of the *guanzhuang* cloth industry came to a halt. Once total output reached roughly 6,000,000 pieces in 1908, it stagnated and remained at that level through at least 1917. This was apparently due to capital limitations and the fact that the relatively small number of *guanzhuang* firms could spread themselves no thinner and still maintain their monopoly of the

TABLE 6.4
Shipments of Nantong Guanzhuang *Cloth from Shanghai, 1922–1931*
(Bolts)

Year	Total shipped	Shipped to Yingkou		Shipped to Andong	
		Amount	Percent of total	Amount	Percent of total
1922	109,415	94,643	86.5	9,725	8.9
1923	123,948	110,110	88.8	10,632	8.6
1924	74,492	70,607	94.8	1,580	2.1
1925	123,042	115,267	93.7	3,125	2.5
1926	100,889	92,402	91.6	3,375	3.4
1927	93,000[a]	82,796	89.9	5,115	5.6
1928	74,894	66,686	89.0	4,842	6.4
1929	80,079	64,192	80.1	12,325	15.4
1930	70,112	50,483	72.0	14,343	20.4
1931	41,625	22,650	54.4	16,895	40.6

SOURCE: "Investigation of the Cotton Cloth Guild, Shanghai," as cited in Lin Jubai 1984: 84.
NOTE: The table does not include the cloth handled by the Qinglanbang, which totaled 38,825 bolts in this period and on average accounted for 4.4% of annual sales.
[a] Estimated amount; the 99,124 cited by Lin does not correspond to his percent of total amounts.

trade. Thus the opportunities were seen to lie in the cotton trade, rather than the further development of the cloth trade.

Furthermore the northeastern *guanzhuang* trade began sliding into decline just at the time that modern bank funding became locally available. As Table 6.4 indicates, there was a more or less steady drop in shipments to Yingkou after 1925, culminating in the virtual loss of the market when the Japanese seized Manchuria (Chen Zengyu 1986: 165–66; Lin Jubai 139–44). The *guanzhuang* merchants tried to compensate by seeking new marketing areas and introducing an improved cloth that more closely approximated the machine-woven goods. But most peasants were too poor to afford the iron-gear loom and additional raw materials necessary to make the new cloth. Thus production levels of improved cloth remained much lower than for *guanzhuang* in its heyday.[9] In 1933 only 9.6 percent of weavers in the industrial districts specialized in the new cloth and another 2.7 percent produced some of it. Nevertheless, this output went partway to offset the cloth merchants' losses: because of its higher price, the market value of improved cloth was slightly more than half that of *guanzhuang* (Peng Zeyi et al. 1957, 3: 761).

The general decline in the cloth trade thus indirectly acted as an additional stimulus to the concentration of capital and the drive among dominant merchants of the commercial-financial complex to monopolize the cotton trade. From the late teens on, it became increasingly difficult for integrated firms and/or their affiliates to fund their expanding cotton purchases from the shrinking proceeds of the cloth trade. Consequently in the 1920's, when the local cotton trade reached an annual volume of business of 24,000,000 yuan—a figure that far overshadowed the value of the *guanzhuang* trade at its height—they began to lean more and more heavily on the modern banks (Shiyebu 1933, 10: 57; Yin Yuepu 1980; Zhang Jintao 1980). Banks with a close relationship with Dasheng, notably the Bank of China, in turn regularly used funds earmarked for cotton business to support Dasheng's cotton collections. Because producers in the reclaimed areas were usually paid in silver rather than notes, with the growing threat of banditry in those parts, the bank even undertook to supervise the safe passage of funds to the collecting areas.[10]

But all this is to tell only part of the story of these banks' activities in Nantong's cotton trade. Of far greater import were those that lay in deeper, more intimate relations between them and the modern commercial elite. Since their dealings were clandestine, it is difficult to gauge the full scope of this relationship. It is clear, however, that direct bank investments were at its core. These investments fueled the rise and expansion of cotton trading firms in the 1920's. The Reshenmao Cotton Company, owned by a *guanzhuang* cloth merchant and heavily invested in by the Bank of China, is a prime example (Cheng Zengchong 1980).

Moreover, as competition intensified in the 1920's and 1930's, covert bank financing supported the machinations of the largest cotton firms, joined in secret alliance, to shut out other firms and take control of collection (Wu Huisheng 1980b; Yu Yikong 1982: 34; Zhang Jintao 1980). The Dechanghe Cotton Company is a case in point. This was the cover name for a coalition of three leading cotton firms, Yuandeji, Luwanchang, and Santaihe. The company was established and kept in funds by the Tailong Native Bank, which itself was a front organization for the Bank of China (Cheng Zengchong 1980).

Covert links of this kind allowed the modern banks, in partnership with the huge commodity trading companies, to dominate Nantong's cotton trade. In this respect the greater sway of merchant capitalism at the local level formed the foundation for the preeminence of bureaucratic capitalists in the larger commodities market, and for an ever-tighter interlinkage between rural producers and the international capitalist economy. Relations such as these allow us to see bureaucratic capitalism not simply as a phenomenon at the highest levels of the state and economy, but as a product of, and indeed dependent on, local society as well. They also bring into fuller light how the local, national, and global interpenetrated in this phase of development of the semicolonial economy.

Commercial Capital and the Collapse of Dasheng

Once the large integrated firms of Nantong city's commercial-financial complex consolidated their hold on the cotton as well as the textile trade,

Dasheng, like other buyers, was forced to purchase cotton on the wholesale market. The shift from guaranteed supplies through *chaozhuang* contracts to wholesale purchase (*dunzhuang*) dealt the final blow to Zhang Jian's self-reliant system. Especially after the cotton trading companies began to construct their own warehouses, Dasheng was unable to secure any special privileges and was forced to compete with outside buyers (Wu Huisheng 1980a). At the same time it was unable to maintain its monopoly over the areas of traditional supply and so had to abandon its collections there. It continued to maintain a collection office at the No. 1 mill to purchase cotton from individual peasant sellers and tried to compensate for the breakdown of the old system by establishing several new collection stations on distant development company lands, but these sources between them supplied only a fraction of the mills' raw material needs (Wu Huisheng 1980b).

Thus during the period when the Chinese textile industry as a whole became extremely unstable, Dasheng lost the pillar of its strength. As we earlier discussed, thanks in large part to rising cotton prices, the Chinese textile industry was in chronic crisis after 1921. In a dangerous survival strategy, textile mills attempted to overcome the problem by purchasing larger and larger quantities of cotton early in the season when prices were lowest. This practice only made a bad situation worse. As Arno Pearse noted in 1929:

> Very large quantities of cotton are bought ahead and not a single bale of such purchases is hedged. Several mill managers in Shanghai did not make any secret of the fact that they were 30,000 bales long in cotton, and they spoke of one company that was at least 50,000 bales long. Some mills have accumulated a special reserve known as the "cotton fluctuation fund." It will be readily understood that the business of cotton spinning is only of secondary consideration under such conditions; it will depend upon the luck or otherwise in the purchase of raw material whether the mill makes a profit or loss. (1929: 196)

At the precise point, then, when all factories were attempting to maximize their purchases, Dasheng's loss of both its monopoly buying system and its guaranteed contracts was particularly disastrous.

As early as 1919, a year of poor local harvest, the No. 1 mill was forced to supplement its supplies with purchases from Taicang ("Minguo banian mianchan" 1920: 24–25). Again in 1921, when the Nantong cotton crop was damaged by heavy rains, it had to buy additional cotton in Hankou (*Tong-hai xinbao*, Dec. 10, 1921: 3). In 1923 both the No. 1 and the Chongming mill faced the worst collection difficulties in their history. Because of a generally poor harvest in many producing regions, outside buyers from Shanghai and Wuxi, and especially the agents of the Japanese-owned Mitsui Company, were, as one newspaper put it, "willing to go to extreme lengths to obtain as much of the Nantong harvest as possible" (ibid., Nov. 8, 1923: 3). These better-financed competitors succeeded in buying up most of the harvest from the trading companies. The result for Dasheng was that, although the Chong-ming mill began weighing in cotton in August, by November it had taken in only 20,000 bales all told. That same month, the No. 1 mill had to stop production for several days because it had exhausted its supplies (ibid.). By then, as we will see shortly, Dasheng was in serious financial difficulty, which partially explains why it could not match the prices bid by the outsiders. Soon thereafter the Chongming mill was forced to suspend operations for six months. When it resumed business in March 1924, it had so little cotton on hand that it could only run a day shift, rather than the normal day-night, two-shift schedule (*Tonghai xinbao*, Mar. 20, 1924: 2).

From this point on Dasheng was plagued with supply problems. It regu-larly had to purchase stocks from Wuhan-Hankou and was sometimes even forced to buy imported cotton (Wu Huisheng 1980a). In short, despite its location in the center of China's premier cotton-producing district, cutthroat competition in a market increasingly controlled by an oligopolist commercial elite forced Dasheng to buy cotton when and where it could. With that, the merchant-industry conflict was resolved: merchant capital would now play a stronger role and modern industry a weaker one in the local economy system.

Still, as hinted at above, some of Dasheng's difficulties were of its own making. Large profits and dividend payments, especially in the "golden years" of the second decade, masked the unsound financial footing of the mill and its branches (Liu Housheng 1965: 257). In the 1920's they entered a period of irreversible decline.

The problem was that, in good times and bad, in line with contemporary practice, Dasheng released most of its earnings as dividends, so that even during the golden age (when over 90 percent of profits were paid out in divi-dends; Yan Zhongping 1963: 172), the company continued to rely on loans for working capital, the expansion of operations, and the support of other projects. By 1923 the No. 1 mill's total indebtedness reached the staggering figure of more than 8,000,000 taels. According to company records, loans to "businesses and individuals," most of them apparently made by native banks, accounted for more than 2,000,000 taels of the debt load; 2,500,000 was obliged for a mortgage loan floated by a consortium of Shanghai banks, made up of the Bank of China and the Communications, Shanghai, and Jin-cheng banks; and the rest had been taken from investment capital (DSXT 1990: 219–23; NT [1] n.d.: 8).

Various outside activities accounted for a significant portion of this in-debtedness, though a lack of detailed records makes it impossible to deter-mine exactly how much was siphoned off for these projects. In 1923 company officials put the figure at around 4,000,000 taels, including 1.3 million spent on welfare and self-government activities (*Tonghai xinbao*, Aug. 17, 1923: 3). The actual amount was probably much greater, since it was common knowledge that Dasheng had used the mortgage loan on the No. 1 plant to aid faltering land development companies and had contributed sizable funds to keep other Capital Group enterprises afloat (DSXT 1990: 218–25; NJ 1959a: 18; NT [1] n.d.: 8). Some sources estimate that the total spent on all additional projects and enterprises may have been three or four times the amount the company officials owned up to (DSXT 1990; NJ 1959a: 18). The No. 2 and No. 3 mills were also by then heavily in debt, both having acquired mortgages for aid to land development companies (DSXT 1990: 221–24; *Tonghai xinbao*, Aug. 17, 1923: 3). In that year (1923), both the No. 1 and the No. 2 mill had operated in the red, and the Haimen mill had barely made a profit (NJ 1959a: 18–19).

At that point, under the direction of the seven leading Nantong native banks, Dasheng's local creditors decided to take matters into their own hands. Headed by the cloth-banking firm owner, cotton firm investor, and former Dasheng board member Zhang Jingpu, the native banks not only cut off Dasheng's credit, but, acting under the authority of a promptly formed Dasheng Shareholders' Association, set out to get their money back (NJ 1959a: 18). The new association first voted for the establishment of a management committee to take over the Nantong mill, then elected seven of the native bank owners to its board of directors and charged them with the supervision of the main mill's operations (ibid.; *Tonghai xinbao*, Aug. 17, 1923: 3). The new management team quickly negotiated a second loan with the Shanghai banking consortium for over 2,000,000 taels and set tight new operating procedures geared to turning an immediate profit (*Tonghai xinbao*, Aug. 17, 1923: 3). These procedures, along with the bank loan, apparently allowed the native banks to recover their funds in short order. In late 1924 they disbanded the management committee, leaving 15,000 of the mill's 75,000 spindles inoperative for lack of maintenance and the cotton inventory entirely exhausted (NJ 1959a: 19). Since the mill was now in an even more precarious position than before, the Shanghai banking consortium soon organized a management committee of its own to oversee the plant's operations (DSXT 1990: 226; NJ 1959a: 19–20).

The man assigned to take over as general manager was Li Shengbo, a highly positioned officer of the Dazhonghua textile mill in Shanghai, and son of Li Jisheng, a prominent figure in Shanghai financial circles (NJ 1959a: 20). Li initiated a complete reorganization, creating new departments, hiring additional managers, and replacing over 30 staff members and technical personnel belonging to the "Zhang Jian group." And with funding from new loans he took steps to increase the mill's efficiency, repairing some machines and replacing others with more modern equipment (NJ 1959a: 19). Thanks to these efforts, by 1928 the mill was again showing a profit, though on a much smaller scale than in its heyday (DSXT 1990: 226–30; NJ 1959a: 20–21).

But the turnaround was only temporary. Like other Chinese industries, the mill fell into decline in the early 1930's. The banking group, unable to recover its debts under the existing agreements, virtually seized the mill and forced new, harsher contracts on Dasheng that upped the mortgage interest to 320,000 taels a year and stipulated that if the plant still had a net profit after meeting these payments, one-half would go to the banks (NJ 1959a: 21–22).

As the general economic crisis in Chinese industry deepened, this crippling burden of interest caused Dasheng's situation to deteriorate further. By 1935, still owing the banks some 4,000,000 taels, the No. 1 mill was operating at a loss. To stay alive, it was obliged to cut its workforce and scale down production for the second time since 1930. The fate of the branch factories was worse. They had by then become bank property or, after repossession, been sold to other companies (DSXT 1990: 232–49; NJ 1959a: 19–22; NT [1] n.d.: 8–11; 19–22; Yan Zhongping 1963: 235, 238).[11]

Commercial Capitalism and the Semicolonial Economy

Although Zhang Jian and his introduction of modern industry to the northern delta have usually occupied the limelight, in important respects the story of cotton and textile growth in Nantong is also that of the accumulation and concentration of commercial-banking capital. Indeed one can argue that the strengths of early industrial development actually contained the seeds of structural weakness, since Zhang's self-reliant system became the primary vehicle for the ascendancy of a modern merchant elite that contributed to its decline. In the end that interlocked urban-rural system paved the way for this relatively small group of merchant capitalists, bound together in an intricate web of overlapping business, personal, and political interests, to exercise oligopolistic control of major arenas of economic activity in the Nantong area.

Yet the development of Nantong's commercial capitalist complex clearly did not occur as an isolated, independent, or even predominantly local phenomenon. Rural industrial expansion under foreign impact first stimulated it, and in the later stages particularly, larger economic forces at the national and international level shaped its course and outcome. From the 1920's, through new linkages with the outside, the very processes that gave merchants control of key aspects of economic activity at the local level simultaneously fueled the growth of a modern national commodities market tied to the world market and, especially in the decade after 1927, to the phenomenon of state-bureaucratic capitalism.

This new formation in the upper levels of the economy denoted the traditional use of state power to pursue private ends (Feuerwerker 1958) and reflected growing state-bureaucratic involvement in the economy. In the 1920's and 1930's it emerged as a new route through which, in the absence of a committed policy of industrialization on the part of the Guomindang government, a small group of well-connected families gained dominance in the industrial sector, and through linkage with the world market, commanded increasing control over the commercial sector at the national level. Parks Coble's study of Shanghai capitalists and the GMD brings to light evidence suggesting that three of the most important economic ramifications of bureaucratic-capitalist growth were, first, a strengthening of merchant capitalism in the social formation as a whole (paralleled, however, by a reduction in the independent functions of merchants); second, the establishment of new conduits for reorienting portions of the economy to the requirements of external economic interests; and third, over time, the absorption of much of Chinese-owned modern industry. Coble's study further suggests that Chinese industries, especially coastal complexes, that remained outside the bureaucratic-capitalists' orbit usually did so only because of their owners' close personal ties with these families (1980: 251–53).[12]

By the early 1920's Nantong's commercial leaders were, of course, aware of the detrimental effects of their cotton policies on Dasheng. Yet despite numerous economic, political, and social linkages with the company—not to mention the local influence of Zhang Jian—they consistently charted an economic course aimed at the greatest possible maximization of profits within the new commercial nexus. Breaking Dasheng's cotton collection system was critical to that aim, and the more so with their declining fortunes in the northeastern cloth trade.

Thus typifying the tendencies of merchant capital generally to monopolize quickly and shift allies when necessary, the cotton policies of Nantong's merchant elite in the 1920's and 1930's were the logical outcome of attempts begun earlier to gain preeminence in the local cotton trade. Though Dasheng was the big loser here, the merchants themselves also lost, in the sense that the price they paid for strengthening their position locally was a greater dependency on a new group of national monopolists and their more distant economic allies. Significantly, however, neither the disappearance of Zhang's semicolonial alternative, nor the ascendancy of commercial capital, nor the interplay of larger national and international forces in both of these developments, altered the basic trajectory of the path to modernity set at the close of the nineteenth century.

7 The Politics of the Peasant and Modernist Paths in the Late Qing-Early Republican Years

NANTONG'S INTERLOCKED urban-rural system and deepening ties to the world market inexorably affected and altered the relations among merchants, landlords, and peasants. Though landlords reaped certain advantages, in the main the growth of urban elite power in the local system weakened their prerogatives. At the same time the rise of a militant peasant movement further challenged their power. By 1911 this movement posed a serious threat to the entire elite-led modernist path. This chapter considers these late Qing developments and their impact on the rural political economy in the early Republican years. It analyzes them as at once reflective and constitutive of contradictions in the local system and in the semicolonial process.

Merchant-Usury Capital vs. Landlordism in the Countryside

Eugene Genovese has argued that the rise of a world market eventually compelled all of the great landowning classes to "think and act like businessmen," even as many of them fought the growth of bourgeois power (1979: 16). Joel Midgal suggests that in the late nineteenth century, as imperialist-capitalist demand for Third World agricultural commodities rose, the bourgeoisification of agrarian elites accelerated. As he and other scholars of the Third World show, this process was played out in a larger context that saw both land and labor become commoditized with astonishing rapidity. For peasant tenants worldwide, the common results were rent increases, a shift to money payment, harsher terms of tenure, and a restructuring of labor processes (Goodman & Redclift 1982; Midgal 1974; Wolf 1969).

This was clearly the case in the northern Yangzi delta once it became linked to the international cotton market. From the 1890's the external demand for and rising prices of cotton increased the attractiveness of the crop

and supported its extension (Da Shiji 1980; Faure 1989: 136–37; Zhang Renren 1915–16). For all of Dasheng's monopolistic pricing policies, the development of local industry stimulated similar trends, especially in the weaving
core where reliance on machine yarns required a greater marketing of raw
cotton. In the 20 years from 1890 to 1910, for example, rents in kind quickly
gave way to money rents in many parts of Nantong-Haimen-Qidong (Mu
Xuan 1980; Qiao Qiming 1926; Zhang Renren 1915–16).

Qiao Qiming's rural survey data on Nantong in the 1905–24 period suggest the dimensions of other attendant changes.[1] They pinpoint an astounding
rise in both land prices and rents over those years, along with a sharp increase
in the percentage of tenants paying rent deposits. Using an index of 100 for
1905, Qiao puts land prices at 250 in 1924 and cash rents at 229 (1926: 17,
23, 47).

At first glance we might assume that these changes would benefit and reinforce rentier landlordism. They did not. For one thing, although rents and
deposits increased, price rises for agricultural commodities, especially cotton, were greater. By Qiao's calculation, unginned cotton reached an index
figure of 296 by 1924, and ginned cotton climbed to 352 (1926: 18–19). Moreover, just when the price of cotton began to rise, the switch to money rents
(which may have accounted for 70–80 percent of all rents by 1924) caused
landlords to lose control of cotton supplies. In Jiangnan landlords were able
to manipulate conversion rates from rent in kind to money to their advantage. But in the northern delta, given the specificities of the cotton trade and
the developing rural-urban system, it was merchants, not landlords, who became the principal beneficiaries of these developments. Thus for landlords,
according to Qiao, as a percentage of land value, cash rents actually yielded
a lower rate of return than fixed rents in kind, sharecropping, and labor rents
(1926: 21, 32; see also Huadong junzheng 1952: 433–46).

Along with merchants, peasant owners and permanent tenants with fixed
rents may have benefited initially, although the greater capital and labor requirements of cotton to a large extent offset its profitability compared with
other crops. Similarly, landlord operators of local cotton firms geared to
peasants who had to sell their crop immediately after the harvest to pay rents
and debts held a favorable position in the rapidly changing economy. But
their activities were circumscribed and superseded by Dasheng's cotton collection system and the expanding scale of operations of urban-based firms.
We earlier saw that as competition for supplies deepened, these firms began
financing auxiliary agents for their purchases in the cotton districts. In the
most highly commercialized districts many of these purchasing agents were
peasants, some of whom rented out their holdings and worked full time for
cotton firms (Shen Shike 1934: 30841).

Urban merchants further eroded the landlords' position and extended their own sway over the countryside by expanding their usurious operations. The key development here was the cotton firms' turn to preharvest loans on cotton crops discussed in Chapter Seven. These loans not only generated huge profits but allowed the large firms to circumvent market buying and increase their leverage over landlords and smaller competitors.

Fertilizer sales provided urban merchants an additional avenue for credit extensions. As expanding cotton acreage created a rising demand for fertilizers, landlords lost another marketing domain that had once been exclusively theirs. Beset on the one side by the urban manufacture of a product they had previously controlled (cottonseed cakes) and on the other by imported substitutes (e.g., soybean cakes), landlords were rather quickly shoved out of the picture by urban merchant firms. By the first decade of the century, during the planting–early growing season, merchant boats selling fertilizer continuously plied the canals and streams of Nantong's cotton districts (Zhang Renren 1915–16, 2.4: 21).[2]

The merchants regularly sold the fertilizer on credit, requiring repayment at harvest and frequently in cotton rather than cash, at a price determined at the time of the loan. A similar situation prevailed in the industrial districts where merchants advanced machine-spun yarn on credit at exorbitant interest (Zhan Ran 1934: 25; Yan Zhongping 1963: 266–67). As Philip Huang notes, agricultural "modernization" of this kind thus came at the cost of new forms of merchant extraction, usually at usurious rates. Sustained by poor peasants increasingly drawn into a cash economy and forced "to borrow at a price that no profit-oriented enterprise would pay" (P. Huang 1990: 133), this brand of modernity deepened the cleavage between landlordism and merchant capital already embedded in the trajectory of the Ming-Qing period and, simultaneously, served to regear the rural economy to the needs of the urban-based system.

The developments in trade-usury capital operations can perhaps best be explained as an emerging strategy of interlocked modes of surplus appropriation by a merchant elite searching for ways to maximize its profit options while competing with landlords and smaller merchants for cotton supplies. As pawnshops increasingly fell under merchant control and the new forms of extraction appeared, this strategy effectively enlarged the merchants' "exploitation space," enabling them to extend appropriation to different activities over time, or sometimes to widen it to include various members of the peasant family.

In examining market mechanisms in China, neoclassical economists, whose analyses are usually fashioned to fit formulaic notions of fully competitive markets or market "imperfections," have generally failed to consider the implications of such interlinked modes. Their really significant impact lay in creating a situation in which peasants faced a shrinkage in their choices, since entry into any one market reduced their options in others (Srivastava 1989: 498). In such situations, as scholarship for other Third World areas shows, it makes little sense to and indeed we cannot infer, as capitalist economic theory does, that the choices of peasants were profit-maximizing, efficient choices made by free decision makers (Bharadwaj 1979: 280; 1985).

On one level, of course, the growth of urban-based trade and usury capital in new interlinked forms acted as a counterbalance to increasing rents and deposits, at once sustaining existing production relations and enabling poor families to continue to exist on the land. Simultaneously, however, in limiting peasants' choices and fostering perpetual indebtedness among them, the regressive dynamics of the new strategy contributed to longer-term peasant marginalization and gave merchants greater control over rural production.

Qiao Qiming's comparative statistics for Nantong and two areas where commercialization was less pronounced, Kunshan in southern Jiangsu and Suxian in Anhui, suggest the impact of these trends by the 1920's. As might be expected, in the areas of lower commercialization, most peasants continued to borrow from landlords. But in Nantong most peasants borrowed from those whom Qiao termed "rich men." This was particularly true of the 64.4 percent of cultivators he classifies as tenants, only 3.3 percent of whom borrowed from landlords (1926: 9, 49, 53).

Qiao's findings clearly suggest the effects of growing merchant dominance over the usury market in the first decades of the century. The tendency toward borrowing from nonlandlord sources also highlights the fact that by the 1920's, in addition to merchants, "semilandlord-like rich peasants" had become an important source of usurious loans, especially to tenants (Shen Shike 1934: 31004; Zhan Ran 1934: 25). We will return to this matter later. For now, the issue is the extent to which the concentration of the benefits of growth in the hands of urban mercantile forces disadvantaged and weakened rural landlordism.

To compound the problem, taxes increased significantly between the late Qing and the 1930's, a development that affected peasant landowners as well as landlords and was only partially offset before 1926 by generally rising agricultural prices. Jiangsu was required to bear the heaviest provincial burden for payment of the Boxer indemnity (2.5 million taels a year) after 1901. But in Nantong-Haimen-Qidong the land tax did not pose a particularly onerous burden since, for a sizable portion of the land, the starting point was the much reduced rate levied on "reed" or "marsh land" (Huang Xiaoxian 1927: 478; Y.-T. Wong 1977: 323; Zhang Renren 1915–16, 2.4). Moreover, in the early Republican years the land tax actually decreased. This reduction, however, was more than offset over the next two decades by spiraling increases in supplementary taxes, both those levied officially and those imposed by self-governing elites. As many scholars have noted, the period of greatest increase came after 1927, with Jiang Jieshi's (Chiang Kai-shek's) seizure of power and imposition of a militarist-bureaucratic state. In Nantong in the first five years of Jiang's rule, the land tax alone rose 64 percent (from 20.176 yuan in 1927 to 33.074 yuan by 1932). Added surcharges and levies by the county government accounted for the bulk of this increase (Sun Xiaocun 1935: 38).[3] In Haimen by 1933, the supplementary taxes were 25 times the regular tax (Shen Shike 1934: 30898–30899).

In the longer run, then, as much as the pull of the developing cotton market, the landlords' relative decline in economic position in the first decade of the twentieth century, coupled with the changing sociopolitical situation, pushed them—in defensive reaction—to develop new strategies. We will examine the economic strategy they finally fastened on in Chapter Eight. At this point they took what seemed to be the best and easiest option: to pass new tax levies on to tenants by raising rents. Their ability to actually collect these rents was, however, quite another matter. For one thing, routine rent resistance, especially the refusal to pay nominal rents, had intensified in the post-Taiping decades (Bernhardt 1992; Liu 1980; Takahashi 1978a). Moreover, by the end of the century, this intertwined with an aggressive new movement among peasants that reconfigured older resistance patterns and placed new stresses and strains on landlordism.

New Trends in Peasant Struggle

Throughout the Yangzi delta and in various parts of the country, peasant collective action steadily mounted in the waning imperial period, reaching a crescendo in the years immediately before and following the 1911 revolution. Interpenetrating with the multiple economic and sociopolitical changes of the period, this escalating struggle powerfully influenced not only the position and actions of landlords, but the entire character of the new order as well.

Moving beyond the standard constructions and dichotomies of modernist China scholarship,[4] new lines of inquiry in recent decades have provided more finely textured and historically contingent analyses of early-twentieth-century peasant struggles. Joseph Esherick's pioneering study of the urban elite in Hunan and Hubei (1976) demonstrates that, in attacking symbols of modernity and resisting the imposition of taxes designed to pay for Westernizing projects, peasants showed a clear perception of the connections between the foreign presence and the discourse and practices of modernity as part of a mode of power developed by and benefiting a new breed of elite. Kathyrn Bernhardt's detailed examination of rent and tax resistance in the southern Yangzi delta (1992) shows that the state, as well as landlords, became the focus of the new wave of peasant struggles in the late Qing. She demonstrates that this focus directly reflected the state's growing intervention in the collection and setting of rents, a development that, in turn, represented the state-landlord response to routine rent resistance.

Yet despite the importance of their contributions, in these and other works, peasants' struggles continue to appear as isolated, separate, and parochial phenomena. Stemming in part from their different analytical focuses, these studies consistently overlook the degree to which the struggles were organically connected.

Part and parcel of the new conditions imposed by semicolonialism and the modern-agrarian-state elite, in the Yangzi delta the struggles of the late Qing-early Republican movement became arenas for the reformulation of the older peasant path and regional political culture as a new collective project. To be sure, older issues of the agrarian class struggle remained central. But in the northern delta and other areas where a restructuring of the labor process was under way, the majority of peasants rejected and sought to short-circuit the roles that were being assigned to them and their reconstitution as a disadvantaged, partially wage-based subproletarian class. On the other hand, as touched on earlier, laborers, poor tenant-workers, middle peasants, and the dispossessed were not the only actors in the northern delta case. Rich peasants and a new group of small semilandlords participated in and indeed sometimes led the protests. The involvement of rich peasants and semilandlords, whose interests diverged in many ways from those of poorer peasants, immediately raises questions about their reasons for joining the movement.

Mao Zedong, in his 1930 investigation of Xunwu in southern Jiangxi, found that only "old rich" small landlords who were experiencing marked economic decline actively supported the "revolutionary culture of the People's Rights Movement," and that the "new rich," who "inclined in a capitalist direction" and formed a "half-landlord-like rich peasant class," were staunchly counterrevolutionary (1990: 152–56).

Did the same sort of economic divisions underlie the semilandlord–rich peasants' participation in the early-twentieth-century movement? The evidence for Nantong and the northern delta suggests that they did not. First of all the movement was not explicitly social revolutionary as in Jiangxi, and thus left an opening for cross-class alliances. More important, economic trends in the late nineteenth century, especially the developing linkages to the world cotton market, favored rich peasants, middle peasant owners, and permanent tenants with fixed rents. To the extent that tenants and part-owners successfully resisted rising rents and deposits, initially they also stood to benefit.

In fact in stark contrast to the trends Mao noted in Xunwu in the 1930's, the northern delta evidence pinpoints *rising* fortunes as the general condition of the semilandlords and rich peasants who supported the late Qing peasant movement. Shen Shike's investigation of Haimen-Qidong, for example, indi-

TABLE 7.1
Semilandlords as a Percent of All Cultivator Groups in Selected
Districts of Haimen and Qidong, ca. 1882–1923

Area	1882–83	1902–3	1922–23
Haimen			
District 6	3.7%	12.5%	14.1%
District 8	1.0	15.1	12.2
District 9	1.7	14.0	9.2
Qidong			
District 1	1.2	12.1	10.2
District 2	1.4	5.5	6.9

SOURCE: Shen Shike 1934: 30855.
NOTE: Spans of time are approximate and districts shown do not necessarily represent the only areas of semilandlord development in Haimen-Qidong.

cates that it was precisely with the growth of the textile and cotton trade in the 1880's and 1890's that semilandlords, who "seized the opportunity to buy more land," appeared as a significant new social group (1934: 30855, 30858–30859). By his definition a semilandlord was a peasant who owned 80 to 120 mu (the range that his local informants identified as typical of small land-lords in the northern delta) and who worked part of his land with additional labor while letting out the remainder. Shen found the phenomenon most pronounced in Haimen's sixth, eighth, and ninth districts and in the first and second districts of Qidong, where the best cotton was grown and cotton farming was most commercialized. As Table 7.1 shows, this development peaked in most of these districts in the early years of the twentieth century. By then, according to Shen, the number of owner-cultivators and part-owners had also markedly increased, whereas larger landlords and tenants had declined.

Shen does not identify the causes of the landlords' decline. Their conflict with the yamen in this period, ending in the rejection of their claims to un-registered *waisha* land in Haimen, may have contributed to the trend (Faure 1989: 190–91). In the absence of any other unusual or extenuating circum-stances, even if Shen's data are inflated, his survey still lends support to the view that the changing economic situation simultaneously disadvantaged landlords and benefited the social classes mentioned above. His description of upward mobility by tenants and small owners presupposes, of course, that these groups were already in a sufficiently favorable economic position to be able to purchase land when it became available.

Broad comparative data reinforce this picture. Seeking, like Thomas Raw-ski (1989), to make a case for economic development, Loren Brandt (1989) argues for the growth of marketed agricultural surplus in the pre–World War Two years. He attempts to explain this growth by demonstrating improv-ing terms of trade for peasants. In fact, however, the terms of trade index of agricultural commodities for products purchased by peasants he constructs shows major improvements only for 1878-1908, with peaks and troughs thereafter, that is, no perceptible trend. Thomas Wiens, noting that Brandt's data are roughly consistent with John Buck's 1907-21 statistics for North and South China, argues that, despite Brandt's intention both he and Buck in fact show that "all of the improvement in the terms of trade occurred before around 1908, and thereafter they did not improve" (1992: 71-72). These findings support our view of improving conditions for semilandlords and rich peasants in particular near the end of the nineteenth and the beginning of the twentieth century. They also resonate with the evidence, as developed in the next two chapters, of deteriorating conditions for the majority of peasants in the succeeding years, especially in the 1911-30 period.

The accumulated evidence unambiguously indicates that the pattern in the northern delta was of the type usually associated with what Maureen Mackintosh (1990) describes as the "normal workings of the market." That is to say, in the 1880's and 1890's new growth trends enabled various peasant strata to benefit. This initial spurt was paralleled, however, by tendencies toward differentiation that, though undoubtedly already present, accelerated under the new stimuli. Consequently, within a short time, even though the opportunities for accumulation were heightened for some peasants, for many others insecurity and economic decline increased.

On the other hand, it was precisely rich peasants and semilandlords, the two rural groups that benefited above all, who were most directly affected by the modern elite's increasing exaction of commercial and supplementary taxes. Take Lin Men, a co-leader in the Pingchao Rebellion of 1912 (to which we will return in due course), for example. In 1912 he reportedly owned 141 mu of land, rented another 48 mu, operated a grain mill, and possessed a large herd of cattle. In the eyes of poorer peasants, these attributes qualified Lin as a "rich man," but they also made him subject to a vast array of commercial taxes and new levies attached to the land tax (Qian Min 1986: 11, 23; Chao Yingbin & Lin Jibe 1981: 127). Since he, like many other rich peasants, was a tenant as well as a landowner, his interests clearly lay in a combined tax and rent resistance struggle.

Thus to return to our original query, it seems clear that the defense of recent gains, not a decline in fortunes, is what prompted the conspicuous activism of a new economic class whose mode of agricultural production was inherently as antagonistic to poorer peasants as it was to landlords. The participation of rich peasants and small, managerial semilandlords in the escalating peasant movement was really about having the freedom and opportunity to continue, unobstructed, on their developmental path.

In sum, despite the inherent contradictions between what might be called a capitalist-like and a communal-egalitarian line, shared opposition to semicolonialism in its multiple modernist expressions formed the basis for the multiclassed village coalitions of the early-twentieth-century peasant movement. Under the banner of and from within this developing political community, different groups advanced their particular class interests. At the same time the movement's multiclass solidarities furthered the conditions already created by changes in the structure of power favoring the joining and reconfiguration of the ideologies of rent and tax resistance. Thus along with economic issues, albeit in immediate local context, the movement contested and vehemently opposed the blurring of official and private power that became a prominent feature of the semicolonial Qing state, and that for both the modern and the landlord elite served as a vehicle for new forms of extraction, coercion, and surveillance. And when, under the imperializing rubric of modernist civilization, the state-elite launched an attack on indigenous cultural forms, the protection of popular culture likewise became an issue of struggle.

To the extent, then, that through its struggles the increasingly radicalized discourses of the late Qing–early Republican movement came to revolve around the issue of the reappropriation of society from an "illegitimate," heterogeneous ruling elite, its antidevelopmentalist critique became the voice of a more distinct, alternative nationalism. By 1911–12 both the meaning of the nation and the form it should take surfaced as key issues in a movement that was triggered initially by the immediate economic, sociocultural, and political issues of the agrarian class struggle. In remarkably similar fashion to the 20-year *campesino* movement in Nicaragua leading up to the Sandinista revolution (Gould 1990), the early-twentieth-century movement thus reconfigured an older line of peasant politics in more radical, cultural form.

Aspects of the 1900–1912 Peasant Movement

To the extent that the early-twentieth-century peasant movement entailed an explicit rejection of semicolonial modernity in its interwoven state and class forms, its two predominant motifs—the struggle against the modern urban elite and the struggle against the state-agrarian elite—often interconnected and overlapped. Collective actions of the first type arose in direct response to economic restructuring, to the expanding range of commercial taxes placed on producers and petty traders, and to elite-directed projects associated with local self-government initiatives.

Throughout the delta these struggles assumed a decidedly anti-Western character, usually attacking, along with their primary targets, new schools, self-government offices, and the homes of the modern elite (Chen Xulu 1955: 63–65). In large collective actions such as the Songjiang rising of March 1911, for example, peasants destroyed no fewer than 12 self-government offices (*zizhi gongsuo*) and 21 elementary schools (Yangzhou shifan xueyuan 1963: 335–36).

Risings and insurgencies of this variety have often been identified as tax struggles. To be sure, anger over taxes, and especially those levied by the tax-farming merchant elite for modern projects, often sparked or played a part in them. But classifying them as merely tax struggles obscures the complex mixture of grievances and the alternative visions usually contained within them.

A 1905 rising in Nantong illustrates the point. In this rising some 500 to 600 peasants (probably all men) from weaving families living nearby marched into Jinsha town to voice their outrage at a new tax on cloth woven from homespun yarn. Things took an ugly turn as they made Gao Liqing, the merchant-owner of a wood and yarn store, a member of the Dasheng staff, and the person responsible for collecting the cloth tax in Jinsha, their central target. They destroyed Gao's store, dumped his stocks of Dasheng yarn in the adjacent river, and then set fire to the private elementary school Gao had founded and to another Western-style primary school in the southern part of the town (Jin Zhihuai 1984: 3–4).

The combination of targets is symptomatic of the times. On the one hand, the peasants were reacting in the main to their declining position in the new textile order. As members of weaving families in one of Nantong's oldest producing districts, where small cloth made with homespun yarn remained the chief product, they were competitively disadvantaged by the growing prevalence of *guanzhuang* cloth and the monopolistic practices of the Dasheng-centered system. The new tax on their product disadvantaged them even more; hence their destruction of the yarn. On the other hand, the burning of the schools well demonstrates the growing hostility in popular consciousness to the new breed of modern elite and, by extension, to both the physical representations of their Western-oriented semicolonial path and the new tax impositions underwriting it. In popular lore the Jinsha rising quickly became known as the "Burning the Foreign School Rising" (Jin Zhihuai 1984: 4).

As the new popular "common sense" took firmer root, multifaceted protests of this sort grew in frequency, scope, and, often, size. Social order became increasingly unstable, so that "uprisings were likely to break out at the slightest agitation, no matter what the slogan of the agitator" (Ichiko 1968: 312). Attempting to stem this tide, frightened elites and officials expanded defense units, chamber of commerce militia, police, and other coercive forces. By 1911, however, they were clearly losing control. In Jiangsu throughout the year, exacerbated by flooding along the Yangzi, food riots, rent-tax struggles, and broad-based insurgencies surfaced, the last becoming larger and more radical after the revolution.

In Haimen and Nantong in the months immediately after the revolution, the control of the countryside by the new elite-led temporary military governments was tenuous at best. The Haimen government, for example, had only enough armed strength to quell the rising at Maojia town. Although this was but one of many risings in the county, officials could not call on the larger and better equipped Nantong forces for support, since many insurgencies were also breaking out there.

Details of one of the small insurgencies that took place in 1911 in Haimen immediately after the establishment of the Republican military government give us another glimpse of the issues involved in the risings of the time. Led by a rich peasant or small semilandlord named Du Jialu, several hundred peasants from around Chuanggang destroyed new schools and the homes of at least a dozen prominent merchants and gentry known to be education advocates. Official reports claimed that the aim of this "anti-Western" rising was to prevent the building of new schools, protect the Qing, and get rid of foreigners. They also indicated that there were at least two class-based constituencies among the insurgents: first, "the rebels," apparently landowners whose "real objective in rebelling . . . was to take advantage of the people's anger" to "attack the education advocates and refuse to raise funds to build schools"; and second, the "common folk," poor peasants and tenants "who joined the rebels because of their objection to cutting their pigtails and personal grievances." But as the writers then went on to intimate, the real source of popular anger was the modern elite's takeover of temples and temple lands in the Chuanggang area for the new schools, or what the peasants called "grabbing land from the people" (Guan Jincheng 1981: 167–68).

What was really at stake, then, was a process in which, as part of the drive for modernist power, private-cum-official self-government elites blatantly commandeered institutions and property commonly regarded as belonging to the "public" or "people's" domain. As public terrain, temples not only formed spiritual and social centers, but were key points in the invisible linkages of heterodoxical religious sects that continued to play an important role in popular political mobilization. From 1908, on the Qing government's instruction, modern elites and their allies increasingly converted temples and their lands into self-government offices and schools. The process was extended under the Republican state, to the point that all the temple land in some counties became the property of elite-run "public associations" (gonghui; Duara 1988: 150). These associations not only took over as managers of the temples' rental lands but often imposed harsh new tenure agreements.

Although records of the Haimen insurgency do not indicate if tenure contracts were an issue, in some temple risings they clearly played a pivotal role. Another so-called "anti-Western" rising, in Chuansha in 1911, for example, revolved in part around harsh new rents introduced by local elites after they took temple lands for the support of a new school.[5] Poorer tenants were particularly hard hit by the new requirement to pay a full year's rent in advance (Faure 1989: 190–91).[6]

Thus in the Haimen, Chuansha, and many other protests the ideologies of rent and tax resistance often fused and reconfigured in new ways. That is to say, the issue was not alone rising rents and taxes, but also the uses to which they were being put. The surfacing and immediacy of what were at heart issues of semicolonial-modernist power necessarily forced peasant activists to debate, rethink, and redefine older notions of the nation, community, and cultural autonomy.

These reformulations were also embedded in struggles against landlords and the state. In the last decades of Qing rule, the state's expanding involvement in rent collection made it eminently clear to peasants where official sentiments lay. Economically squeezed by staggering debts to the imperialist powers and landlords' reluctance to pay taxes in the face of routine rent resistance, the Qing state threw its organized power behind the landlord class.

First in Suzhou—the stronghold of landlord-gentry influence in the southern delta—as part of the post-Taiping reorganization, and by the turn of the century in other areas as well, the Qing government authorized the establishment of rent dunning bureaus (*zhuizuju*) that also served as tenant debtor prisons, and it granted greater quasiofficial powers to landlords to deal with rent resistance. Signaling unprecedented state support for an increasingly challenged landlord rule, the first measure separated the prosecution of defaulting tenants from the regular judicial system, thereby enabling landlords to dispense with costly litigation and bypass the courts entirely. By authorizing them to submit arrest warrants directly to the bureaus, the second measure even made it unnecessary for landlords to file formal complaints at the yamen (Bernhardt 1992: 145–47; Takahashi Kosuke 1978a). The new measures thus at once made the state's coercive forces more readily available to landlords and further blurred official and private power. At the same time, however, trying to neutralize mounting peasant discontent, the government cautiously assumed a new role in setting rent ceilings, a trend that briefly reappeared in the late 1920's during the momentary ascendancy of the left-Guomindang.

Precisely because of the state's expanding role as an enforcer and arbiter of rents, its officials and dunning bureaus emerged alongside landlords (and the new rent collection agencies they were establishing) as the targets of peasants' rent struggles. In these struggles peasants not only came to grasp how the practices of the landlord and official elites impacted them; they turned those very practices against their adversaries. In a totally unprecedented development, for example, they appropriated the grounds on which landlords had always argued for tax relief. Seizing on the practice of "reporting a poor harvest" (*baohuang*), peasants began collectively requesting that government officials inspect their fields in years of low yield to set an appropriate reduction. Behind this new tactic lay the threat that they might turn the peaceful action into its more violent counterpart (*naohuang*) if a reduction was denied (Bernhardt 1992: 193). The effect of this maneuver when it succeeded, as it often did, was to force a policy of appeasement through which the state and landlords regularly agreed to rent reductions. It also encouraged collectivities to form to press for tax as well as rent reduction. Consequently struggles against the agrarian elite surfaced as another arena for the development of multiclass solidarities. Other new practices, especially tenants' assumption of taxes in return for permanent tenures with low fixed rents, extended the material basis for the joining of tax and rent struggles (Kojima 1973).

Finally, a variety of new organizational forms at once underlay and became expressions of the developing insurgent politics of the movement. Though still heavily flavored by religious elements—in the northern delta, for example, apparently in reaction to the increased use of modern weaponry by state-elite forces, new invincibility rituals similar to those practiced by the Boxers and Red Spears in North China became part of local political culture[7]— these groups were predominantly secular, were frequently multiclassed, and tended to be explicitly political. As such, they intersected with and extended the politics of older secret societies such as the Big Swords (Dadaohui).[8]

In what was one of the most important subaltern developments in the period and a trend that started well before the mobilization of antipeasant forces after 1911, associations of this type spread among the peasantry from 1900 on, taking such names as the One Dime Society (Yijiaohui), the Thousand Person Society (Qianrenhui), and the Tenant Society (Dianhuhui) of [X] village or district (Bernhardt 1992: 194). Some of these new groups may have been forced into being by the vacuum created by the expropriation of temples by the elite, but most were far from being mere replacements for the temple societies that had historically formed part of the organizational field for rent struggles. The aims were now more explicitly political and pursued through an integration of peasant and proletarian techniques. This integration became evident, especially, in rent and tax strikes that sometimes extended over a county-wide area. Although these groups usually received official-public notice only in moments of collective action, thus creating the impression that they were temporary and ephemeral, several were in fact enduring, operating secretly over time on both sides of the Yangzi. In some instances as well, they became the organizational heart of mass campaigns around specific issues.

The One Mind Society (Qixinhui), for example, initially served as the principal organizational network for the large-scale multiclass Pingchao Rebellion in Nantong (1912), which began as a protest against a new dike tax proposed by Zhang Jian and other members of the modern elite. In organizing the rising, the five chief leaders specifically decided to make use of the Beishan temple (mentioned in Chapter Three) and the One Mind Society to mobilize peasants into a broader organization, the Public Security Society (Baoanhui), which they conceived and formed in direct opposition to the Dike Protection Society (Baotanhui) of the elite (Qian Min 1986: 10–12).[9]

The One Mind Society surfaced again in 1917, when it served as the organizational base for a large rent resistance action that engulfed most of Jinshan in the southern delta (Bernhardt 1992: 195–96).

In sum, although the political associations that appeared during the 1900–1912 movement usually took a localist form, they supplied a key organizational grid for the development of a new regional political discourse among peasants. During more than ten years of semicolonial struggles through which that evolving discourse took shape, peasants, like members of the elite, traversed the long political distance from tacit acceptance of the state to notions of their own independent domain. By 1911–12, in refusing to give their consent to a version of modernity and governance that stripped away gains of those who were rising, compounded the suffering of the many who were disadvantaged, and gave no peasant a public voice, they were at once struggling for cultural autonomy and advancing an alternative nationalist discourse, the demands of which (to borrow from Gramsci) if not organically formulated nevertheless added up to a revolution.[10]

At the end of the Ming, bondservants, serfs, servile tenants, and subaltern laborers in the Yangzi delta justified their actions by proclaiming that the state had fallen, so they were free. In 1911, when the Qing collapsed, signifying another moment of political change, delta peasants defiantly declared that since the dynasty was gone, land no longer belonged to the original owners (Y.-T. Wong 1977: 336). Shortly thereafter, when they saw that the members of the new elite—who were not, in their eyes, rulers at all but merely illegitimate "grabbers of the people's land"—aimed to establish a repressive, more extractive state, peasants took another ideological step.

In the Pingchao Rebellion of 1912 in Nantong, what began as a "tax protest" quickly came to involve thousands of peasants who, constituting themselves as a Nation and fashioning their own military command, declared their independence from the new Republican state. The rebel Nation lasted for over a month before, as we shall discuss further below, it was bloodily conquered. In the southern delta in 1911, the Thousand Person Uprising in Changshu-Wuxi-Jiangyin had likewise generated a declaration of independence and the establishment of an autonomous domain (Qian Min 1986; Yangzhou shifan xueyuan 1963: 163–65). Marking the culmination of more than a decade of continuous struggle in the delta, these rebellions stood as penultimate transformations of elite practice, clear rejections of the legitimacy of the elite-led military governments of the Republic, and logical outcomes of the reformulation under new conditions of an older peasant path in more distinct alternative nationalist terms. Thus in the semicolonial moment, viewed in light of the development of a radical politics among peasants, arguably, both the conditions and the prerequisites for the Communist revolution deepened.

The Urban-Rural Elite Alliance

The crisis produced by mounting peasant insurgency in the first decade of the century and the spread of rural rebellion once the Qing collapsed had the effect of dissolving differences between the modern elite and the more conservative landlord-gentry. Abandoning their past positions and in essence establishing a new coalition, in an abrupt about-face they quickly came over to the side of the revolution. As we earlier noted in our discussion of Zhang Jian, they did so with clarity of focus and purpose: to control and purge both the revolution and the peasantry of their more radical social impulses. Their support and financial backing were essential to the success of the revolutionary project since the revolutionaries only dimly grasped the significance of the agrarian question—and by extension the possibility of mass peasant involvement. In fact, then, by acting as a stimulus for the conversion of the elite, peasant action as much as the machinations of revolutionaries produced the 1911 revolution.

Following the events of 1911, the relation of political forces became all-important and involved two key aspects: first, the reassertion of elite control over the countryside to smother the peasants' move toward autonomy; and second, the practical working out of a suitable equilibrium within the urban elite-landlord alliance, but in a way that still placed the modern urban elite in a directing position. The acquiescence of the revolutionaries to the modern elite's assumption of power was not a particularly serious problem since, most often, the group's leadership of the new military governments was the understood condition for its participation: hence, immediately upon his joining of the revolution, in December 1911, Zhang Jian's designation as commander of the temporary military government of Tongzhou.

Concerning the first relational question, that is, the peasant problem, throughout the delta and beyond after the urban elite and their conservative allies seized power, and once they amassed sufficient armed strength, a pattern of unequivocal repression and reprisal emerged. During the last decade of the Qing, the framework of the state had placed constraints on the elite's ability to suppress the rising tide of peasant action. Once the dynasty was overthrown and the local modern elites became the State in their own areas, these constraints disappeared. Using all available force, they moved to suffocate the insurgent fire. This crackdown brought into full view the new levels of violence and brutality forming the underside of the modernist-semicolonized path.

The repression and massacre of peasants who took part in the multiple risings in Nantong-Haimen in 1911–12 clearly illustrate this trend. Under the general authority of Zhang Jian, as head of the military government, and Zhang Cha, who assumed leadership of the antipeasant garrison and bureau of civil affairs, the Republican-revolutionary forces set out on a campaign of terror, property destruction, and mass shootings. The Pingchao rebels were an immediate target. The official troops no sooner penetrated territory of the rebel Nation, according to one eyewitness account, than they "shot everyone they saw and burned house after house" until entire villages had been razed. In four core villages of rebel strength, taking reprisal to an unprecedented level in the Nantong area, they burned down at least 360 homes (Fei Fanjiu 1986: 8; Qian Min 1986: 18–23; Guan Jincheng 1991).

Pacification in the southern delta was pursued with similar intensity. In places where tenants rejected both the legitimacy of the Republican state and the legitimacy of landlords' rights to the land in the new situation, the Republican rulers were even more heavyhanded than their Qing predecessors in dealing with rent resistance. On the order of Governor Cheng Dequan, for example, four Suzhou tenants were brought before a firing squad for the simple offense of refusing to pay their rent (Y.-T. Wong 1977: 336). In this manner the military forces of the new state squelched the insurrectionary momentum—although in some parts of Jiangsu it took several years to do so—and reestablished the semblance of control. Yet if expedient, and temporarily successful, this solution to the peasant problem could not cure the deepening rift between peasant political culture and ruling ideologies. On the contrary, the momentary equilibrium achieved through terror, force, and the steadfast refusal of new ruling blocs to incorporate any aspect of popular political discourse into their agendas only added, in the longer run, to the homogeneity of peasants as a permanently organized force in opposition, that is, as one among whom it became almost impossible to reconstruct a hegemonic apparatus.

Consequently, in the northern delta, as in many other localities, coercive force became more deeply implanted as a permanent attribute and requirement of the new mode of modern power. Although it has rarely been analyzed as such, the modern elite had a hidden military character from the outset, something that became more and more pronounced as it added to the forces directly at its disposal, including most notably the industrial police guard, the "defense" guard of the new city police, the rural rent dunning agencies, and the self-government "protection" units in the reclaimed land areas, backed up by growing numbers of rural militia and, of course, the regular garrisons. If the elite now had to confront an insurgent population, in part that was because this indirect mode of military-bureaucratic rule had escalated the level of violence in class politics and in local society as a whole. As such it duplicated and added to the overdevelopment of similar tendencies at higher levels.

On the other hand, the working out of an equilibrium between the modern and conservative landlord elite came to involve above all a sharing of political space, expressed through landlord-gentry support for the modernizing path and self-government initiatives. This trend had begun to appear in the pre-1911 years, especially after 1908, when the state abolished the examination system. It accelerated after the demise of the Qing. At the same time, precisely because of the volatile agrarian situation, there was a pressing need in the new self-government administrations for landlords to function politically to repress and oppose peasants' attempts to ameliorate their existence (Fei Fanjiu 1986; Gramsci 1971; Qian Min 1986; Zhang Renren 1915–16; Zhu Mingxia & Bian Xiaozhi 1986).

Thus their overnight conversion to the modernist path did not mean that conservative landlords had fundamentally changed their outlook. On the contrary, as in joining the revolution, their principal goal was to "expand their influence" (Ichiko 1968) and "to grasp the power to lead" (Mao Zedong 1990: 149), if in ways that were largely being defined by the modern elite. Expanding activism also frequently provided conservative landlord-gentry with lucrative new possibilities; many seized the opportunity for example, to pocket revenues raised for public projects. In Nantong-Haimen maneuvers of this sort served to deepen the opposition of peasants to the ruling bloc and induced conservative rural elites who little more than a decade earlier had protested en masse against Zhang Jian's plans to establish Dasheng to become ardent advocates of self-government and elite initiative.

Developments connected with the Dike Protection Society in Nantong that culminated in the Pingchao Rebellion illustrate both points. During the last half century of Qing rule, in parts of western Tongzhou dikes and embankments along the Yangzi steadily deteriorated. Leakage and flooding increased in frequency. In 1907 Zhang Jian and other members of the modern elite founded the Dike Protection Society, which hired a Dutch engineering firm to survey southeastern Tongzhou, where the problem was most acute. In 1910, on the firm's recommendation, the county assembly approved the society's plan to levy a dike tax for the construction of new stone embankments in four southwestern ports. The work began in 1911, following a disastrous flood that demolished 30 dikes in Changshu, Jiangyin, and southwestern Tongzhou (Qian Min 1986: 10–11).

Meanwhile, attracted mainly by the prospect of dike tax collection as a new source of income, several landlord-gentry from Pingchao, located to the northwest of the dike construction areas near Nantong city, began vying for inclusion in the project. In 1912, at a meeting with Zhang Cha and others arranged through old family connections with members of the dike society, the Pingchao landlords—all of whom were former *baojia* trustees—were formally accepted into the organization. Subsequently, the society expanded its construction plans to include dikes at four locations in the Pingchao district. It also revised its guidelines for assessing the tax, setting a rate of four yuan

per mu on land that would directly benefit from the embankments (designated as within three li of the river) and two yuan on the land beyond. The
tax was to be split evenly between tenants and landlords and was payable for
20 years (Qian Min 1986: 11). These rates almost doubled the relatively moderate land tax established for the four southern areas and brought it to a level
that matched or exceeded the rents of many permanent tenants in the area
(Fei Fanjiu 1986: 5–6). For the landlords of the society, with their monopoly
on tax collection, the upped rates created, as one report put it, "a new life-
time rice-bowl" (ibid., p. 6). The imposition of the tax in Pingchao and the
dike society's subsequent refusal to rescind or reduce it ignited the Pingchao
Rebellion.

Special initiatives like the dike tax, and the heading and staffing of various self-government offices, thus formed vehicles for conservative landlord-
gentry to enter and claim space in the new field of power created by the semicolonial state and the modern elite. Their entry was nowhere more evident
than in their association with the push for modern schools. In the years after
1911, once a semblance of social control had been forcibly reestablished, they
entered this arena in full force as founders of schools and heads of education bureaus. Although no one has yet fully analyzed the socioeconomic and
political composition of these particular circles of reform, the main trends
are clear. Whereas in 1907, spearheaded by the modern elite, only 47 new-
style schools had been founded in Nantong, in 1919 the total number reached
207, with many of the newest dotting the landscape of outlying rural districts (Chauncey 1992: 62, 65–67). By that time, as well, education circles
themselves, rather than the yamen or other self-government agencies, were
directly collecting and managing educational taxes (ibid., p. 133).

In 1930 Mao Zedong found that the educational circles in Xunwu were
composed chiefly of conservative large and middle landlords who had
"jumped on the bandwagon" of Westernized education to gain power and
money (1990: 149).[11] There, possibly, as in Nantong, this leap coincided with
another significant development in the late teens: the return to the countryside of many large and middle-level landlords. This shift marked a new
offensive by landlords determined to extend their social control and claim
economic as well as sociopolitical space in the shifting and contingent urban-
oriented order. Their resumption of rural residence to directly manage and
orchestrate agricultural production brought the agrarian economy further in
line with the needs of urban-based capital and, thus, produced new developments in rural class relations and struggle.

8 Constituting 'Semicolonial Capitalisms': Modern Landlordism, Commercial Farming, and Rural Labor

FROM THE TEENS to the 1930's, the processes fostering changes in rural class relations accelerated and deepened. Viewed broadly, this acceleration was closely tied to developments we have already examined, namely, the disintegration of Zhang Jian's self-reliant system and the greater integration of the cotton economy into the commodity market structures controlled by local merchant and state-capitalist monopolists. It also intertwined with a change we have yet to examine, the blossoming of modern landlordism. Though the reconstitutions of class and changes in class relations of this period continued to underpin local modernist power, they also expressed precisely the maturing of the semicolonial economy. As such they denoted, in an economic sense, the further erosion of the boundaries separating the local and the global.

These socioeconomic changes in the countryside are the subject of this chapter and the next. Together the two chapters identify the development of commercial managerial farming among larger landlords, semilandlords, and rich peasants and the subproletarianization of the vast majority of peasants as key trends and concomitants of growing urban-based commercial power. Contradicting the *a priori* analyses of modernist scholarship, this chapter argues that, as a specific constitution of semicolonial modernity, these rural "capitalisms" did not foster the dissolution of older, "precapitalist" labor forms. On the contrary, to a significant degree, in the agriculturally specialized districts, they entailed the expansion of indentured and disguised wage labor, a development that contributed to the repeasantization and marginalization of peasant families.

The Issue of Managerial Farming

Research on North China spotlights the rise of managerial farming among medium-sized and large landlords as a significant socioeconomic development of the Qing period; and it emphasizes its expansion, especially among smaller landlords and rich peasants, in the late nineteenth and early twentieth centuries under the growing influence of the international capitalist market (P. Huang 1985; Jing Su & Luo Lun 1959). In contrast, students of the Yangzi delta have either automatically assumed that managerial farming was so unimportant that it did not warrant attention; or, more commonly, taken developments in the southern delta as characteristic of the region as a whole. The effect has been to narrowly analyze landlordism; to ignore signs of the development of managerial farming; or to explicitly argue against its existence based on assumptions about the situation in Jiangnan.

In his treatment of the delta, David Faure (1989), for instance, notes that during the teens many Nantong landlords evicted tenants so as to convert to managerial farming, but he does not go on to discuss this phenomenon. On the related question of rich peasant agriculture, he simply states that in the delta "the practice of managing sizeable estates of rented land by the employment of hired laborers seems to have been uncommon" (1989: 149). On the other hand, Philip Huang (1990) explicitly argues against the development of managerial landlordism in the delta, citing high labor costs as the principal deterrent.

While such images and assumptions may hold true for parts of Jiangnan, comparative statistical data make them problematical for the delta as a whole. John L. Buck's indexes show that full-time agricultural wage labor was actually *more pronounced* in the Yangzi rice-wheat region than in other areas: 18 percent of the farms in the Yangzi area hired workers by the year, as compared with the 17 percent average for China as a whole, and only 17.5 percent in the north (1937a: 291). More important for our consideration of the northern delta, notions of the nondevelopment of managerial farming simply will not do and must be radically revised. The survey data for Nantong-Haimen-Qidong unambiguously point to landlord and semilandlord–rich peasant managerial farming with wage labor as significant developmental trends in the first decades of the twentieth century (Huang Xiaoxian 1927; MMT 1941; JS [5] 1933; Qiao Qiming 1926; Shen Shike 1934; Zhang Renren 1915–16).

What actually happened in these areas was the continued development of the semilandlord–rich peasant class on the one hand; and on the other, the expansion of managerial farming among large and medium-sized landlords,[1] especially in Nantong, where many landlords gave up urban residence and returned to the countryside to supervise farming activity. These twin processes, as we will see, occurred in the context of declining opportunities for less advantaged small owners and tenants and contributed to the downward differentiation among them.

Semilandlord–Rich Peasant Agriculture

As noted in the last chapter, according to Shen Shike, a new social group of semilandlords, men who farmed part of their land with wage labor and rented out the remainder, first emerged within the upper layers of the peasantry in the last decades of the nineteenth century when the cotton trade began to expand. Shen goes on to track that line of development as the northern delta fell under the influence of Shanghai, the world market, and the Dasheng mills:

> Because . . . prices rose and harvests were good, there were many land mergers. The profits made by independent peasants helped them take land from those less fortunate and become semilandlords. But the unfortunate ones were reduced to tenants or part-owners. At the same time, new settlers swelled the ranks of the tenants, so that their number gradually increased while that of independent, owner-cultivators decreased. (1934: 30858–59)

What Shen suggests here, if only in broad strokes, is a kind of rural differentiation in which rich peasant agriculture and semilandlordism grew stronger. The corollary to this strengthening was the more pronounced delineation of a "poor peasant economy," accompanied by declining access to land for the majority of peasants. This process intersected with three related trends: the fragmentation of holdings, which has usually been attributed solely to population growth; the imposition of new, typically harsher rental forms; and the swelling of the outlaw population by "seasonal" peasant-bandits and the dispossessed, who from the late teens congregated in growing numbers along the Rugao-Nantong-Haimen periphery and, especially, in the unreclaimed portions of development company lands (Barkan 1983; Liu Daosong 1980; Shen Shike 1934; Yin Yuepu 1980).

These trends deepened during the 1920's. Permanent tenants working land owned by large absentee landlords from Chongming and other localities continued to predominate in the areas along the Yangzi, but semilandlord–rich peasant farming grew stronger in all districts. By 1927, as a field report of Haimen put it: "most small landlords are also farm managers . . . who not only hire field hands but participate in agricultural production. . . . Independent owners with more land [i.e., rich peasants] also hire 2–3 [full-time] laborers, male or female, to work for them" (Huang Xiaoxian 1927: 475). Shen Shike likewise found a wide use of hired labor among semilandlords and rich peasants (and among many medium-sized landlords as well; 1934: 30996). An investigation of rural Qidong made by the Rural Rehabilitation Committee in the early 1930's found a similar situation there. Its survey team noted the degree to which, under the influence of Nantong and the Dasheng mills, commodity production had assumed a "controlling influence in agriculture . . . and constituted a special feature of the area"; and it emphasized

TABLE 8.1
Agricultural Groups in Haimen and Qidong by District, ca. 1932
(Percent)

District	Semilandlords	Owner-cultivators	Owner-tenants	Tenants
Haimen				
1	11.5%	33.2%	27.0%	28.0%
2	10.1	29.4	26.2	34.3
3	9.3	25.4	23.1	42.1
4	10.3	31.9	27.8	30.1
5	12.4	29.3	28.1	30.2
6	12.6	27.7	32.4	34.3
7	12.5	18.8	33.3	36.4
8	12.6	11.2	34.1	42.1
9	7.1	33.6	18.1	41.2
10	6.3	35.8	15.1	42.8
Qidong				
1	8.2%	30.6%	18.1%	43.1%
2	7.1	29.2	23.6	40.1
3	6.3	24.1	19.6	50.1
4	2.0	22.1	21.7	54.1
5	4.0	25.1	12.5	58.4
6	9.2	30.1	19.1	41.6
7	3.0	27.1	9.5	60.4
8	3.0	24.1	8.7	64.2

SOURCE: Shen Shike 1934: 30853.

the extent to which, alongside tenancy and absentee ownership in the villages, the development of "rich peasant agriculture" based on comparatively large farms and both long- and short-term hired laborers formed a second distinguishing characteristic (JS [5] 1933: 3, 6).

Table 8.1 presents the composition of the agricultural population of Haimen and Qidong as Shen Shike found it in the early 1930's. It shows that in Haimen the greatest concentrations of semilandlordism occurred in the sixth, seventh, and eighth districts, where the best cotton was grown. Relatively lower percentages of owner-cultivators (the latter category presumably including rich peasants) and higher levels of owner-tenants and tenants, who together comprised roughly 66, 69, and 76 percent of the cultivators in these districts, paralleled semilandlord development. This table also indicates some decline in the total number of semilandlords from the teens to the 1930's (cf. Table 7.1), a trend to be expected as differentiation proceeded. It almost certainly marked the demise of weaker, more fragile members of this new social group as the terms of trade changed after 1910 and as the stronger members consolidated their positions and expanded their holdings. In a continuation of the earlier pattern, the Qidong data show relatively less development of semilandlordism and a higher percentage of owner-cultivators. This is also to be expected given the usually high concentration of landownership in Qidong by Chongming landlords and the particular strength of rich peasant farming noted in the Rural Rehabilitation Committee's survey.

That survey further refines this picture by designating rich peasants as a specific category. It found that in Qidong, although rich peasants constituted only 7.2 percent of the population, they owned 22.5 percent of the land. Moreover, owned land accounted for only 64.2 percent of the total land that rich peasants actually managed; they rented the other 35.8 percent from landlords. Those who were full tenants (i.e., 19 percent of all rich peasants, as against just 4 percent of owner-tenants) held most of the rented land. The result of this pronounced development of rich peasant farming and land concentration among landlords was that together the two groups controlled fully 90 percent of the land (JS [5] 1933: 11–14, 41–43, 51–52).

Thus in the teens and 1920's, as Haimen and Qidong became more fully constituted cotton peripheries of local and international capital, a relatively small number of semilandlords and rich peasants gained control of a substantial portion of the land. Built up on the basis of "many land mergers" that effectively reduced the land available to the majority of peasants, the growth and consolidation of these "semicolonial capitalisms" exacerbated the already existing situation of declining opportunities for less advantaged small owners and tenants and contributed to downward trends among them.

Reconstituting Landlordism in Modern Form: Nantong

In Nantong, paralleling and in certain respects overshadowing the expansion of rich peasant–semilandlord agriculture, another significant new trend appeared: a turn to commercial farming by large and medium landlords, many of whom left Nantong city and smaller towns to take up residence in the countryside. Although a key development in its own right, the turn to managerial farming was part of a broader economic offensive among landlords that, after 1911, also involved the introduction of new labor forms and controls on labor, the imposition of new tenurial arrangements with harsher terms for tenants, an attack on tenants' topsoil ownership rights, and an unprecedented mobilization, achieved organizationally through the creation of landowner associations, the expansion of rent collection bursaries, and other new associational forms.[2]

Both the conditions underpinning this offensive and the class-based mobilization that fueled and reflected it bring to mind Gramsci's observation that social groupings constitute themselves as associations in order to influence the situation at moments that are historically vital for their class (1971: 211). By the 1910's the semicolonial process had resulted in such a moment for the northern delta landlords. As we have seen, they were weakened economically by merchant capital's growing power in the countryside, challenged sociopolitically by the modern urban elite's drive for hegemony, and threatened fundamentally in both respects by peasants' mounting insurgencies and endemic rent resistance. Through their launching of what was effectively a "historically vital" offensive and an economic counterpart to their overnight conversion to the modernist path in 1911, the older wielders of conservative local power thus moved to recoup some of their social and economic dominance. In the process they reconstituted themselves as modern landlords.

Studies in world history pinpoint the pivotal role of landed classes in key moments of agrarian change. They also show that a common thread in Third World developmental patterns has been the tendency of landed ruling classes to seek to maintain their dominance by resisting any significant alteration in the social structure, while nevertheless adapting economically to changing conditions generated by imperialist, colonialist, and neocolonialist market forces (see, for example, Moore 1966; and Byres 1991). In key respects the turn to managerial farming among Nantong's landlords typifies this pattern. Framed by rising prices and escalating competition in the cotton trade, it became the front line of the new offensive. It was a clearly accelerating trend in the teens and early 1920's, when according to Qiao Qiming, "many landlords returned to the countryside to take up farming" (1926: 44). It enabled landlords, or at least those who were in a position to evict tenants and take over land management themselves, to reassert control over cotton supplies and trading activities previously eroded by money rents and, increasingly, merchants' usurious operations.

Although we do not have statistics on the number of landlords who actually returned to the countryside, Qiao's findings on the percentage of resident landlords are suggestive (see Table 8.2).[3] The usual assumption among China scholars is that by the Republican period most large and medium landlords in the Yangzi delta had taken up permanent urban residence, leaving only smaller landlords in the countryside. But Qiao found that in 1924 the vast majority of Nantong landlords—84.2 percent—were rural residents, as compared with 34.1 percent for Kunshan (1926: 42). Moreover, as can be seen in Table 8.2, proportionally far more large and medium landlords lived in the countryside than small landlords. In this respect Nantong stood in direct contrast to Kunshan (and so far as large landlords are concerned, even bore some resemblance to Suxian, an area of low commercialization in Anhui).

As with semilandlordism and rich peasant agriculture in Haimen-Qidong, commercial farming among larger landlords reached its fullest development in the districts where the best cotton was grown and where landlords were, therefore, in the best position to take advantage of rising market prices (Qiao Qiming 1926: 44). Rich peasants and small semilandlords also expanded

TABLE 8.2
Resident and Nonresident Landlords in Nantong,
Kunshan, and Suxian by Size, 1924
(Percent of group)

County	Resident landlords	Nonresident landlords
Nantong		
Large	98.1%	1.9%
Medium	98.2	1.8
Small	56.7	43.3
Kunshan		
Large	30.4	69.6
Medium	32.7	67.3
Small	38.6	61.4
Suxian		
Large	77.2	22.8
Medium	23.2	76.8
Small	25.6	74.4

SOURCE: Qiao Qiming 1926: 43.
NOTE: By northern delta standards, the holdings of large land-lords roughly averaged 800–1,200 mu; of medium landlords 200–300 mu; and of small landlords 80–120 mu.

TABLE 8.3
Land Tenure in Nantong, 1905–1924
(Percent)

Year	Owner	Owner-tenant	Tenant
1905	20.2%	22.9%	56.9%
1914	15.8	22.7	61.5
1924	13.0	22.6	64.4

SOURCE: Qiao Qiming 1926: 9.

their holdings in these areas. Thus it was precisely in the premium cotton areas that tenant evictions, landlord repossession of tenants' holdings, and the gobbling up of land by lesser managerial farmers proceeded furthest. Consequently, though modern landlordism and semilandlord–rich peasant farming contributed in various ways to the downward differentiation of peasants reflected in rising tenancy rates in the county as a whole (Table 8.3), in premium cotton districts like Liuqiao the spread of managerial farming actually underpinned a decline in tenancy (Qiao Qiming 1926: 11, 44).

As a result, where managerial farming became most pronounced, pockets of relative depopulation appeared. Viewed in this light, descriptive accounts from the teens and 1920's that paint a picture of a sparsely populated countryside inhabited mostly by middle and rich peasants, along with a few landlords, clearly captured part of the rural reality. As Zhang Renren, who authored a report on agriculture in Nantong following a brief visit to the county in 1915, states:

> Rural Nantong is situated in a great plain and is an ideal place for farming and living. Three to five residences scatter in a one-*li* area or so, presenting a classical picture of pastoral life. The houses mostly comprise reed stems, standing as high as a *zhang* [3.3 m]. Some houses have no windows, some, a half-door. A few houses have brick walls and a tile roof. The walls are white-washed, or the upper portion is painted black. These houses are quite spacious, usually used as residences for upper-level households. Willows grow around the houses and vegetable plots are arranged beside them. What a beautiful pastoral scene! (1916, 2.6: 13)

On the other hand, to the extent that, in the agricultural districts, the spread of capitalist-style farming in both its larger and smaller-scale modes resulted in shrinking access to land for the many, it had the added effects of forcing the growing numbers of disadvantaged peasants to live in over-crowded village clusters and into farming on increasingly fragmented, often poorer quality holdings or, even worse, out of agriculture altogether. Even in the premier cotton districts, large managerial landlords seldom farmed all of the land they owned. As in North China, where approximately 200 mu constituted the upper limit for maximum returns from direct management (P. Huang 1985: 172–73), their farming activities were centered in their best acreage and usually extended only up to the point where the diseconomies of distance grew at a faster rate than the economies of size (Banaji 1980: 74); they rented out the remaining holdings.

Although for different reasons, the densely populated industrial districts replicated the fragmented landholding pattern, but there, as we will see in the next chapter, the huge numbers of marginalized peasants managed to carry on as owners, if only of minuscule plots of land. In the county as a whole, then, the intertwining of semicolonial economics, the strategies for domi-nance of the heterogenous rural-urban elite, and the expansionist projects of those who were attempting to rise led to overpopulation and fragmented holdings in some parts of the countryside and depopulation and larger-scale management in other parts. Owing largely to the first phenomenon (and the specific demographic trends to which it gave rise, especially in the indus-trial districts), as we shall also discuss more fully in the next chapter, by the 1920's Nantong had one of the highest person-to-land ratios of any county in Jiangsu province.

In short, if Zhang Renren's "idyllic" description of a sparsely populated countryside suggests one dimension of this combined and uneven develop-mental pattern, what it fails to portray is its underside: the overcrowded agricultural communities that flanked the managerial farms. In those com-munities from the first decade of the century, the increasingly disadvantaged poor eked out a precarious existence farming ever smaller holdings, paying

TABLE 8.4
Cultivated Farm Area in Nantong and Kunshan by Group, 1905-1924

Year	Index number (1905 = 100)			Average farm size (mu)		
	Owner	Owner-tenant	Tenant	Owner	Owner-tenant	Tenant
Nantong						
1905	100	100	100	16.6	18.8	19.0
1914	77	76	79	18.8	14.2	15.0
1924	60	59	62	10.0	11.0	11.8
Kunshan						
1905	100	100	100	23.1	23.4	24.6
1914	63	88	99	14.5	20.5	24.3
1924	41	72	94	9.4	16.9	23.2

SOURCE: Qiao Qiming 1926: 14.

harsh new "cotton rents," and working the lands of the better-off managerial farmers as hired or indentured laborers. Indeed, forced depopulation through tenant evictions and the repossession of the land not only formed the precondition for managerial landlords' farming activities, it also furthered the processes through which a majority of peasants were, structurally speaking, repeasantized as an unstable and underprivileged labor force that met the needs of modern landlords, rich peasants, and various forms of urban capital for cheap labor.

Qiao's survey data give us further insight into this overall picture. As reproduced in Table 8.4, they show a decrease in average farm size for all categories of peasant farming from 1905 to 1924. The rate of decrease not only was much greater among owner-tenants and tenants in Nantong than in Kunshan (by 1924 their holdings in Nantong averaged only 60 percent and 59 percent, respectively, of the 1905 farm size); it began much earlier. Bearing out the argument we have been making that downward trends began to accelerate after the first decade of the century, these data show that by 1914 tenants' holdings had reached the minimum size considered necessary for subsistence in Nantong, that is, 14-16 rented mu (or a minimum of 7-8 mu for owners; MMT 1941). By 1924 tenants' holdings (and possibly owner-tenants' too) were well below this minimum, calculated at a rental rate of 50 percent. In terms of actual rents, this figure may have been lower or higher, but the trend was toward higher rents.

Changes in Land Tenure

Throughout the northern delta new tenurial arrangements that brought higher rents and deposits to tenants accompanied the deepening of commodity production in the agrarian economy. These changes in the land system formed part of the modern landlords' offensive to regain lost ground by extending their control over the peasantry and, simultaneously, under the impetus of cotton grade growth, contributed to the regearing of the agrarian economy in the service of urban capital.

Accordingly, it was in the most productive and highly commercialized cotton districts that managerial farming, the highest rents, and the most complex forms of tenure converged. In Haimen, for example, by the early 1930's rents ranged from 14 yuan to 32 yuan for 1,000 *bu* (four mu), and in Qidong, where productivity was lower, they ranged from 14 to 24. But those peak rates prevailed only in Haimen's districts 5–8 and in Qidong's districts 1 and 2, that is, in the districts of greatest cotton production and semilandlord–rich peasant concentration (Shen Shike 1934: 30921).

Those districts, like Nantong's leading cotton areas, also had the highest percentage of flexible leases giving either party the right to cancel at any time before the next planting season (MMT 1941: 57–58; Shen Shike 1934: 30942). Capping the trend toward shorter contractual periods that began near the end of the nineteenth century, such leases allowed landlords to convert to managerial farming whenever they wished and, as they were more and more inclined to do, to evict tenants in order to raise rents (MMT 1941: 61–66; Shen Shike 1934: 30914).

The new arrangements detrimentally affected agriculture as well as tenants. Shen Shike notes that in the districts where flexible leases prevailed, it was common to see, among poor peasant farmers, "reckless cultivation" and "the plundering of land" with little regard for fertility. Shen suggests that in such cases tenants, knowing that their leases might be canceled at any time, were afraid to undertake long-range farming operations (1934: 30913). But reckless cultivation, which generally meant concentrating solely on cotton in order to maximize returns, also flowed directly from the high "cotton rents" and "cotton deposits" that tenants in these districts were forced to pay. From the turn of the century on, as land prices, rents, and deposits rose, and as cash became the only medium of exchange, poorer peasants really had little option but to intensify cotton cultivation, whether they had security of tenure or not. Growing crops of lesser value while paying "cotton rents" was simply out of the question. The more intensive cultivation of cotton thus also brought less diversification as peasants shied away from interplanting and turned land previously used for rice, beans, hemp, and corn to cotton (Zhang Renren 1915–16, 2.6: 9).

By the 1920's many of these peasants were being required to pay a full year's rent in advance under a type of contract called *yuzu*. That contractual form, also known as *quanyu* (full payment in advance), seems to have appeared on both sides of the Yangzi during the first decade of the century, but its greatest development in the northern delta came in the teens and 1920's (Qian Min 1986: 5; Zhan Ran 1934: 25). By the early 1930's these contracts accounted for 54.7 percent of all rents in district 6 of Haimen, for 58.1 percent in district 7, and for fully 72.6 percent in district 8 (Shen Shike 1934: 30943). A derivative form, called *banding*, in which the tenant paid half the rent in advance and half at harvest, also spread in the 1920's (Shen Shike 1934: 30945).

Both rental types worked to counteract rent default. At the same time they expanded the "exploitation space" of usury capital and further reduced peasants' options by forcing them to borrow to secure the required advances. Still worse, by 1916 rent deposits, which were more the rule than ever (even in 1905, 72.9 percent of peasants in Nantong had paid this older insurance against default; by 1924 fully 88.9 percent did so; Qiao Qiming 1926: 49), had risen to the point where they typically equaled or even surpassed annual rents (Zhang Renren 1915-16, 2.6: 8). By the early 1940's tenants in some districts were putting down a full year's rent plus two and a half times that amount as security (MMT 1941: 44).

Furthermore, rising deposits were often attached to a third and equally harsh rental form that also spread in this period. Known as *xianzu*, it usually maintained existing rent amounts and involved only higher deposits. The one significant innovation lay in requiring tenants to pay full rent regardless of harvest amounts (Shen Shike 1934: 30948-30949; Zhan Ran 1934: 24). In other words, with the use of this rental form landlords effectively undercut the *baohuang* tactic that peasants had used in the Qing with some success to achieve rent reductions. *Xianzu* was most common in Haimen's fourth, fifth, and sixth districts, where it accounted for 45.1 percent, 54.2 percent, and 31.1 percent of rents, respectively, in the early 1930's (Shen Shike 1934: 30948).

High rents and deposits between them increasingly shut off the poorer peasants' access to land. Even though many were willing to pay dearly for land with which to set up their own households, when large amounts of cash were needed for advance payments and deposits, they frequently lost out to richer peasants. In the best cotton districts, where competition for land was fiercest, as Shen Shike put it, "those who can offer the highest rents, get the land" (1934: 30945). By indirectly favoring rich peasant agriculture, the new cotton rents and deposits thus compounded the problem of shrinking access to land for the many that was already occurring under the impetus of various rural "capitalisms."

Since poorer peasants who did succeed in obtaining contracts often did so only by resorting to usurious borrowing, the new rental forms also cut into and even negated the higher market return for cotton compared with other crops. The high cost of cotton production was another problem. In 1924 in Nantong, for example, between rents and production costs, especially for fertilizer, the capital requirements of medium-level tenant households averaged

725.30 yuan. That was almost twice the amount needed by their counterparts in rice-producing Kunshan (371.82 yuan) and almost three times the requirement in Suxian (248.10 yuan; Qiao Qiming 1926: 48).

On top of all this, by the early 1920's almost half the tenant households in Nantong were attempting to meet these costs and maintain production while farming with insufficient tools and livestock. According to Qiao, only 56.8 percent of them possessed "sufficient farm tools to secure a living" and only 21.8 percent owned livestock. Figures for owners were not much better, at 65.3 percent for tools and 24.2 percent for livestock (1926: 65). Since Qiao's category "owners" includes rich peasants, the averages do not suggest a more secure and stable middle peasantry above the poor peasant-tenant strata. As we have already seen, the downward slide affected the middle as well as the poor.

Middle peasants have generally been regarded as the social group in the countryside most closely approximating self-sufficient owner-cultivators. Based on the criteria the Chinese Communist Party (CCP) used in determining class status during the land revolution, they usually owned most of the land they tilled, used only small amounts of hired labor, and did not hire-out. But in the northern delta by the early 1930's, many middle-level peasants more closely resembled poor peasants. In the Rural Rehabilitation Committee's 1933 survey of Qidong, for example, the so-called middle peasants owned only 24.4 percent of the land they farmed, and thus rented 75.6 percent (as compared with poor peasants, who owned only 10.5 percent and rented 89.5 percent). Most of the middle peasants were in fact either owner-tenants (13 percent) or full tenants (59 percent; JS [5] 1933: 52–52).

In sum, paralleling and in some cases accompanying their turn to managerial farming, modern landlords' efforts to reposition themselves by combating endemic rent resistance in new ways and extracting more of the peasants' surplus altered the terms of and intensified the class struggle. The harsher rents and deposits they imposed in the teens and early 1920's instantly reduced the options and opportunities of a growing majority of poorer peasants, yet indirectly favored those of rich peasants. On the other hand, politically, the repercussions of these developments extended well beyond the issue of extraction. Just as peasants viewed the modern elite (and the state they represented) as illegitimate usurpers of power who rapaciously imposed new taxes and "grabbed the people's land," in peasants' eyes (modern) landlords had become "just like" and "no different from tax officials" (Shen Shike 1934: 30945). The landlords' offensive thus not only heightened antagonisms in the countryside; it became another point through which peasants formulated an understanding of and opposition to the reconfigurations of class within the evolving semicolonial system.

The Rich Peasant–Poor Peasant Divide

The developments in land and class relations after 1911 figured prominently in a new wave of peasant collective action that surfaced in the late teens and gathered momentum through the 1920's. Unlike the multiclass movement of 1900–1912, however, as we will discuss more fully in the next chapter, it assumed a more pronounced poor peasant–subproletarian character. The evidence suggests that, as rich peasants and semilandlords gained access to poorer peasants' land, and as their usurious operations became more vital to peasant survival, the same developments that produced the new wave of struggles also drove a wedge into and splintered the "new village community" of the late Qing movement.

In the cotton districts the spread of advance-payment contracts and large deposits hastened the process whereby, along with merchants, rich peasant entrepreneurs became major lenders to tenants. Since by now landlords in Nantong were dealing almost entirely in secured-mortgage loans or grain loans connected with indentured labor (discussed below), tenants had little choice but to pay the exorbitant rates of interest demanded by merchants and, increasingly, rich peasants. Rich peasant loans in those districts, or what peasant borrowers commonly referred to as "double exploitation-heavy interest loans," carried the highest interest rates in the northern delta, often amounting to 50–60 percent and for particular types of emergency loans much more (Huadong junzheng 1952: 439–40; Huang Xiaoxian 1927: 480; Zhang Yiyong 1935).

Other practices worked to divide the peasantry and promote landlord-rich peasant unity. Rich peasants, for example, in a sense became more landlord than peasant when they sublet some of their rental property at higher rental rates to poorer peasants (Huadong junzheng 1952: 437–38). Similarly, part of the money rich peasants lent to tenants came from funds borrowed from landlords and merchants at much lower rates of interest than peasant borrowers paid (ibid., p. 440). In this period larger absentee landlords developed bursary-warehouses to handle rent collection, especially in the central districts of Haimen and Qidong and along the Yangzi, where permanent tenancy and rent-in-kind prevailed. Many of these bursaries also handled rent collection and dunning for semilandlords and rich peasants (Huang Xiaoxian 1927: 475).

No less important, in the Republican period landlords lost the special tax exemptions they had enjoyed under the Qing. The equalization of tax responsibility among landowners created a new arena of shared interest between landlords and rich peasants, enabling the latter, who in the past had often led struggles involving tax issues, to defer to landlords in pressing for tax reductions. Land tax struggles consequently declined in number (Bernhardt 1992:

208). Simultaneously, that is, as small landlords and semilandlord–rich peasants shifted their allegiance to larger landlord allies, part of the foundation for the multiclass alliances of the late Qing peasant movement disintegrated. In the 1920's what tax struggles there were tended to be waged by tenants and poor peasants protesting special taxes and were often mounted in conjunction with rent resistance (Zhu Mingxia & Bian Xiaozhi 1986).

As a result of these various factors, rich peasants increasingly pared off from the poor peasants to link up with larger landlords. These landlords' underwriting of rich peasant activity acted to heal some of the wounds of the repression of the 1900-1912 movement and to rebind the lower landlord-semilandlord and upper peasant strata to the dominant political-economic structure. The historically significant criticism of the poor that "today the hearts of people are . . . more greedy" (Mao Zedong 1990: 155) not only applied equally to modern landlords and "high-interest" rich peasant "exploiters," but in a certain sense fastened on the similarity of outlook and the intertwining interests of the two. On the other hand, there was, of course, a continuing contradiction of a fundamental nature between them. Thus despite the points of affinity, in actively supporting the crushing of the new village politics of the 1900-1912 peasant movement and then moving to tighten their control over land and labor, modern landlords created definite barriers to both the political and the economic potentialities of rich peasant-semilandlord agriculture. In imposing these limitations so as to maintain and strengthen their own position, one could argue, landlords likewise stimulated, albeit indirectly, the overdevelopment of the economic practices that, after 1911, made rich peasants-semilandlords "the most rapacious class in the countryside."

Disguised Wage Labor and Modes of Labor Control

In assigning a determining role to the market, in both their neoclassical economic and positivist "Marxist" forms, the narrative teleologies of linear progressivist history assume that commercial/capitalist development inexorably generates more "advanced" labor forms in agriculture, including especially competitive labor markets and free wage labor. In this scenario older, "precapitalist," forms disintegrate and disappear. But, as a large body of literature now shows, this was not and is still not the case in various parts of the world. In fact, the effect has often been just the opposite. Particularly in the contemporary Third World, the systemic role of bonded, unfree, and other types of disguised wage labor as preferred relational forms is now perceived as central to the accumulation processes of agrarian capitalisms. Indeed, in the circumstances where unfreedom and older labor forms are initiated or reintroduced by capital for the purpose of accumulating surplus value, it is simply no longer possible to categorize them as "relics of the past" (Brass 1997: 337–38; see also Brass 1986; and Daniel et al. 1992).

The labor arrangements associated with the shift to commercial farming among larger landlords and the expansion of semilandlord–rich peasant agriculture in the northern delta provide an early example of such patterns. To a considerable degree these arrangements involved wide reliance on "hired" workers who were not necessarily paid in cash, which is to say, on a disguised labor force. Farm managers secured the labor of these workers through tenure contracts, usury, debt-bondage, outright purchase of the laborer (in the case of women), and other means, rather than in a competitive labor market. Accordingly, estimates of the rural labor force based only on calculations of wage workers at once obscure the significance of disguised and unfree labor and the degree to which the strengthening, not the demise, of older labor arrangements promoted both the various "capitalisms" of the northern delta countryside and the semicolonizing modernist path.

In general in the northern delta, as the German socialist Karl Kautsky once observed of similar trends elsewhere, the same developments that, on the one hand, created the demand for wage laborers, on the other, created the wage laborers themselves (Banaji 1980). That is to say, only a portion of the hired/disguised rural labor force came from the fully proletarianized agricultural laborer class, which even in the late 1920's still constituted at most 12 percent of the rural population in Nantong and 8 percent in Haimen (Huang Xiaoxian 1927: 473; MMT 1941: 97). Instead, much like the situation in North China Philip Huang (1985) describes, poor peasant, mostly tenant, households unable to meet all their subsistence needs were the backbone of the rural labor force.

But contrary to Huang's analysis, in these circumstances the "survival" of fragmented, overburdened, proletarianized peasant holdings was not so much a reflection of the ability of poor peasant agriculture to compete with larger managerial holdings as of the fact that in crucial respects it ceased to compete under a path of modernity fostering the survival of both. Downward differentiation, as we noted earlier, generated the cheap day-labor for commercial farming enterprises. Simultaneously, precisely because of the need of poor peasant families to secure longer-term employment for some members, and much like capitalist enterprises, to cast out other, "redundant," members, it produced the seasonal and long-term labor that was integral to the expansion of large-scale farming. In this process, as agriculture became more fully bound up with urban social development as a whole, the old sexual division of labor disintegrated. The demand for cheap peasant labor not only transformed males into auxiliary and subsidiary wage workers but created new space for women as undervalued, hired agricultural laborers. We will examine these developments in greater detail in due course.

Suffice it to say, in the present context, that in the agriculturally specialized districts landlords and rich peasants were able to capitalize on the lack of industry and the peasant family's limited employment options to meet a portion of their labor needs in cheaper, nonmarket forms. They typically secured disguised labor in three, sometimes overlapping, ways: labor-rent or share-harvest contracts; usurious loans requiring repayment in labor rather than money or goods; and outright purchase and bondage, most often involving the buying and selling of women.

LABOR RENTS, CONTRACT LABOR, AND USURY

Labor rent was most commonly used to meet seasonal needs. It developed not only in Nantong-Haimen but in Rugao, Taizhou, and other areas (Huadong junzheng 1952: 441) and tended to take two forms. In some cases the tenant-laborer was required to work a set number of days on the landlord's land in return for the rental of a plot. In others the tenant (and often family members) had to till a specified amount of the landlord's land. Both forms were variable, but the first was particularly so, with labor days sometimes falling as low as 62–72 per mu of rented land but conventionally numbering 101 in the cotton districts (Shen Shike 1934: 30918). Tenants who contracted by acreage generally tilled two to four mu of the landlord's land for each mu they rented (Huadong junzheng 1952: 441).[4] Both arrangements required tenants to abandon work on their own plots whenever the landlord was in need of their labor. In yet another variation, landlords simply allowed regular tenants to defer paying their rents by providing labor in the interim (Shen Shike 1934: 31008).

Semilandlord–rich peasants, as well as larger landlords, negotiated labor-rent contracts. Most often, in the first case, a man would sublet the poor quality land he rented in return for a tenant's labor on his own better quality holdings. Larger landlords were likewise apt to lease out their least desirable land (Huadong junzheng 1952: 437).

Contract labor, in which owners typically signed laborers on for a specified amount and type of fieldwork, was a seemingly straightforward cash exchange. It was used most in the busiest agricultural seasons and was especially favored in the cotton districts (Zhang Renren 1915–16, 2.6: 8). Often, however, especially among semilandlords and rich peasants, contract labor became a means of acquiring labor and engaging in usury. In one common practice fieldwork was contracted and paid for in advance, usually in kind, through the negotiation of a usurious loan. Most loan contracts occurred in the spring, when poorer peasants were forced to borrow grain or money for food. Borrowers repaid the loans by working creditors' fields during the busy season at a much lower "wage rate" than the prevailing wage (MMT 1941: 156). Lenders often provided tobacco or spirits (but apparently not meals) during the work period; these were also charged against the "wage." This was thus not contract labor at all in the true sense but, as one survey put it, "a distinct type of farm labor made possible by the practice of usury" (Institute of Pacific Relations 1939: 72–73). In some instances, operating in classic debt-peonage fashion, loan contracts led to mounting indebtedness that required years of labor to clear (Huadong junzheng 1952: 444).

SHARECROPPING

Sharecropping was of course a very old contractual form. As we discussed earlier, sharecropping declined during the Qing to the point where it may have persisted only in the more isolated districts of northern Nantong-Haimen organized along patron-client/kinship lines. But it made a comeback as managerial farming spread and the plight of poor tenant households grew worse, especially in the premium cotton districts from Rugao to Chongming but also in some rural industrial districts (Gu Li 1981: 51; Huang Xiaoxian 1927: 474, 476–77; JS [8] 1913: 11; Qiao Qiming 1926: 24; Shen Shike 1934: 30966–30967). By the early 1920's it accounted for perhaps 10 percent or more of all contracts, and it then expanded through the rest of the decade (Gu Li 1981: 50–51; Huang Xiaoxian 1933; Qiao Qiming 1926: 21).

As an invisible form of modern labor-hiring, sharecropping contracts could involve only a simple share-harvest agreement. But to the extent that they drew on the most destitute peasant strata, landlords were normally expected to provide the seeds and fertilizer, and frequently the tools.[5] In addition, landlords assumed the power to supervise and direct production. Landlord-owners commonly received 70–80 percent, or at the lowest 60 percent, of the main harvest, depending on the district and land quality. Most often tenants and landlords equally divided the secondary harvest (Gu Li 1981: 51; Huadong junzheng 1952: 442, 444; Huang Xiaoxian 1927; Qiao Qiming 1926: 24).

Twentieth-century sharecropping contracts thus reversed the 40-60 landlord-tenant split that seems to have become the standard fixed rent during the Qing. Although sharecropping has not usually been considered part of managerial farming, I argue that as an arrangement that allowed landlords to supervise production, it became a characteristic feature of this mode in its modern semicolonial form. In other words sharecropping, like disguised labor generally, was integral to the formation of modern landlordism and thus to the landlords' economic offensive. Its spread was consequential in making modern northern delta landlords "think and act like businessmen." In short, sharecroppers, functioning "virtually like hired farmhands" (Huang Xiaoxian 1927: 474), provided a source of long-term, directable labor at reduced cost to managerial landlords.

To be sure, the need to meet all capital expenditures could make share-cropping arrangements costly for landlords, especially when large amounts of land were involved. But usually landlords did not have to furnish meals and board, still a standard part of hired-labor costs in the teens and 1920's. Buck, for example, found little difference in the actual wages of agricultural laborers in the Yangzi rice-wheat area and those in North China. On average actual wages of an annual laborer in the Yangzi area totaled 37.78 yuan, compared with 34.46 yuan in the winter wheat–gaoliang area and 36.93 yuan in the winter wheat–millet area. But in the Yangzi area, the value of food and board was much higher, totaling 47.41 yuan, or a figure that was well above actual wages paid. Consequently, there were marked differences in total wage costs between the north and the south, the cost of an annual laborer in the Yangzi area averaging 89.08 yuan, compared with an average of only 75.55 for the two northern regions (Buck 1937b: 328).

Sharecropping thus enabled landlords to eliminate a sizable portion of the wage labor bill by leaving it to peasants to make do on their rented plots. Given the small harvest share that they now received, this labor arrangement undoubtedly resulted in lower quality foods and lower consumption levels among sharecroppers than among hired workers who received meals.[6] Qiao's 1924 survey indicates the considerable monetary advantages it had for landlords. As a percentage of land value, sharecropping on medium quality land gave an 11.3 percent return, as against only 4.6 percent from money rents (1926: 32). Furthermore, in cheapening labor power, the spread of sharecropping and other forms of disguised-unfree labor appear to have contributed to changes in wage labor relations by the 1930's, especially the move by managerial landlords and rich peasants to reduce costs by eliminating the customary practice of providing meals to contract and day-laborers (or by cutting the wage in half if meals were still included). These arrangements gained ground in the 1930's, particularly in the cotton districts (MMT 1941: 102).

As is perhaps already evident, sharecropping, like labor rents, not only provided low-cost labor but assured managers of fieldhands during the peak periods of the agricultural year when competition for hired help was greatest. Although scholars have frequently emphasized underemployment as a feature of the prerevolutionary Chinese countryside, during the busiest agricultural seasons hired-labor shortages were frequently acute. Over half the localities surveyed by Buck in the Yangzi rice-wheat area reported shortfalls during the planting and harvesting seasons (1937a: 301). Guaranteed access to labor was thus critical to successful managerial operations, and a sometimes shaky proposition for semilandlord–rich peasants, who, as one report put it, "need a great deal of seasonal labor for planting and harvesting, but are always in fear that they will not be able to secure an adequate number of people" (Institute of Pacific Relations 1939: 71).

DISGUISED FEMALE LABOR

By the 1920's the features of the rural family system bearing directly on women—female infanticide, child marriage, contract prostitution-concubinage, and the buying and selling of females—were clearly on the rise (Fei Hsiao-tung 1939; Guo Zhenyi 1938; Luo Qing 1935). This situation has usually been imputed to deepening rural decline, commonly referred to in contemporary literature as the agrarian crisis of the 1920's.

A more accurate assessment, it seems to me, should take into account the interlocking of economic growth and rural decline as a generalized feature of the semicolonial economy. Rural decline (in the sense of the downward differentiation of the majority of peasants tied to new growth trends) unquestionably became one of the key factors influencing rural families to sell their daughters or to place them, in return for a cash payment, into some form of servitude for a specified period of time. On the other hand, viewed in light of the growing demand for labor generated by the expansion of commodity production and the appearance of various rural "capitalisms," the disguised intent in at least some of these practices was purely and simply to procure free or cheap female labor. Indeed, the growing use of female labor, especially in agriculture, stands as one of the significant features and dynamics of semicolonial growth patterns.

Studies of women in late-nineteenth–early-twentieth-century China have created a very different picture. Early feminist writings suggested that southernmost China was the only place where women played more than an insignificant role in family agriculture.[7] The question of agricultural wage labor among women was rarely addressed, but the presumption was that to the extent it existed at all, it likewise did so only or mainly in the south.[8] Socioeconomic analyses have begun to provide a more realistic picture of women's growing role in family farming in different regions, but often these same studies argue that the hired agricultural laborer market remained exclusively male.[9] Yet just as notions of the lack of managerial farming in the delta must be radically revised, clearly it will not do for us to continue to imagine that there or even in North China, women remained outside of the agricultural labor market. Although systematic investigation of hired agricultural labor among women must await future research, the accumulated evidence shows incontrovertibly that a female labor market developed in North and Central China, as well as in the south. This was certainly the case in cotton-producing regions, where there was widespread movement of poor peasant women into the cotton fields as cheap hired laborers.

The growing preference for hired female labor in the cotton districts of the northern delta in fact replicated a similar trend in the cotton belt of North China, where managerial farming had developed earlier. At the close of the nineteenth century, according to eyewitness accounts such as Arthur Smith's early village study, not only had the cultivation of cotton become largely the work of women, but a female agricultural laborer market was already operating there (1899: 167, 261, 276). In the Nantong area, by at least the mid-teens, women and girls became the preferred form of hired labor for cotton weeding and picking/harvesting (MMT 1941: 100–102; Zhang Renren 1915–16).

Underlying this development in both regions lay an intertwining of gender, class, and the high labor requirements of cotton cultivation, which, according to Buck, required roughly twice as much labor per mu as rice (1937b: 314–17). In the northern delta these requirements were even higher, since weeding was more intensive, typically occurring five times as compared, for example, with only three or four times in the southern delta. In the prewar period women usually received 10 cents a day for this work and 10–20 cents for picking; male farm workers made 20–30 cents a day in the same period (MMT 1941: 74, 102). Thus in creating a sexual division of labor in the hired labor market for cotton weeding and picking that replicated the gender hierarchy, employers further devalued the peasant-based labor force on which commercialized production depended. These developments in the northern delta, as in North China, provide early examples of the widespread tendency in the contemporary Third World (including the Chinese countryside during the last two decades) for commercial farming to be built up on the basis of a conversion of peasant women into an undervalued, hired labor force, a process also entailing the displacement of males from agricultural work.

To return, then, to our original point, the development of a multifaceted market in disguised female labor at once reflected and expressed women's growing role as agricultural laborers and their greater commoditization under new growth trends. It enabled rich peasants and modern landlords to acquire needed female labor even more cheaply by circumventing and, in a certain sense, inhibiting the developing female wage-labor market.

In the northern delta–Subei in the 1920's and 1930's, the market in women flourished. Girls were frequently sold more than once, taken on first as child-servants in the homes of the affluent and then resold as concubines, workers, or wives. In the early 1930's a three- or four-year-old girl routinely sold for 10 yuan, a seventeen- or eighteen-year-old for 50–60 yuan or slightly more than twice the annual wage of a male agricultural laborer (Luo Qing 1935: 109). As rural investigations of Nantong indicate, many of these girls were put on the market by desperately poor families (MMT 1941: 180–81). They also strongly suggest that upper-strata families used the market to purchase women for use as field labor (MMT 1941: table 2), but because the investigators did not specifically collect data on disguised or unfree female labor, the extent of its use remains unclear. Nevertheless, given the growing importance of cheap female labor in commercial agriculture, we cannot conclude our discussion of disguised labor without at least briefly identifying some of its specifically female forms.

Concubinage and early marriage came to be two of the rich peasants' favorite means of acquiring indentured-disguised labor. As one contemporary report noted:

> Instead of hiring wage earning agricultural laborers by the year, many rich peasant families take in concubines who are considered from the point of view of field work to be much less expensive. To begin with, concubines receive no wages. . . . Then they do housework in addition to the field labor, a combination which is difficult to obtain from a hired laborer. Finally, the concubines are apt to work harder than hired women laborers because often they are put in the position of managing hired laborers, and they are more apt to identify their own interests with that of the farm. It is said that concubinage has been made use of among the owners of handweaving establishments . . . but such a system of concubinage is certainly more common among the families requiring additional field workers. (Institute of Pacific Relations 1939: 84)

The use of concubines in precisely these ways, that is, as both laborers themselves and overseers of female workers, seems to have been common among rich peasant-like families in Nantong's industrial districts (MMT 1941: tables 1, 2, 10).

In some places rich peasant families took a different tack: marrying their sons off at age thirteen or fourteen to girls four or five years older. The motive behind this growing practice is encapsulated in a popular saying in those parts, "To acquire a daughter-in-law is far more advantageous than to hire a laborer by the year" (Institute of Pacific Relations 1939: 83).[10]

In many areas, including the northern delta, sharecropping or labor-rent agreements, though ostensibly contracted with only a male household head, actually extended to his wife and perhaps other family members as well. The wife was expected, on call, to perform fieldwork or other tasks with no monetary remuneration or change in the share of the harvest. Some sources see in this commandeering of female labor a remnant of the older "right of possession" invoked by Chinese landlords to justify their raping of tenant-peasant women (Huadong junzheng 1952). But the requisitioning of unremunerated female/family labor was far from unique to Chinese overlords. Indeed, it is probably one of the foremost reasons why landlords in various parts of the Third World even now prefer sharecropping to other arrangements. As Gillian Hart notes of contemporary Indonesia: "[An] important characteristic of *kedokan* [sharecropping] is that, by adding extra tasks to the contract with no corresponding increase in the harvest share, employers can readily lower wages. Moreover, in the process of requiring additional tasks the employer is likely to gain access to the labor of additional household members" (1986: 181).

Usury and debt bondage also intersected and intertwined with disguised female labor. In the northern delta and on Chongming, for example, it was not uncommon for a (usually) destitute family to make a "daughter deposit," that is, to offer a daughter at a low price to a landlord or rich peasant in exchange for an emergency loan. In this usurious arrangement the daughter became a laborer for the lender until she was of marriageable age, at which time the family had the option of buying her back (Huadong junzheng 1952: 445). In other cases families mortgaged one (or more) of their members as a laborer-servant to a lender when they were unable to repay a loan (ibid.).

These randomly drawn examples, combined with the outright purchase of women for use as cheap field-domestic labor, give us a glimpse of the degree to which the accelerating commercialization of the rural economy and spread of unfree labor coincided with the commoditization of women. Although the precise contours of the market in women remain illusive, it is nevertheless clear that female labor acquired in nonwage forms became a significant part of the disguised labor force that fueled the growth of modern landlord–rich peasant farming in the northern delta.

DISGUISED LABOR RELATIONS AS A MECHANISM OF CONTROL

Emerging within the context and as part of the process of agrarian class struggle, disguised labor relations not only became a method whereby employers imposed or reimposed their authority over the labor process; they also served as a form of social control. In the latter respect the expansion of these relations in the northern delta again bears a striking resemblance to the spread in recent decades of similar practices in Indonesia, India, and other parts of the Third World experiencing rapid commercial change. "The *active* resort by the rural bourgeoisie in contemporary India to loans and debt," writes Tom Brass, "[has become] a preferred method of controlling, cheapening or disciplining labor-power in order to set the capitalist labor process in motion" (1997: 338; italics in original).

Similarly, Gillian Hart, in her study of rural Java, pinpoints sharecropping and debt-related contracts as the labor arrangements that expanded most rapidly under the stimulus of the Green Revolution and that were utilized "above all by the most 'entrepreneurial farmers' " (1986: 179). As she writes of a field investigation carried out in 1975–76 in a district where less than 10 percent of the population controlled nearly 60 percent of the land:

Demand for agricultural labor over the course of the survey rose with the spread of pest-resistant rice technology. . . . Access to work was, however, highly differentiated and was mediated in part by . . . land-debt contracts. . . . These arrangements were designed *to keep labor cheap and manageable* by providing job security to a select group of workers, while simultaneously excluding others. . . . Many of those excluded [were landless households whose] survival was contingent upon the deployment of huge amounts of male, female and child labor to activities yielding very low returns. (1986: 15; italics in original)

Emphasizing the degree to which employers' needs to exercise control can arise from social and political forces as well as from the labor process itself, Hart argues that debt-labor contracts and sharecropping arrangements enable rural employers to use job security as an indirect means of disciplining and controlling peasant-workers (1986: 178). Stated differently, even though highly exploitative, those practices function as both mechanisms of control and worker performance precisely because the job security they provide is preferable to the far more tenuous position of families in the pool of underemployed, casual labor (1986: 13, 177–83).

Similar dynamics operated in the northern delta in the teens and 1920's, the key difference being that, instead of landless laborers, the pool of underemployed was composed chiefly of tenant families whose employment options, even low-paying casual work, were limited. As one sharecropper put it, "You can gain little from tilling the fields [in this way], but you would starve if you didn't work on the rented [sharecrop] land" (Huadong junzheng 1952: 446). I further suggest that, in the aftermath of the early-twentieth-century peasant risings (as in Indonesia in the 1970's following the crack-down on the communist-left), disguised labor relations were crucial to the landlord offensive to reestablish control in the countryside.

OTHER ASPECTS OF DISGUISED LABOR RELATIONS

The controlled labor arrangements, especially sharecropping, also meshed well with the sociopolitical and cultural dimensions of modern landlordism. They made it possible for owners to derive many of the benefits of managerial farming with only a modicum of effort and time. This was an important consideration, especially for large and medium landlords whose holdings exceeded the size that could be easily or profitably managed directly. As noted, Nantong's managerial landlords solved this problem by renting out surplus land. Letting it out to sharecroppers or labor tenants still allowed for supervision, but because only a few simple instructions during daily visits to the fields were normally required, it freed them to carry out the other duties that now attached to the modern rural elite.

After 1911, as we have seen, for large and medium landlords the shift to the modernist project entailed greater participation in local political, self-government, and educational activities. Thus precisely when they were becoming deeply involved in managerial farming, modern landlords were also obliged to devote considerable amounts of time to maintaining and strengthening relations with supravillage authorities and groups. This situation, as Hart also argues for contemporary Indonesian landlords with comparable involvements (1986: 191) intensified the rural elite's need for a reliable and easily managed agricultural labor force.

Virtually all managerial landlords also, having achieved greater control of local cotton harvests, now participated in the cotton trade. As one of the former members of Nantong's merchant community I interviewed observed: "Any landlord who could get his hands on some cotton became involved in the cotton trade" (Zhang Zhiqing 1980). Some acted as agents for the large cotton companies; most headed the small one- or two-person cotton firms that, as we noted earlier, doubled in number in the course of the 1920's. By the 1930's these small cotton *hang* spread around the countryside accounted for over two-thirds of the region's total cotton firms (Shiyebu 1933, 4: 52; *Tongruhai mianye gonghui* 1924; Zhang Zhiqing 1980). The effective result of gaining greater control of cotton supplies, then, was to enlarge the landlords' field of operations and make their conversion as the economic allies of the Nantong merchant complex more complete.

Semilandlords and rich peasants also pursued many nonfarm activities, often in nearby market towns and cities. Unlike larger landlords, however, they on the whole lived up to their reputation as the most "rapacious class in the countryside," focusing on money-making activities to the exclusion of political involvements (a development that, as noted earlier, also reflected the stifling of coalitional peasant politics after 1911; Qiao Qiming 1926: 68; Shen Shike 1934: 30997). Among them, as among the newly rich small landlords and "half-landlord-like rich peasants" Mao observed in Xunwu, nothing was more important than making money. Thus, any time left over from farming was mostly devoted to loan-sharking, to cotton-trading operations, and to other small businesses. Above them stood small landlords and some lower-middle landlords with similar inclinations toward moneymaking rather than cultural and political pursuits. In parts of Haimen and Qidong, as one report noted, they went beyond trade and some usury to a bit of country lawyering:

> The small and medium landlords usually hire farmhands and they work on the land too. Every day, besides providing supervision over the farmhands, they frequent the pubs and tea houses, adjudicating peasant disputes. . . . They gain some profits from doing so. The peasants have no place to get justice. How bitter their words are if you listen to them! Is this the remnant of feudal society? (Shen Shike 1934: 30996) [11]

The reporter not only touches on the economic activities of many small and medium landlords but, if inadvertently, suggests the growing antagonism and increasingly conflictive relations that underlay legal disputes in the 1920's.

This antagonism was not in fact a "feudal remnant," as he seems to imply. It flowed directly from the elite project of modernity we have been describing, and more specifically, from the attempts of managerial landlords and land development companies to evict tenants and peasants from their land. By the mid-1920's, if not earlier, things were brought to a still more feverish pitch when larger landlords moved to annul the topsoil rights of permanent tenants and repossess the land.[12]

The Attack on Tenants' Topsoil Rights

Although the precise contours of the attack on tenants' ownership rights in various districts of the delta remain to be fully studied, it at once clearly marked another front of the larger, "historically vital" landlord offensive to reestablish control over peasants and their surpluses and a dimension of the related processes whereby capital took greater hold of agriculture. The job was made easier by the erosion of customary restrictions on land transactions, such as priority and redemption rights, as the landlords moved to make land-ownership more complete (Institute of Pacific Relations 1939: 21–26).[13]

In the northern delta landlords holding subsoil rights were confronted with the problem not only of low fixed rents and rising tax payments, but of a widening gap between the value of subsoil holdings and that of surface land. In the early 1930's in Qidong, for example, the subsoil of a mu of good quality land was worth only eight yuan, compared with 60 yuan for the top-soil (ibid., p. 27). Seeking to work themselves out of this economic impasse while inexorably being pulled into the vortex of business and profits, land-lords opted to break up the compromise established in the Qing between peasant-communal and landlord property in the dual-ownership system.

The impetus for this initiative came from the large absentee landlords of Chongming and northern Zhejiang when those areas became the focus of Guomindang land reforms in 1927–29. Conceived and sponsored by the left-GMD during its brief period of ascendancy, the proposed reforms included such measures as rent reduction, the prohibition of dunning bureaus and debtor prisons, and the establishment of arbitration committees to handle rent disputes.

The reforms had little impact in most of the delta for lack of implementa-tion. But both Qidong, which was formally constituted as a county in 1928 and thus removed from Chongming's jurisdiction, and parts of northern Zhe-jiang, especially in Jiaxing, had local GMD party committees with strong leftist leanings (some or many of their members were probably Communists) that attached great weight to carrying out the reforms. At the same time higher administrative leaders may have designated the two localities as areas of particular focus. Qidong, for example, might have drawn unusual interest because of the high concentration of landownership by Chongming landlords. In addition, landlord-tenant relations there had become particularly fractious, apparently because (on top of the types of rental changes discussed earlier) absentee landlords had already begun moving some years before to challenge permanent tenants' rights. As a result litigation, late payments, and outright peasant refusal to pay full rental amounts had all increased. By the late 1920's few peasants appear to have been paying the specified rents (Institute of Pacific Relations 1939: 29).

In any event, the Qidong party committee whether pushed or on its own, took an explicit anti-landlord stand. According to the committee, the warehouses or rent-collecting bursaries of landlords in Qidong

> much resemble governmental yamen or bureaus of the traditional type. The tenants who deliver the grain are subject to beating by the collector at the slightest excuse and even the local Bureau of Public Safety is used as a prison. It is also a matter of ordinary practice for the people connected with rent collection to make miscellaneous exactions from the tenants. (Ibid., p. 28)

To remedy this situation the committee went beyond standard proposals for rent reduction and outlined a more radical reform program aimed at eventually eliminating landlordism altogether by giving permanent tenants both subsoil and topsoil rights (ibid., pp. 28–29). Local committees in parts of northern Zhejiang took a similarly strong stand, carrying out rent reduction and establishing arbitration committees in a number of localities.

As a result conflict between landlords and the local GMD committees, as well as that between peasants and landlords, escalated. In Chongming the landlords' reaction was swift and intense. They instantly mounted a united attack against the Qidong committee, including publicly accusing its members and some of the district authorities of "insidious communism" (ibid., p. 29). Comparable hostilities emerged in Zhejiang (Huai Pu 1933: 74–75).

In this volatile situation the Guomindang, in 1928, issued new regulations. Kathryn Bernhardt argues that the intent was to protect tenants who insisted on rent reduction from retribution by specifying the conditions under which a landlord might legally evict a tenant: if he wished to farm the land himself or if the tenant had defaulted. What enraged landlords, however, was the provision that these conditions were not applicable to tenants who had paid a deposit or held topsoil rights (Bernhardt 1992: 186). The new regulations thus offered a considerable measure of protection to permanent tenants, who were also eligible for rent reduction under the new GMD guidelines.

The result was open warfare. In a show of force and blatant defiance of the new regulations, landlords escalated both the evictions of permanent tenants and rent hikes. In so doing they explicitly challenged the authority of the left-GMD reformers and, in an ingenious move, took this attack on their prerogatives as an opportunity to eject permanent tenants from the land. In the past such a blatant assault would have been unlikely, but there were now two new elements in the mix. Landlords themselves had never been under so sharp an attack; the stand of the left-GMD reformers and growing peasant militancy stirred landlord opposition of the most reactionary type. Put differently, the social contradictions underlying the landlords' launching, after 1911, of an offensive that was historically vital to their class had by the late 1920's reached an extreme level of intensification. At the same time by 1928 landlords were emboldened by the development of new forces of reaction in the state that directly reflected and expressed that intensification, namely, Chiang Kai-shek's (Jiang Jieshi's) militarist takeover of the Guomindang in 1927, followed in the next two years by his rightist attack on the revolution and the wholesale ousting or neutralization of the left-GMD at all levels of the party administration. On the other hand, the landlords' capacity to instantly stand united in their opposition to the (left-) GMD regulations reflected precisely their more general and ongoing mobilization after 1911.

As a result of the concentrated landlord attack, rents in Qidong doubled in a matter of years (Institute of Pacific Relations 1939: 28, 94). It is uncertain how many permanent tenants were evicted in this period, and details of the ploys landlords used to accomplish this remain murky for that area, though they were no doubt much of a piece with those used in Zhejiang. In one of the favorite tactics there, new landlord purchasers of subsoil rights demanded that tenant topsoil owners produce their contracts. This seems to have been done with the intent, in the first instance, of providing grounds for evicting tenants who had only oral contracts. Although written contracts for all forms of tenure arrangements became more common in the twentieth century, many new contracts as well as older ones continued to be secured by oral agreement. Even in the early 1930's only 60 percent of existing contracts in Haimen were written, and only 70 percent in Qidong (MMT 1941; Shen Shike 1934: 30901–30902). For tenants who did have formal documents, the demand that they produce them served a second purpose to the same end: it allowed new owners to write directly on the contract that they had the "right" to buy back the topsoil at any time they wished to till the land themselves. This tactic became increasingly common after 1928, suggesting that it was the product of concerted landlord action (Huai Pu 1933: 73).

In that year landlords who were already holding subsoil rights—regardless of whether the original contract was written or oral—started demanding that permanent tenants recognize their right to redeem the topsoil at any time. In this scenario, which actually reversed the general trend toward the disintegration of redemption rights and interjected them anew into the dual-ownership system, the landlord "agreed" to inform the tenant one year in advance of repossession. Instead of paying for the topsoil, however, the landlord only canceled the last year's rent (Huai Pu 1933: 73–74). In other more blatantly illegal and often violent instances, landlords simply evicted permanent tenants and confiscated the land (Institute of Pacific Relations 1939: 94).

Records from the arbitration committees established in Zhejiang provide a rough gauge of the impact of these developments on landlord-tenant relations. Fully 70 percent of the 49 unresolved disputes referred to the Zhejiang Reconstruction Office in 1928–29 by local arbitration committees involved the eviction of tenants by landlords wishing to take over cultivation themselves or to rent to another tenant (most of the rest, 22 percent, hinged on the proper amount of rent under the GMD's rent reduction program; Bernhardt 1992: 171). Similarly, nearly one-third (31 percent) of all cases brought before the Jiaxing county committee over the course of 1930 turned on landlord seizure of tenant land (ibid.).[14] Since dual-ownership predominated in northern Zhejiang, as in Qidong, we must assume that the majority of these cases involved permanent tenants. Whether the Zhejiang landlords actually wished to take over land to farm themselves, as they often stated, or simply wished to avoid rent reduction remains obscure.[15] But whatever the case, the fact that 70 percent of unresolved cases concerned eviction issues suggests that landlords largely refused to back down.

Furthermore, it became increasingly unnecessary for them to do so. After the establishment of militarist rule in 1927, the move toward reform in the land system disintegrated. Not only were reforms such as those proposed for Qidong never seriously acted on (Institute of Pacific Relations 1939: 29–30), but landlords found new support for their ownership claims in the Guomindang's revised land and civil laws of 1930.

The new code placed dual and multiple ownership under the single legal category of permanent tenancy and set out a series of laws governing it. Permanent tenants with topsoil rights were still afforded some protection, but to a lesser extent than before. One new provision allowed landlords to evict permanent tenants and terminate their contracts if they fell two years behind in their rent payments (art. 846). Another set new legal precedent by requiring written contracts for valid permanent tenure (art. 759). In short the laws that thereafter became the basis for many of the suits initiated by landlords nullified oral contracts and supplied landlords with the legal right to evict tenants who held them. The revised code thus legalized a practice that landlords had already developed and used. In addition, it undercut the well-established view in customary law of surface rights as ownership rights by failing to specify that tenants could mortgage, pledge, sublease, sell, or inherit them. Beyond specifically prohibiting subletting, it simply stated that the right to permanent tenure could be transferred to others (arts. 845, 846; P. Yang 1988: 167–69, 213–14; Yao Ruiguang 1967: 163–176).[16]

To the extent, as Partha Chatterjee has argued, that the result of class struggle at any given moment is the relative recognition of peasant rights in the established structure (1988: 378), in one swift move of the pen the Guomindang lawmakers erected a new barrier to a central trajectory of peasant struggle since the early Qing. At the same time they legitimated, and thus gave fuller reign to, much more recent processes in which landlords attempted to at once expropriate peasants' land and their rights in the established structure. In the northern delta the consequence was to bring peasants still more fully under the sway of the system of exploitation emanating from Nantong city.

Structure and Process

Thomas Rawski (1989) and Loren Brandt (1989) are prominent among the scholars who would have us believe that, in the first decades of the twentieth century, China entered a new phase of sustained economic development that was as beneficial to the countryside as to the cities. In their revisionist view, under the impetus of internationally contextualized market expansion and urban industrial growth, technical levels and productivity rose, peasants stopped being peasants and became instead a vast sea of petty capitalist entrepreneurs, and on the whole conditions improved. Compatible analyses insist that where there was little improvement and social inquities "persisted," this was "not the result of a spreading market economy . . . so much as evidence that significant parts of rural China were still excluded from the new commercial opportunities" (Feuerwerker 1990: 209). In fact, however, in making such generalizations about the market, development, and modernity, these interpretations seem to tell us much more about the predetermined assumptions and stylized models on which they are based than about the history they purport to reveal. Indeed, the semicolonial history of the northern Yangzi delta flatly contradicts them.

For the countryside, that history gives us a composite picture of rural decline and deterioration amid intense commercial growth. Underlying it, in the last analysis, is the fact that peasant family production had been brought more fully under the control of capital, or its formal subsumption under capital as Marxists describe it.[17] Formal subsumption has often been used as a structural concept, but clearly it is a processual concept as well.[18] In the northern delta, it was in one sense the outcome of a half century of *repeasantization*, in which the peasant family more fully became both a locus of petty commodity production and a marginalized labor force working in the service of capital.

This subtle transformation was not simply the result of the playing out of stylized market forces; nor was it a mechanical reflex of abstract processes of capital accumulation. Its dynamics interconnected with the making of a huge subproletarian class within the peasantry and with the development of a variety of capitalist-style productive relations in city and countryside that were themselves inseparable from new strategies for power and class formation within the elite and the upper layers of the peasantry. It was the historical content of these class relations and the social struggles emanating from them that gave repeasantization its specific form and character in the northern delta.

In the late nineteenth century and in the first decade of the twentieth, international, comprador, and local urban-based capital all assumed key roles in the framing of what became a defining moment in this processual story: the creation of a distinct spatial division between agriculturally specialized and rural industrial districts, which to a considerable degree undermined the unity of agriculture and commercialized home industry that had formed a source of independence, strength, and stability among peasants since the Ming. Thereafter in the agriculturally specialized districts, as this chapter has detailed, though still framed by the other forms of capital, it was really modern landlordism that moved onto center stage.

In an offensive that was historically vital to their class, landlords in effect reconstituted themselves in modern form and simultaneously accelerated the conversion of peasants into subproletarians. Contradictorily, their actions also favored and limited the expansion of semilandlord–rich peasant agriculture, which in competing with and allying with modern landlordism likewise contributed to the downward trends among the majority. Although this layering of capitalist-style commercial farming increased the demand for wage labor, it led as well to the spread and development of various forms of unfree and disguised labor. The latter tells not only of the cheapening of labor power and its decommodification under the semicolonial thrust, but of the way in which the sociopolitical requirements of dominance, as well as the demands of the productive process, influenced the direction of change in the relations and forms of labor.

As a means by which landlords and other classes imposed their authority over the labor process and thus as an expression of the agrarian class struggle, that direction was not at all toward fully proletarianized labor but rather toward reconstituting large numbers of poor, destabilized peasants as a cheap and partially unfree labor force. In this situation family farms in the northern delta were not a strange survival of an older economic order or of an independent, isolatable peasant economy with some sort of inherent structural logic all its own. In repeasantized, subproletarian form, they stood as the essential counterpart to the development of multiple "semicolonial capitalisms." Thus in the agriculturally specialized areas of the northern delta, the expanding numbers of poor subproletarian peasants carried out production processes not as entrepreneurs, as Rawski-Brandt would have it, but as workers exploited and permanently disadvantaged by new and reconfigured forms of capital.

9 *Subproletarianization in the Industrial Districts*

IN THE RURAL industrial districts, as in the agriculturally specialized areas, the semicolonial process fostered changes in rural class relations that were no less than transformative. Yet because rural industry created a particular set of dynamics, subproletarianization there assumed a distinctive form. It entailed the more complete subjection of peasants to petty commodity production and the vagaries of the market, giving them a marked proletarian character. Contradictorily, it simultaneously came to involve the overdriving of—in the sense of further retreat into—subsistence farming. The result was a form of marginalization of the most dismal and socially reprehensible type.

Rural investigators working for the South Manchurian Railway Company (Mantetsu) who came to Nantong in 1940 after just having surveyed several localities in Jiangnan were clearly shocked and appalled by the impoverishment, squalor, and misery they found. Thanks to the household data they gathered and other assorted materials, we have an unusually full if painful picture of peasant life in the industrial districts.

Landholding

The team of nine investigators, one of several deployed by the railway's Shanghai Research Office in 1939–40, compiled detailed data on the village of Touzongmiao, located approximately 40 kilometers northeast of Nantong city and only a third of a *li* from Jinsha, which as we noted previously was one of the oldest weaving centers and a premium cotton-producing area as well. The Nantong survey was part of a larger research project aimed at creating a typology of agricultural communities in the Yangzi delta. Touzongmiao was chosen as representative of rural communities that combined commercialized cotton farming with household cotton textile industry.[1]

TABLE 9.1
Profile of Touzongmiao, 1940

Category	Landholding (mu)				
	<5	5 to 10	10 to 15	>20	Total
Population	313	49	14	17	398
Households	79	9	3	3	94
Average family size	4.0	5.4	4.7	5.2	4.2
Working-age population					
(11–65)	194	29	12	12	247
Workers per family	2.4	3.2	4.0	4.0	2.5
Total cultivated land[a]	207.6	41.3	19.3	105.1	373.3
Amount owned	115.6	40.3	17.3	105.1	278.3
Amount rented	92.0	1.0	2.0	—	95.0
Average farm size	2.8	5.9	6.4	35	4.3

SOURCE: MMT 1941: 37–38, 93, table 1.
NOTE: All the subsequent tables in the chapter are based on the 1940 survey data.
[a] Figures apply only to the 86 agricultural families that owned or rented farmland. The 8 excluded households fall in the two lowest categories: <5 mu (6 households) and 5 to 10 mu (2).

The researchers interviewed residents of 94 households containing 398 members in all.[2] Eighty-seven of the surveyed households can be classified as agricultural, all but one of which engaged in some form of land management; the remaining household, which neither owned nor rented farmland, derived its agricultural income from wage labor. The members of the other seven households made their living from retail selling, peddling, carpentry, spinning and weaving, agricultural labor, transport work, dyeing, fishing, and begging (MMT 1941: table 1).

What is immediately clear from the Touzongmiao data is that the average farm in the rural industrial districts was far smaller than in the agriculturally specialized districts. Whereas the average peasant holding (owned and rented) in the agricultural districts appears to have hovered at 8–10 mu, the average for Touzongmiao's 86 farming families (including managerial landlords) was only 4.3 mu (Table 9.1), and for owned land alone, only 3.8 mu (Table 9.2). Most, nearly 85 percent of these families, averaged only 2.8 mu. In fact, then, 93 percent of the farming households fell far short of the 7–8 mu of (owned) land required for subsistence.

On the other hand, as Table 9.2 indicates, tenancy rates were relatively low: only about 21 percent of the farming households were full tenants, and about 29 percent part-tenants. These figures contrast sharply with Qiao Qiming's findings for the county as a whole in 1924, when fully 87 percent of the peasants were either tenants (64.4 percent) or part-tenants (22.6 percent; see Table 8.3 above).[3]

Obviously what enabled these peasant families to exist on such small parcels of land while forestalling complete land loss and tenancy was house-

TABLE 9.2
Landholding in Touzongmiao by Resident Group

Category	Managerial landlord and semilandlord	Owner	Owner-tenant	Tenant	Total
Households					
Number	5	38	25	18	86
Percent	5.8%	44.2%	29.1%	20.9%	100.0%
Total land owned	127.9	124.5	65.4	4.3	322.1
Farmland	114.8	107.2	56.3	–	278.3
Other[a]	13.1	17.3	9.1	4.3	43.8
Average land owned	25.6	3.3	2.6	0.3	31.8
Percent of land owned	39.7%	38.7%	20.3%	1.3%	100.0%

SOURCE: MMT 1941: Table 1; 37.
[a] House and grave land.

hold industry. Weaving and spinning in fact supplied 55.8 percent of total family income for the 85 percent of farming households with less than five mu of land (MMT 1941: 94). This tells us that in villages like Touzongmiao, as in many other areas of commoditized household industry, peasants tended to value land as much for the opportunity to set up a household as for farming. That in turn shows how over time, but especially under the influence of foreign yarn and then the Dasheng system, rural industrial expansion accelerated the rate of population growth and consequently the demand for land (Banaji 1980: 78). In the industrial districts, in a word, the tendencies toward land fragmentation, overcrowding, and the proletarian character of the peasantry developed to an extreme.

Landlordism in the village manifested something of the same tendency. Though landlords collectively controlled a large portion of the land, ownership was dispersed among many individuals. The five resident managerial landlord and semilandlord families (four of which were related by kinship) together owned about a third of the village land (with almost half the rented holdings of four located outside the village). Only one of the 43 owner-tenant and tenant families rented village land from these landlords. The other 42 families rented a total of 91.8 mu from 36 landlords living in nearby villages, Jinsha town, or cities as far away as Shanghai.[4] Half of these outsiders were managerial landlords, and six rentier owners. Most of the others were merchants (9). One was a teacher, and the other two were of unknown background (MMT 1941: 50). Breaking down the ownership of all village land, peasants held 44.2 percent, the resident landlords 31.1 percent, and the 36 nonvillage landlords 24.7 percent, or a total of 56 percent for landlords (-semilandlords) as a whole.

In sum the pattern of landownership simultaneously combined the relatively high degree of peasant ownership usually identified with low levels of commercialization and the tendency toward landlord concentration commonly theorized for commercialized areas. Landlordism displayed similar ambiguity, encompassing both the resident-managerial pattern of the agricultural districts by the 1920's and the absenteeism associated with Jiangnan and other commercialized areas. At the same time, however, like the tiny peasant plots that formed the seedbed for the further development of landlordism, many of the landlord properties tended to be highly fragmented. This fragmentation explains why land in such villages was measured in *bu* (250 = 1 mu = 1/6th of an acre) rather than the much more widely used mu.

Landholding and Rural Industry

Although Jinsha was one of the oldest weaving districts, these patterns were not unique to it. Investigations of Nantong's household weaving industry in the 1930's indicate that overcrowding, poverty, and destitution obtained throughout the rural industrial areas, where all together the producing population totaled at least a half million persons, and landholding may have averaged no more than one mu per capita (Peng Zeyi et al. 1957, 3: 758; Yan Zhongping 1963). As we noted in Chapter Eight, the tightly packed populations of these districts account, to a large extent, for the unusually high population density in the county as a whole. In 1929 Nantong had the most households of any county in Jiangsu (269,479) and the highest person-to-land ratio—only 1.01 cultivated mu per person (Nankai Weekly Statistical Service, April 17, 1933: 74–75; *Tongji xuebao* 1929, no. 5: 44–48).

In Europe of course, as a large body of literature now shows, poverty and overcrowding were characteristic in the areas of rural industry, both during processes of protoindustrialization and after the appearance of the factory system. It was in fact precisely these features, in combination with its generally exploitative character, that led scholars like Marx and Kautsky to single out rural industry as the worst side of the capitalist system. As Kautsky put it: "Home-based industries are characterized by long hours of work, exhausting labor, the worst sort of dwellings, in short, they are characterized by revolting conditions. They form the worst kind of capitalist exploitation and the most degrading form of peasant proletarianization" (cited in Banaji 1980: 80).

In the European context, as well, demographic trends and the proletarianization of peasants often intertwined. Under the organizational impetus of merchant capitalists, as many scholars have noted, rural industrial systems usually emerged among the poorest peasant strata, who were rather quickly proletarianized. Once this occurred, that is, once producers became completely subject to the exploitative wages commonly offered by merchants, they were often able to survive only by marrying early to maximize the family workforce and thereby, total household income — a pattern that fueled demographic growth and further proletarianization (Kriedte et al. 1981; Medick 1976; Mendels 1972; Tilly 1979).

These European trends have led not a few scholars to view proletarianization as both a key dynamic and a consequence of rural industrial expansion. In arriving at this conclusion, moreover, they have often neglected the obvious, namely, the key role that the merchant-peasant nexus played in determining the pattern of change. Most important, full proletarianization typically emerged only as the generalized outcome of rural industrial expansion under putting-out systems — precisely because those systems *stimulated* and *made possible* the abandonment of agriculture by poor peasant producers.

Thus, although rural industry was just as exploitative in Nantong, and its organization enabled merchants to establish considerable control over the conditions of peasant production, the lack of a putting-out system precluded full proletarianization. Consequently, agriculture and home industry continued to interlock. This is not to say that there were no effects on agriculture. Yan Zhongping describes well the potentially negative effects on agriculture of rural industrial expansion:

> A contradiction arises between the two aspects of production, agriculture and industry, which formerly were mutually coexistent and intertwined. . . . Since rather continuous production [of industry] must be maintained if output is to be raised and income increased, agriculture necessarily becomes secondary to weaving, and the original unity of the two is lost. Compared with agriculture, the amount of capital that one must invest is relatively small, but the rate of cash turnover is quicker. Consequently, in the process of the expansion of the local market, hand-weaving [comes to have] a tremendously powerful influence on peasant producers, causing them to begin to disregard agricultural labor, even to the point of setting it aside to concentrate their labor power on weaving. At this point, the two industries, agriculture and handicrafts, have already begun to separate. (Peng Zeyi et al. 1957, 3: 784)

But Yan, like many scholars of Europe, assumes that the commercialization of household industry will eventually lead to the complete separation of industry and agriculture, that is, to the full proletarianization of producers. The problem with this generalization, as with the assumption that agricultural commercialization automatically leads to development, is that it abstracts markets and processes of commodification from the historically specific context in which they occur.

As we will see later, the development of rural industry did have negative effects on agriculture of the type Yan notes, but precisely because land formed the basis for industry, there was rarely a full separation of the two. Even by 1940 only two families in Touzongmiao relied solely on spinning and weaving for cash income (MMT 1941: table 2).

TABLE 9.3
Spinning and Weaving in Touzongmiao by Landholding

| Landholding[a] (mu) | Households | Spinning-weaving households | | |
		Number	Percent of all households	Percent of spinning-weaving households
<3				
2–2.9	20	14	70.0%	1.7%
0–1.9	28	14	50.0	23.7
3–4	14	13	92.8	22.0
4.1–8	26	17	65.3	28.9
>8	6	1	16.6	1.7
Total	94	59	62.8%	100.0%

SOURCE: MMT 1941: Tables 1, 2, 11
[a] Includes rented land.

Moreover, landholding served as a barometer of the type and amount of textile production undertaken by various households. Table 9.3, for example, shows that families in the middle landholding range (3–4 mu) had the highest rates of participation in textile production, followed by those with holdings of 2–2.9 mu. Table 9.4 indicates that though the poorest families (<3 mu) produced and sold the most cloth in absolute terms, their average output was far lower than that of the other households. Plainly peasants with insufficient land to provide (through the sale of crops, loans, or other means) for the purchase of yarn, and initially, of course, for the expense of a loom, simply could not afford to weave and were forced to engage in the less remunerative work of spinning.[5] Table 9.5 shows the proportion of agricultural and nonagricultural income for representative managerial landlord/semilandlord, owner, owner-tenant, tenant, and landless families. Though the figures spotlight their proletarian character, most families in the village, if they had any land at all, continued to identify themselves as peasants.

The Overdriving of Subsistence Farming

One reason why 85 percent of poor Touzongmiao villagers with holdings so negligible as to supply only 14.7 percent of their income (MMT 1941: 94) continued to think of themselves primarily as peasants was that they counted heavily on their land for their subsistence. If in one sense their tiny holdings functioned principally as a means for them to earn a living from textile production, in another, as the Mantetsu investigators noted, they "had meaning only for domestic consumption" (ibid., p. 149). Most farmed across two seasons, using the bulk or all of their cotton crop to purchase or make yarn and pay rents and debts, and retaining as much of the second harvest as possible.

TABLE 9.4

Cloth and Yarn Production in Touzongmiao by Landholding

| Category | Landholding (mu) | | | | |
	<3	3–4	4.1–8	>8	Total
Total households	48	14	26	6	94
Number of spinning and					
weaving households	28	13	17	1	59
Self-supplied cotton					
Amount (jin)	87	186	214	19	506
Value (as percent of					
year's harvest)	17.0%	40.1%	21.9%	41.3%	—
Purchased yarn					
Amount (jin)	1,212	598	825	23	2,658
Value (yuan)	2,251	1,178	1,437	51	4,917
Total production					
Yarn (jin)	220	76	53	—	349
Cloth (pieces)	1,367	955	1,015	46	3,383
Total sales of yarn					
Percent marketed	100.0%	100.0%	100.0%	100.0%	100.0%
Value (yuan)	200	68	53.5	—	321.5
Total sales of cloth					
Percent marketed	99.0%	100.0%	99.7%	100.0%	100.0%
Value (yuan)	3,020	1,892	2,200	90	7,202
Average sales per					
household					
Yarn (jin)	7.9	5.8	3.1	—	
Cloth (pieces)	48.4	73.5	59.5	46.0	

SOURCE: MMT 1941: Tables 1, 2, 11.
NOTE: All total figures are rounded up; and all percentages are rounded to the first decimal place.

TABLE 9.5

Agricultural and Nonagricultural Income of 17 Touzongmiao Families by Group

(Yuan)

| Group | Households | Total income | Agricultural income | | Nonagricultural income | |
			Amount	Percent	Amount	Percent
Managerial landlord						
and semilandlord	2	635.00	635.00	100.0%	—	—
Owner	6	1,042.75	237.75	22.5	808.00	77.5%
Owner-tenant	6	875.90	142.70	16.3	733.20	83.7
Tenant	1	144.00			144.00	100.0
Agricultural laborer	2	230.90	3.00	1.3	227.90	98.7

SOURCE: MMT 1941: 133.

TABLE 9.6

Average Annual Household Consumption of Domestic Crops in Touzongmiao by Group

(Shi)

Product	Managerial landlord and semilandlord	Owner	Owner-tenant	Tenant	Agricultural laborer
Barley	4.40	2.38	2.30	3.00	—
Broadbeans	1.50	0.22	0.72	—	—
Onions	0.45	0.50	0.28	0.50	0.01
Peanuts	0.20	—	—	—	—
Rice	3.00	—	—	—	—
Soybeans	0.70	0.18	0.45	—	—
Wheat	0.25	0.75	0.07	0.20	—

SOURCE: MMT 1941: 146.

NOTE: Villagers also grew and consumed sweet potatoes in some quantity, but the researchers did not include that item in their data.

The overdevelopment of this second or subsistence economy stands out as a special feature of repeasantization in the rural industrial districts and corollary to the emergence of subproletarian families.

Barley became the central crop around which this "natural" subsistence economy revolved. From the turn of the century it progressively replaced wheat and various other supplementary crops as the second crop to cotton. In Touzongmiao by the time of the Mantetsu investigation, it occupied 80 percent of cultivated land during the second season (the rest being devoted mainly to wheat and broad beans; MMT 1941: 163). Barley's main appeal was that it was more compatible with cotton than wheat since its growing period did not overlap with that of cotton and it could be planted immediately after the cotton harvest. Although it was slightly more labor intensive than wheat and had a lower market value, it gave a higher per-mu yield. Peasants in Touzongmiao made it their primary dietary staple and marketed virtually none of their barley (ibid., pp. 86–88). Many were thus able to sustain themselves for much of the year with little else beyond some corn flour and dried sweet potatoes (a summer crop that thrived and was only grown in poor soil; ibid., pp. 88, 163–64; Shen Shike 1934: 31000; Zhang Renren 1915–16).

Table 9.6 shows the predominance of barley in the diet of peasant owners and especially among tenants. (The larger figure for the landlord households is of no importance here, since barley constituted 80 percent of the food they provided to hired agricultural workers; MMT 1941: 101). The question to ask, then, is to what extent each of the peasant groups relied on its own production. That can be roughly determined by weighing the cash value of barley, 10 yuan per shi in 1940, against the total food costs for the three groups. The results, in Table 9.7, clearly show the increasing importance of subsistence farming as economic status declined. This pattern stands in direct contrast to the pattern for agricultural income we saw in Table 9.5.

TABLE 9.7
Subsistence Farming in Touzongmiao by Group
(Yuan)

Category	Owner	Owner-tenant	Tenant
Cash value of barley[a]	23.80	23.00	30.00
Price of purchased food	96.88	44.86	42.00
Total food cost	120.68	67.86	72.00
Barley as percent of total	19.7%	33.9%	41.6%

SOURCE: MMT 1941: 140, 146.
   [a] These figures are arrived at by assigning a cash value of 10 yuan per shi to the consumption amounts shown in Table 9.6.

Thus though agriculture accounted for only a fraction of total income for the poor peasants, it remained central to their reproduction, providing—largely *outside the market economy*—subsistence for many of them for four to seven months of the year (MMT 1941: 164). But that came about only because they accommodated to their situation by shifting to a food crop that promised to give them a measure of household autonomy, for at least part of the year (cf. Kulinkoff 1989; Mies 1986).

For those who have sought to understand the "competitive viability" of small peasants vis-à-vis big commercial producers, this Janus-face of the poor peasant majority as at once subproletarianized workers and repeasant-ized subsistence farmers provides an important key. The retreat into the second economy enabled them to circumvent total market dependency and continue to eke out a partially autonomous existence on the land. As such it represented both an economic and a political strategy of resistance to the downward pressures of the semicolonial-modernist path. In the last analy-sis, however, this very independence lowered the wage costs for cloth mer-chants, managerial landlords, transporters, and various other employers of cheap labor on whom peasants were dependent. No less important, though the point is often overlooked in treatments of peasant production, northern delta peasants subsidized the price of their commercial crops by not calculat-ing the costs of their labor in their subsistence production and consumption (cf. Mies 1986: 153). In these respects, in the rural industrial districts, as in the agricultural areas, the formation of a class of peasant-workers who were also marginalized subsistence producers developed in conformity with, not in competition with, the economic system emanating from Nantong.

The retreat into greater subsistence production also exacted tremendous costs. In classic Chayanovian fashion it required a simultaneous reduction of consumption among the poorest strata to levels far below the minimum re-quirements set by the Nankai Institute of Economics in 1933 (Walker 1986: 477–79). When producers have been able to maintain older subsistence regi-mens, the nonintegration of consumption has often allowed them to maintain better health standards than among producers with integrated, market-based consumption patterns (Mies 1986: 153; Rau 1990). But in Nantong, framed by the requirements of cotton growing and thus of the larger economic system, the recentering of subsistence production in barley led over time to marked deterioration in the health of poor peasant producers. As the Mantetsu team noted, along with insufficient food, the disproportionate consumption of barley, a grain of low caloric value and less digestible than wheat or rice, probably explained why farmers in the area had such poor physiques and suffered from chronic stomach illnesses (MMT 1941: 164).

Agriculture fared no better. The most intensive barley season coincided with one of the peak periods of demand for cloth, and hence of cloth production (Yan Zhongping 1963: 264). Many families had to neglect their crops and maintain almost continuous cloth production during periods of high merchant demand to offset times of low demand (Huang Xiaoxian 1927: 477). As we will see, many also had to take wage-paying jobs to tide themselves over, most often as fieldworkers, openings that came exactly when their own farms needed attention, during the busiest, most important periods of the agricultural year. Combined with more intensive cropping, soil deterioration from lack of fallowing, and among the poorest, too little fertilizer, these factors contributed to the decay of cultivation even as subproletarian families were becoming more dependent on it.

Thus counterbalancing equivalent trends in the agricultural areas, the intertwining of the cotton economy, rural industry, and subsistence farming in the industrial districts accelerated the deterioration of cultivation, imposed new subsistence crops of a lower nutritional value, and from the standpoint of both human and agricultural development, gave peasant production an increasingly irrational character. This irrationality mirrored precisely the very rational struggle for survival among the poor, marginalized peasant-workers who made up the majority of the population. It also formed a reflexive image of the discourse of modernity reigning in Nantong through which those at the helm of the merchant-industrial complex rationalized the concentration of the benefits of growth in their own hands.

Reconstituting the Sexual Division of Labor

We have seen how the interpenetration of the local and the global in the semicolonial process effected changes in the sexual division of labor. This was even more strikingly the case in the areas of concentrated rural industry. Without an adequate base in land to sustain them, peasant households were pressed into developing new labor systems aimed at maximizing total family income. These systems also satisfied the demand within the Nantong-centered economic nexus for an optimal packaging of various kinds of cheap labor. But undergirding them—and highlighting its position as a structural problem of both the family and the larger society—lay the redefining of the sexual division of labor. As I have argued elsewhere (Walker 1993a), recognizing its role as a central dynamic in social change, that is, in the creation of the subproletarian family, helps us to understand how in the first decades of the century changes in family labor systems at once reflected and affected interrelated processes of economic growth, class formation, and the replication of sexual inequality.

On one level, the reordering of the older division of labor involved a radical readjustment in textile production. In contrast to the earlier division where weaving had been the preserve of women, in weaving households men as well as women now wove (MMT 1941: table 11). That trend had begun at least by the 1880's as a response to the specificities of the *guanzhuang* trade. As we earlier saw, the Shanghai guild established four transaction periods for *guanzhuang* cloth during seven months of the year (February–August). Merchant demand was greatest during and immediately preceding these seven months. Weaving households accordingly intensified production, leading in the heaviest buying periods to the nonstop operation of the loom, 24 hours a day, with all able-bodied family members, male and female, participating (Huang Xiaoxian 1927). Thus although production continued to bear some relation to the older pattern of greatest output during the slack agricultural seasons, the rhythm was largely determined by the requirements of Nantong merchants (Yan Zhongping 1963: 264).

As in the agricultural districts, the second significant alteration in the sexual division of labor was the movement of women into agriculture. Most likely this change developed earlier in the industrial than in the agricultural areas, beginning first in family farming but related, indirectly, to the emergence of a market for agricultural labor in Jiangnan. By the mid-nineteenth century families in some of the oldest and most crowded textile districts along the Yangzi and near the Nantong-Haimen border, such as Xingren, were already assuming subproletarian characteristics. Male members of these families regularly found work on the migrant agricultural labor circuits in Jiangnan (Guan Jincheng 1956; Walker 1993b). Female family members undoubtedly assumed responsibility for farming family plots during the periods of male absence.

In any case what is of chief concern to us is not the time or even the particular situations in which this change in the division of labor first began to occur, but rather the circumstances under which it accelerated and became widespread. Quite clearly, in the industrial as in the agricultural districts, the generalized movement of women into agriculture—as both a function and a dynamic of new growth trends—intimately intertwined with the expansion

TABLE 9.8
Agricultural Hiring-Out Among Touzongmiao Households with Less Than 10 Mu

Category	<5 mu	5 to 10 mu	Total
Households	79	9	88
Members hiring-out	46	1	47
By gender			
Male	35	1	36
Female	11		11
By work arrangement			
Annual	3		3
Seasonal	1		1
Daily	38	1	39
Contract	4		4
Labor days			
Total	2,763	20	2,783
Average by gender			
Male	35	20	
Female	60		
Agricultural wages (yuan)			
Total	461.85	5.0	466.85
Average	5.84	0.55	

SOURCE: MMT 1941: 100.
NOTE: None of the members of 6 households with 10 or more mu hired out for agricultural work.

of the semicolonial cotton trade. Although references to women working in agriculture (except for weeding) do not begin to appear until the twentieth century, by the teens a market for female labor was clearly operating, and by the time of the Mantetsu investigation, women not only were widely engaged in family farming but formed almost 33 percent of the hired agricultural labor force (MMT 1941: tables 1, 2, 10; Zhang Renren 1915–16). Like the other changes in rural political economy associated with the growth of the cotton trade, the relative rapidity with which this redefining of the old division of labor occurred really should not surprise us. The reappearance in the 1980's of feminized family farming and a gendered agricultural labor market provides a much more recent example of the swiftness with which, on a massive scale, such changes can be effected.

The data in Table 9.8 suggest the heavy reliance of the poor peasant families of Touzongmiao on women's hired agricultural work. We note first of all that, in this village, the poorest families (0 to 5 mu) supplied virtually all of the hired agricultural laborers; only one man in a family with more land, 5 to 10, hired out for farmwork. Two-thirds of these workers were men. Women, however, worked a much higher number of days than men, an average of 60 compared with 35. This reflected the fact that more than men, they tended to be stably employed. All four of the contract workers, for example, were women who hired out to pick cotton at harvest time. The only seasonal worker and one of the three annual workers were also women. The first worked for a landlord living outside the village from April until October, doing cotton cultivation, cotton harvesting, clothes washing, and other household labor. Because she brought her children with her, her wage was extremely low, only six yuan for the half year (MMT 1941: 101). The other worked as a farmhand in a nearby village (and thus still lived at home) for a landlord who was a relative. She too made a comparatively low wage (15 yuan) because she took a child with her to work (ibid.). All the other women hired out as daily workers for cotton weeding and picking.

The Feminization of Family Farming and Male Off-Farm Employment

All of the labor systems that developed within and characterized different strata of subproletarian families reordered women's labor so that it became the mainstay of family subsistence and commercial farming. Although men also now wove, it was women who typically did the farming and weaving for much of the year and, among the lower strata, helped keep the family going as agricultural workers. Men more fully became permanent off-farm or auxiliary wage workers in the casual labor force. It is in this development that the significance of the movement of women into agriculture can be most fully comprehended: the feminization of family farming, along with women's continued participation in weaving, provided the cornerstone for male wage work. In this respect women were not merely left behind as men moved into off-farm work but were deliberately "defined back" to the home and farming, where their added roles in agriculture became, in effect, a new variant of older seclusion norms (cf. Mies 1986: 26).

As semicolonial commercialization accelerated in the late nineteenth and early twentieth centuries, poor peasant families in various parts of China increasingly relied on nonagricultural work to supplement their income from family farming and agricultural employment. It was important to remember, a 1930's report cautioned,

> that in general the hired agricultural laborers in China are at the same time poor peasants who cultivate land either owned or leased, and in intervals are also hired out as coolies. While the general phenomenon among the rural rich is a trinity of landlord, merchant, and usurer, that among the rural poor is another trinity of poor tenants, hired farm hands, and coolies. According to a field investigator who in 1933 worked throughout Henan province, the landless peasants and those with insufficient lands have to change rapidly from one farm to another. One day they do field work on their own land or the land they have leased; the next day they work as hired laborers in someone else's field; and the day after that they work as

coolies transporting goods from the shops in the city. These partially hired laborers in Henan far outnumber the full-time hired laborers, and the same situation is to be found in many other provinces. (Institute of Pacific Relations 1939: 71)

But in Nantong's industrial districts, this tripartite, poor peasant economic mode arose not merely in the scarcity of land. It was a function as well of the preference for cheap female hired labor in commercial cotton farming and the proletarian role that rural households played in the Nantong-based system. Consequently, nonfarm work there, like household industry, came to occupy much greater importance in family income than agricultural labor. In short it overdeveloped, not only causing men to take on nonfarm jobs, but often forcing them to spend substantial periods of the year away from home.

Source-of-income data for the 17-household sample of Touzongmiao families illustrate this point. They suggest that among the 85 percent of the population whose holdings fell in the 0–5 mu range, agricultural wage labor accounted for only 6 percent of total cash income; as against fully 21.7 percent from nonagricultural wage labor (MMT 1941: 994). (The rest, it will be recalled, came from weaving, 55.8 percent, and agriculture, 14.7.) This pattern clearly did not obtain among all families in the village. Nevertheless, the figures are significant. Forty percent of the farming families had one or more members hiring out as agricultural laborers, and 47.7 percent had one or more members working in off-farm jobs (both occasional and full-time; MMT 1941: 173–76, tables 2, 9, 10). Though all the agricultural laborers were from families with fewer than five mu, most of the off-farm workers came from the lowest (<3 mu) and upper (4.1–8 mu) strata. The small group in the middle (3–4 mu) remained closest to the earlier norm of maintaining the family principally by combining farming and weaving (as noted, these families had the highest average cloth output in the village).

Although both the upper and the lowest strata came in this way to straddle the boundary between the rural and urban worlds, it was for quite different purposes and to quite different effect.[6] Families in the upper strata hired almost half of all the village's agricultural dayworkers, and although 65 percent of them wove, they produced substantially less cloth on average than the families in the middle (3–4 mu). At first glance that disparity appears surprising, since their larger farms would have increased the potential for weaving. It is simply that a higher percentage of men in this group worked in full-time and subsidiary nonfarm jobs. A tendency toward joint-family formation paralleled this trend (MMT 1941: table 2). Joint families eliminated the necessity of land division on inheritance and created a dual labor force that could be divided along sexual lines between farm and nonfarm employment. With slightly better education, men in these strata were in a position to obtain relatively good jobs.

Since farming in this management category required a labor force of roughly two adult men or three adult women, the typical pattern was for women to farm and weave. Male family members—or at least the family head—often worked at commercial and skilled jobs, such as shop clerking or carpentry, in nearby Jinsha or in Shanghai. When better jobs could not be obtained, sons often worked full- or part-time as rickshaw pullers, agricultural laborers, or porters. When male family members were absent and women could not handle all of the farming, they relied on hired labor—often that of women from the poorer peasant classes. Straddling the rural and urban thus helped upper-strata families to forestall a downward slide and maintain their "cumulative advantages." Conversely, it contributed to processes through which the majority of peasant families were more permanently converted into a marginalized casual labor force.

For these lower-strata families, and specifically the 51 percent whose less than three mu of land could support only 1–1.5 persons (MMT 1941: 175), off-farm employment was not an option but a requirement for family subsistence. Accordingly, the division of labor in these families was highly flexible, with all members trying to find work when and where they could. As in the case of contemporary Java cited in the last chapter, it was this unstable casual labor force, along with its equivalent in the agricultural districts, that formed the foundation for the expansion of disguised labor. The men and women of these disadvantaged families shared weaving and farmwork, and during the busy agricultural seasons, both worked as agricultural laborers. Men also worked at menial, below-subsistence-wage jobs that often took them away from home for extended periods of the year. Some may have become part-time bandits, joining outlaw groups when there was little farm or wage work and returning home to their families and a respectable existence when work became available (see Billingsley 1988). When both transport and weaving were possible, whether men chose one or the other often depended on the current price of cloth. As one contractor who hired porters in the village put it, when the price was high it was difficult for him to get coolies, but when it was low he had no trouble at all (MMT 1941: 180).

Ultimately, many of these families had no choice but to send sons and daughters away from home permanently. Here the purpose was not, as among upper-strata families, to bolster the household's income, but to eliminate surplus labor and especially, it would seem, to avoid land division among brothers. In the twentieth century casting members out to prevent further division became common practice among poverty-stricken families in various parts of China (M. Cohen 1978: 187–88).[7] Like many of the peasants forced out of farming in the agricultural districts, men who could not find work swelled the ranks of the lumpenproletariat, surrogate bandit "families," and the other groups of dispossessed operating on the fringes of—and increasingly from the late 1910's as part of—rural society. Few of the men in this village who did secure permanent jobs continued to live at home. Most seem to have settled in Shanghai and to have worked as rickshaw pullers or porters or in similarly low-paying jobs. Many attempted to maintain contact with the family by returning home for a short time at New Year, though apart from the few who had succeeded in securing better-paying jobs, such as factory work, and sent home small amounts of money each year, they did not contribute to the family's support. Others neither remitted money nor returned home. Once they left the village, the family lost all contact with them (MMT 1941: 105–6). In most cases out-work and migration eventually led to a breakup of the family.

The fate of women and girls who were forced out was as dismal or worse, since at best they faced child marriage and, at worst, prostitution or indentured labor. For some women, as we earlier discussed, this fate was unquestionably a fact of village life. But most stayed on as the linchpin of family farming and household industry. So thoroughgoing was this change that, as the Mantetsu investigators pointedly noted, at any one time there were few able-bodied men in the village (MMT 1941: 91).

Complicating Rural Differentiation

The relegation of women to household industry and family farming among the upper-strata peasants (5 to 10 mu) made it possible for men to move into full-time, off-farm jobs. It also led to a new mode of family farming in which part of the fieldwork was performed by hired laborers. Consequently, although the landholdings of this group were still typically of below-subsistence size (most fell in the 4.1–8-mu range), in Touzongmiao those families took on the characteristics of a rich peasant class.

Indeed Table 9.9 shows that the proportion of work done by hired labor on farms of five to 10 mu exceeded the 25-percent norm developed during the land revolution to demarcate the rich-peasant class. Table 9.10 shows, in addition, that they hired 30 percent of all labor, compared with only 28 percent for families in the 10-to-15-mu range, though that small group of families hired workers for far more days, 254.3 compared with only 91.4. Predictably, managerial landlords and semilandlords hired workers for the greatest number of days overall.

Viewing rural differentiation and labor hiring in this light enables us to place in clearer perspective Yazawa Kozuke's (1961) contention that the Republican period saw a capitalist transition in agriculture. Based on these same Touzongmiao data, Yazawa's influential formulation posits the labor-hiring strata as a "surplus-oriented" bourgeois class, and those who hired out as belonging to a "subsistence-oriented" proletarian class. But our analysis re-

TABLE 9.9
Family and Hired Labor in Agriculture in Touzongmiao by Landholding

Category	Landholding (mu)				
	<5	5 to 10	10 to 15	>20	Total
Households	72	9	3	3	87
Total family members	289	49	14	17	369
Average family size	4.0	5.4	4.7	5.7	4.2
Working-age population (11–65)	179	29	12	12	232
Working-age members per family	2.5	3.2	4.0	4.0	2.7
Total labor days	14,490	3,143	1,723	1,921	21,277
By family[a]	14,320	2,320	960	960	18,560
By hired labor	170	823	763	961	2,717
Percent hired	1%	26%	44%	50%	—

SOURCE: MMT 1941: 98–99.
[a] Assumes 80 labor days per person a year.

TABLE 9.10
Hired-in and Hired-out Agricultural Labor in Touzongmiao by Landholding

Category	Landholding (mu)				
	<5	5 to 10	10 to 15	>20	Total
Households	72	9	3	3	87
Hired-in days	170	823	763	961	2,717
Household average	2.3	91.4	254.3	320.3	31.2
Percent of total	6.3%	30.3%	28.1%	35.3%	100.0%
Hired-out days	2,757	20	—	—	2,777
Household average	38.3	2.2	—	—	31.9
Percent of total	99.3%	0.7%	—	—	100.0%

SOURCES: Table 9.9; MMT 1941: 93.

veals the principal problem with Yazawa's interpretation: because he ignored the role of women in managing agriculture while male family members went off to other jobs, he misinterprets the reasons why labor hiring assumed such marked proportions in Touzongmiao. Moreover, despite his line of argumentation, Yazawa is unable to demonstrate any significant differences in farming techniques or management style among the various landholding groups. Nor could he, for there is no evidence within this so-called "bourgeois class" (or among managerial landlords, for that matter) of the innovation and rising productivity that his notion of capitalist transition suggests. In transferring the responsibility for farming to women (who still had to manage most of the weaving and all household duties), these families sought no more than to maintain existing levels of production. Stated differently, the directional line in this rich peasant–like group was toward agricultural stultification, not development.

On the other hand, Yazawa's depiction of two differentiated classes resonates with the evidence presented here for a countryside marked by an increasingly proletarianized poor peasant population working in the service of, and to a considerable degree subsumed by, various forms of (interpenetrating) local and international capital. Certainly to the extent that Nantong's modernist path fostered "intensified exploitation, greater insecurity, and increas[ed] human misery" (Thompson 1963: 212), it exhibited key features of a classical-style capitalist transition. It did so, however, as the preceding chapters have argued, without simultaneously generating the momentum and sustained development also typically associated with processes of capitalist growth.

This Janus-faced modernity found its fullest expression in the rural industrial districts. But in complicating the usual picture of two broadly differentiated classes, the emergence there of an "added" group of rich peasant–like families whose landholdings were too small to provide family subsistence only serves to illustrate the point. Like the poor peasant majority beneath them, they were subject to downward pressures and exhibited many of the characteristic traits of subproletarian families: they relied on wage earnings and their farm produce to sustain themselves; their consumption levels fell below minimum subsistence standards; they often showed a loss of net income; and they were chronically in debt (MMT 1941: 140–57).[8] Nevertheless, their ability to ensure greater stability, thwart the downward slide, and maintain slightly better living standards rested in part precisely on their exploitation of the poor peasant majority. Like those to whom they were themselves subject, they contributed to a larger, multifaceted process of rural-urban social differentiation and inequity through which the vast majority of peasants were turned into a disadvantaged, market dependent, and proletarianized poor peasant labor force. Consequently, in the industrial as in the agriculturally specialized districts, class-like demarcations within peasant society became more pronounced while the conditions fostering poor peasant demands as those of the majority of peasants developed further.

Poverty and the Question of Cloth Consumption

As both cotton farmers and producers of handwoven cloth, subproletarian families in the industrial districts were doubly linked to the Nantong-based system and were most damaged by it. By the 1940's they were among the most destitute and marginalized of the northern delta's rural dwellers. What constitutes poverty is of course at once historically and geographically specific. Even for similar locations and time periods, attempts to set the poverty level have often been foiled by large discrepancies in standard-of-living analyses

(Himmelfarb 1983: 7–9). But the Mantetsu investigators were never in doubt about what their data told them: that Touzongmiao was a village made up almost entirely of people who were poverty-stricken and barely surviving. They could see for themselves, and were profoundly affected by, the human devastation—the makeshift, dilapidated housing, ravaged and unhealthy physical appearance, and tattered clothing of the villagers.

Let us weigh this visible evidence against one of the central pieces of "inferential evidence" on which recent revisionist arguments for rising living standards hinge: the increase in per capita consumption of cloth in China during the Republican period. After credibly demonstrating high growth rates in the tiny industrial sector, Thomas Rawski (1989), for example, attempts to show that the agricultural sector grew at comparable rates, the latter being essential to his argument of sustained economic development overall. He accomplishes this goal, but only by constructing, as one of his critics emphasizes, "dubious" and "unreliable estimates" for agricultural investment and growth (T. Wiens 1992: 66–67). He then uses these and other cumulations "of mistaken inference" (ibid., p. 69) to argue for rising per capita income and living standards in rural China. Given the lack of any direct evidence for these assumed trends, he argues that the rising consumption of cotton cloth substantiates the conclusion that living standards were improving (1989: 289).

In countering Rawski's argument, Philip Huang (1990) makes the important point that, in the main, rising per capita consumption of cloth (which Xu Xinwu estimates to have increased about a third from 1840 to 1936; as cited in Huang, p. 137) can be attributed to the fact that machine-made cloth was less durable than handwoven, at a ratio of 2:3. This alone, as Huang notes, would account for an increased total consumption of 28.4 percent (ibid., pp. 137–38). On the other hand Huang offers no explanation for the rather significant shift to machine-woven cloth implied in these figures.

It is precisely on this question that the pattern of cloth consumption in Touzongmiao gives the lie to Rawski's inference. To the Mantetsu team, the dress of these villagers was one of the most visible signs of peasant impoverishment. They found it astonishing that in this cloth-producing village almost all of the residents wore "miserable, raglike clothing," and in the case of many children, so little that they were half-naked (MMT 1941: 162). Equally startling to the investigators initially was the fact that most villagers purchased their clothes or the fabric to make them instead of using the more durable cloth they produced themselves.

A detailed profile of 18 of the families clearly indicates this tendency. The accounts of 12 of the 18 showed expenses for clothing totaling 73.34 yuan, or an average of about six yuan per family (MMT 1941: 140). If this item had shown up in only two or three households, one could assume that silk or cotton had been purchased for special purposes, but that will not do when it was part of the budget of two-thirds of the sample. This finding directly correlates, moreover, with the fact that, as shown in Table 9.4, the villagers marketed virtually all the yarn and cloth they produced. It was simply that, as the team correctly concluded, the cash income from spinning and weaving was so vital to family subsistence that producing families could not afford to retain any of the cloth they produced. Instead, at the last minute, when their rags could be pieced together no more, they purchased the cheapest varieties of clothes on the market, including mainly the ready-to-wear sold to the Shanghai working and underclass made of inferior handwoven cloths and, increasingly, the flimsy, less durable varieties of machine cloth, especially those produced in Japan (*Ershinianlai zhi Nantong* 1930, 4: 19; Lin Jubai 1984: 83; Liu Ruilong 1986: 5).

The Touzongmiao villagers were in much the same fix as the peasants in the south of England who lost their land during the late eighteenth century in the course of capitalist development. Unlike the better-off peasants who could still afford to have the women of the family make their clothing, the poverty-stricken southern agricultural laborers "could spare practically nothing for clothes":

> Even those [women] who were provident enough to supply themselves with a small stock before marriage were reduced to a ragged state from their inability to renew their garments afterwards, "and then [critics of the day jeered] the women spend as much time in tacking their tatters together, as would serve for manufacturing new clothing." . . . Although the clothing sold by the shops was often cheaper in the initial outlay, home-spun garments were generally considered superior in warmth and durability. But the women in the South and wives of the poorest labourers in the North could not even afford to purchase the raw material to spin at home. If any surplus remained for clothes at all, necessity demanded the finished article at once, and the purchase was made from the second-hand dealer or the village shopkeeper. Because they had no reserves . . . the practice of providing clothing at home fell into disuse, and dependence upon the slop shop, the result in the first place of economic conditions, was wrongly imputed to idleness and lack of skill. (Pinchbeck 1930: 51)

To be sure, the author pinpoints the importance of time in this pattern (as well as the availability of cheap machine-made products), rather than the desperate need for cash income from weaving as emphasized above for Touzongmiao. The central point, however, is the same: systemic impoverishment accounts for the villagers' otherwise seemingly irrational replacing of homemade cloth and clothing with market goods, most often in inferior, less durable forms.

Thus, far from providing an index of rising standards of living as Rawski and others would have it, the growing consumption of cloth in Touzongmiao was a barometer of peasant pauperization. That the Mantetsu investigators considered these Nantong peasants worse off in this respect than those of

Changshu, Wuxi, and Taicang, the Jiangnan communities they had already surveyed, does not invalidate this line of argument for those or other localities. Given the fact that the "poverty line" was and remains higher in the southern delta than farther to the north, similar dynamics could easily have been operating among the poor, even if they were slightly better off.

Community and Class

As in the making of the English working class, the downward slide of subproletarian families in Nantong's industrial districts undoubtedly generated, at times, hopelessness and demoralization. Yet in the face of this "catastrophic experience" (Thompson 1963: 212), decidedly different impulses and developmental lines emerged within the evolving poor peasant community. One was the strengthening of older forms of mutual aid, exchange labor, and work sharing.

The intensification of this collective aspect of village life among poorer peasants stemmed directly from the conflicting demands of maintaining their farms and earning what was now an essential part of their income from wage-paying jobs. For those who relied on employment as agricultural laborers, the problem was compounded, since work was often available only at a time when they were most needed on their own farms. To obtain wage income, they frequently let the work on their own farms go and then banded together or exchanged labor with each other to catch up on planting, harvesting, or other tasks they had been forced to postpone.[9] In Touzongmiao only families with holdings of six mu or less participated in the roughly 45 labor exchange arrangements the Mantetsu team recorded, with the largest number concentrated among families with two to four mu. Only three of the families involved in these relations also hired-in day labor, whereas over half had members who hired out (MMT 1941: table 9).

At the same time the poor residents in Touzongmiao assumed collective responsibility for neighbors so destitute that they were reduced to begging. A minimum of 5 percent and perhaps as many as 10 percent of the villagers were "professional" or "seasonal beggars" (MMT 1941: 180). In earlier times family and kin would have been the first to offer support to people in such desperate straits. But as families fragmented and disintegrated under the pressures of marginalization, out-migration, and long-term away-from-home work, obligations to kin dissolved (and with them, their last resort, since the "moral imperatives" that might have once brought them aid from the local Xu lineage landlords had long since ceased to operate; ibid.). Under these circumstances responsibility for the needy shifted to the community. As the Mantetsu team concluded:

When poverty is so extreme the bonds of families and kinship that have developed uniquely in China and are still tenacious are of no use. . . . Kinship ties work effectively only so long as financial interests are guaranteed. . . . But in other areas of actual life the mutual ties of kinship are completely severed and only the village community guarantees the existence of the bottom-most level of rural society. (Ibid., p. 182)

In practice, given the growing divisions between richer peasants and those who were poor, leading to the isolation of the former, it was really the poor peasant community that supported and "guaranteed the existence" of those who were unable to otherwise survive.

Subproletarianization, Class Struggle, and Peasant Politics

This moment of a heightened community consciousness in the industrial districts coincided with a resurgence of peasant mobilization throughout the northern delta that coalesced in a single poor peasant–subproletarian politics as the 1920's wore on. The community that shaped and was shaped by this experience must not be viewed, however, as operating only at the village level. To the extent that in the 1920's the material conditions fostering a poor peasant worldview as the predominant outlook of peasant political action took firmer root, it intertwined with intensifying class struggles in which most often, rather than the village, shared work experiences and broad-based opposition to developing forms of power and labor control became the basis for collective political activity. Put another way, in the sense that in any particular setting, peasant ideology is a cultural and ideological formation that has specific social and historical roots, the struggles of the 1920's not only bore the imprint of but deepened the development of peasants as a subproletarian class.

Reflecting both the powerful influence that the international cotton market was exerting on the local economy and, more specifically, the multipronged landlord offensive to regain lost ground, tenants' actions became one of the central theaters of the new wave of struggles. From the early 1920's landlords faced mounting resistance on the part of tenants, ranging from widespread refusal to pay the full rents demanded, to actions against specific landlords, to violent mass protests. Organized resistance by permanent tenants against landlords who were attempting to usurp their property rights and risings against corrupt and abusive warehouse managers who oversaw the collection of rents in kind for absentee landlords became typical of the period (JS [6] 1983; Liu Ruilong 1986: 7).

So, too, did large-scale risings against landlords-cum-local trustees who tried to pile taxes on top of rent payments. The attempt to impose a new tax in the reclaimed land areas of Dongtai in 1922, for example, stirred a rising of 8,000–10,000 tenants. When attempts to collect the tax continued, a much larger area-wide mobilization of at least 30,000 tenants occurred in 1923. Violent protracted struggles against land development companies, especially the Dayoujin, Dafeng, and Tonghai companies, also took place. Arising when the companies prohibited the transfer or sale of tenure rights and attempted to get out of fixed contract agreements by imposing higher rents, these struggles literally turned the new land areas into a war zone. They also assumed a proletarian-like character. Lacking the lineage and village connections from which peasants in other areas drew organizational support, but having the advantage of being able to direct their attack at a single enemy, peasants in the reclaimed areas mobilized horizontally against individual companies (Huang Xiaoxian 1927; JS [1] 1983: 24–85 passim; Shen Shike 1934; Zhang Youyi 1957, 2: 372–73, 3: 1015–1018; Zhu Mingxia & Bian Xiaozhi 1986).

The further development of the kinds of coercive landlord power and administrative control discussed in Chapter Seven also became a source of intensifying class conflict. Especially in the outlying, peripheral areas, individual landlords had managed by the 1920's to erect comprehensive anti-peasant administrations that included bureaus to collect special taxes and levies, accounting offices to press for rents and debts, police forces to go after rent offenders, and courts and tribunals to try and punish them (Liu Ruilong 1986; Shen Liangpan 1980: 78).

Landlords with strong governmental connections, such as Lu Xishan, who was an assembly member and owned 10,000 mu of land in the Lugang area of Rugao, were in a position to assume virtual rule in the countryside, often by having family members head various offices. Lu, with the aid of his son, who worked in the Civil Administrative Office in the town of Banjing, reportedly ran roughshod over the peasant population in Lugang (Liu Ruilong 1986: 6).

Peasants were acutely aware of the implications of these developments, in terms of both the expansion of landlord power and their own position in the class struggle. Consequently, opposition to the "illegal yamen," as they appropriately labeled the new landlord accounting offices and tribunals, and to the landlords who headed or supervised them, formed the subtext of many of the 1920's struggles. In the 1922–23 mass risings in Dongtai, for example, peasants killed several of the local trustees responsible for collecting the various special local taxes, but, symbolically, deposited the corpses at the home of the leading landlord organizer of "peasant affairs" in the area (Zhu Mingxia & Bian Xiaozhi 1986).

A large-scale rising in 1923–24 in the Henxiang area of Taixing provides another illustration. A large landowner named Huang Bichen, who also was an assembly member, fashioned a feudal-like administration over peasants in

108 villages surrounding Zhendong, where he lived. He established his own court, issued regulations, collected taxes, and trained a group of policemen to supervise the tenants and peasants in his fiefdom. Led by an old peasant known as Yu the Daoist (Yu Xuexian), peasants in the villages rose in armed rebellion when Huang attempted to impose a new tax on pigs, but the entire system of control he had imposed quickly surfaced as the central issue. When Yu was captured, another peasant, Yu Dahua, assumed leadership. The rebellion lasted for three months, during which the town of Zhendong was set on fire three times, and both Huang and the county magistrate had to flee. In the end troops suppressed the insurgents and killed the leaders. Although Huang was able to reestablish his position, he was forced to rescind the tax, and the peasants were emboldened enough to commemorate their insurgency by building a small temple in honor of their slain organizer, Yu the Daoist (Liu Ruilong 1986: 6–7). In struggles such as "Burning Zhendong" (so named by the insurgents), as had long been the customary expectation in collective peasant actions, all the residents of the insurgent villages may have participated. Nevertheless, in their violent escalation of resistance to "local bullies and evil gentry"—and thus to the developing forms of coercive modern power—such struggles at once assumed the class character and bore the imprint of a more explicit poor peasant–subproletarian politics.

Reflecting precisely the structural positioning of most peasants in the northern delta by the 1920's, those politics also crossed urban-rural boundaries. It was not only "porters and poor peasants" who banded together in urban uprisings such as those in Taizhou in 1921 (Liu Ruilong 1986: 8). Marginalized subproletarian peasants found strong allies in other groups of urban poor who were disadvantaged by the growth of modern merchant hegemony in Nantong, especially petty traders, small merchants, and hawkers. Instances of concerted action by peasant-weavers and petty traders (an alliance that dated back to the late Qing) clearly demonstrate that in the industrial districts, along with more typically agrarian issues, control of the conditions of production and marketing had become the central issues in class conflicts with merchant capital (Bernstein 1979; Lin Jubai 1984: 265).

The largest of these actions occurred in 1935, when peasants from weaving households and their petty trader–merchant allies attempted to prevent the opening of, and then moved to destroy, the new Nantong Cloth Market established by the cloth merchant elite. As the peasants clearly recognized, they were going to lose virtually all control over their own production if the merchant elite succeeded in this effort to tightly regulate the kinds and quality of cloth accepted for sale. At the same time, under the auspices of the Chamber of Commerce and with the full support of the Nantong police, the cloth merchants declared older marketing areas at the west gate of the city illegal, a move that was calculated to eliminate smaller cloth traders or at least bring them under the control of the new market. Although peasant resistance lasted for several weeks, in the end local authorities quelled all public protests, leaving the closely supervised market in operation (Lin Jubai 1984: 289–98; Miao Qingping 1935; *Tongtong ribao* Oct. 20, 1935: 3, Nov. 3, 1935: 3).

Viewed in its totality, then, the evidence strongly suggests that the coalescence in the 1920's of a more explicit poor peasant politics and its expression in escalating class conflict cannot be separated from the deepening of subproletarianization. At the level of ideology and consciousness, that politics clearly appears to have reflected the fact that the majority of rural producers were not merely tenants and part-tenants. They were at the same time also agricultural laborers, disguised hired and indentured laborers, household industrial producers, porters, rickshaw pullers, casual laborers, beggars, and farmer-bandits. As we have seen, various combinations of labor predominated in different households. Yet the key point is that, for a majority of rural families, subproletarianization involved a shared experience of semicolonial modernity as marginalization. Virtually no poor peasant household was exempt from its effects.

The various productive and occupational endeavors of the unstable subproletarian family thus simultaneously produced multiple alignments, which in turn formed the loci for multidimensional struggles. In this respect poor, subproletarian families became the essential matrix for a distinctive consciousness—one born of the multiplying structures of daily life and work, and through which collective actions such as tenants' risings in the countryside and risings crossing urban-rural boundaries became equally characteristic.

This is not to suggest that in this conjunctural moment northern delta peasants suddenly developed a "class consciousness" of the type, as modernist formulations would have it, that was necessarily taking them in the direction of revolution, but simply to link the deepening of subproletarian class formation to growing peasant militancy. That militancy expressed the intensification, by the 1920's, of what might be termed the central contradiction of the semicolonial mode—that between subproletarians and the many "capitalisms" of the semicolonial economy. As in the 1900–1912 movement, it is really only in light of the continuing development of this contradiction, both structurally and in an ideological sense, that the variegated strains of peasant politics in the 1920's can be fully understood as those of a single, historically particular subproletarian peasantry.

To some extent the escalation of rural class struggles in poor peasant-subproletarian form also interconnected with the development of a militant proletarian politics. In the early 1920's, well before students in the Nantong-Rugao area began to organize local Communist Party branches, the collective discourses of subproletarian peasants and the urban poor were already influencing and becoming infused with radical working-class ideas in Nantong city and Shanghai. Workers at the Dasheng mills, most of whom were, for example, women from subproletarian families in nearby rural districts, not only took to the workplace mentalities based at least in part on intimate knowledge of the multiple work-life experiences of their family members, but brought back home news of and thoughts about slowdowns, strikes, and the meaning of modernity. In such families strict boundaries between the mental "universes" of urban and rural simply dissolved (Liu Ruilong 1986: 8; NJ 1959b). Viewed in this light, the appearance in 1921 of the first strike actions in both the Dasheng No. 1 and Chongming branch mills, the urban rising of porters and poor peasants in Taizhou mentioned previously, and insurgencies among tenants in various parts of the northern delta hardly seem coincidental.

Similarly, many of the members of subproletarian families in Nantong, Haimen-Qidong, Rugao, Taixing, and other localities who were working as casual and permanent laborers in Shanghai in the early 1920's were in all likelihood veterans of the militant struggles of the delta-wide 1900–1912 movement. They thus took to the cities a commonsensical understanding of ruling structures as unjust and illegal, as well as poignant memories of specific struggles, such as the forming of the radical Pingchao Nation, that undoubtedly contributed to working-class activism and militancy. Conversely, on their periodic return trips home, they spread the news and ideas of workers' strikes (in which, in some cases, they had participated; Liu Ruilong 1986: 8) and took back to the cities knowledge of the new directions of cultural politics and economic struggles in their home areas. Studies of the revolutionary buildup in China have usually stressed the movement of radical ideas from the cities to the countryside, but the evidence shows that such boundaries cannot be so easily drawn.

In sum in the late 1920's, when a small group of Communist Party organizers finally came to the northern delta countryside, they stepped into a situation of escalating class conflict in which they found themselves working, not with a population of primordial holdovers from the past waiting to be awakened, or groups of disaggregated agriculturalists motivated only by petty-bourgeois individualist concerns, or a victimized mass that was somehow being inexorably propelled toward social revolution, but with a politically seasoned, "long-prepared force." It consisted of people who for over a quarter of a century had been developing an alternative nationalist critique of modernity built on ideas of autonomy, equality, and social justice. In that process they had come to understand their situation, define themselves, and articulate their shared relationship and vision of the world in increasingly politicized fashion.

In the brief period before Jiang Jieshi's (Chiang Kai-shek's) counterrevolutionary move (1927) made an impact north of the Yangzi, many northern delta peasants supported the Communists' bid for the future. Party organizers made rapid headway among both poor subproletarian peasants and the burgeoning bandit populations along the borders of Nantong, Rugao, and

Taixing. When counterrevolution did come, in the spring of 1928, Lugang, the home base of the local despot Lu Xishan, became the site of the first Communist uprising in the northern delta (Barkan 1983: 465, 477–80; NT [5] 1983; "Rugao nongmin douzheng zhi jingguo" 1983). At the same time Communist organizers quickly recruited peasants, groups of Big Swords, and others into the new Fourteenth Red Army and formed one of the first Communist base areas in China. It encompassed a broad stretch of territory that extended northward from Qidong, through western Haimen-Nantong and northern Rugao (almost reaching Jinsha, and including parts of the Dayoujin, Huafeng, and Dayu development company lands), and into western Rugao and Taixing. The base lasted only three years, a failure that owed not to a lack of peasant support but to the Nationalists' military superiority, the mutiny of one of the larger bandit gangs, and the fact, as the Party candidly admitted, that the organizers showed much less political acumen than the peasants they organized (Barkan 1983; JS [1] 1983: 290–300, 377–84; JS [7] 1983; Liu Ruilong 1986: 35–113).[10]

The exact relationship between the deepening peasant militancy of the 1920's and the Communist movement is a subject that needs to be explored in a separate study. Nevertheless, like working-class struggles in Chinese cities such as Shanghai (Perry 1993), peasant history in the northern delta compellingly suggests the importance of understanding alliances from the bottom up (see Winn 1986) in the development of revolutionary politics. As the important work of scholars like Elizabeth Perry argues (1980, 1993), it also suggests that revolutionary politics began with peasant politics, a politics growing out of both the longer line of peasant political culture in the delta and the radicalized semicolonial struggles that marked a crucial moment in this alternative history.

Over the last decade detailed empirical research based on newly available sources has given us more finely textured analyses of the revolutionary process in China (notably, Chen Yongfa 1986; Dirlik 1997; Hartford & Goldstein 1989; and Odoric Wou 1994). The resulting view of "many revolutions," which interconnected with yet depended on the dialectical interaction of peasant and Party, and indeed of a Party that was able to succeed only by paying attention to local concerns, marks an advance over older treatments. Mao Zedong, in fact, in 1933, outlined precisely this procedure as essential to revolutionary success (1971). Yet as the peasant history of the northern delta forces us to confront, the course of the Revolution, especially its success or failure in particular areas, cannot be fully explained by limiting the focus of inquiry to Party-peasant interaction. To understand its patterns, treatments of the Revolution in different localities are, in the last analysis, going to have to come to terms with the semicolonial process and the clear evidence of an older, deeply rooted peasant path.

Semicolonialism and the Peasant Path

DOMINATION, violation, and resistance framed semicolonial China. During the late nineteenth and early twentieth centuries in Nantong and the northern Yangzi delta, the semicolonial encounter took shape in two broadly interconnecting yet decidedly different and conflicting trajectories. The first trajectory emanated from imperialism and indigenous wielders of power. Wrapped in a universalizing discourse of progress and modernity, it produced a restructuring of the Yangzi delta economy under the impetus of the Shanghai treaty port and the Nantong urban-based elite, aided by rural allies. To be sure, there were trenchant points of contradiction between imperialism and Nantong's local elite, as well as among its constituent members. Nevertheless, the points of economic convergence between them and the colonizing representation of history, development, and the world that to greater or lesser degree they also eventually shared meant that, in the last analysis, the elite-fashioned path in Nantong furthered imperialist domination as well as that of its local architects.

This modernist path ran up against an independent developmental line emanating from the peasantry, which coalesced in a popular politics that demonstrated continuing peasant concern with issues of social justice, opposed processes that were disadvantaging the majority of rural dwellers, and by the second decade of the century, explicitly contested the form that the nation was going to take. Despite elite attempts at its suppression, the peasant path represented a historical alternative to the development of social inequities rooted in the elite project, and through its persistence, it profoundly affected the character and course of sociopolitical change. As much as imperialism or the elite, this alternative peasant history shaped the semicolonial moment and formed a crucial part of the hybridized modernity that was its product.

The aim of this book has been to delineate and explore the multiple layers and dynamics of these dominant and alternative lines so as to simultaneously trace out a key moment of globalization and draw attention to semicolonialism as a crucial category of analysis in the study of modern China. In recovering this semicolonial history—and thereby situating major issues of imperialism and global process within a specific local context—the findings presented here spotlight semicolonialism as a mode of control that operated through fragmented, multiple, and multilayered forms of domination.[1] In the northern delta the domestic power of imperialism framed that mode, both in terms of its evolving political and economic privileges and in terms of its totalizing cultural agenda. But its specific expressions can be fully understood only in light of older historical trends and patterns in agrarian class conflict, the contemporary social struggles that formed an integral part of the semicolonial process, and changes in gender relations that crucially affected the way that society was replicated and work organized. Unraveling the interpenetrations and points of opposition of these external and internal dynamics, in the sense of social dialectics, as well as the dialectic between society and economy, has necessarily involved critically confronting and moving beyond the developmentalism that has supplied the analytical framework for much of the work on modern China.

The Semicolonial Mode: Many "Capitalisms"

Fortunately, as one scholar recently put it, "the image of colonialism as a coherent, monolithic process seems, at last, to be wearing thin" (Comaroff 1997: 165). Colonies were never empty spaces to be made over in the colonizer's image, any more than imperialist states were "self-contained entities that at one point projected themselves overseas" (Stoler & Cooper 1997: 1). The recent turn in colonial studies has thus begun to emphasize the tensions and contradictions of empire, including not only various forms of engagement and resistance, but the degree to which conflicts in metropolitan countries shaped colonial encounters (Stoler & Cooper 1997; Comaroff 1997).

Still, compared with semicolonial contexts, whether viewed in terms of their administrative regimes, armies, or control over economic processes, colonialisms assumed a certain coherence with greater power to dominate and directly pursue their hegemonic projects. In key respects, then, despite many similarities, the study of semicolonialism presents a different set of problems. In China, most obviously, given the absence of a colonial state, lacking direct access to most of the interior, and with only limited assistance from the Qing, the agents of global capitalism had to depend on linkage and alliance with a range of Chinese elites to realize their economic aims—elites that were for the most part intent on building, protecting, or expanding their own bases of power. Consequently, of necessity, imperialism became a crucible fostering multiple hegemonies, or what Frederick Cooper has referred to as a subcontracted power structure.[2]

We saw for the Yangzi delta the crucial role that the Shanghai treaty port initially played in this process—as the site of a foreign-controlled financial-commercial network through which foreign business interests used their unequal trading privileges to disseminate manufactured goods and procure agricultural commodities and raw materials. Nantong surfaced as one of the beneficiaries of the restructuring of the delta economy that took shape under the influence of that network, the new global framework acting simultaneously as a powerful stimulus to its textile and cotton trades and as a dissolvant of its older peripheralized status. By the late 1920's powerful state capitalist forces, functioning as the economic allies of global capitalism through their growing monopolization of a new-style national commodities market, added to this patterning.

Yet in the last analysis economic restructuring in the delta and, by extension, the realization of imperialist objectives depended on and were fundamentally tied to an expansion of commodity production, most of it in rural-based form, paralleled by attendant changes in labor. This was quite simply because the accumulation of capital lying at the heart of imperialist economic activity in China, as in fully colonized areas, could primarily derive only from the exploitation of workers and not from international trade. Accordingly, throughout much of the colonial world, as scholars of late-nineteenth- and early-twentieth-century colonialisms have emphasized, the operation of the capitalist mode of production involved an organic linkage with domestic and peasant-based subsistence economies.

That heterogeneous linkage contradicts standard developmentalist images of "crushing" capitalist "progress" as inherently antithetical to such economies and ultimately promoting both their dissolution and the separation of labor from the means of production. Indeed, it was precisely by establishing *organic relations* between capitalist and domestic peasant economies that imperialism set up the mechanism, as Claude Meillassoux argues, for "overexploiting" and reproducing cheap labor power. Although domestic peasant economies remained largely outside the sphere of capitalist production, by continuing to form the site for the reproduction and to a large extent the feeding and maintenance of labor power, they in effect subsidized the low wages within it. At the same time they nevertheless came under capital's sphere of influence, being totally involved with the market economy as the principal suppliers of the labor and commodities that it required. As a result, these economies were simultaneously maintained and destroyed, and under the sway of processes that were contradictory in essence, they at once continued to exist and no longer existed (Meillassoux 1981: 90–98).

Viewed in this light, the Yangzi delta stands a prime example of a region where, because imperialism could not directly orchestrate an expansion of the peasant-based petty commodity economy or the particular labor relations needed to carry it out, the directive role of local elites and other rising classes became crucial to the imperialist project. Accordingly, the specific transformations of this semicolonial process and the social struggles in which they were embedded have lain at the heart of our examination.

Among other things, that examination has led to a central finding of this book: that in the northern delta a variety of competing "capitalisms," supported and extended by new political and cultural practices, became the chief expression of the fragmented, multifaceted, and multilayered mode of semicolonial domination. As a specific modernity that took shape in the half century from 1880 to 1930, these many "capitalisms" reflected precisely the differential impact of imperialism and the world market on local processes and both the making and the contesting of new forms of power by various groups and classes. In turn, the competition among these many "capitalisms," despite their points of alliance and interconnection, actualized and furthered the operation of semicolonial power in partial and multiple forms.

In certain respects these "capitalisms," particularly the modern industrial enterprises established by Zhang Jian as a "nationalist" counter to imperialism, as well as a source of independent economic power, complicated and thwarted imperialist aims. Nevertheless, even Zhang's Dasheng mills interlocked with and deepened the petty commoditized productive mode of the peasant economy. Indeed, as outlined in the preceding chapters, at the close of the nineteenth century, under Zhang's direction modern industry became the linchpin in the creation of a combined and uneven subregional economic system that entailed production and marketing relationships embracing towns, financial institutions, commercial and subsistence farming, and rural household as well as urban industry. The interlocking of modern industry and peasant production underpinning this system concentrated the benefits of rapid economic growth in the hands of Nantong's modern urban elite, firmly established Nantong city as the center of exploitation of a type that united city and countryside in a single structural process,[3] and produced a more distinct separation of agriculturally specialized and rural industrial areas. The last reinforced the older functional role of much of the northern delta as a peripheral supplier of raw cotton, but now it did so to meet the needs of the Nantong rather than the Jiangnan elite. At the same time, it drove a wedge into and undercut the sources of economic stability that had been a source of peasant strength since the end of the Ming.

Compounding economic trends that imperialism was already generating and that intensified in the first decades of the twentieth century, and appearing at once as a planned accompaniment to and an unintended consequence of its organization, Zhang's integrated urban-rural system also stimulated the development of other local "capitalisms." In Nantong city it hastened the expansion and integration of large merchant capitalist–native banking firms that assumed greater control over the conditions of peasant-based household industry and, eventually, hegemony over both the cloth and the cotton trade. In the countryside, complementing and in tension with growing competition for cotton on an international scale, it prompted the appearance and expansion of various forms of capitalist-style commercial farming—among modern landlords who took up farming with wage and disguised wage labor; rich peasants who expanded their operations in a similar manner; and even upper-strata families within the subproletarianized peasantry who developed a mode of rich peasant–like farming.

To the extent that these rural productive formations either directly or indirectly fostered the rapid expansion of wage labor, they assumed the face of capitalism. In intensifying commodity production and generating other associated trends, they accelerated rural and urban class differentiation and the regearing of the rural economy in the service of urban-based capital, both local and distant. Yet if in these respects they bore classically capitalist traits, they also shared the distinctive features of what might best be termed semicolonial capitalisms.

In the first instance, in the volatile and rapidly changing economic environment of the time, which was creating opportunities for some and threatening others, the real name of the game became the control of labor and commodities as a means of securing a foothold or dominance in the expanding, hierarchically ordered circuits of trade. Consequently, rather than productive innovation as in the classical models, the principal thrust of these many competing "capitalisms" became the greater extraction of absolute surplus value. In both intent and expression, and whether organized by merchants or by members of rural classes, they operated like commercial capital instead of productive capital of the improving variety.

For landlords and to some extent rich peasants, this particular economic course also assumed political dimensions—as a counter to, on the one hand, the growing influence of monopolistic industry and merchant-usury capital over the countryside and, on the other hand, the intensification of rent and other forms of resistance among peasants. It was precisely because of the dual need to ensure access to and control over labor that disguised forms of wage labor and the reappearance of sharecropping became predominant features of the emergent rural "capitalisms." In this sense, like the operations of the modern industrialists and Nantong's merchant capitalist elite, they, too, quickly assumed a monopolistic dimension.

Furthermore, and again bearing much closer resemblance to imperialist-colonial than to classical capitalist models, these various "capitalisms" did not use or stimulate the development of fully proletarianized labor, but instead drew on peasant-workers from destabilized peasant families as their primary labor force (even the bulk of the workforce in the Dasheng mills was made up of women from nearby peasant families). Destabilization, in fact, lay at the heart of the semicolonial process, in the sense that it accompanied and formed the necessary condition for the conversion of peasants into peasant-workers. In this respect it both reflected and expressed the devastating impact of global and local capitalisms on the majority of rural dwellers and, by extension, the operation of imperialism as a "mode of reproduction of cheap labor power." It is only when semicolonialism is viewed in this light that we can begin to understand what was actually involved: the invasion of international capitalism into local systems "without offering," in the words of one scholar, "a secure source of income to pay the penalties of lost self-sufficiency" (Stover 1974: 84).

A host of associated changes, including the disintegration of the older combination of agriculture and household industry in the structure of family farming and an entire range of new and harsher tenurial forms contributed to peasant destabilization and forced the members of downwardly differentiating families, even when they considered it undesirable, more deeply into commodity production and wage labor. These processes of change were, in turn, closely bound up with increasing inequalities in access to land that cannot be explained by simplistic demographic arguments.

Paradoxically, along with the fuller generalization of the commodity economy and wage labor, this specific agrarian transition also brought a deepening of the subsistence or *second economy*. On the one hand, this process reflected the fundamental economic rationale of the entire semicolonial formation, that is, the need of both imperialism and (subcontracted) local "capitalisms" to preserve, albeit in more precarious and unstable form than before, the peasant-subsistence economy in order to realize and perpetuate primitive accumulation.[4] But retreat into the subsistence economy also became part of a survival strategy among destabilized families and a means by which they sought to maintain autonomy and independence from the market. Isolation from commodity exchange meant that the family farm, if of meager and dwindling size, continued to provide a real historical alternative to wage labor (Post 1982).

Under the multipronged assault of imperialism and various local capitalisms, the vast majority of rural dwellers were thus repeasantized as an unstable and largely impoverished poor peasant wage labor force, which though it remained on the land, nevertheless met the needs of local and imperialist capital for commodities, cheap labor, and resources. The routine casting out of family members, either permanently or on a rotating basis, which also became a characteristic feature of this process, produced a continuous flow of rural migrants into the towns and cities, thereby keeping industrial and casual wage rates low. As the indispensable component and appalling social outcome of the expanding market relations of the semicolonial mode, the transformation of destabilized peasant families into subproletarians marked what in fact was the (generalized and systematic) appearance of a historically new peasantry.

In the northern Yangzi delta, then, many competing "capitalisms"—as a form of economy and control and as requisite intermediate organizers of organic economic relations between imperialism and local labor—became a defining feature of semicolonial domination. Emerging at the interstices of local society, these semicolonial capitalisms at once propelled new wielders of economic and political power into the limelight, brought older extractors of surplus value to find new strategies to maintain their positions, and created a context in which those who occupied lower positions in the emerging economic hierarchy might at least hope to forestall a downward slide. For the vast majority of families, however, the result was impoverishment and subproletarianization. Traversing urban-rural "boundaries," their multiple identities as commercial and subsistence farmers, agricultural laborers, home textile producers, porters, rickshaw pullers, and low-paid casual workers of various other sorts marked a pattern of dynamic economic growth that hinged (the momentary flowering of modern industry notwithstanding) on the intensification of petty-commoditized production through the exploitation of rural labor. In short, that development marked a pattern in which capital had taken greater hold of agriculture, in the sense that it had been penetrated by capitalist relations if not at all thoroughly by capitalism (see Byres 1991).

This economic trajectory created very limited demand for improved instruments of production and little need for the emergence or expansion of industries producing the means of consumption. Instead, it showed that, in the form of many "capitalisms," the strategy for power fashioned by Nantong's urban elite and then rather quickly modified by older and would-be wielders of power had produced a specific semicolonial modernity in which development as generally conceived was not part of the agenda for the countryside and would occur only on the most limited and halting scale in the cities.

Gender and the Differentiating Rural Society

Marking the appearance of a historically new peasantry particular to semicolonialism,[5] subproletarianization involved changes in the labor process within as well as outside the family. Indeed, it was only through a rearticulation of the older sexual division of labor within peasant households that the subproletarian family took shape. Stated differently, class analysis alone cannot reveal the complex nature or key dynamics of subproletarianization. It must be understood as an engendered process of class formation, in which the recomposition of (unequal) gender relations in the household became the essential locus for the organic linking and (partial) subordination of peasant labor to imperialism and local "capitalisms."

At the end of the Ming, the solidification of the older division of labor played an equally important role, giving new stability to peasant production at the same time that it brought women under more intense familial control. In the semicolonial moment, as multiple economic forces undercut peasant stability, the radical rearticulations of the older division did not necessarily weaken familial controls over women. But they did make possible the intensification of subsistence and commercial farming, rural industry, and the various forms of wage labor that enabled many families to survive. In that new embodiment of the Chinese peasant, women became the mainstay of family farming, subsistence, and reproduction. They thus stood at the center of a process through which the replication of sexual inequality, though in altered form, established the basis for continuous primitive accumulation by imperialism and local capitalisms and the transfer of the surplus from agriculture to industry. Outside the family, the social reconstruction of poor subproletarian women as a significant part of the hired agricultural labor force devalued women's labor and deepened the overexploitation of peasants even more.

The latter development calls attention to another key point: the relation of changes in the sexual division of labor to stratification among subproletarianized peasants and thus to a process that was much more complex than standard two-class analyses of rural differentiation usually suggest. In this case, however, the central dynamic was not so much quantitative in the sense of producing pronounced economic differences as qualitative. Interconnecting with urban differentiation, it entailed a sharpening of differences within villages and in patterns of work that added to the cumulative advantages of some peasants and the cumulative disadvantages of the majority.

Precisely because a feminization of family farming lay at the core of the changing division of labor, this form of differentiation enabled men in subproletarian families with slightly more land to obtain permanent off-farm jobs that were usually better paying than the temporary menial and casual work common among men *and women* of the poorer families. Because of the absence of male family members, the better-off families also became a significant labor-hiring group, women farm managers supplementing their own labor with that of hired workers—often also female—drawn from the poorer peasants. Along with the activities of modern landlords and semilandlord-rich peasants, the management style of these rich peasant–like families at once expanded the demand for agricultural labor and contributed to processes whereby the vast majority of subproletarian families more *permanently* (that is, noncyclically, which is not to say irreversibly) became a marginalized labor force. It was precisely this cumulation of disadvantages among the many that created the large pool of families who were willing to agree to sharecropping and other forms of disguised wage labor. Although these forms further disadvantaged the already marginalized, they often offered the only prospect of security.

Yet the rich peasant–like management style of upper-strata subproletarian families was not aimed at achieving a greater productivity of labor; it was simply a means of maintaining agriculture through the intensification of the labor of women, who were still responsible for textile production and the care of family members. Consequently, like the other rural "capitalisms," it contributed to transformative developments in the countryside in which, the initial increases in production notwithstanding, the primary dynamism and theater of action became changes in transferring shares of the surplus to particular groups and classes.

In terms, then, of the economic relations between peasants and the non-producing and partially producing classes, as well as those among peasants, the recasting of the sexual division of labor brought changes in both the form and the function of production relations, and in the ways in which different groups and classes gained access to the products of their own and others' labor.[6] At the same time women's labor became the essential foundation for the creation and perpetuation of the subproletarian family. Attention to women's labor roles within it thus forms an essential vantage point for understanding the real issues of agrarian social reproduction and in key conjunctural moments, the dynamics of social change. This vantage point takes us well beyond the historical distortions—and, in the final analysis, replication of gender hierarchies—contained in standard depictions of Chinese peasants as "male" and of women's work as belonging to the less important categories of "auxiliary," "surplus," or "low opportunity cost" labor.

Modern Industry, Merchants, and the State

Flowing from the common understanding of industrialization as the sine qua non of economic development, recent studies on both sides of the on-going debate about the nature of the prerevolutionary Chinese economy have uncritically equated modern industry with urban development.[7] The evidence for Nantong shows, however, that the character, substance, and trajectory of modern industry—as indeed of the various other local "capitalisms" of the northern delta—were determined not by some transhistorical essence but *in their making*. Although imperialism and older historical patterns continuously conditioned and intervened in that making, most often, as I have repeatedly emphasized, external determinations were articulated with internal agency. In other words, that making was largely the product of specific local struggles.

Viewed in terms of the semicolonial process as a whole, the social struggles between subproletarianized peasants and the heterogeneous ruling elite assumed the greatest significance. Yet the tensions, contests, and conflicts, as well as the shifting alliances among the elite and rising groups and classes, made a difference. In an economic sense, these various struggles revolved in part around the degree to which, as T. J. Byres (1974) expresses it, a *net* marketed surplus was produced for and delivered to local industry, and thus also around the intersectoral terms of trade between industry and agriculture.[8] Such production and delivery goals lay at the center of both the monopolistic contours of modern industry in Nantong and the geographic and economic unevenness of Zhang Jian's integrated urban-rural system. But the actual degree to which that transfer was made and by whom was a matter of class relations and struggles. Furthermore, the issues of social control and labor relations often intersected with those struggles, as did questions of politics and ideology that could not be reduced simply to economic class practices.[9]

Considered in this light, modern industry in the northern delta, far from being a "nutritive source" of sustained development, urban or rural, appears as a fleeting and largely unsuccessful attempt to counter the growth of imperialist power in China. On one level, its demise, by the 1920's, as a *dynamic* local "capitalism" stemmed from its own internal limitations—limitations that reflected its sudden historical grafting onto existing economic organization. Among these, unsound financial policies that to a significant degree were dictated by merchant-usury capital's continuing control of the investment market loomed most important.

Yet equally if not more important were the attempts by impoverished producers, rich peasants, modern and old-style landlords, and merchant-usurers to block the transfer of the net marketed surplus from the countryside or, at the very least, to share in the benefits of that transfer, thereby reducing the portion for industry. It is in the latter respect that the growing tension between monopolistic local industry and merchant-usury capital (and by extension modern landlords, who despite a different political agenda nevertheless functioned as the economic allies of urban-based cotton merchants) assumed particular significance.

Initially, Dasheng's monopoly system provided unusual strength and momentum to industrial development in Nantong. But it held firm only through the first decade of the century before falling victim to Nantong's modern merchant elite, which had accumulated and concentrated enough capital to launch its own drive for monopoly in the cotton sector. Revealing the growing economic contradictions in Zhang Jian's "nationalist" developmental path, the details of that specific history spotlight the way in which within the fragmented mode of semicolonial control, different fractions of capital related to the world market. No less importantly, they document a strengthening of merchant capital in the economic formation rather than its subsumption by modern (local) industry.

The complex changing relations between merchants and industry also throw into bold relief the state's pivotal role in local economic processes. Just as Zhang Jian's ability to superimpose a monopolistic industry on local economic organization owed much to the support of the semicolonizing Qing state, so it was the intervention of new state forces in the form of modern banks and bureaucratic capitalists that finally sealed the victory of the Nantong merchants, and the fate of local industry. With the banking takeover of the Dasheng mills in the mid-1920's, local industrial growth virtually came to a halt.[10] In that moment when "development" came to rather narrowly mean the further concentration of commercial capital through trade and monopoly, paralleled by the new controls placed on merchant capital by the foreign-backed state capitalist regime, Nantong's merchant leaders most fully assumed the traits of a semicolonial elite.

After the early 1920's, with the single exception of the costly Chamber of Commerce building, no new industrial enterprise or significant architectural symbol of modernization appeared in Nantong. Following on the heels of three dynamic decades for Nantong city and modern industry, this visual silence eerily marked the semicolonial character of a path of modernity that, in the end, pinned its hopes on a marginalized countryside and left towns to function as mere transshipment depots for exports to nonlocal and more distant international markets.[11]

This history in some respects resembles that of Wuxi in the southern delta. As in Nantong, the elite-led modernist path in Wuxi emerged in the context of the semicolonial restructuring of the delta economy. Centered on developing the local silk industry for the export market, the Wuxi pattern likewise entailed urban-rural linking. At the helm of the industry, as the work of Lynda Bell shows (1994; forthcoming), stood the magnate Xue Shouxuan, who in the 1930's, much like Zhang Jian at the turn of the century, used connections with the state to obtain monopolistic control over peasant cocoon producers and other advantages.

But there was a key difference between the two areas. In Nantong the emergent bureaucratic-capitalist system, which at once functioned as part of the state and as a fraction of capital, contributed to the weakening of modern industry and the strengthening of merchant capital. In Wuxi, in contrast, the system facilitated the consolidation of industrial power—to the point where, by the early 1930's, Wuxi ranked third in the country in industrial output. At that stage most Chinese industries that remained outside the state-capitalist orbit were able to do so only because of close personal or family ties between their owners and functionaries near the top of the state apparatus (Coble 1980). At the same time, the Guomindang state, principally to convince foreign backers of its modernizing intent, sought to develop several showplace localities. Wuxi became one of the few beneficiaries of both sets of circumstances.

Outside of the treaty ports, Nantong's experience, and the story of industrial capital within it, may well provide the more representative image. On the other hand, highlighting the plurality of the forms and forces of semicolonialism, both Nantong and Wuxi illustrate well how imperialism and an expanding global capitalism interconnected with the driving forces in Chinese economic life to influence social relations and local economic systems at all levels of the economic hierarchy. The differing trajectories of modern industry in the two localities drives home the point that understanding why, historically, particular ruling classes or fractions within them acquired a higher or lower degree of autonomy must entail analysis not only of structures but of processes (Cooper 1993: 142; Leys 1978). Those trajectories remind us all too clearly as well that, from the inception of modern industrial technology to the present, the history of imperialism and capital accumulation has been synonymous with processes of uneven development and "the constant emergence, realigned interaction, and transformation of local capitalisms" (Pred & Watts 1992: xiii).

The Peasant Path and Semicolonial Politics

The resistance and alternative history peasants fashioned in the first decades of the twentieth century formed a critical dimension of the semicolonial process in the northern delta. Through their struggles peasants developed a mass nationalist critique of semicolonial modernity and simultaneously shaped the entire character and viability of the local regime. On one level these struggles formed key textual moments recording both peasants' opposition to the multiple "capitalisms" that were disadvantaging them and their efforts to prevent the consolidation of the modernist ruling bloc. But in bringing their own histories and interests to the engagement with semicolonial power, they also mapped the reformulation of a much older, deeply rooted peasant path.

Scholarly research on peasant social movements in colonial settings, many of which were likewise strongly nationalist-autonomist, indicates that they typically arose under two, frequently interlinked conditions: first, when common forms of hidden "everyday" resistance could no longer be sustained; and second, when the practices of colonial capitalism threatened peasants' autonomy in unprecedented ways (Feierman 1990; Isaacman 1993; G. Joseph 1990; Mallon 1987b; Ranger 1985). In key respects these same conditions, albeit in semicolonial expression, formed the context for the new moment of peasant action in the northern delta in the decade prior to 1911.

Several factors converged to produce these conditions. The move by landlords and the state to take the weapon of rent resistance away from peasants was one of the most important. As we saw, the development of a radical regional political culture among delta peasants at the end of the Ming and their routinization of rent resistance in the Qing forced the state to back landlords by intervening in the landlord-tenant relation. If this policy failed to significantly deter the evolving peasant path, it became even less effective in the post-Taiping years when, empowered by the radical Taiping legacy, "everyday" rent struggles increased throughout the delta. Claiming that taxes came out of rents, delta landlords again turned to the state for help. Faced with mounting foreign debt and thus seeking to ensure tax collection from landlords, the Qing state acquiesced by granting them greater quasi-official powers and intervening in rent collection in unprecedented ways.

Other measures initiated by landlords, who not only had to contend with an economically and culturally strong peasant community but bore the brunt of the growing influence of imperialism and the world market on the domestic economy, compounded the state-elite line. Their manipulation of conversion rates as money rents replaced rents in kind raised real rents, while their creation of private dunning "armies" as appendages of the new rent collection bursaries extended the repressive turn. In short, in attempting to simultaneously roll back the gains of and intensify the pressures on rural labor, landlords and the state changed the contours of the class struggle. Although there is little indication that their attempt to make the old peasant strategy of routine rent resistance more difficult and riskier was all that effective, it plainly did heighten class and peasant-state antagonisms. In defining new terms in which power was articulated and contested, these measures led to the further militarization of local society and stimulated the broad-based mobilization of, first, peasants and then landlords.

After the turn of the century, older forms of everyday rent resistance were in any case an insufficient strategy against the multitude of new taxes levied by the local elites in support of their modernist projects or against the emergent "capitalisms" that were undermining the independence and stability of peasant households in multiple ways. Put most simply, then, the changing field of power forced peasants to broaden the targets of and develop new approaches to struggle.

Resonating with popular mobilization in other parts of China, the rising tide of multifaceted peasant action that appeared in the years from 1900 to 1912 quickly assumed the character of a delta-wide movement. Reminiscent of the late Ming, when in regional and transregional discourses bondservants and servile tenants reformulated older notions in new contextual terms, the multidimensional struggles of the early-twentieth-century delta combined an evolving critique of modernity with more deeply rooted concepts of equality, of property rights for the many instead of the few, and of the state as a principal deterrent to freedom and autonomy. In the northern delta they also specifically became struggles *about class*, in which peasants at once resisted the deepening inequalities of elite-centered modernism and their own transformation into a subproletarianized labor force.

The fact that they (initially) failed in this endeavor does not, however, tell the entire story, or in the longer run, even the most important aspect of it. By 1911–12, in what can only be viewed as an expression of a different way of seeing and interpreting the world, peasant struggles became even more radical and emancipatory. Manipulating and transforming constructs and ideas of the elite, in both the northern and the southern delta multiclassed peasant alliances definitively rejected the legitimacy and self-appointed "leadership" of the heterogeneous modernist elite by declaring their independence from the new Republican state. They thus radicalized their praxis through an emerging commonsensical understanding of the ruling bloc and its structures as unjust and "illegal" and by actualizing the notion of an autonomous peasant community-Nation free from the control of both elite and state. In this conjuncture the organic crisis and bifurcation of Chinese society not only took another qualitative turn, but *politically*, despite the movement's momentary defeat, both the conditions favoring the continuation of a unified peasant project and a new moment in a longer line of independent peasant development had appeared.

At the same time, this militant peasant line necessarily shaped the local regime. The antecedents of repressive local rule were firmly embedded in the prior history of the peripheralized northern delta, augmented as noted above by semicolonial pressures on landlordism. But the fact that, by 1911–12, the elites saw the countryside as virtually "out of control" sealed both the conservative urban-rural elite alliance and the deepening of the "hidden" military character of its modernist mode of power. In characterizing peasants as inferior and belonging to a different time, the imperialist discourse of progress and modern civilization supplied a ready-made rationale for the antipeasant contours of that mode.

To be sure, semicolonialism had created the opening in which the urban entrepreneurial-commercial elite could impose its specific project on local society and, thus, "wield an influence quite out of proportion to [its] limited numbers and relative economic and social weakness" (Bergère 1989: 60). Yet in the face of growing peasant nationalism and particularly because the urban elite made no attempt to curry public favor by incorporating popular demands into its program or to gain popular consent for its "leadership," it still needed the support and cooperation of the pivotal holders of local power — the landlord-gentry. Repression and militarism thus united the urban elite and rural landlords, who when faced with a serious challenge from below closed ranks to preserve and extend their control of land and labor. Both joined the

1911 revolution to crush its more radical impulses and reestablish rule over the peasantry. In the years after 1911, through a certain rationalization of the political order, the authoritarian and militarist dimensions of their roughly hewn coalition became more pronounced. Zhang Jian and his brother Zhang Cha first headed the civil-military bureaus that ruthlessly crushed the forces of peasant Nation-ists. Thereafter, in local self-government and other institutional forms in central zones and a more exclusive wielding of power by landlord magnates in peripheral areas, the ruling bloc expanded its coercive apparatus and established an antipeasant administration in the countryside. In the process conservative "modern" landlords moved to improve their declining economic position by balancing political-military levers with a new economic offensive that combined labor-tying and social control with greater surplus extraction.

Scholars of agrarian transitions have long emphasized the crucial positioning of landlord classes in processes of transformative agrarian change. In certain respects the emergence of both the conservative rural-urban alliance and modern landlordism in the northern delta bring to mind Barrington Moore's (1966) now classic comparative historical sociology of landlord power, or what he calls the "repressive [landlord] adaptation" to capitalism. In this model, of course, Moore argues that the central role in modern authoritarian political trajectories is played by a reactionary alliance among landlords, the state, and (later) a dependent bourgeoisie, in which landlords maintain their position by gaining support from the state and intensifying pressures on rural labor, especially through labor-repressive agriculture. On the other hand, Moore also emphasizes that the consummate expression of this repressive, modernizing road—the Prussian case—depended as much on the "capture of the village community and destruction of its autonomy" (1966: 460–67) as on the enserfment of peasant producers for commercial farming by landed Prussian elites. Paralleling his consideration of the strength or weakness of conservative elite alliances, Moore thus situates his analysis in the processes and outcomes of agrarian class conflict.

In the northern delta the urban-rural alliance and, especially after 1912, the multipronged political and economic offensive of modern landlords bore the familiar traits of Moore's repressive modernist route. But in colliding with an agrarian social movement that could not be "captured" or destroyed, the northern delta elite encountered profound political limits. Despite the brutal crackdown in the years after 1911, peasant activism reappeared in full force within a decade. Contradictorily, then, precisely when both the landlord offensive and subproletarianization were reaching new levels of intensity, the same processes that were more fully subordinating peasants in an economic sense formed the context for class struggles that made them even more uncontrollable politically. Reflecting also state-elite practices after 1911 that to some extent neutralized the rich peasant–small owner component of the pre-1912 peasant coalitions, the resurgent mobilization assumed a more explicit poor peasant–subproletarian character.

To the extent that consciousness is generated in and changed by social action (see Marshall 1983), this mobilization reflected and deepened the class formation of subproletarian peasants. Its history directly contradicts recent postmodernist and compatible analyses contending that the complex "internal differentiation" of peasants with subproletarian characteristics suppresses class-based political action.[12] Against such formulations the record for the northern delta unambiguously indicates that interpenetrating with an alternative vision of community(-nation), the shared experience of subproletarianization—as defined by multiple social relations of production and the political project of the modern elite, and as an evolving awareness in consciousness of one's identity so formed—became the crucial nexus for the development of an oppositional peasant politics along increasingly class-based (poor peasant–subproletarian) lines.

As articulations of the shared experience of semicolonialism and an alternative imagined community, the mounting struggles of the 1920's continued to combine the ideals of a radical social program with opposition to the fraudulent "nationalist" state. But their main focal points became the social relations and coercive forms of semicolonial power, especially those associated with modern landlordism. Bringing class conflict to a new level, in those struggles and the deepening rent resistance that left few landlords with the rental payments they demanded, peasants not only thwarted the landlords' move to rebuild a system of local landowner control underwritten by and as part of the state, but destabilized and laid bare the contingency of the entire modernist route. In turn, the obvious inability of the local power bloc to consolidate its position and, by extension, the continuing crisis of authority, stood at the center of a defining within the elite of national political options that paved the way for the ascendancy of the militarist Guomindang regime. In sum, in the first decades of the century, despite and yet integral to the backdrop of many "capitalisms," subproletarianization, and repressive modernist power, the peasant path was effecting a certain transition of its own—one that formed an essential part not only of semicolonial history but of the prehistory of the revolution.

Thus here again against standard developmental images of stability, peacefulness, and the relative insignificance of the military component in commercially advanced areas (commonly represented in China scholarship in the construct "peaceful cores and troubled peripheries"), the realities of semicolonial politics in Nantong and the northern delta present a strikingly different history. They highlight the analytically autonomous role of politics and the degree to which the strength and opposition of "subordinate" peasant classes, especially as articulated in multifaceted struggles that provided the terrain for the nonlinear development of a coherent regional political culture, must be incorporated into explanations of political trends and outcomes.[13] In so doing, they throw into bold relief as well the limitations of analyses viewing state formation as relating only to formal governmental institutions or to the growth of centralized power abstracted from processes of class formation and conflict in local society.[14]

Peasants and History: Rethinking the Nation

The evidence of a separate and long-term line of peasant development in the delta compels us, I would argue, to take a close look at our concepts of the nation. With some notable exceptions, historians have tended to take the nation-state as their starting point. Whether as an imagined community (Anderson 1991), as a homogeneous culture tied to the state (Gellner 1983), or as various fragments (Chatterjee 1993), the nation is generally understood, analytically and historically, as being interlocked with capitalist development, the appearance of bourgeois elites, and the rise of the modern state. Accordingly, nationalism is treated as a distinctly modern phenomenon involving a fundamental epistemological break in consciousness with the past, and history is conceived as essentially a linear, progressive (elite-)nationalist process in which the Nation(-State) as subject gathers self-awareness (Duara 1993, 1995).

These concepts serve up the notion of a single "real" nationalism as objective truth inextricably tied to the modern state. Shaping the ways in which reality is imagined and acted upon, they "set up the world as a picture" and suggest that this representation is not only an orderly system but the movement of history (Escobar 1995). In fact, however, as I have repeatedly emphasized, under the weight of this restrictive teleological narrative, which functions as an ideological construct supporting particular forms of power, the real and varied contexts in which any particular history is to be comprehended recede from view, are suppressed, or erased.

Recently, in part because of global developments that contradict the modernist metanarrative, scholars have taken renewed interest in questions of nationalism and the nation. New lines of critical inquiry have begun to appear. In China studies, for example, Prasenjit Duara (1993) confronts standard images of the radically novel and modern nature of nationalist consciousness and their privileging of modern society as the only social form capable of generating political self-awareness. He argues that in China, from the Song, a statist discourse that blended the Confucian notion of community with the idea of racial uniqueness knitted the "nation" together. In contrast

Florencia Mallon's (1995) pathbreaking analysis of four regions in Mexico and Peru tackles head-on the conventional association of nationalist ideology with the bourgeois elite and of nationalism as a predefined ideology. Reconceptualizing nationalist consciousness as analytically separate from—though historically connected to—the politics of the modern nation-state, she convincingly shows the pivotal significance of alternative peasant nationalisms both in constituting and in shaping the nation.

In different ways both Duara and Mallon dismantle the notion of a single real nationalism. Duara's depiction of a stabilizing statist discourse of the nation enriches our understanding of hegemony in China. Yet his elite-centered formulation ignores the views of the vast majority of the population, and hence like the genealogical discourse he describes, it fails to consider the possibility of popularly based alternative nationalisms and movements of history.[15] On the other hand, although Mallon's history from below brings these alternatives into fuller view, it continues to connect them historically to a Euromodeled statist project whose contours and sources lay in the "triple knot" of bourgeois democracy, capitalism, and colonialism.

I suggest that the accumulated evidence for China now makes it possible—and intellectually necessary if we are to close the gap between theory and history—to take this decentering further and begin to examine the nation as *both* analytically and historically separate from the state. Specifically, I propose what might be tentatively termed a peasant-nation thesis, in which I view the stirrings of nationhood as grounded in new developments in peasant production, culture, and politics. This view shares the older anthropological concern with state-class formation as a framework for the emergence of an oppositional and to some extent relational identity. Most important in this respect are formulations suggesting the possibility of *ethnogenesis*, in which domination inherent in processes of state formation might supply the context for the appearance of an oppositional national identity based on ethnic lines or rooted in the common experience of subordinated groups as producers (Patterson & Gailey 1987; Sider 1976). For purposes of the present discussion, I am not centrally concerned with the issue of state domination as such. The question is instead whether and how certain conjunctural conditions might conduce to new imaginings and forms of unification among subaltern groups and classes.

Viewed in this light, both the evidence for the coalescence in the late Ming of a distinct subaltern cultural domain of regional and even transregional scale and the evidence for an independent developmental line among the peasants of the delta tantalizingly suggest the formation of a peasant nation. I have argued in the preceding chapters that the new imaginings about and constructions of community in the Yangzi delta did represent a radical break with the past—in the sense that at least in part peasants stopped believing what they used to believe. But though this change was linked to the expansion of commodity production, it was not part of a project leading toward a modern nation-state. Indeed the nation of which I speak was not a statist project at all, but one submerged and confined within the contours of the state. As a genuine community of shared interests, it appears to more closely approximate Stanley Diamond's view of a nation "as the basis of culture, the generator of custom, the creative aspect of a whole people" (1974: 37). In the sense that this provisional peasant nation was bound up with the formation of a belief system that contained elements of the past, but endowed them with new meanings antithetical to those of the state and elite, it can also be viewed, most broadly speaking, as a political community. Its discourses articulated a broad vision for organizing society and project for collective identity, both of which are central to Mallon's definition of nationalism.[16]

Yet the new "national" subaltern culture encompassed far more than a changed view of things. It opened up new political and ideological space in which peasants and their allies waged concrete struggles—struggles that turned on both regional and local concerns, informed by a vision of community based on the premise of equality. The significance of the late Ming as a watershed thus appears in the broad social and economic changes that supplied the context for the formation of this "national" culture and, specifically in the Yangzi delta, produced material changes that structurally empowered peasants and enabled them to initiate a sustained line of development. In short, I propose that the uprisings of bondservants and servile tenants in the Yangzi delta at the end of the Ming should be viewed not solely as struggles for freedom and liberation, but quite literally as a nationalist impulse in which peasants acted to bring society closer to their vision of what the nation (as an "unbounded" community) should be.

Similarly, albeit with a qualitative difference, the widespread peasant protests of the first decade of the twentieth century, though mostly local or confined to a few villages, also appear unquestionably as a nationalist movement in which the central issues became the meaning of the nation and the form it was going to take. In that semicolonial context, to the extent that the modern "nationalist" elite attempted to accumulate power through the violent exclusion of all popular discourse, clearly no class outside of the peasantry could genuinely claim to speak for the nation. Strategically, from the late 1920's, in localities such as the northern delta, the decision of poor, destitute, and subproletarianized peasants to embrace both a symbol of Revolution and new Communist allies in the furtherance of their project marked a crucial moment in the making of a national peasant history.

In sum, understanding peasant history as incorporating both localcommunal and regional-nationalist dimensions helps us to overcome the gap separating, on the one hand, standard assessments of peasant politics as only localized and parochial and, on the other, the contradictory evidence of regional political cultures and peasant discourses that, though largely expressed in local struggles, occurred simultaneously on a transregional and even national scale. Whether subsequent scholarly inquiry will enable us to bring the outlines of a peasant-based national history into fuller view remains to be seen. At the very least, however, if we are to bring history back in, we must, finally, come to terms with the compelling evidence for the nation as a site of contestation and, given this dialectic, take account of the different contexts in which Chinese history is to be comprehended (Dirlik 1996).[17]

The Peasant Path in Contemporary Perspective

My findings for a long-term tendency toward unification and an alternative line of development among peasants impact as much on assessments of China's present and the road ahead as they do on interpretations of the revolution and the past. If the revolutionary Communist program resonated in many ways with peasants' discourses and provided a radical new context for the realization of their aims, it made only limited progress toward those goals in some areas. On the other hand, many peasants are now nostalgically counterremembering the Maoist period as a time when, compared with the present, their voices carried much more weight and power. In company with that is an increasingly militant opposition to the current modernist path, which—with hundreds of recorded peasant uprisings, protests, and collective actions in the last several years alone—is assuming the proportions of a national movement. Indeed, the situation today is remarkably reminiscent of the peasants' critique of modernity in the first decades of the century.

As they did then, peasants are now protesting a policy that is disadvantaging them economically and dispossessing them of any effective political voice or influence while stereotypically denigrating them, their skills, and their way of life as backward and impeding China's development. What they are pinpointing, of course, is precisely the pretension by the leaders and new elite of China (and their peers in other development-oriented Third World countries) that modernization justifies, as Henry Bernstein puts it, "the exploitation and oppression of peasants that the state organizes or otherwise colludes in" (1990: 70). In short, as in the early twentieth century, they are opposing a development process that is based on their disempowerment and is bent on defining them politically and ideologically as people who have to be "developed" by someone else (Cooper 1993: 195).[18]

Questions of social and economic justice, cultural autonomy, legitimacy, and self-determination have thus reemerged at the center of peasant political-nationalist discourse. This book has argued that in two pivotal historical moments, the Ming-Qing transition and the passage into semicolonialism, peasant action became decisive. Both moments were marked by mounting peasant struggles and the fall of the state. In both, as well, the peasants took their struggles beyond the boundaries of the existing situation and their own ideologies to envision and create something entirely new, in the second instance by linking their autonomous project with that of a new group of revolutionary-minded allies.

In the 1920's and 1930's, when this alliance was effected, the visionary power of Communist Party leaders like Mao Zedong was in understanding that, if in loosely structured and contradictory form, the project of poor, sub-proletarianized peasants represented that of the nation, and that their stance against Western-style development in fact represented an alternative vision of modernity. In the same decades, in a different part of the world, the Communist Antonio Gramsci also began to reject the developmentalism of the then orthodox Marxist narrative. He saw that Italian peasants were not only not disappearing as they were supposed to do but were effectively resisting the centralizing tendencies of capitalism, and that their condition of "backwardness" was in fact linked to modernity and advancement in the north, the two reproducing each other as it were. As a result of these insights, like Mao, Gramsci retheorized the social and political role of peasants, taking the position that they had to be won over through an understanding of their way of seeing the world, that is, on the basis of their own materially rooted ideology and culture. Carried further, his theoretical constructs in effect challenged the orthodox privileging of urban-industrial society and suggested instead that the ethos, values, and moral codes of peasants would have to be incorporated into any Marxist theory of socialist transition. In short, Gramsci had begun to posit peasant popular culture as the starting point for a socialist view of the world—a world in which "the terms were and would be 'town and country'" (Davidson 1984: 146–47).

In drawing attention to Mao's original insights and Gramsci's theories, I am not implicitly advocating a utopian national populism as a preferred path for China in the future or subscribing to the romantic view of peasants as uniformly virtuous and deserving of some nonstate variant of people's capitalism (Bernstein 1990). Clearly China's peasants are no more uniform in the present than they were in the first decades of the twentieth century, or for that matter in the Ming-Qing. Class formation at present, as in the past, is entailing competition and struggle among peasants as well as between peasants and others. Race and gender continue to compound the complexities of the process. Clearly, too, given the rapid expansion in recent years of global capitalist markets and homogenizing cultural forms in the Chinese countryside, peasant culture is being subjected to powerfully corrosive forces and influences.

Nevertheless, the fact remains that peasant opposition to the current route of modernization is once again reappearing as a unified discourse of the many. To the extent that this discourse is now grounded historically in socialist ideology and practice, as well as in older egalitarian visions of morality and justice, it not only remains generally compatible with socialism, but continues to stand as a fundamental critique of the inequities and alienation of modernist civilization.

In the last analysis, what peasant history, the growing militancy of contemporary peasant opposition, and Gramsci's and Mao's insights all suggest is that, in China, the road to the future will ultimately have to come to terms with an enduring peasant path. Stated differently, any truly *national* agenda is going to have to give full consideration to both the place of agriculture and the views of peasants. Since antipeasant biases have become increasingly pronounced in the postsocialist context of the last two decades, it seems doubtful that such an agenda will emerge from the existing leadership. If peasants seize the initiative—and past history is any indicator—then, arguably, the future is wide open.

Reference Matter

Notes

For the abbreviations used in the in-text citations and these Notes, see the References, p. 285.

INTRODUCTION

1. Many of these complexities were rooted in the Third World, including among others, national liberation struggles, the failure of blueprints for development to transform new states, the success of social revolutions, and the catapulting of peasants to the center of the modern historical stage. By the 1960's and 1970's, the proliferation of Third World conditions in the First World and the voices of the permanently excluded there contributed to the global reverberations fostering rethinking and paradigm shifts. The global capitalist restructuring, demise of socialist states, reappearance of popular communisms within former socialist states, and resurgence of ethnic nationalisms in current train have further undermined older certainties.

2. For an excellent discussion of these general developments by Latin American and African scholars, see Cooper et al. 1993. For provocative discussions of paradigmatic issues in China scholarship, see Marks 1985; P. Huang 1991; and Dirlik 1996.

3. Building on positivist notions of Western Enlightenment and 19th-century conceptions of evolution, modernization theory assumes that all societies follow certain unilinear and evolutionary stages of development, some proceeding through these stages more quickly than others. Analyses of the 1950's–70's emphasized social-psychological traits, as expressed in values and attitudes, as central to the timing of the "evolutionary progression," but Third World peoples were usually cast as victims of their own traditional and parochial orientations. More recently, stemming from the requirements of global capitalism and criticism of the racist premises of those analyses, emphasis on the market as a universalizing force has come to replace the older cultural focus (see n. 7, below). But in both formulations the proposed solutions remain the same: increased contact between the developed world and the Third World so as to advance cultural diffusion and the benefits of trade and technology. The narrative teleologies of modernization thus impose a partial vision of Western society as a universal theory of growth and equate civilization with the displacement of indigenous cultures and people by modern (read Westernized) citizens and states.

4. For an early critique of the culturalist impact-response variant applied in Cold War China scholarship, see Peck 1969; for a more recent discussion, see Barlow 1993. For a critique of the market as a suprahistorical force, see Marks 1985. For an excellent discussion of paradigm and its implications in China studies, see Dirlik 1996.

5. After 1949, Mao Zedong's statement (1939) that imperialism diverted China from and blocked further development along an incipient capitalist path formed the

interpretative framework for modern Chinese history. Research necessarily had to verify or resonate with this thesis.

6. Philip Huang's seminal work *The Peasant Economy and Social Change in North China* (1985) stands as a landmark in this genre of scholarship. See also Bell 1985; Esherick 1987, 1976; Grove 1975; Marks 1984; Perry 1980; So 1986; Walker 1986; and Yip 1988. In contrast to scholarly trends in the West, Japanese Marxist scholars took the formation of the semicolonial economy as a central problematic. Focusing principally on North China, they pointed to the formation of a poor peasant semi-proletariat as a pivotal development. See, for example, Kotani 1977; and Takahashi Kosuke 1978b.

7. Accordingly, the analyses of "early modern" scholars of the Ming-Qing reproduce the Eurocentric narrative in Chinese form (D. Johnson et al. 1985; Ownby & Heidhues 1993; Rowe 1984). Advocates of the emergence of a so-called public sphere in the Qing adopt a similar stance (Rankin 1986). And, avoiding the problem of defending imperialism by socially and historically decontextualizing the market and presenting it instead as a universalizing, objective force that produces standarized, predictable, and beneficent modernizing results, neoclassical economic and other historians turn older formulations on their head by contending that, in the early 20th century, China began to experience sustained economic development (Brandt 1989; D. Johnson et al. 1985; Rawski 1989). Anthropological treatments complement these economic analyses by proclaiming that by then Chinese peasants were really no longer peasants at all and should properly be called "farmers," since in both practice and attitude they had become petty capitalist entrepreneurs (M. Cohen 1993).

8. Similarly, bound by the limitations of an *a priori* view of China as backward and feudal, Chinese Marxist historians have often *essentialized* peasants and their struggles. Although they give greater play to the proactive and egalitarian impulses of peasant struggles, these "peasant wars" (as they are usually termed) nevertheless appear as "generic protests" (Esherick 1983) with little impact on an intransigent feudal society.

9. Socialist-collectivized labor forms have not altered this fundamental autonomy. Rather, collective productive units replace the family as its chief expression, which also carries crucial implications for the development of forms of social power. Herein lies, as well, the relative continuing strength of peasants in socialist societies as they have been constituted thus far, compared with workers in collectivized industrial settings.

10. I draw here on the conceptualization advanced by William Roseberry (1993). Roseberry stresses both structured fields of power and particular household economies in the formation of particular peasantries. I add the productive dimension, so as to allow for historical instances in which internal developments in peasant production, i.e., of the productive forces, form the economic basis for alterations in the field of power.

11. For a bibliography of some of the most important Western, Chinese, and Japanese works on these developments, see Zurndorfer 1989: 105–12. Grove & Esherick 1980 and Kamachi 1990 review major Japanese works in social and economic history for the Ming-Qing and Republican periods. Shigeta 1984 and Mori 1980 review important Japanese works on the gentry.

12. Underlying this framing, of course, is the broader and equally problematical assumption of a universal teleology in which feudalism must culminate in and be replaced by the capitalist mode of production. For a consideration and critique of this linear strain in Chinese Marxist historiography, see Dirlik 1985.

13. World-system theory as posited by Immanuel Wallerstein (1974) became the leading analytical critique of the modernization paradigm in the 1970's. Drawing on and reformulating older notions of dependency (Frank 1967), it exposed underdevelopment as being inextricably intertwined with the development of capitalism in Europe. Yet in privileging capitalism as the motor of modern world history, and thus giving one-sided emphasis to global processes, it obscured the coherence and internal dialectics of social formations encountered by an expanding capitalism. Consequently, as critics increasingly argued, it could not account for why, in various world areas, and even within them, different systems of production and struggles for control of land and labor—occurring in the context of international capitalist expansion but not as mere reflections of it—led to structures with different potentials for continual growth (Cooper 1993: 96-97). For detailed critiques, see Brenner 1977; and Stern 1988.

14. According to Pierre Bourdieu, systems of domination are reproduced over time because of the way actors understand their world: "the cognitive and meaning structures making up the *habitas* [have] been shaped by the workings of relations of domination which produce the structured structures of the *habitas*" (1977: 72-78). But in fact subaltern political cultures can produce "structuring structures" of their own that help to sustain resistance over time.

15. Subei, also known as Jiangbei (lit., northern Jiangsu), commonly refers to the portion of Jiangsu province lying north of the Yangzi and south of the Huai River.

16. To more precisely capture the specific features of semicolonial modernity, I intentionally reverse the common formulation, the "development of underdevelopment" (Frank 1967; Lippit 1978).

17. The works cited stand at the core of the current debate on the 20th-century rural economy. On one side Rawski and Brandt unconvincingly attempt to show that China began to experience sustained economic development in the first decades of the 20th century; on the other Huang argues that commercialization did not produce development in the countryside. For the contours of this debate, see the special issue dealing with perspectives on the rural economy in *Republican China*, 18.1 (1992), especially the articles by Thomas Wiens and Philip Huang. See also Ramon H. Myers, "How Did the Modern Chinese Economy Develop?—A Review Article," *Journal of Asian Studies*, 50.3 (1991): 604-28, and Huang's reply, pp. 629-33; R. Bin Wong, "Chinese Economic History and Development: A Note on the Myers-Huang Exchange," *Journal of Asian Studies*, 51.3 (1992): 600-611; R. Bin Wong, "The Development of China's Peasant Economy: A New Formulation of Old Problems," *Peasant Studies*, 18 (1990): 5-26; and Albert Feuerwerker, "An Old Question Revisited: Was the Glass Half-Full or Half-Empty for China's Agriculture Before 1949?," *Peasant Studies*, 17 (Spring): 207-16.

18. In contrast to Gates's generalized, market-oriented formulation, many Chinese historians treat "peasant petty-commodity production" (*nongmin de xiaoshangpin shengchan*) as a specific productive form involving both market and subsistence production (see, for example, Fang 1986). I adopt that usage in this book. In high-

lighting the subsistence element, it draws attention to a key difference between urban and rural "petty commodity producers." Viewed from the perspective of peasants that difference becomes significant, both in the economic sense of subsistence production as a historical alternative to the market and as a key factor in the mapping of alternative political strategies.

CHAPTER ONE

1. On the delta's economic and agricultural geography, see Tregear 1970; and JS [2] 1979. For an excellent discussion of its ecosystem and historical geography, see P. Huang 1990: chap. 1; and P. Yang 1988: chap. 1.

2. Karen Sacks emphasizes the need for an analytical framework that comprehends class, race, and gender oppression as parts of a unitary system (1989: 545).

3. Nishijima Sadao, whose pioneering research (1948–49) first detailed cotton and cotton textile development, considers state policies the major stimulus for the expansion of production. Other scholars, most notably Oyama Masaaki (1984), reject Nishijima's "external" thesis and argue that small peasant producers were responsible for the growth. As will become apparent below, I subscribe to Oyama's argument.

4. Since much of this scholarship interprets China's past from a modernizationist perspective, this association is usually analyzed as symptomatic of the inertia of the so-called traditional economy. Chao Kang, for example, characterizes it as an institutional bottleneck to industrial capitalist development (1977: 80).

5. Textile production also developed in the cities and towns of the cotton districts in the Ming. It was carried on principally by female spinners, whose work probably constituted only one aspect of household economic activity; and by professional weaving households that specialized in official cloth and such high-quality cotton textiles as three-shuttle cloth. Small weaving workshops that produced high-quality cloth and probably employed no more than 20 weavers also appeared. In professional households and workshops producing specialty cloth (including silk as well as cotton), men appear to have displaced women as principal weavers (Fu Yiling 1956: 12). In general the product of the urban weaving industry stood in sharp contrast to the coarse cloth (*cubu*) turned out by peasant producers (Nishijima 1984: 58–59).

6. In what proportion and to what degree the Ming labor force was held in servitude is impossible to say. The term *nupu* has been variously translated as bondservant, serf, tenant-serf, tenant, and slave. Much of the problem stems from the complexities of the period, namely, that there were many kinds of tenants; that the status of tenants and serfs was often confused and frequently blurred; and that within a given category there were marked regional and even local differences (Fu Yiling 1981–82, 1961: 68–153; Wakeman 1985: 617). Following recent convention, I will use the word bondservant to denote someone in servitude, that is, as a general translation for *nupu* and its various subcategories, including *dianpu*, which specifically refers to agricultural serfs. Since bondservantry was not restricted to agricultural workers, the term seems preferable to "serf," which carries both agricultural and European connotations. For discussions of the legal distinctions among bondservants, tenants, and hired workers, see McDermott 1981: 677–80; and Niida 1962a: 150–68. See also Wakeman's excellent summary of social subordination in the Ming (1985: 616–23).

7. Mark Elvin finds the roots of Ming bondservantry in the manorial order and the serfdom and serf-like tenancy established in the Song (1973: 235; see also Takahashi Yoshiro 1978). At the outset of the Ming, this was undoubtedly so on many delta estates. But some bondservantry originated in the Yuan, when soon after the invasion of the Mongol armies and the establishment of the dynasty, many Jiangnan peasants were taken into bondage and shipped to the north. Kublai Khan was quick to respond to the enslavement of his new subjects. In an imperial decree of 1293, he stated: "Eighteen years have lapsed since Jiangnan was subjugated and the inhabitants there became our subjects. That notwithstanding, we hear that those engrossed in money making are openly selling men as commodities and are trading *liangmin* [free peasants/commoners] after kidnapping and bringing them [north] under the pretext of their having 'begged to be adopted.' . . . Hereafter all itinerant traders traveling to and fro between south and north and engaged in human traffic shall be banned" (translated in Ebisawa 1983: 29). Despite such attempts by the Yuan rulers to enforce their prohibition against the enslavement or involuntary servitude of *liangmin* except when they were captured in war, the acquisition and selling of bondservants—by merchants, officials, and soldiers—continued well into the 14th century (ibid., pp. 30, 47).

8. But the first Ming emperor, Hongwu, did succeed in breaking down some bondservantry in the delta—at least for a time. In an attempt to eliminate local bases of power and establish a stable peasant tax base, he confiscated a portion of the estates of powerful delta landlords and forcibly moved their families to Fengyan (Anhui), the early Ming capital. The confiscated lands were added to government holdings acquired during the Song and Yuan, and the bonded laborers on them were converted to state tenants who paid taxes in amounts roughly equal to the prevailing rents on private land (M. Wiens 1988: 18–19). These maneuvers gave the state a total of 45% of cultivated land in the southern delta, with especially high proportions in Songjiang and Suzhou prefectures, over 86% and 62%, respectively (Mori 1961: table 1; M. Wiens 1988: 18).

9. Instances of even well-to-do families commending their land to avoid taxation were not uncommon (McDermott 1981: 684). Thus in some cases landlords were also bondservants.

10. For further discussion of these points, see McDermott 1981. He indicates that under the Ming code only dukes (*gong*), marquises (*hou*), and, eventually, officials of the third rank or higher could legally hold bondservants. The state sometimes bestowed bondservants on members of these groups.

11. Members of this upper bondservant stratum often acquired considerable wealth and local influence. In the late Ming they increasingly defied their masters—sometimes to the extent of usurping control of a landlord's holdings or mobilizing his workers against him (Elvin 1973; McDermott 1981; M. Wiens 1979).

12. China's deepening involvement in the global monetary system is now well substantiated. By the late 16th century, principally via Manila and the Spanish galleon trade, China was importing at least a third, and perhaps more, of all silver mined in the New World (Chaunu 1960: 269; Wakeman 1985: 2–3). It also imported substantial amounts from Japan (Atwell 1977). Almost all past scholarship has assumed that the dynamism for this development lay with the West, that is, that silver flowed into China *because* of a constant deficit in the balance of payments in favor of Chinese

goods (silks, porcelains, etc.). In a pathbreaking analysis, however, Frank Perlin challenges this formulation by spotlighting how, from the 16th century, internal commercialization—especially that connected with cotton textiles in countries such as India and China—"which emerged independently of that in Europe, but within a common international theater of societal and commercial changes" (1983: 33), acted as a key stimulus for global monetary formation. Perlin emphasizes the multi-centered nature of this developing system. It was driven by merchants in these various independent centers of commercial development who, to further the monetization of their domestic economies, aggressively imported silver as a commodity. In his view this broad-based, varied, and massive demand for the "instruments of monetization," together with simultaneous long-term developments in the production and supply of monetary media, formed the precondition for flows of American silver and for Euro-Asian trade.

13. As with cotton textiles, managerial landlords or their wives often supervised all aspects of sericulture. Fu Yiling cites, for example, the case of the Mao lineage landlords in Huzhou, "who planted hundreds of thousands of mulberry trees" and "managed agriculture personally, improving techniques and implementing a variety of management [forms] for agriculture, mulberry cultivation, silkworming, and weaving" (1981–82: 63).

14. The criticism of landlord-gentry practice by the "righteous gentry" overlapped with that raised by members of the Donglin faction, whose advocacy of a "hegemony of rural villages" has been interpreted as representing the interests and opposition of lesser landlords to growing land concentration and wealth among the more powerful landlord-gentry (Mizoguchi 1978). But the *xiangping* community (i.e., the community formed on the basis of public criticism) extended well beyond the small Donglin school, which had only 115 members in all of Jiangsu and Zhejiang provinces in the years 1592–1626 (ibid.).

15. For two excellent studies on urban risings and struggles, see Fuma 1993; and von Glahn 1991.

16. During the Ming Jiangsu province ranked second in the country for the number of *jinshi* degree-holders produced, all together 2,721. An astounding 77% of these came from the three southern delta prefectures of Songjiang, Changzhou, and Suzhou (P.-t. Ho 1964: 227, 248). The northeastern prefectures of Zhejiang province, which ranked first (with 3,280 *jinshi*), were also located in the southern delta. Whereas the large number of upper-level gentry reflected the economic and cultural development in the area, that development in turn attracted wealth and talent (ibid., p. 232).

17. The 1557 rebellion revolved around a preacher/teacher named Li, who called himself a White Lotus Master *(bailian jiaozhu)*. From 1547 onward Master Li was active in the market town of Wu and its surroundings, where his followers developed into 72 groups. In early 1557, interpreting the drying-up of nearby Lake Tai as an omen, he prophesied the approach of the apocalypse. At this, two of his followers, the martial arts instructors Li Nan and Jiang Peng, along with low-ranking military officers they recruited, laid plans to launch a rebellion with an attack on the city of Huzhou. Their mentor, Master Li, joined in the effort to mobilize the rebel forces. But authorities learned of the planned insurgency beforehand, and after only minor skirmishes, 46 people were arrested. Of these, 10, including Li Nan and Jiang Peng, were executed. Many more of Master Li's followers fled to escape arrest.

18. Because of these rumors, later literati writers would hold a "magician" (and possibly a White Lotus teacher) called Patriarch Ma, who had a large following in the area to the southwest of Huzhou and who was said to have organizational linkages to Master Li and to a man named Li Fuda, who had been a participant in a White Lotus rising in Shaanxi in 1513, responsible for the 1557 rebellion (Hamashima 1982: 583–84; Ter Haar 1992: 159–63, 172–95). Like officialdom as a whole, these writers saw the practice of magic as one of the essential ingredients of an archetypal White Lotus movement. The simultaneous spread of millenarian teachings and violent insurgencies reinforced the official view of a magico-religious conspiracy. For details, see Ter Haar 1992. As Ter Haar suggests, because of our reliance on elite constructions, our conception of White Lotus activity may be oversimplified. The central historical point remains, however, that whether of White Lotus or some other affiliation, sectarianism spread rapidly and widely in the late Ming.

19. The line of political development reflecting and furthering this transregional cultural movement did not appear in homogenized form. In North China, where the specter of the state was more direct and overpowering, through much of the Qing massive, implicitly anti-statist millenarian rebellions and larger-scale religious risings formed its characteristic expressions (Esherick 1987; P. Huang 1990; Naquin 1976).

20. For theoretical treatments of these points, see Harry Harootunian's discussion of ideology as conflict in 18th-century Japan (1982); Herman Ooms's brilliant analysis of Tokugawa ideology (1985); and Antonio Gramsci's observations on the state and civil society in periods of organic crisis and on the process of cultural formation (1971: 210, 275–76, 340–41).

21. In some pockets of the country where "the actually existing relations" retained a patriarchal character, servile relations appear to have persisted well into the 20th century. Ye Xianen (1981) documents the existence of bondservantry in prerevolutionary Huizhou (Anhui). Field investigations in Guizhou province in the 1930's revealed that in several counties large landlord families relied on bondservant-serfs to carry out both house and fieldwork. In these households the master still selected his servants' marriage partners, and children were set free only after reaching adulthood. Even at this late date, as in the Ming, women were still used also as the vehicle for acquiring indentured male workers (Institute of Pacific Relations 1939: 80, 83). Similarly, travelers in Fujian in 1916 found one village in which there were 300-odd bondservant-serfs. Their ancestors had sold themselves into serfdom in the Ming in return for wives. Their marriages were still controlled by landlord-masters who permitted them to marry only other serfs (Amano 1940: 369). See also Potter & Potter 1990 for the most recent documentation of relations of this type in early 20th-century Guangdong. As we will see in chap. 8, a continuity of practice cannot be assumed in all these cases. In the 20th century under new processes of commercialization, older labor forms expanded or were reintroduced.

22. Dual ownership also developed in those parts of the cotton districts where salt flats and marshes were reclaimed and converted into farmland, namely, along the northern banks of the Yangzi, at the perimeter of the southern cotton belt, and on the outer parts of Chongming Island, which lies at the mouth of the Yangzi. Niida Noboru has in fact suggested that permanent tenancy emerged on Chongming's reclaimed lands during the Yuan (1962c: 183–86, 189–90; see also Fujii 1975). Some

scholars place its origins even earlier. Phil Yang suggests that some Ming cultivators who commended their land to tax-exempt families may have relinquished de jure ownership while retaining topsoil rights (1988: 208, chap. 6). See also Fujii 1984; and Kusano 1977, 1975, 1970.

23. Oyama Masaaki (1957–58) argues that when tenants did assume authority for water control themselves, the (often multivillage) collectivities they formed to carry it out became an added organizational nexus for rent and political struggles. Scholars such as Hamashima Atsutoshi reject Oyama's claim that new water control communities filled the vacuum caused by landlord neglect, although contradictorily Hamashima provides evidence suggesting precisely that type of involvement (e.g., 1980: 78). On the other hand, Hamashima is clearly correct in arguing that the late Ming state attempted to assert its authority over the social relations of water control by nullifying the landlord-gentry's exemption from corvée and requiring, on the basis of land owned, that "landlords shall provide the food and tenants shall provide the labor" for repair work to dikes, the dredging of creeks, and so forth (ibid., p. 87). But given landlords' opposition, it is unlikely that the new policies were widely implemented.

24. Andrew Turton emphasizes this point in his consideration of nongovernmental ideological institutions of the dominant classes, including "development, educational, religious and welfare associations, professional groups, privately owned media and publishers, [and] some kinship and domestic structures" (1984: 39). Quite clearly, however, this is no less true of the institutions of subaltern classes. Such institutions may contribute to the "contradictory consciousness" of subordinate groups and classes, but they are also integral to the operation of hegemony.

25. I draw the notion of patriarchal peasant households as the basic units of the state from Niida Noboru's (1962b) critique of the idea of the separation of state and society. By enabling us to understand how changes in peasant families and communities can bring about changes in the state, this concept allows us to move beyond notions of villages and peasant families as merely encapsulated in the state (see Harriss 1982: 17).

26. In these respects the reconstitution of patriarchy in peasant households in late Ming–early Qing China bears some resemblance to state formation in places where the kin group was the chief obstacle to state power. In England, for example, "the power of kings and heads of households grew in parallel with one another in the sixteenth century" (Stone 1975: 55). Similarly, feminist scholars have suggested that new states have historically consolidated their power by allowing household heads to usurp some of the kin group's authority, especially over land, women, and children (Hartmann 1981: 374–75; Muller 1977; see also Gailey 1987a; Rohrlich 1980; and Silverblatt 1978).

CHAPTER TWO

1. Tongzhou was a department of Yangzhou prefecture during the Ming. It was made an independent department (*zhilizhou*) in 1724, with jurisdiction over Rugao and Taixing counties (TZZ 1875; 1: 3).

2. Disasters of this type continued in the Qing. Haimen lost 80%–90% of its land area in the great tidal flood of 1662. As a result the county administration was dis-

solved, and the remaining land was incorporated into Tongzhou (Zhu Zhangmin & Cheng Yun 1984: 7). Later, in 1775, Haimen was resurrected as an independent subprefecture (*ting*). In the Republican period it once again fell under Nantong's administration, and in 1928 its southeastern sections became part of the new county of Qidong ([Qianlong] Jiangnan tongzhi 1737, 20: 23; Shen Shike 1934).

3. And Songjiang's production steadily expanded until the 19th century, except for a period in the 17th century, when output declined because of changes in world trade and fluctuations in the supply of silver. For details, see Wakeman 1985: 632–33.

4. Kenneth Pomeranz (1993) takes a different line on the peripheralization of inland North China. He argues that the presence of the state in the north stimulated the economy of the whole region, and that it was only in the late 19th century, when imperialist pressure caused the Qing state to shift its focus to new localities, that the inland became a peripheralized hinterland. Although Finnane's and Pomeranz's arguments might appear contradictory, in fact they are not. Together, they substantiate a well-known feature of states, namely, that they are formed in and perpetuate inequalities and uneven development.

5. Thanks to an eastward shift of the coastline, tidal erosion and damage to the dike diminished during the Qing. As the coastline receded, many of the salt flats dried up, and new land and marsh accumulated. The reclamation of these coastal lands by development companies in the early 20th century is discussed in Chap. 4.

6. Monks from nearby Lang Mountain also financed reclamation work in this period (Xu Chaoming 1985: 2). By the 19th century the Lang Mountain temple had become one of the largest landholders in the district (Guan Jincheng 1956: 14).

7. As Chap. 1 discusses, one impetus for the decline of this Jiangnan class (which would also have been operative in the northern delta) was the early-16th-century change in state policy that made tax collection, till then carried out by a small circle of people for life, the joint or rotating responsibility of a relatively large number of people, frequently landlord-gentry (Mori 1980: 45).

8. Behavior of this type was common in many parts of China. Even in cosmopolitan Jiangnan through much of the Ming, force was one of the major means by which the elite acquired bondservant-slave labor and land (McDermott 1981; Li Wenzhi 1981).

9. Available sources do not indicate whether uxorilocal residence was a new practice in the area or an older one that gained new strength from the social and economic changes of the times. There is increasing evidence that, in the late imperial period at least, the consolidation of patrilineal/patriarchal practices among the upper classes effectively undercut both women's property claims and women's rights. During this period regulations reinforcing the negative image of uxorilocal marriage and "lineage rules requiring the adoption of male heirs rather than succession by daughters" became common (R. Watson 1991: 361–62).

10. In 1894 Zhang Jian, whose career will be discussed in detail in Chap. 5, attained national renown by placing first in the *jinshi* metropolitan examinations. He was the first person from Tongzhou since remote times to achieve this distinction (Bastid 1988: 33).

11. As Albert Memmi so eloquently writes of the colonialist: "He, of course, is resolutely conservative. It is on just that point [preserving the status quo] that he is most rigid, that he compromises the least. [His] nationalism is truly of a special

nature. He directs his attention essentially to that aspect of his native country which tolerates his colonialist existence. A homeland which became democratic, for example, to the point of promoting equality of rights even in the colonies, would also risk abandoning its colonial undertakings. For the colonialist, such a transformation would challenge his way of life and thus become a matter of life or death. . . . Finally, political and economic considerations cause a real antagonism between the colonialist and the residents of his homeland. And in this connection, the colonialist is, after all, correct when he speaks of not feeling at home in his native country. He no longer has the same interests as his compatriots. To a certain extent, he no longer belongs to them" (1991: 61-62).

12. On the other hand, as I have noted elsewhere, the nonlocal origins of migrant producers sometimes created "reverse discrimination." Especially in the *waisha* areas, Tongzhou-Haimen landlords appear to have used the "cultural difference" and "outsider" origins of southern tenants as justification for harsh tenure agreements (Walker 1993b; see also Guan Jincheng 1956: 43).

13. In the early Ming, as in the Yuan period, most pirates were Japanese, and the targets of attack were the imperial tribute ships. In the 15th century, however, Chinese pirates began to predominate. Their growing numbers along the Yangzi and the Zhejiang-Fujian coast reflected the reappearance, despite state prohibition, of private trade. Frequently operating with as many as 100 ships, pirate legions often occupied coastal towns for prolonged periods while mooring their fleets. In one such incident in 1521, in the Lang Mountain district of Tongzhou, hundreds of people lost their lives when government troops surrounded the harbor town in the hope of recapturing it. In this incident, as was often the case, troops were hesitant to engage pirates in direct battle because they were unequipped for nautical pursuit (*Tongzhou zhi* 1577, 8: 27-28). Although pirate bands often preyed on the wealthy in local communities, not infrequently coastal elites became involved with them, principally by supporting and dealing in the illegal smuggling trade on which they thrived (Higgins 1980: 30-33).

14. Illicit communities of this type, which were already significant by the late Ming, continued to build up along the Yangzi and the coast with the recession of the coastline and drying up of salt flats in the Qing. By the early 20th century, according to an investigation of the Jiangsu provincial government, at least one-fifth of the land in Nantong was *shatian* (lit., sandland), and most of the land in Haimen-Qidong had once been sandy shores (Shen Shike 1934: 30831; Zhu Fucheng 1977).

15. Armed rebellions in fact erupted in 1644 in the greater Tongzhou area and again in 1645, when rebels held the Rugao county capital for three months before government troops finally subdued them (Mao Daolai 1980: 13; TZZ 1875, 1: 43-44).

CHAPTER THREE

1. The permanent topsoil rights acquired by peasants in the "one field, two owners" system made it difficult for landlords to amass the contiguous holdings usually associated with and necessary for larger-scaled capitalist-style farming with hired labor (Mann 1990). In contrast, in North China, where in the 18th and 19th centuries, there was significant development of managerial farming, managerial landlords were often able to accumulate large contiguous holdings totaling several hundred or more mu.

See, for example, Jing Su & Luo Lun's study of Shandong (1959); see also, P. Huang 1985.

2. Although research on the topic has hardly begun, the significant exception to the above pattern appears to be the development of a vibrant rich peasant agriculture in semicolonial Jiangnan. Even in that context of growing demand for wage laborers, however, the economic gains and security afforded peasants by topsoil rights, household industry, and better-paying off-farm employment created a pattern of social reproduction in which many peasant families continued to avoid hiring out as agricultural laborers. Instead, through regularized migrant circuits, poorer peasants from the northern delta and, especially, northern Subei (supplemented by those from particular Jiangnan communities where new social and economic processes were weakening peasants) formed the cheap labor force for rich peasant farming. A systematic examination of the historical development of this migrant labor force and the rich peasant-managerial agriculture that fueled it, as well as the ways in which both trends interconnected with patterns of economic difference among specific Jiangnan localities, stands as a pressing research task for investigation of the semicolonial process in Jiangnan.

3. In developing his thesis of an "involutionary peasant family economy," Philip Huang (1990: 44–57) constructs a picture of greater flexibility in the division of labor in the delta during the Qing than I have outlined here. But since he draws his evidence almost exclusively from 19th-century sources and the recollections of informants of the pre-1949 situation, his data, far from contradicting the developmental outline suggested above, actually support the argument for accelerating change in family labor systems in the late 19th and early 20th centuries. Nantong, as the following chapters will show, exemplifies this pattern.

4. The fact that the author fails to take note of gender roles in the productive work described in this quotation should not be taken to mean that no sexual division of labor existed in the Wuxi-Jinkui area. Other sources clearly indicate that the standard division relegating women to household industry and men to farming prevailed in this area. Recall, for example, that Xu Guangqi's list of places where families were dependent on women's skills included Changzhou prefecture in which Wuxi-Jinkui were located.

5. Shiraishi Hirō (1960) suggests that rent deposits may have emerged in conjunction with a transition from shared to fixed rents. In his view, under the shared harvest system deposits were unnecessary since landlords could generally count on taking their share of the harvest. With growing absenteeism, however, sharecropping became impractical. Fixed rents proved to be a solution, but they did not protect landlords from the possibility of rent resistance. Deposits thus became the corollary to the fixed-rent system.

6. The above interpretation differs from the recent strain in Western scholarship, best exemplified in the works of Rankin (1986) and Rowe (1985; 1984), that views public management and associated aspects of landlord rule as a separation of "society" (i.e., elites) and the state. This scholarly line also suggests that this separation bears resemblance to the so-called bourgeois "public sphere" that emerged in opposition to feudal states in some parts of Europe during capitalist development. Critics of this approach for China spotlight the fact that characterizations of the "autonomous local

management of public sphere activities" are "marred by evidence of top-down, official sponsorship" (Wakeman 1993: 131); and that in adopting a "one-sided interpretation of two-sided evidence" its characterizations ignore the "persistent and prominent role of the state" (P. Huang 1993: 220).

7. The different types of merchants engaged in the silk trade in the vicinity of Huzhou included, for example, representatives of larger wholesalers/brokers/retailers (*chaozhuang*); middlemen between producers and wholesalers (*duozhuang*) and their agents (*chenghanchuan*); and peddlers who sold small amounts of silk to weaving households (*chaisizhuang*) (Tanaka 1984a: 99).

8. Even in the finishing processes—over which they exercised considerable control—merchants did not directly manage production. In the calendaring industry, for example, an intermediate stratum of bosses or managers organized the workshops and workers. These managers took orders from merchants in what resembled a form of putting-out. Yet despite the impressive dimensions of this type of development—in 18th-century Suzhou at any one time there were probably 10,000–20,000 silk calenders—the important point remains that it was generally confined to those aspects of the productive process requiring special skills and equipment (Yokohama 1960–61).

9. In urban areas and suburban-industrial villages, however, there were many instances of collective action against merchants, especially among spinners, weavers, and small peddlers. The rising in Jiaxing prefecture in the 1670's is typical. More than 2,000 weavers and small peddlers allied against the merchants of Puyuan market town, an important collection and distribution center for raw silk and a production center for pongee. Claiming that the town merchants "dominated the market," the weaver-peddler force broke into merchant shops and burned them to the ground (Tanaka 1984a: 100).

10. The development of this culture and long-term offensive problematizes common assumptions of scholars of comparative peasant politics, especially those of moral economists who generally view these politics as "backward looking" and "defensive." Moral economy interpretations also often argue that the vertical ties of dependence that bind poor peasants to a dominant class of rich peasants and/or landlords inhibit their militancy and proclivity for collective action (Alavi 1973; Scott 1976; Wolf 1969). In light of this analysis they advance a "middle peasant thesis," suggesting that because middle peasants are not directly dependent on landlords for access to their means of livelihood (and thus are free to engage in political action without jeopardizing their subsistence), they are more likely to form horizontal alliances and, in initial stages of mobilization, are thus more militant than poor peasants. They add, however, that for these hypotheses to hold true, poor peasants must not have alternative means of livelihood. The actions of peasants in the Ming and Qing periods substantiate the importance of additional forms of livelihood (and security of tenure or land rights) in making it possible for poor peasants (and other strata) to act. But they also clearly show that peasant politics are by no means limited to "defensive reaction."

CHAPTER FOUR

1. By the imperial decree of 1757, foreigners were further required to conduct all their business in the port city with the Cohong, a small group of Chinese merchants (numbering about a dozen).

2. The Tianjin-Beijing treaties of 1858–70 provided for the opening of 11 other ports. The figure steadily climbed, from 29 before the signing of the Sino-French treaty of 1885 to 45 in 1899.

3. Paul Baran, in his pathbreaking study *The Political Economy of Growth* (1957), was one of the first scholars to pinpoint the proliferation of merchant capital in the Third World as a product of global capitalist expansion. Subsequent studies have verified many of Baran's original postulates. Many stress the dual role of merchant capital in the expansion of capital, i.e., as an agent of industrial capital and as an autonomous force. They also show that because of this duality and the fact that through most of the 19th century merchant capital was the primary form of capital in the Third World, it often competed with industrial capital for the right of surplus extraction at the local level, even to the extent of assuming control over the conditions, if not the actual organization, of production (Bernstein 1979; Shenton & Lennihan 1981; and for fuller expositions, de Silva 1982; Goodman & Redclift 1982; Kay 1975; and McGaffey 1987). Such studies thus spotlight how continuing struggles between merchants and industrial capital, both locally and internationally, have profoundly affected Third World development.

4. *Chitaobu* measured approximately 2.2 *zhang* (1 *zhang* = 3.581 m), or close to 8 m, by a little less than 1 *chi* (= .33 m), compared with only 15 *chi* (roughly 5 m) by a little over one-half *chi* for *xibu* (Da Shiji 1980; Lin Jubai 1984: 29).

5. Contrary to conventional wisdom, Shanghai was not simply a fishing village before 1843. As indicated in Chap. 1, it was one of the major cotton markets in the Songjiang area in the Ming. With the reopening of foreign trade after the disruptions of the transition, the city gradually reemerged as a "conduit for interregional and international commerce" (Rowe 1993: 4)—a position it had held before the relocation of the Ming capital, in 1421, from Nanjing to Beijing. On its pre–treaty port development, see Elvin 1977; Johnson 1993; Jones 1974; and H. Lu 1992.

6. Between 1880 and 1890 imports of foreign cotton goods at the Yingkou port doubled, to make the northeastern provinces one of the principal markets in China for machine-made foreign cloth. Most of this cloth was sold in cities rather than the countryside, where the market for handwoven cloth still predominated (Oyama 1960: 8–9). Nevertheless the influx of machine-made cloth placed pressure on Nantong merchants to imitate the wider product.

7. The term *guanzhuang* reflects the fact that the major marketing area for goods handled by these merchants was to the north of Shanhai Pass, the eastern end of the Great Wall. In other words, it denotes the northeastern provinces.

8. Technically speaking, the Ningbo *bang* and the Zhejiang clique were not the same. The Greater Ningbo clique (*da Ningbo bang*) formed the core of a group that included people from many localities in Zhejiang. It was so influential within the Zhejiang group that the names were often used interchangeably (Jones 1974: 80).

9. Declining yarn prices had much to do with the rise in yarn imports. The relatively expensive English yarn was pushed out of the market first by the products of Bombay spinning mills and then, beginning in the 1890's, by Japanese yarns as well. From 1884 until 1902 yarn prices remained below the 1893 price (Feuerwerker 1969: 21–23).

10. Similarly Jiangnan's handweaving industry, which had been harder hit than

the northern delta's by imports of piece goods, began to recover as yarn imports increased and their price declined. Subsequently it provided an outlet for the products of Chinese spinning mills established in Shanghai near the end of the century (Chen Zengyu 1986; Lin 1984). But between the continuing rise in cloth imports until the 1920's and the greater specialization of peasant households that accompanied semi-colonial restructuring, Jiangnan never regained its earlier prominence in cotton textile production. For a discussion of the decline of the complex management patterns that were common among Jiangnan families who resided outside the cotton-growing districts, see Lynda Bell's (forthcoming) excellent examination of the demise of cotton weaving and the intensification of silk production in the peasant households of Wuxi.

11. To some extent these offices also enabled them to bypass and act independently of brokers. Of particular importance in this respect was the opening of Chinese-owned textile mills in Shanghai after 1896, which provided new, if limited, sources of machine-spun yarn (Lin Jubai 1984: 64).

12. In practice cloth prices were pinned to the market price of yarn. At the time of the guild's founding, it set a minimum cloth price of 10 *liang* silver for every 100 *zhang* of yarn, with prices rising by cloth quality up to 1.5–2.2 *liang* above the basic price (Yu Yikong 1982: 35). In contrast, prices paid to peasant weavers were set by informal agreement by the merchants in Nantong, and thus frequently bore no direct relation to the selling price in Shanghai.

13. Reflecting the inaccessibility of the Yingkou port during the winter months, these selling periods opened approximately every two months from January 5 through July (Peng Zeyi et al. 1957, 3: 715).

14. In 1889 or 1890 Jiuda changed its name to Xinji. Li Yongchang, one of its joint owners, operated the new firm. It owned nine oceangoing junks (Lin Jubai 1984: 78).

15. A fourth group of merchants from Shanghai, who had originally dealt in the homespun cloth of the Shanghai-Pudong area, by now handled Nantong cloth as well. Known as the *qinglanbang* (black-and-blue group), they had no dealings with the *guanzhuang* firms since the narrow, colored cloth was their main stock in trade. They did purchase small quantities of wider cloth, but only moldy cloth that was discounted down to half the regular price. *Guanzhuang* merchants looked down on these firms, considering their dealings "shady" and their cloth "cheap." *Qinglan* merchants often went to Nantong to purchase cloth themselves, probably working through the "county merchant" firms. They marketed their best cloth in Guangdong and Guangxi for transshipment to Vietnam and Singapore. Medium grades went to Jiangxi, Zhejiang, and Shanxi. The lowest quality cloth sold in Shanghai, to stores that specialized in making cheap working-class clothing (Lin Jubai 1984: 83–85; *Shanghai shi mianbu shangye* 1979).

16. Like every trade guild of the time, the cotton guild worshipped a patron deity. The Empress of Heaven (lit., the Goddess of Latter Heaven, Tianhou Shengmu), was expected, above all, to provide safe passage for the shipments to the northeast. Though most guilds held their sacrificial rites on the patron's birthday, the cloth guild set two dates, March 3 and September 9 (lunar calendar), for its days of worship. The first date represented the time of the year when the ice in the Yingkou port began to melt, the second the time when a hard freeze set it. These holidays were marked by board of directors' meetings, and following sacrificial ceremonies, evening dinners to

which guild members, brokers, and clerks in the *guanzhuang* firm offices in Shanghai were invited (Yu Yikong 1982: 44; Lin Jubai 1984: 65).

CHAPTER FIVE

1. Many Western studies of local elites and patterns of dominance apply the inherited categories of a (problematic) "European" model to China and/or focus almost exclusively on political relations between the state and the elite, thus ignoring crucial economic and class contexts. For important recent research that is sensitive to both the economic dimension and the culturally prescribed framework of elite action, see Bell 1985; and especially Bell 1990. For three of the best treatments to date debunking the notion of a single "European" developmental route, both economically and sociopolitically, see Brenner 1976 and 1985; and Tibebu 1990.

2. At the end of 1897, circumventing conservative control at court, radical intellectuals led by Kang Youwei persuaded the young Guangxu Emperor to issue an edict on national affairs that, in effect, marked the beginning of an attempt at modernizing change commonly known as the Hundred Days. During this three-month period members of Kang's group assumed administrative posts and ordered significant changes in administration, education, and the economy. These changes were cut short, however, when, with the backing of the Empress Dowager Ci Xi, conservatives reclaimed power, took the emperor prisoner, canceled his policies, and arrested many of the modernizers.

3. Some members of the delta's urban elite establishment, like Li Houyou and Xu Shulan—both close friends of Zhang Jian's—lived in Shanghai, but maintained business interests and carried out managerial activities in their native places. Most, including Zhang himself and Tang Shouqian, also a close friend, continued to reside in the smaller provincial cities of Zhejiang-Jiangsu, though they regularly visited or sojourned in Shanghai (Rankin 1986: 83-84, 178, 182-83).

4. Through the control of new mass media and the establishment of regional and transregional associations, the leaders of the urban elite further defined their sociopolitical role. In organizations such as the Jiangsu and Zhejiang Railway associations (established by Zhang Jian and Tang Shouqian) and the Society to Prepare for Constitutional Government (organized by Zhang Jian in Shanghai in 1906), and subsequently, in the provincial assemblies that grew out of the constitutional movement (Zhang Jian headed the Jiangsu assembly), they developed new mechanisms for simultaneously institutionalizing political power and protecting the new economic structures under its control (S. Chu 1965: 61-67; Rankin 1986: 258-68).

5. Another strain of scholarly inquiry emphasizes the longer-term oppositional character of local elite activity and the disintegration of state power from the 18th century on (Esherick & Rankin 1990; Rankin 1986), but as noted in Chap. 3, n. 6, it has come under considerable criticism.

6. In the final analysis, the Qing state's own weakness and self-interest were what made it incapable of withstanding the foreign commercial offensive, establishing adequate tariff protection, or enforcing crucial tax exemptions to increase China's competitive edge in the domestic market. Moreover, despite its encouragement of patriotic sentiments, in financial pinches such as the Stock Exchange Crisis of 1910, the

state clearly demonstrated a willingness to sacrifice the interests of Chinese nationals and contract new debts in order to safeguard foreign loans (Bergère 1968: 248). The Republican government did not provide any greater protection; and its commercial policies continued to favor foreign over Chinese interests.

7. For a comparative example, see Kahn 1993: especially chap. 6. Drawing on the work of Robert Elston (1989) and his own study of colonial Indonesia Kahn suggests that from the last decades of the 19th century, five major features began to characterize modern colonial state formation in Southeast Asia; (1) an enormous growth in the size of bureaucracies corresponding to the managerial requirements of a new order; (2) an expansion in the scope of bureaucratic functions; (3) an increase in the intensity of governance; (4) new styles of governing, marking a move from personal ties and followings; and (5) a greater centralization of state powers.

8. Samuel Chu's pioneering work (1965) provides the fullest English-language account of the Dasheng founding process. See also Walker 1986. For the impassioned report Zhang Jian presented at the 1907 shareholders' meeting, recounting the major events and difficulties of these first four years, see TZ 1910, 1:111–22.

9. The disruptions of World War One delayed the acquisition of European machinery and spindles for the Haimen branch. It did not open until 1921.

10. I am grateful to Wu Huisheng of the Historical Records Department of the Nantong No. 1 Textile Factory (formerly Dasheng No. 1) for providing me with a detailed description of Dasheng's cotton collection system. His two lengthy reports provide new detailed data on that system and Dasheng's relationship with Nantong's commercial-banking complex.

11. The mill employed a number of devices inside and outside the factory compound to effect this subterfuge. It stationed factory patrolmen wearing uniforms almost identical to those of the Qing military at the factory and buying office entrances, where peasants coming to the factory to sell cotton could not help noticing them. In the buying area *benzhuang* personnel weighed the cotton and put it in the warehouse before stating the price being offered. Peasant sellers were then sent inside the office to be paid at a counter designed to closely resemble the desks used by county magistrates in court hearings. It was quite high, forcing payees to stretch hard for the money they were owed (Wu Huisheng 1980a). Thus from the moment peasants reached the factory until the cotton sale was concluded, they faced officially clad functionaries, symbols of state authority, and official-style behavior.

12. Although Zhang consulted with his closest associates in planning and establishing the subsidiaries, he apparently did not regularly involve the Dasheng board of directors. By 1907 at least one of the directors had joined certain shareholders in speaking out against Zhang's cavalier handling of the company's funds. To forestall more serious criticism and further legitimate his authority, Zhang called the first-ever shareholders' meeting that July. Unwilling to criticize Zhang publicly these men remained silent at the meeting. The 50-odd shareholders in attendance voted unanimously for Dasheng to continue to support the subsidiary companies. A new company, the Nantong Industrial Company, was created to amalgamate and manage these enterprises. Dasheng provided 600,000 taels for the organization of the company. Zhang Jian became its president, and Zhang Cha its vice president (NJ 1959b, 2: 6–7; Sun Yutang 1957: 1076).

13. Zhang's closest business associate was his older brother, Zhang Cha. In 1902 Zhang Jian persuaded his brother to relinquish his post as a county magistrate in Jiangxi province and return home to Nantong to help him with Dasheng and other projects. Zhang Cha turned out to be an indispensable aide. Shortly after his return, he became chief executive of the Dasheng mill. Over the next 20 years, he collaborated with Zhang Jian in founding many enterprises and land development companies. Some contemporary observers ranked his business acumen higher than his brother's (S. Chu 1965: 34). Zhang Jian strongly relied on other family members as well. One of his nephews organized and managed several of the enterprises. And Zhang's son, Xiaoruo, on his return from the United States, entered the business, to manage the Huaihai Bank and organize several land development companies (*Ershinianlai zhi Nantong* 1930, 2: 54; NJ 1959b, 2: 13). Another nephew, Zhang Cha's son Zhang Ren, headed the Industrial Police Guard (*shiye jingweituan*), the unit Zhang Jian organized to maintain order and security at the Dasheng plant. Zhang Ren perfected and enlarged the organization, making it an efficient instrument of control in the mills and their subsidiary plants, and in the new land areas of the development companies. As a local publication propagandizing Nantong's industry proudly proclaimed in 1920 of Zhang Ren's directorship of the guard: "Owing to his efforts, Nantong's industries are not affected by [the labor] troubles plaguing other areas of the country" (NT [7] 1920: 33). This labor peace did not last. Within a few years, a militant movement emerged in the Dasheng mills.

14. Over time Zhang Jian also used Dasheng funds to promote commercial ventures among family members and friends, both in Nantong and Haimen. This activity may have added to the criticisms of him that prompted the shareholders' meeting of 1907. Several of the beneficiaries were women. Sometime before 1908, for example, Zhang funneled funds to Xu Yinyi's wife, presumably a female relative, to establish 13 businesses in Haimen, including a cloth firm and a cotton firm. In the same period he helped the wife of his brother's son to establish the largest general goods store in Haimen, the Gonglu Silk, Cotton, and Grocery Store. And in 1918 Zhang directed funds to the wife of an associate to establish a new-style hotel with modern baths in Nantong city. In 1925, when Zhang instructed his son and grandson on how the family property was to be divided, he indicated that some of his personal holdings had been established by his wife, his son's wife, and his grandson (NJ 1959b, 2: 10–11).

15. Though the Dasheng companies, or the Nantong Group as they were commonly known, were the first in the field, more than 20 other reclamation companies were founded after 1914. Most were organized by merchants and bankers from Shanghai, Tai county, and Nantong, who had a vested interest in developing cotton production (Chen Hongjin 1939: 35; Shiyebu 1933: 264). Between them, the two groups of companies claimed most of the coastal land north of the Yangzi and south of the Huai.

16. The chambers were to demonstrate that political power in 1911. In the words of one contemporary observer: "With the downfall of the Manchu regime . . . the government of almost every city in China was for months virtually carried on by the chambers of commerce and associated guilds" (cited in Bergère 1968: 268).

17. Two years later, in 1904, at the request of Shen Xiejun, founder of the Haimen Cloth Association, the organization changed its name to the Tongchonghai General Chamber of Commerce for Cotton Cloth (Tongchonghai mianbu zongshanghui). The

three county offices then operating, in Nantong, Chongming, and Haimen, took their guidance from the Nantong city office. In 1910, with the incorporation of Taixing county, the name was changed again, to the Tongchonghaitai General Chamber of Commerce (Tongchonghaitai zongshanghui; NT [2] n.d.: 71–72; Yu Yikong 1982: 46–47).

18. Resistance to state extraction of local resources, especially through commercial taxes on cotton goods, can also be viewed as part of the chamber's promotion of local economic autonomy. For a discussion of this aspect of the chamber's activity, see Walker 1986: 320–31.

19. In the administrative reorganization of 1928, Jiulong became part of the new county of Qidong.

20. Peripheralization and landlordism did not preclude, however, the development of rich peasant–semilandlord farming in Chongming (-Qidong). Spurred by the cotton trade, as Chap. 8 examines, in the first decades of the century a pronounced rich peasant agriculture paralleled and to some extent challenged entrenched landlord power.

21. This structure was maintained in a subsequent reorganization in 1913, when the counties of Rugao, Tai, and Dongtai were incorporated (*Ershinianlai zhi Nantong* 1930, 2: 51–52).

22. According to the 1929 census of Jiangsu, Rugao had 266,835 households and a total population of 1,373, 441. Nantong county had the second-largest population, with 1,347,393 people and 269,479 households ("Population Census of Jiangsu [Kiangsu], 1929" 1933: 74).

CHAPTER SIX

1. Native banks acted much like savings and loan associations, using deposits from individuals to support their commercial loans (McElderry 1976: 11; Xu Guangqi 1982: 50). The interest rate paid to depositors varied, depending on their relationship with the manager and the amount of the deposit. The rate was kept secret. Since these arrangements could work to the advantage of people who made sizable deposits, regular customers generally preferred dealing with *qianzhuang* rather than modern banks whose operations principally revolved around the commercial trades (Xu 1982: 59).

2. Chen Hongjin argues that because shareholders saw these enterprises as a means of acquiring land, the companies were pressed to concentrate on gaining title to lands already under cultivation (1939: 38–39). The rapidity with which the Dayujin Company managed to divide 80% of its holdings certainly suggests that a sizable proportion of what purported to be land acquired for reclamation was farmland. It normally took several years to bring reclaimed land into production.

3. This is in stark contrast to 1913, when the foreign-owned mills in Shanghai, the site of most modern enterprises at the time, possessed only 39.8% of all spindles (Chao Kang 1977: 117).

4. Despite yearly variations in yarn prices and cotton costs, the margin between the two steadily closed, dropping from 27% in 1928 to 15% in 1936 (Chao Kang 1977: 122).

5. There was also a considerable rate of concentration in the Chinese industry as the leading firms absorbed unsuccessful mills in the 1920's. In 1930, as a result, seven Chinese and seven foreign companies between them owned 61 of the country's 127

cotton mills and controlled almost 60% of the spindles and looms (Chao Kang 1977: 124). The Rong brothers' Shen-Xin complex in Wuxi-Shanghai, which between 1916 and 1936 increased the number of spindles under its control from 12,960 to 567,248, is the leading example of the tendency toward concentration among Chinese companies (Yan Zhongping 1963: 188–90). Its ability to do so lay in part in close relations with the GMD state.

6. In 1924 leading Shanghai native banks agreed to use the Bank of China's bank notes. Native banks found that arrangement attractive because it alleviated the perennial problem of silver supply by specifying that security against the notes would consist of 60% silver, 30% government bonds, and 10% *zhuangpiao* (McElderry 1976: 144–45). But the agreement marked a victory for modern banks in the extending of notes and was later regularized among Bank of China branches and native banks in other localities, including Nantong (Xu Guangqi 1982; Zhang Zhiqing 1980).

7. Miyashita Tadao's investigation of the proportion of bank drafts issued in Shanghai by modern and native banks shows a rapid shift after the late 1920's. In 1926 native banks issued 80% of the drafts, against only 10% for the modern banks (commercial firms or other financial institutions accounted for the remainder); in 1931 the respective shares were 50% and 40%; and in 1936, now leading decisively, modern banks issued 70% of the drafts, *qianzhuang* only 20% (1942: 141).

8. In mid-1937, for example, the Bank of China controlled 15 textile mills with a total of over 350,000 spindles. In conjunction with the Bank of Communications, it had taken over seven of these mills through foreclosure; four had been founded with bank capital; and the other four had been purchased through satellite agencies (Zhang Yulan 1957: 120).

9. Several leading cloth merchants also attempted to deal with the demise of the northeast trade by organizing improved cloth production in four small weaving workshops. But these simply could not compete with production based on the cheap labor of peasant households. All four shut down within a few years (Lin Jubai 1984: 242–46).

10. Conventionally, for example, funds had been sent to Dasheng's collecting station in Dongtai county by boat. In the early 1930's, however, after the crushing of the Communist base area, bandit and communist activity remained so severe that the water route was unsafe. As a counterstep, a Bank of China employee was assigned to transport the silver by plane. The plane made regular flights to a 200- to 300-mu landing strip belonging to the Dazhong Transport Company, a Dasheng subsidiary (Yin Yuepu 1980).

11. During the war years Dasheng No. 1 fell under Japanese control. After the war T. V. Soong attempted to absorb it into his Chinese Textile Company empire by having it declared government property. Dasheng personnel avoided this maneuver by enlisting the aid of the Chens, another of the "four great families" at the pinnacle of the bureaucratic-capitalist structure. Under their sponsorship a temporary management committee was established in 1945, and then ownership and management reverted back to members of Zhang Jian's family and the Dasheng company. They continued to operate the mill with fluctuating losses and meager profits until the People's Republic nationalized it. It is now called the No. 1 Textile Mill of Nantong. (NJ 1959a: 35–36).

12. Coble's study (1980) is the fullest recent examination of bureaucratic capital-

ism. Although he equivocates in his interpretation of this phenomenon, the evidence he presents plainly outlines the formation and contours of this structure at the national level. It thus reinforces the findings of older studies, such as Fang Zhiping 1946; Kang Zhongping 1948–49; and Xu Dixin 1947.

CHAPTER SEVEN

1. Qiao Qiming's survey and other studies of its kind are open to criticism since they rely on random sampling and the impressions and recollections of informants. They are nevertheless useful in presenting popular perceptions of local developments and their causes; and the similarities in their findings and consistency with other evidence tend to bolster their reliability.

2. Peasants had long preferred bean cakes for fertilizer because at least 60% of the cottonseed cakes were hulls. After the turn of the century, however, when oil-pressing factories like the Guangsheng Oil Factory, a Dasheng subsidiary, began using machines that could hull the cotton before the oil was pressed, cottonseed increased in popularity and was widely marketed throughout the northern delta (Zhang Renren 1915–16, 2.4: 2).

3. During this five-year period the prime tax for Nantong remained constant at 9.10 yuan but the supplemental tax rose from 11.076 to 23.974 yuan. In 1927 the county kept less than half of the supplemental tax (5.20 yuan); in 1932, it retained 22.518 yuan, or almost the entire levy (Sun Xiaocun 1935: 38, 41). Thus not only did the county's total revenues increase dramatically, but the percentage of tax revenue transferred to the provincial government plummeted. For a discussion of competition among local elites and different levels of government for tax revenues, see Bell 1985: especially chap. 3.

4. Lucien Bianco's construction of peasants as primordial, immutable, and prepolitical typifies the modernist perspective. Bianco finds little difference between peasant action in the 17th century and that in the 20th. In his view peasant politics in both periods reflected the "spontaneous orientation of peasant anger" and a peasantry "more conscious of state oppression than of class exploitation" (1986: 301).

5. For a discussion of other issues in the Chuansha rising, see Prazniak 1986. As she shows, another impetus for the rising came from the elite's expropriation of the Yugong temple in the town of Tangmoqian for a local self-government office. Ding Fei, the lay sister who managed the temple, played an instrumental role in mobilizing the rising.

6. The Chuansha rising not only brought owners and tenants together in unified action but was supported by the yamen officials in a "rift" with the modern urban elite over the control of the temples and temple lands (Faure 1989: 191). Though Faure considers the Chuansha situation atypical, entrenched state functionaries quite frequently aligned with, and even incited, collective action against the modern elite. The Jinsha area of Nantong, for example, saw yet another rising when, soon after the 1911 revolution, the self-government council decided to make the Jinsha Salt Yamen into a court of first resort. The council reasoned that since Jinsha no longer produced salt, salt authorities should not have jurisdiction over civil and criminal cases. Yamen personnel, including the salt chief, were afraid that with this conversion, they might

lose their jobs, and one of the runners mobilized the salt workers, apparently on the same grounds. In early 1912 several thousand people, armed with hoes and rakes, invaded the Jinsha council headquarters to protest, and when discussions did not go well, demolished the council office. In the end troops quelled the rising, the runner was prosecuted and sentenced to death, and salt workers paid for the damages they had incurred. Soon after the head of the salt yamen did lose his job, and Zhang Jian's friend Sun Jinchen, who had originally proposed the change, became the head of the court (Chao Yingbin & Lin Jibe 1981: 124–25).

7. In examining the Junshan Rising of 1863 in Nantong and other pre-20th century insurgencies in the area, I have encountered no evidence of invincibility rituals or practices (Walker 1993b). These were clearly present, however, in risings such as the Pingchao insurgency of 1912 in which participants believed that if they wore wet clothing bullets could not harm them (Qian Min 1986). By the 1920's, if not earlier, they were also present in secret societies like the Big Swords (see following note).

8. Well into the 1920's bandit groups and older secret societies such as the Big Swords continued to play pivotal political roles. In 1928–29, for example, when Chinese Communists began organizing a base area in the northern delta and established the Fourteenth Red Army to protect and expand it, they took groups of Big Sword "spirit troops" (*shendaodui*) who believed themselves to be invincible to bullets into the army, where they fought as separate units (*Shibao*, Oct. 6, 1930: 2).

9. The five leaders were of widely mixed background, suggesting the cross-class character of the rising as a whole. One, as previously noted, was an entrepreneur-managerial farmer with (owned and rented) holdings of almost 200 mu. The others were a poor peasant, who co-rented 5 mu of land with his brother; an ex-soldier and tenant; a former Red Gang (*Hongbang*) member–salt smuggler; and a rich peasant who tilled 50 mu of land and ran a beancurd shop (Fei Fanjiu 1986: 8; Qian Min 1986: 11–12).

10. I am here drawing on the following passage: "In every country the process [of state upheaval] is different, although the content is the same. And the content is the crisis of the ruling class's hegemony, which occurs either because the ruling class has failed in some major political undertaking for which it has requested, or forcibly extracted, the consent of the broad masses (war, for example), or because huge masses (especially of peasants and petit-bourgeois intellectuals) have passed suddenly from a state of political passivity to a certain activity, and put forward demands which taken together, albeit not organically formulated, add up to a revolution. A 'crisis of authority' is spoken of: this is precisely the crisis of hegemony, or general crisis of the state" (Gramsci 1971: 210).

11. More progressive landlords of course also became active in this arena. As Mao noted for Xunwu (1990: 150), and as was undoubtedly true to some extent in Nantong as well, the conservative-progressive split often coincided with divisions between old and young.

CHAPTER EIGHT

1. At the upper extreme Qidong, Haimen, Nantong, and Rugao all had landlords whose holdings totaled 8,000 mu or more, but of the four counties this phenomenon

was least pronounced in Haimen (Huang Xiaoxian 1927: 473; Liu Ruilong 1986; Mu Xuan 1980).

2. Groups of bursary owners often supplied the critical mass for the formation of a landowner association (usually known as *tianye hui* or *tianye lianhehui*). The influential Suzhou landlords set the precedent for this type of mobilization when they organized a 200-member association in 1910. After 1911 landowner associations spread throughout the delta (Bernhardt 1992: 164–65; Gu Li 1981: 51; Huai Pu 1933: 72–75; Qiao Qiming 1926: 109).

3. Qiao defined "resident landlords" as those living in the countryside or near the lands they owned. "Nonresident landlords" were those who lived in cities and towns or relatively far away from their farmland (1926: 42).

4. There was still another arrangement in which in exchange for rented land the tenant in effect became a long-term hired worker for the landlord, either for a fixed time or permanently. When a fixed term was agreed upon, the landlord usually ceded 2–3 mu of land to the tenant at the conclusion of the contract period. Although the few pockets of "hereditary tenancy" in northern Haimen may have been remnants of this form, it seems to have been practiced principally in Huaibei (Huadong junzheng 1952: 442).

5. In the northern parts of Liuqiao and Shigang in Nantong, landlords frequently also supplied a waterwheel and a stone roller for milling grain (Qiao Qiming 1926: 24).

6. Many researchers have noted that one of the tragedies of peasant proprietors in disadvantageous economic circumstances is that they tend to cut expenses at the cost of their own consumption. Karl Kautsky perhaps best illustrates this tendency in his discussion of the farming incomes on a medium-sized holding of 11 hectares cultivated exclusively by wage labor and a smaller family-run holding of 5.5 hectares in Bischoffingen, Germany. "The bigger holding," he notes, "ended with a deficit of 133 marks, the smaller with a profit of 191 marks. The difference consisted in this, that on the holding run on wage labor the diet was fairly good, the equivalent of almost 1 mark per person per day, while on the smaller farm where the family was fortunate enough to be working for itself, the cost of consumption amounted to only 48 pfennings per person per day, not even half as much as on the other farm. If the peasant proprietor's family had been as well fed as the wage laborers of the bigger farm, instead of a profit of 191 marks, they would have shown a loss of 1,256 marks. The profit did not mean that his barns were full; it meant that their stomachs were empty" (cited in Banaji 1980: 70).

7. Since no systematic study of rural female labor in China had been undertaken, most of these scholars relied on J. L. Buck, whose data indicate that in North China women performed only 5 percent of all farmwork and in China as a whole only 13 percent (the largest proportion of female family labor was in the double-cropping rice area, 30%; the smallest in the rice-tea and winter wheat–millet areas, 5% and 6%, respectively; 1937a: 292–93). But as is now widely understood, in many instances Buck's data overrepresent middle peasants. Such overrepresentation makes his findings on farmwork among women problematical at best, since women of that strata appear to have performed much less farmwork than those in either poor or rich peas-

ant families. Utilizing household data, Chap. 9 illustrates this point for Nantong's industrial districts.

8. Even here a distorted picture emerges. Judith Stacey, for example, does suggest that in response to rural decline, families in the southern Yangzi delta began to transfer responsibility for agricultural work to women, and that in South China women became a higher proportion of the agricultural laborer force (1983: 101). Yet in noting the latter phenomenon, she uncritically accepts Chen Hanseng's problematical suggestion that "when rural employers increase the proportion of women laborers, this is a sign that male labor has become scarcer or less docile or sufficiently less efficient to make the employment of women preferable" (1936: 103). Thus Chen, one of the most perceptive scholars of China's rural political economy, fails in this instance to consider the possibility that the growth of the market for female agricultural labor could simply reflect capital's move to cheapen labor power as commodity production expanded. Certainly, as Chap. 9 illustrates, increasing casual labor, full-time off-farm employment, and migration among men have often formed the counterpart to a feminization of family agriculture and agricultural wage labor among the poorest women. But in many parts of the Third World, as the work of Maria Mies (1986) and other scholars shows, instead of the scenario Chen suggests, this turn among men has often been the product of their displacement from agricultural wage work as the market for cheaper female labor expanded.

9. In his seminal study of North China, Philip Huang concludes, for example, that "as things were . . . the overabundance of surplus labor in a stagnant economy ruled out such employment opportunities for women" (1985: 201). And of the Yangzi delta, he states: "Most important so far as the delta is concerned is . . . that a substantial part of the productive labor force—especially women—remained outside of the labor market. Cultural constraints against women venturing outside the home, plus the logistical difficulties of managing female labor that came with those constraints, kept the market for their labor from developing. [This] had the paradoxical effect of sustaining artificially high wages for . . . male adults who did sell their labor . . . The result . . . was the effective elimination of managerial farms from the delta countryside" (1990: 111).

10. In Guangxi and other parts of South China, in a pattern reminiscent of the use of women in the patriarchal landlord system of the Ming, the market in women, debt bondage, and the spread of modern sharecropping arrangements also intersected. Male agricultural laborers worked for 7 to 10 years without wage payment in return for a slave-girl wife. On their marriage, the couple usually received a small parcel of sharecrop land and a residence from the landlord, but they were also subject to his call for fieldwork at any time. Thus, as one account stated, "what would be free labor is actually transformed to slave labor and the slave girl is used, in such cases, to effect the change" (Institute of Pacific Relations 1939: 83). Whether this practice was a continuation of earlier patterns or new to the semicolonial economy remains to be clarified. On the other hand, my current research on rural labor in early-20th-century Guangxi, an area usually depicted as having been peripheral to new growth trends, has already revealed the outlines of a flourishing commercial agriculture in the 1920's serviced by a large migrant labor force composed of men *and women*.

11. In Xunwu Mao Zedong found this practice, too, but among larger landlords

and mainly for the purpose of allowing them to indulge in the pleasures of brothel life. To this end, as he notes, they overcharged their peasant-clients outrageously: "Why [is it] the gentry [who now visit prostitutes the most?] Because they are involved in litigation and stay in brothels throughout the year. Only at New Year's and other holidays do they return home. Where does the money for this come from? In lawsuits, country folk give them 100 yuan when only 20 yuan is needed for legal fees. They pocket the 80 yuan and in this way are provided with the means to cover their expenses for prostitutes" (1990: 113).

12. Strictly speaking, permanent tenancy implied hereditary tenancy and differed from the holding of permanent topsoil rights (which could be bought, sold, mortgaged, and transferred) by tenant-owners. Hereditary tenancy was virtually extinct in the Nantong area by the 20th century. Only three peasant families in the 8th district of Haimen, for example, fell into this category in the early 1930's, all of whom had been child-servants of a certain landlord Wang (Shen Shike 1934: 30908). Our concern here is not with tenants of this sort but with those who held permanent topsoil rights, a form of tenure that was predominant, as we have seen, along the coastal and river districts, especially in Haimen-Qidong. For convenience I will variously refer to that group as permanent tenants or topsoil owners.

13. In contrast to the property systems common in capitalist societies, in Ming-Qing China land was generally regarded as the property of the family or clan rather than the individual. Landownership was also often "incomplete," and its transfer subject to various kinds of restrictions. Owners of contiguous neighboring fields, or in some areas lineage members, had first right of purchase to a piece of property that came up for sale; and the original owner generally had the right to redeem a piece of property after its mortgage and even after its sale. But in the 20th century, as land and rents became monetized, the trend was toward complete transfer and sale. In Haimen by the early 1930's, according to one rural investigation, complete transfers accounted for 56.9% of all land sales; the figure was much lower in Qidong, only 27.7% (Shen Shike 1934: 30868). On the other hand, the trend toward complete transfer and sale developed only for fully owned property and for subsoil in the dual-ownership system (P. Huang 1990: 107). In the case of topsoil property, reflecting its predominantly peasant base, the first right of purchase by kin and neighbors continued to be the norm.

14. This was the year, as discussed below, that the new land and civil laws went into effect. Since they allowed landlords to evict permanent tenants who did not possess written contracts, most of these Jiaxing cases were probably brought before the arbitration committee by landlords, in contrast to the preceding years, when evicted tenants apparently lodged the bulk of the complaints.

15. There is some indication of the development of managerial farming in the Jiaxing area. Amano Motonosuke (1940) noted the presence of large rich peasant tenants in Jiaxing who farmed with wage labor; other data indicate that, by the 1930's, 19% of all farm labor in the county was performed by hired labor, or an amount that was slightly higher than the average in the delta and North China alike (Institute of Pacific Relations 1939: 77).

16. The consequence was a clear ambiguity about what constituted legal ownership. Why dual and multiple ownership was placed in the category of permanent

tenancy to begin with was never explained, but it ended up in the anomaly of having laws pertaining to permanent tenancy in the section on ownership, while those pertaining to fixed tenure fell under creditors' rights. Part of the problem of course was the murkiness of ownership rights at the time. But the problem was compounded, as Phil Yang notes, by the drafters' reliance on Japan's Meiji code as a model (1988: 213). In 1937 the Supreme Court clarified the issue by ruling that surface rights did not constitute ownership but were only a local variation of permanent tenancy.

17. I use the term formal subsumption in the sense outlined by Karl Marx, that is a situation in which the actual material form of production does not change, but its management does. As Marx states: "This change does not in itself imply a fundamental modification in the real nature of the labour process, the actual process of production. On the contrary, the fact is that capital subsumes the labour process as it finds it, that is to say, it takes over an existing labour process. . . . If changes occur in these traditional established *labour processes* after their takeover by capital, these are nothing but the gradual consequences of the subsumption. The work may become more intensive, its duration may be extended, it may become more continuous or orderly under the eye of the interested capitalist, but in themselves these changes do not affect the character of the actual labour process. [Formal subsumption] is the general form of every capitalist process of production; at the same time, however, it can be found as a *particular* form alongside the *specifically capitalist mode of production* in its developed form, because although the latter entails the former, the converse does not necessarily obtain" (1977: 1019–21; italics in original). Marx thus contrasted formal subsumption with what he termed "real subsumption" involving, in his view, a specifically capitalist mode of production, "which transforms the nature of the labour process and its actual conditions" (p. 1019). "Only when that happens," he states, "do we witness the real subsumption of labour under capital" (ibid.).

18. Christopher London (1997) makes this point well in his treatment of subsumption in the Colombian coffee industry.

CHAPTER NINE

1. The other villages surveyed were in the five counties of Songjiang, Wuxi, Changshu, Jiading, and Taicang (MMT 1941: 8, 27). The Mantetsu surveys of the delta and North China are generally ranked at the very top of the ethnographic materials available for China. I discuss their quality and reliability in Walker 1986: 360–63. See also P. Huang 1985: 34–36.

2. The 94 households represented approximately 54% of the households in the village. The researchers originally intended to survey all 178 of the households, but when they arrived, the northern section of Touzongmiao, which was separated from the southern part by a small stream, still lay outside Japanese lines. After two days of interviewing in the northern section, the Mantetsu team decided the situation was too dangerous to continue. Thereafter they restricted their work to areas of the village covered by Japanese lines. Although this omission limits the conclusiveness of the survey, it does not substantially affect its usefulness. The team reported that they could discern no visible differences in economic status, occupation, or standard of living between the surveyed and non-surveyed sections of the village. They were con-

vinced that the 94 surveyed households provided a reliable cross-section of economic divisions and life within the village as a whole (MMT 1941: 28).

3. Qiao's data are based on sample areas of Nantong county, but he appears to have sampled mostly or only the agricultural districts. If his sample includes industrial areas, then the rate of tenancy in the agricultural districts would have been even higher than Qiao's figures indicate.

4. The five managerial landlords rented out 92 mu all told, 52 of which lay inside the village. Since just 3.2 mu of this land was being rented out to the lone local tenant, the Mantetsu team assumed the remaining 48.8 mu of village land was rented by nonvillagers. The interview questionnaires were not structured in such a way as to determine the identity of landlords who owned land outside the village but rented to Touzongmiao residents (MMT 1941: 50).

5. Yan Zhongping (1963: 268) calculates that, at minimum, peasants needed about 75 yuan in start-up costs for improved cloth in the 1930's: 46.30 yuan for an iron-gear loom; roughly 24 yuan for enough yarn to produce 10 *pi* of cloth, the standard amount they used to avoid the waste of materials and labor power that more frequent warping incurred; and 4 yuan for miscellaneous items like starch. This figure represented almost twice the average annual rent for 8 mu of land. The prohibitive cost of an iron-gear loom was what kept most peasants (i.e., the poor peasant majority) from shifting to improved cloth; the wooden loom used for *guanzhuang* cloth cost only 9 yuan. But with yarn expense, start-up costs could still total 20 yuan or more. That amount generally formed the dividing line between those who could and could not afford to weave.

6. In a very real sense, through such straddling, rural and urban differentiation intersected and intertwined. For discussions of this phenomenon in other Third World countries, see Berry 1980; Kitching 1980; and Stitcher 1985.

7. This practice has typified other agrarian societies as well. Studies of the European rural economy suggest that regardless of how strongly implanted the principle of equal inheritance was in an area, once landholdings became so small that inheritance threatened subsistence, peasant families routinely employed a variety of measures to circumvent division. See, for example, Berkner & Mendels 1978.

8. For a discussion of consumption, income and loss, and indebtedness patterns within different peasant strata in Touzongmiao, see Walker 1986: 471–81.

9. In some localities the provision of a draft animal in exchange for human labor represented another form of disguised labor. It is not clear that this type of exchange took place in Touzongmiao. Only one family had an ox. During the single plowing season of the year, this family regularly hired-out to turn the fields of others with its ox (MMT 1941: 101).

10. Even after the base area was abandoned, the GMD could not reestablish complete control. Bandits, Communist guerrillas, and peasant insurgents contrived to make large areas along the coast and peripheries of the development companies unconquerable. At the same time, local Party organizations continued to operate clandestinely within the GMD-controlled areas. Largely because of these operations, when Japanese troops entered Nantong, they had to withdraw twice before they finally, in 1938, established control of localities such as Jinsha. But even then their hold was precarious at best. In 1940, when the Mantetsu team arrived in Touzongmiao, it deemed the northern part of the village too "unsafe" to carry out field investigations. Local

CCP activity continued to expand in the early 1940's. In 1945 the New Fourth Army liberated part of the Nantong area, including Jinsha. The GMD regained limited control in 1946 and maintained it until its final demise three years later. See Jin Zhihuai 1984: 5–7; NT [9] 1985, 5: 1–16; and for full details, JS [1] 1983; and NT [9] 1986–87, vols. 6–7.

CONCLUSION

1. Shu-mei Shih (1996) develops this definition in her examination of gender, race, and semicolonialism.

2. Cooper makes the important point that even in colonial context, notably that of Africa with which he is specifically concerned, the limited spatial and cultural domains over which early colonial regimes actually exercised power often necessitated alliances with the very people whose "tyranny" their imperialist rhetoric pledged to uproot. He refers to the continuation and elaboration of this pattern of rule through connections to a variety of elites—itself symptomatic of compromise and weakness in African colonialism—as a "subcontracted power structure" (1997: 409–10, 412).

3. I draw on Frank Perlin's (1983) formulation for this description.

4. See, for example, Claude Meillassoux's discussion of primitive accumulation (1981: 104–9). He argues that Marx's conception of primitive accumulation as an initial historical phenomenon (i.e., as the point at which, through the dissolution of feudalism, capitalism took off) did not take into account the "real process of capitalist growth and expansion which is achieved through the continuous incorporation of new lands and, still more, of new peoples under the influence of colonialism and imperialism" (p. 105).

5. See also n. 12 below.

6. For further discussion of these points, see Benjamin White's excellent essay (1989) on problems in the empirical analysis of agrarian differentiation.

7. In the standard model of neoclassical economics, as noted earlier, Thomas Rawski (1989) insists, for example, that modern industry was not only generating sustained urban development but was propelling the countryside in the same direction. On the other hand, although Philip Huang (1990) argues that, in the Yangzi delta, rural-urban linking generated a pattern of rural underdevelopment, he in effect creates a dual-economy model by contending that in the cities modern industry produced development. To a serious degree this uncritical equating of modern industry with sustained development stems from the fact that neither Rawski nor Huang situates his economic analysis in the context of social structures and struggles. Once the analytic compass is broadened, modern industry becomes not a given but something that must treated problematically, structurally and processually.

8. Byres has been concerned chiefly with the question of agrarian transition as the mobilizing of resources for industrial capitalist accumulation in the Third World. He argues, for example, that though in various Third World countries land reform would generate an increase in output, that output would be consumed mostly within the agrarian sector; thus gross marketed surplus would increase but a net marketed surplus would not (1974: 244–45). For comments on Byres's approach, see Bernstein & Brass 1996–97: 8–9.

9. See Henry Bernstein's (1996–97) excellent discussion of this point in his consideration of the problematic of agrarian transition in the work of T. J. Byres.

10. In Nantong the reversals in urban development trends paralleled by a slowing or stultification of agricultural growth persisted until liberation, at which time the Dasheng No. 1 mill was still operating at a lower output capacity than in the teens. After 1949, however, when the overdeveloped local structure of many "capitalisms" and modern landlordism was dismantled, the renamed No. 1 Mill expanded, giving impetus to the simultaneous redevelopment of rural industry in cooperative form. The new framework and presence of local industry placed both Nantong city and rural producers on sounder economic footing than their counterparts in counties, including those in Jiangnan, lacking a comparable, local industrial base.

11. Barrington Moore (1966) discusses a similar situation in different context.

12. Formulations of this type also argue, first, that as the product of internal and external differentiation, this "multivocality" is a recent phenomenon tied to contemporary globalization; and, second, that this complex differentiation makes the category "peasant" obsolete. But formulations of this sort are only possible because they adopt a problematic, ahistorical definition of peasants as autonomous agriculturalists engaged in subsistence production. This categorization ignores the actual historical characteristics of peasants in many parts of the world for well over a century or, as in the case of China, much longer. Indeed, given the development of differentiated, commercialized production, it would hardly apply to peasants in various areas of China from the late Ming. Moreover, as suggested above, from the mid-19th century under the global structuring of imperialism-colonialism, internal (and external) differentiation became a globally generalized characteristic of peasants (i.e., the emergence of semi- and subproletarianized peasants, or at the very least "peasant-workers"). Accordingly, rather than denoting the appearance of "postpeasantries" in the contemporary world, internal differentiation actually becomes a generalized feature of what we might call "modern" peasantries. Elsewhere, as in the northern delta, the political histories of these modern peasantries problematize postmodernist and related "new social movement" assertions about the impossibility of class-based collective action. For one of the most detailed presentations of the "postpeasant" position, see Kearney 1996.

13. Recent research on peasantries and subordinate classes for other world areas spotlights this point as well. See, in particular, Florencia Mallon's (1995) examination of regional histories in Mexico and Peru. On regional cultures, see also the recent study of David Faure and Helen Siu, who advance a notion of a region as "a conscious historical construct that may be captured in the cultural expression of those involved in creating it" (1995: 1).

14. I make a distinction here between state building and state formation. In recent decades several China scholars have adopted the model of European state making proposed by Charles Tilly (1975) and others to suggest a *continuous* process of state building (involving bureaucratization, the penetration of local communities, greater surplus extraction, and the consolidation of power by a centralizing state) from the Qing through the Republican period. See, for example, Bernhardt 1992; Chauncey 1992; Duara 1988; and Jones 1978–79. Unlike the European studies, however, most

of these analyses artificially separate economic and political developments. Consequently, they tend to focus on state-elite relations without considering the significance of class formation in larger political processes. They are the more problematical because of their insistence on a continuous process of state building. As one of their critics, Lloyd Eastman, points out, "the nearly complete political breakdown . . . in many rural areas makes it utterly ahistorical to depict the warlord era as a time of state building" (1990: 226–34). On the other hand, Eastman and other critics, like those they criticize, continue to focus on formal state-bureaucratic trends emanating from centralized sources of power as the key determinants and characteristics of state building. If, however, one shifts the focus from state building to state formation as a process resting in the political subordination of the majority of a population and a redirecting of part of their production toward the maintenance of one or more nonproducing classes, that is, to see state formation as "a tense and contingent means of reproducing class relations" (Gailey 1987b: 35), then the possibility of totally new lines of analysis appears. In the case of China, such a view allows us not only to move beyond the artificial separation of the political and the economic, but to recognize local society as a key terrain of intertwined class and state formative processes.

15. Duara comes closest to such a consideration in his *Rescuing History from the Nation* (1995, especially chap. 3) when he examines alternative narratives of the nation within the elite and suggests that popular religion and the collective actions of secret societies provide the outlines of oppositional counternarratives that resisted and subverted the totalizing discourse of the "nationalist" elite. Unfortunately, he does not explore the latter in detail or consider how historically such counternarratives (along with other elements of popular culture) may have coalesced into a national "rhetoric of popular dissent."

16. Because Mallon continues to place nationalism historically within the context of modern nation-state formation, I have here presented only part of her definition. The full definition runs: "A broad vision for organizing society, based on the premise of citizenship, with individual membership beginning from the assumption of legal equality" (1995: 4). The power of her formulation lies in the recognition that modern state formation does not rest in a single ready-made (bourgeois-liberal) vision, but involves multiple visions and competing hegemonies, which in the end are incorporated, excluded, or modified to produce the final "national" vision. In viewing nation-state formation as a process of both contestation and alliance, her formulation thus marks an advance, I suggest, over that of Benedict Anderson (1991). Despite its many provocative elements, in the last analysis Anderson's influential notion of the nation as imagined community, that is, as a bounded community in which people imagine themselves as one, not only continues to conflate the nation and state, but reinforces the view of nationalism as the preserve of a modern "national" elite.

17. Any notion of a peasant nation as a line of alternative development is of course complicated by class, gender, and ethnicity.

18. Li Lianjiang and Kevin O'Brien (1996) offer insight into some of the current forms of peasant political action, but their analysis is ahistorical. Couched solidly within the modernist model, it neither recognizes the degree to which, since the Ming, "policy-based resistance" has been common to the repertoire of peasant protest, nor

considers how three decades of socialist ideology and practice might be structuring peasant thought and action today. For one of the most fascinating treatments to date of the recent cultural politics of peasants, see Kipnis 1995. He details how they are redefining themselves—in the face of the depredations of development-oriented modernizers—as the only legitimate heirs and transmitters of traditions from the past.

References

Jiangsu and Nantong entries are cited by bracketed numbers preceded by the abbreviations JS and NT. I have used a few other abbreviations in the citations as follows:

DSXT   *Dasheng xitong qiyeshi*
MMT   Minami Manshū tetsudō kabushiki kaisha Shanhai jimusho
NJ   Nanjing daxue lishixi, *Dasheng fangzhi gongsi*
RG   *Rugao wenshi ziliao*
TZ   *Tongzhou xingban shiye zhi lishi*
TZZ   *Tongzhou Zhili zhouzhi*, 1875

Alavi, Hamza. 1973. "Peasant Classes and Primordial Loyalties," *Journal of Peasant Studies*, 1: 23–62.

Amano Motonosuke. 1940. *Shina nōgyō keizairon* (On the Chinese agricultural economy). Tokyo: Kaizōsha.

Anderson, Benedict. 1991. *Imagined Communities: Reflections on the Origins and Spread of Nationalism.* 2d ed. London: Verso.

Arnason, Johann. 1987. "The Modern Constellation and the Japanese Enigma, Part 2," *Thesis Eleven*, 17: 4–39.

Arnold, David. 1984. "Gramsci and Peasant Subalternity in India," *Journal of Peasant Studies*, 11.4: 155–77.

Asad, Talal. 1992. "Conscripts of Western Civilization," in Christine Ward Gailey, ed., *Dialectical Anthropology: Essays in Honour of Stanley Diamond*, vol. 1: *Civilization in Crisis: Anthropological Perspectives*, pp. 333–52. Gainesville: Univ. of Florida Press.

———, ed. 1973. *Anthropology and the Colonial Encounter.* London: Ithaca Press.

Atwell, William G. 1977. "Notes on Silver, Foreign Trade and the Late Ming Economy," *Ch'ing-shih wen-t'i* 8. 3: 1–10.

Banaji, Jarius. 1980. "Summary of Selected Parts of Kautsky's *The Agrarian Question*," in Harold Wolpe, ed. *The Articulation of Modes of Production*, pp. 45–92. London: Routledge & Kegan Paul.

Baran, Paul. 1957. *The Political Economy of Growth.* New York: Monthly Review Press.

Barkan, Lenore. 1990. "Patterns of Power: Forty Years of Elite Politics in a Chinese County," in Esherick and Rankin, listed below, pp. 191–215.

———. 1983. "Nationalists, Communists, and Rural Leaders: Political Dynamics in a Chinese County, 1927–1937." Ph.D. diss., Univ. of Washington.

Barlow, Tani E. 1993. "Colonialism's Career in Postwar China Studies," *Positions*, 1.1: 224–67.

Barrera, Mario. 1979. *Race and Class in the Southwest: A Theory of Racial Inequality.* South Bend, Ind.: Univ. of Notre Dame Press.

Bastid, Marianne. 1988. *Educational Reform in Early Twentieth-Century China*. Tr. Paul J. Bailey. Ann Arbor: Univ. of Michigan Center for Chinese Studies.

—— [-Bruguiere]. 1980. "Currents of Social Change," in John K. Fairbank and Kwang-ching Liu, eds. *The Cambridge History of China*, vol. 11: *Late Qing, 1800-1911, part 2*, pp. 536-602. Cambridge, Eng.: Cambridge Univ. Press.

——. 1976. "The Social Context of Reform," in Paul Cohen and John Schrecker, eds., *Reform in Nineteenth Century China*, pp. 117-27. Cambridge, Mass.: Harvard Univ. Press.

Bell, Lynda S. Forthcoming. *One Industry, Two Chinas: Silk Filatures and Peasant-Family Production in Wuxi County, 1865-1937*. Stanford, Calif.: Stanford Univ. Press.

——. 1994. "For Better, For Worse: Women and the World Market in Rural China," *Modern China*, 20. 2: 180-210.

——. 1990. "From Comprador to County Magnate: Bourgeois Practice in the Wuxi County Silk Industry," in Esherick and Rankin, listed below, pp. 113-39.

——. 1985. "Merchants, Peasants, and the State: The Organization and Politics of Chinese Silk Production, Wuxi County, 1870-1937." Ph.D. diss. Univ. of California, Los Angeles.

Bergère, Marie-Claire. 1989. *The Golden Age of the Chinese Bourgeoisie, 1911-1937*. Tr. Janet Lloyd. Cambridge, Eng.: Cambridge Univ. Press.

——. 1983. "The Chinese Bourgeoisie, 1911-37," in John K. Fairbank, ed., *The Cambridge History of China*, vol. 12: *Republican China, 1912-1949, part 1*, pp. 722-827. Cambridge, Eng.: Cambridge Univ. Press.

——. 1968. "The Role of the Bourgeoisie," in Mary C. Wright, ed., *China in Revolution: The First Phase, 1900-1913*, pp. 229-96. New Haven, Conn.: Yale Univ. Press.

Berkner, Lutz K., and Franklin F. Mendels. 1978. "Inheritance Systems, Family Structure, and Demographic Patterns in Western Europe, 1700-1900," in Charles Tilly, ed., *Historical Studies of Changing Fertility*. Princeton, N.J.: Princeton Univ. Press.

Bernhardt, Kathryn. 1996. "A Ming-Qing Transition in Chinese Women's History? The Perspective from Law," in Gail Hershatter, Emily Honig, Jonathan N. Lipman, and Randall Stross, eds., *Remapping China: Fissures in Historical Terrain*, pp. 42-58. Stanford, Calif.: Stanford Univ. Press.

——. 1992. *Rents, Taxes, and Peasant Resistance: The Lower Yangzi Region, 1840-1950*. Stanford, Calif.: Stanford Univ. Press.

Bernstein, Henry. 1996-97. "Agrarian Questions Then and Now," *Journal of Peasant Studies*, 24. 1-2: 22-59.

——. 1990. "Taking the Part of Peasants?" in Henry Bernstein, Ben Crow, Maureen Mackintosh, and Charlotte Martin, eds., *The Food Question: Profits Versus People?*, pp. 69-79. New York: Monthly Review Press.

——. 1979. "African Peasantries: A Theoretical Framework," *Journal of Peasant Studies* 6.4: 421-43.

Bernstein, Henry, and Tom Brass. 1996-97. "Questioning the Agrarians: The Work of T. J. Byres," *Journal of Peasant Studies*, 24.1-2: 1-21.

Berry, Sara. 1980. "Rural Class Formation in West Africa," in Robert H. Bates and Michael F. Lofchie, eds., *Agricultural Development in Africa: Issues of Public Policy*, pp. 401-24. New York: Praeger.

Bharadwaj, Krishna. 1985. "A View on Commercialization in Indian Agriculture and the Development of Capitalism," *Journal of Peasant Studies*, 12.4: 7-25.

———. 1979. "Towards a Macro-economic Framework for a Developing Economy: The Indian Case," *The Manchester School*, Sept: 270-302.

Bianco, Lucien. 1986. "Peasant Movements," in John K. Fairbank and Albert Feuerwerker, eds., *The Cambridge History of China*, vol. 13: *Republican China 1912-1949*, Part 2, pp. 270-328. Cambridge, Eng.: Cambridge Univ. Press.

Billingsley, Phil. 1988. *Bandits in Republican China*. Stanford, Calif.: Stanford Univ. Press.

Bix, Herbert. 1986. *Peasant Protest in Japan, 1500-1884*. New Haven, Conn.: Yale Univ. Press.

Bourdieu, Pierre. 1977. *Outline of a Theory of Practice*. Cambridge, Eng.: Cambridge Univ. Press.

Brandt, Loren. 1989. *Commercialization and Agricultural Development: Central and Eastern China, 1870-1937*. Cambridge, Eng.: Cambridge Univ. Press.

Brass, Tom. 1997. "Immobilised Workers, Footloose Theory," *Journal of Peasant Studies* 24.4: 337-58.

———. 1986. "Unfree Labor and Capitalist Restructuring in the Agrarian Sector: Peru and India," *Journal of Peasant Studies*, 14.1: 23-56.

Braudel, Fernand. 1972. *The Mediterranean and the Mediterranean World in the Age of Philip II*, vol. 1. London: Collins, Ltd.

Brenner, Robert. 1985. "The Agrarian Roots of European Capitalism," in T. H. Aston and C. H. E. Philpin, eds., *The Brenner Debate: Agrarian Class Structure and Economic Development in Pre-Industrial Europe*, pp. 213-328. Cambridge, Eng.: Cambridge Univ. Press.

———. 1977. "The Origins of Capitalism: A Critique of Neo-Smithian Marxism," *New Left Review*, 104: 25-92.

———. 1976. "Agrarian Class Structure and Economic Development in Pre-Industrial Europe," *Past and Present*, 70: 30-75.

Buck, John Lossing. 1937a. *Land Utilization in China*. Shanghai: Nanjing Univ.

———. 1937b. *Land Utilization in China: Statistics*. Shanghai: Nanjing Univ.

Byres, T. J. 1991. "The Agrarian Question and Differing Forms of Capitalist Agrarian Transition: An Essay with Reference to Asia," in J. Breman and S. Mundle, eds., *Rural Transformation in Asia*, pp. 1-76. Cambridge, Eng.: Cambridge Univ. Press.

———. 1974. "Land Reform, Industrialization and the Marketed Surplus in India: An Essay on the Power of Rural Bias," in D. Lehmann, ed., *Agrarian Reform and Agrarian Reformism*. London: Faber & Faber.

Cai Shaoqing. 1987. *Zhongguo jindai huidangshi yanjiu* (Research on the history of secret societies in modern China). Beijing: Zhonghua shuju.

Calhoun, Craig. 1983. "The Radicalism of Tradition: Community Strength or Venerable Disguise and Borrowed Language," *American Journal of Sociology* 88.5: 886-914.

———. 1982. *The Question of Class Struggle: Social Foundations of Popular Radicalism During the Industrial Revolution*. Chicago: Univ. of Chicago Press.

Chang, John K. 1969. *Industrial Development in Pre-Communist China: A Quantitative Analysis*. Chicago: Aldine.

Chao Kang. 1977. *The Development of Cotton Textile Production in China*. Cambridge, Mass.: Harvard Univ. Press.

Chao Yingbin and Lin Jibe. 1981. "Tongzhou guangfu chuqi de sande fengchao" (Three uprisings in Tongzhou after the overthrow of the Qing dynasty), in NT [9], listed below, vol. 1, pp. 124–27.

Chatterjee, Partha. 1993. *The Nation and Its Fragments: Colonial and Postcolonial Histories*. Princeton, N.J.: Princeton Univ. Press.

——. 1988. "More on Modes of Power and the Peasantry," in Ranajit Guha and Gayatri Chakravorty Spivak, eds., *Selected Subaltern Studies*, pp. 351–90. New York: Oxford Univ. Press.

——. 1986. *Nationalist Thought and the Colonial World: A Derivative Discourse?* London: Zed Books.

Chauncey, Helen R. 1992. *Schoolhouse Politicians: Locality and State During the Chinese Republic*. Honolulu: Univ. of Hawaii Press.

Chaunu, Pierre. 1960. *Les Philippines et le Pacifique des Ibériques (XVI, XVII, XVIII Siècles): Introduction Méthodologique et Indices d'Activité*. Paris: S.E.V.P.E.N.

Chen Hanseng. 1936. *Landlord and Peasant in China*. New York: International Publishers.

Chen Hongjin. 1939. "Land Division Through the Land Development Companies in Northern Jiangsu," in Institute of Pacific Relations, comp., *Agrarian China*, pp. 35–42. Chicago: Univ. of Chicago Press.

Chen Ji. 1984. "Jinsha beishan" (North Hill in Jinsha), in NT [6], listed below, vol. 2, pp. 14–18.

Chen Shiqi. 1979. "Jiawu zhanqian Zhongguo nongcun shougongye mianfangzhiye de bianhua he zibenzhuyi shengchang de chengzhang" (Change in China's rural handicraft cotton textile industry and the growth of capitalist production in the period before the Sino-Japanese War), in Huang Yiping, ed., *Zhongguo jindai jingjishi lunwen xuanji*, vol. 4, pp. 958–97. Shanghai: Shanghai shifan daxue lishixi.

Chen Shouhua and Du Wenqing. 1980. "Lueshu jiefang qian Rucheng de qianzhuang ye" (A brief account of the native banking industry in Rugao city before liberation), in *RG*, vol. 2, pp. 52–55.

Chen Xulu. 1955. *Xinhai geming* (The 1911 revolution). Shanghai: Renmin chubanshe.

Chen Yongfa. 1986. *Making Revolution: The Communist Movement in Eastern and Central China, 1937–1945*. Berkeley: Univ. of California Press.

Chen Zengyu. 1986. "Tonghai diqu yuanzhuangbu xingluo shilue" (A historical sketch of the rise and decline of *guanzhuang* cloth in the Tonghai district), in JS [9], vol. 18, pp. 157–65.

Cheng Zengchong. 1980. "The Relations Among Cloth Firms, Cotton Firms, and Native Banks in Nantong." Report and personal interview at round-table meeting, Nantong Library, Dec. 17, 1980. [Cheng's father managed a Linji cloth firm.]

Chesneaux, Jean. 1971. *Secret Societies in China in the Nineteenth and Twentieth Centuries*. London: Heinemann Educational Books.

Chiba Masaji. 1986. *Asian Indigenous Law: In Interaction with Received Law*. London: Kegan Paul International.

Chu Hua. n.d. [late 18th century] *Mumianpu* (On cotton), in *Shanghai zhanggu congshu*. Shanghai, 1936.

Chu, Samuel C. 1965. *Reformer in Modern China: Chang Chien [Zhang Jian], 1853–1926*. New York: Columbia Univ. Press.

Chu, Yung-deh R. 1967. "An Introductory Study of the White Lotus Sect in Chinese History with Special Reference to Peasant Movements." Diss., Columbia Univ.

Cihai (The Cihai dictionary). 1979. 3 vols. Shanghai: Cishu chubanshe.

The Civil Code of the Republic of China. 1930. Shanghai: Kelly & Walsh.

Clifford, James, and George E. Marcus, eds. 1986. *Writing Culture: The Poetics and Politics of Ethnography*. Berkeley: Univ. of California Press.

Coble, Parks M. 1980. *Shanghai Capitalists and the Nationalist Government, 1927–1937*. Cambridge, Mass.: Harvard Univ. Press.

Cohen, Myron L. 1993. "Cultural and Political Inventions in Modern China: The Case of the Chinese 'Peasant,' " *Daedalus*, 122.2: 151–70.

———. 1978. "Developmental Process in the Chinese Domestic Group," in Arthur P. Wolf, ed., *Studies in Chinese Society*, pp. 183–98. Stanford: Stanford Univ. Press.

Cohen, Paul A. 1984. *Discovering History in China: American Historical Writing on the Recent Chinese Past*. New York: Columbia Univ. Press.

Comaroff, Jean. 1985. *Body of Power, Spirit of Resistance: The Culture and History of a South African People*. Chicago: Univ. of Chicago Press.

Comaroff, John L. 1997. "Images of Empire, Contests of Conscience: Models of Colonial Domination in South Africa," in Cooper and Stoler, listed below, pp. 163–97.

Cooper, Frederick. 1997. "The Dialectics of Decolonization: Nationalism and Labor Movements in Postwar French Africa," in Cooper and Stoler, listed below, pp. 406–35.

———. 1993. "Africa and the World Economy," in Cooper, Isaacman et al., listed below, pp. 84–201.

Cooper, Frederick, and Ann Laura Stoler, eds. 1997. *Tensions of Empire: Colonial Cultures in a Bourgeois World*. Berkeley: Univ. of California Press.

Cooper, Frederick, Allen F. Isaacman, Florencia E. Mallon, Steve J. Stern, and William Roseberry. 1993. *Confronting Historical Paradigms: Peasants, Labor, and the Capitalist World System in Africa and Latin America*. Madison: Univ. of Wisconsin Press.

Da Shiji. 1980. "The Development of Cotton Textile Production in Nantong." Report and personal interview at round-table meeting, No. 1 Guest House, Nantong, March 28. [Da formerly managed a *guanzhuang* cloth firm.]

Daniel, Victor, Henry Bernstein, and Tom Brass, eds. 1992. *Plantations, Proletarians and Peasants in Colonial Asia*. London: Frank Case.

Dasheng xitong qiyeshi [DSXT] (Business history of the Dasheng system). 1990. Nantong: Jiangsu gucang chubanshe.

Davidson, Alastair. 1984. "Gramsci, the Peasantry and Popular Culture," *Journal of Peasant Studies*, 11.4: 139–54.

de Silva, S. B. D. 1982. *The Political Economy of Underdevelopment*. London: Routledge.

"Diaocha Tongchonghai mianzuo shouhuo fanyun qingxing baogaoshu" (Report of an investigation of the situation of cotton cultivation, harvesting, and marketing in Nantong, Chongming, and Haimen). 1918. *Nongshang qongbao*, 4.6: 65–66.

Diamond, Stanley. 1974. *In Search of the Primitive: A Critique of Civilization*. New Brunswick, N.J.: Transaction Publishers.

"Dimensions of Ethnic and Cultural Nationalism in Asia—A Symposium." 1994. *Journal of Asian Studies*, 53.1: 3-131.

Dirks, Nicholas B. 1992. "Introduction: Colonialism and Culture," in Dirks, ed., *Colonialism and Culture*, pp. 1-26. Ann Arbor: Univ. of Michigan Press.

Dirlik, Arif. 1997. "Narrativizing Revolution: The Guangzhou Uprising (11-13 Dec. 1927) in Workers' Perspective," *Modern China*, 23.4: 363-97.

———. 1996. "Reversals, Ironies, Hegemonies: Notes on the Contemporary Historiography of Modern China," *Modern China*, 22.3: 243-84.

———. 1985. "The Universalisation of a Concept: 'feudalism' to 'Feudalism' in Chinese Marxist Historiography," *Journal of Peasant Studies*, 13.2: 197-227.

Dobb, Maurice. 1946. *Studies in the Development of Capitalism*. New York: International Publishers.

Duara, Prasenjit. 1995. *Rescuing History from the Nation: Questioning Narratives of Modern China*. Chicago: Univ. of Chicago Press.

———. 1993. "Bifurcating Linear History: Nation and Histories in China and India," *Positions* 1.3: 778-804.

———. 1988. *Culture, Power, and the State: Rural North China, 1900-1942*. Stanford, Calif.: Stanford Univ. Press.

———. 1987. "State Involution: A Study of Local Finances in North China, 1911-1935," *Comparative Studies in Society and History* 29.1: 132-61.

Eastman, Lloyd. 1990. "State Building and the Revolutionary Transformation of Rural Society in North China," *Modern China* 16.2: 226-34.

Ebisawa Tetsuo. 1983. "Bondservants in the Yuan," *Acta Asiatica*, 45: 27-48.

Elston, Robert E. 1989. "International Commerce, the State and Society in Southeast Asia: Economic and Social Change from the Early Nineteenth Century to the Depression." Unpublished paper. [As cited in Kahn 1993, listed below.]

Elvin, Mark. 1977. "Market Towns and Waterways: The County of Shanghai from 1480 to 1910," in G. William Skinner, ed., *The City in Late Imperial China*, pp. 443-73. Stanford, Calif.: Stanford Univ. Press.

———. 1973. *The Pattern of the Chinese Past*. Stanford, Calif.: Stanford Univ. Press.

Ershinianlai zhi Nantong (Nantong for the last 20 years). 1930. 2 vols. n.p.

Escobar, Arturo. 1995. *Encountering Development: The Making and Unmaking of the Third World*. Princeton, N.J.: Princeton Univ. Press.

Esherick, Joseph. 1987. *The Origins of the Boxer Uprising*. Berkeley: Univ. of California Press.

———. 1983. "Symposium on Peasant Rebellions: Some Introductory Comments," *Modern China*, 9.3: 275-84.

———. 1976. *Reform and Revolution in China: The 1911 Revolution in Hunan and Hubei*. Berkeley: Univ. of California Press.

Esherick, Joseph W., and Mary Backus Rankin, eds. 1990. *Chinese Local Elites and Patterns of Dominance*. Berkeley: Univ. of California Press.

Fan Baichuan. 1983. "Ershi shiji chuqi Zhongguo zibenzhuyi fazhan de gaikuang yu tedian" (The situation and special characteristics of Chinese capitalism in the early 20th century), *Lishi yanjiu*, 4: 11-24.

Fang Xing. 1986. "Lun Qingdai qianqi nongmin shangpin shengchan di fazhan" (On the development of peasant commodity production during the early Qing), *Zhong-guo jingjishi yanjiu*, 1: 79–94.

Fang Zhiping. 1946. *Lun guanliao ziben* (On bureaucratic capitalism). n.p.

Faure, David. 1989. *The Rural Economy of Pre-Liberation China: Trade Expansion and Peasant Livelihood in Jiangsu and Guangdong, 1870 to 1937*. Hong Kong: Oxford Univ. Press.

———. 1985. "The Plight of the Farmers: A Study of the Rural Economy of Jiangnan and the Pearl River Delta, 1870–1937," *Modern China*, 11.1: 3–37.

Faure, David, and Helen F. Siu. 1995. *Down to Earth: The Territorial Bond in South China*. Stanford, Calif.: Stanford Univ. Press.

Fei Fanjiu. 1986. "Minchu Siyugang fankang mujuan fengchao" (The struggle against the field tax in Siyugang at the beginning of the Republic), in NT [9], listed below, vol. 6, pp. 5–9.

———. 1981a. "Xinhai geming qianhou shang nong jiaoyu gejie chuangli zuzhi (The founding organizations in commercial, agricultural, and educational circles before and after the 1911 revolution), in NT [9], listed below, vol. 1, pp. 140–41.

———. 1981b. "Xinhai geming qianhou Nantong zizhi tuanti de xingqi (The emergence of self-government associations in Nantong before and after the 1911 revolution), in NT [9], listed below, vol. 1, pp. 136–39.

Fei Hsiao-tung. 1939. *Peasant Life in China: A Field Study of Country Life in the Yangzi Valley*. New York: Oxford Univ. Press.

Fei Hsiao-tung and Chang Chih-i. 1945. *Earthbound China: A Study of Rural Economy in Yunnan*. Chicago: Univ. of Chicago Press.

Fei Hsiao-tung et al. 1986. *Small Towns in China: Functions, Problems and Prospects*. Beijing: New World Press.

Feierman, Steven. 1990. *Peasant Intellectuals: Anthropology and History in Tanzania*. Madison: Univ. of Wisconsin Press.

Feldman, Shelley. 1991. "Engendered Class: Family Labor Relations in Subsistence Production." Paper presented at the annual meeting of the Association for Asian Studies, New Orleans, April 1991.

Feng Hefa, comp. 1935. *Zhongguo nongcun jingji ziliao xubian* (Materials on the Chinese rural economy. Supplement). Shanghai: Liming shuju.

———. 1933. *Zhongguo nongcun jingji ziliao* (Materials on the Chinese rural economy). Shanghai: Liming shuju.

Feuerwerker, Albert. 1990. "An Old Question Revisited: Was the Glass Half-Full or Half-Empty for China's Agriculture Before 1949?" *Peasant Studies*, 17.3: 207–16.

———. 1969. *The Chinese Economy, ca. 1870–1911*. Ann Arbor: Univ. of Michigan Center for Chinese Studies.

———. 1958. *China's Early Industrialization: Sheng Hsuan-huai (1844–1916) and Mandarin Enterprise*. New York: Atheneum.

Finnane, Antonia. 1993. "The Origins of Prejudice: The Malintegration of Subei in Late Imperial China," *Comparative Studies in Society and History*, 35.2: 211–38.

Fong, H. D. 1936. "The Growth and Decline of Rural Industrial Enterprise in North China: A Case Study of the Cotton Handloom Weaving Industry in Baodi," *Nankai Social and Economic Quarterly*, 8.4: 691–772.

———. 1935. "Rural Weaving and Merchant Employers in a North China District," *Nankai Social and Economic Quarterly*, 2 parts, 8.1: 73–120; 8.2: 274–308.

Fortune, Robert. 1847. *Three Years' Wandering in the Northern Provinces of China.* London: Murray.

Fox-Genovese, Elizabeth, and Eugene Genovese. 1983. *Fruits of Merchant Capital: Slavery and Bourgeois Property in the Rise and Expansion of Capitalism.* New York: Oxford Univ. Press.

Frank, Andre Gunter. 1967. *Capitalism and Underdevelopment in Latin America.* New York: Monthly Review Press.

Fu Yiling. 1981–82. "A New Assessment of the Rural Social Relationship in Late Ming and Early Qing China," *Chinese Studies in History*, 15.1–2: 62–92.

———. 1980. "Capitalism in Chinese Agriculture," *Modern China*, 6.3: 311–16.

———. 1975. "Mingmo nanfang de 'dianbian' 'nubian'" (Tenant and bondservant risings in South China in the late Ming), *Lishi yanjiu*, 5: 61–67.

———. 1963. *Mingdai Jiangnan shimin jingji shitan* (An inquiry into the urban economies of the southern Yangzi delta during the Ming). Shanghai: Renmin chubanshe.

———. 1961. *Ming-Qing nongcun shehui jingji* (Rural society and economy during the Ming and Qing). Beijing: Shenghuo shudian.

———. 1956. *Ming-Qing shidai shangren ji shangye ziben* (Merchants and merchant capital in the Ming-Qing period). Shanghai: Renmin chubanshe.

Fujii Hiroshi. 1984. "Shoki ichiden ryōshusei no shinkenkyū" (New research on the early dual ownership system), *Tōhōgakuhō*, 69: 89–104.

———. 1979–80. "Ichiden ryōshusei no kihon kōzō" (The basic structure of the dual ownership system), *Kindai Chūgoku*, 4 parts, 5 (Apr. 1979): 83–150; 6 (Sept. 1979): 70–119; 7 (Feb. 1980): 34–87; 8 (Oct. 1980): 53–118.

———. 1975. "Sōmintō no ichiden ryōshusei" (The one field, two owners system of Chongming Island), *Tōhōgaku*, 49: 55–68.

Fujioka Kikuo. 1985. *Cho Ken to shingai kakumei* (Zhang Jian and the 1911 revolution). Sapporo: Hokkaidō daigaku toshokan kōkai.

Fuma Susumu. 1993. "Late Ming Urban Reform and the Popular Uprising in Hangzhou," in Lynda Cooke Johnson, ed., *Cities of Jiangnan in Late Imperial China*, pp. 47–80. Tr. Michael Lewis. Albany: State Univ. of New York Press.

———. 1976. "Mindai Byakurenkyō no ichi kōsatsu—keizai tōsō to no kanren to atarashii kyōdōtai" (A study of the White Lotus in the Ming—the new community and its relationship to economic struggle), *Tōyōshi kenkyū*, 35.1: 1–26.

Gailey, Christine W. 1987a. *Kinship to Kingship: Gender Hierarchy and State Formation in the Tongan Islands.* Austin: Univ. of Texas Press.

———. 1987b. "Culture Wars: Resistance to State Formation," in Thomas C. Patterson and Christine W. Gailey, eds., *Power Relations and State Formation*, pp. 35–56. Salem, Wis.: Sheffield Publishing Co.

Gates, Hill. 1996. *China's Motor: A Thousand Years of Petty Capitalism.* Ithaca, N.Y.: Cornell Univ. Press.

Geisert, Bradley K. 1979. "Power and Society: The Kuomintang and Local Elites in Kiangsu Province, China, 1924–1937." Ph.D. diss., Univ. of Virginia.

Gellner, Ernest. 1983. *Nations and Nationalism.* Ithaca, N.Y.: Cornell Univ. Press.

Genovese, Eugene D. 1979. *From Rebellion to Revolution: Afro-American Slave Revolts in the Making of the Modern World*. Baton Rouge: Louisiana State Univ.

Gledhill, John. 1994. *Power and Its Disguises: Anthropological Perspectives on Politics*. London: Pluto Press.

Goodman, David, and Michael Redclift. 1982. *From Peasant to Proletarian: Capitalist Development and Agrarian Transitions*. New York: St. Martin's Press.

Gould, Jeffrey. 1990. *To Lead as Equals: Rural Protest and Political Consciousness in Chinandega, Nicaragua, 1912–1979*. Chapel Hill: Univ. of North Carolina Press.

Gramsci, Antonio. 1971. *Selections from the Prison Notebooks*. New York: International Publishers.

Grove, Linda. 1975. "Rural Society in Revolution: The Gaoyang District, 1910–1947." Ph.D. diss., Univ. of California, Berkeley.

Grove, Linda, and Clifton Daniels, eds. 1984. *State and Society in China: Japanese Perspectives on Ming-Qing Social and Economic History*. Tokyo: Univ. of Tokyo Press.

Grove, Linda, and Joseph Esherick. 1980. "From Feudalism to Capitalism: Japanese Scholarship on the Transformation of Chinese Rural Society," *Modern China*, 6.4: 397–438.

Gu Li. 1981. "Guanyu 'Rugao shatian qingkuang de diaocha' de yixie buchong" (Some supplementary comments to "An investigation of conditions in Shatian, Rugao"), in RG, vol. 4, pp. 47–52.

Guan Jincheng. 1991. "Xinhai Tongzhou guangfu shimo" (The 1911 revolution in Tongzhou), in *Nantong Jingu*, no. 5. Comp. Nantong jingu bianxiezu. n.p.

——. 1981. "Tongzhou duli hou haimen de raoluan" (The social disturbance in Haimen after Tongzhou prefecture's independence), in NT [9], listed below, vol. 1, 167–70.

——. 1956. *Nantong Junshan nongmin giyi shili* (Historical materials on the Junshan peasant rising, Nantong). Nanjing: Jiangsu renmin chubanshe.

Guha, Ranajit. 1992. "Discipline and Mobilize," in Partha Chatterjee and Gyanendra Pandey, eds., *Subaltern Studies VII*, pp. 69–120. Delhi: Oxford Univ. Press.

——. 1983. *Elementary Aspects of Peasant Insurgency in Colonial India*. New Delhi: Oxford Univ. Press.

——. 1982. "On Some Aspects of the Historiography of Colonial India," in Ranajit Guha, ed., *Subaltern Studies I*, pp. 1–8. Delhi: Oxford Univ. Press.

Guo Zhenyi. 1938. *Zhongguo funu wenti* (The problem of Chinese women). Shanghai: Shanwu yinshuguan.

Hamashima Atsutoshi. 1982. *Mindai Kōnan nōson shakai no kenkyū* (Studies on rural society in the southern Yangzi delta during the Ming). Tokyo: Tokyo daigaku shuppankai.

——. 1980. "The Organization of Water Control in the Kiangnan Delta in the Ming Period," *Acta Asiatica Bulletin of the Institute of Eastern Culture*, 38: 69–92.

——. 1974. "Minmatsu Shinsho Kōnan deruta no suiri kankō no saihen ni tsuite" (The reorganization of water control practices in Jiangnan in the late Ming–early Qing), *Shakai keizai shigaku*, 40.2: 23–42.

Harootunian, Harry. 1982. "Ideology as Conflict," in Tetsuo Najita and J. Victor Koschmann, eds., *Conflict in Modern Japanese History: The Neglected Tradition*, pp. 25–61. Princeton, N.J.: Princeton Univ. Press.

Harriss, Michael. 1982. *Capitalism and Peasant Farming: Agrarian Structure and Ideology in Northern Tamil Nadu.* London: Oxford Univ. Press.

Hart, Gillian. 1986. *Power, Labor, and Livelihood: Processes of Change in Rural Java.* Berkeley: Univ. of California Press.

Hartford, Kathleen, and Steven M. Goldstein, eds. 1989. *Single Sparks: China's Rural Revolutions.* Armonk, N.Y.: M. E. Sharpe.

Hartmann, Heidi I. 1981. "The Family as the Locus of Gender, Class, and Political Struggle: The Example of Housework," *Signs: Journal of Women in Culture and Society,* 6.3: 366–94.

He Binghua. 1981. "Lunxian yu Rikou qian hou de Rugao" (On Rugao before and after the occupation by Japanese bandits), in RG, vol. 4, pp. 43–47.

He Menglei. 1977. "Suzhou Wuxi Changshu sanxian dianzuzhidu diaocha" (An investigation of the land tenure system in the three counties of Suzhou, Wuxi, and Changshu), in Xiao Zheng, ed., *Mingguo ershi niandai Zhongguo dalu tudi wenti ziliao,* vol. 63. Taibei: Chengwen chuban youxian gongsi.

Hechter, Michael. 1977. *Internal Colonialism: The Celtic Fringe in British National Development, 1536–1966.* Berkeley: Univ. of California Press.

Higgins, Roland L. 1980. "Pirates in Gowns and Caps: Gentry Law-Breaking in the Mid-Ming," *Ming Studies,* 10, Spring: 30–37.

Himmelfarb, Gertrude. 1983. *The Idea of Poverty: England in the Early Industrial Age.* Chicago: Knopf.

Ho, Ping-ti. 1964. *The Ladder of Success in Imperial China.* New York: Science Editions.

Honig, Emily. 1992. *Creating Chinese Ethnicity: Subei People in Shanghai, 1850–1980.* New Haven, Conn.: Yale Univ. Press.

———. 1989. "The Politics of Prejudice: Subei People in Republican-Era Shanghai," *Modern China,* 15.3: 243–74.

Hosono Koji. 1967. "Minmatsu Shinsho Kōnan ni okeru jinshi doboku kankei" (Relations between landowners and their bondservants in the late Ming–early Qing), *Tōyō gakuhō,* 50.3: 1–36.

Hsiao, Kung-chuan. 1960. *Rural China: Imperial Control in the Nineteenth Century.* Seattle: Univ. of Washington Press.

Hu Huanyong. 1947. "A New Cotton Belt in China," *Economic Geography,* 23.1: 60–66.

Hu Xianru. 1981. "Rugao xian shatian qingkuang de diaocha" (An investigation of the situation of "sand-lands" in Rugao county), in RG, vol. 3, pp. 79–95.

Huadong junzheng weiyuanhui tudi gaige weiyuanhui, ed. 1952. *Huadong nongcun jingji ziliao: Jiangsusheng nongcun diaocha* (Source materials on the rural economy of eastern China: survey of rural villages in Jiangsu province). n.p.

Huai Pu. 1933. "Zhejiang Chongde xian nongcun guanchaji" (A record of an investigation of villages in Chongde county, Zhejiang," in Feng Hefa 1933, listed above, pp. 72–75.

Huang, Philip C. C. 1993. " 'Public Sphere'/'Civil Society' in China? The Third Realm Between State and Society," *Modern China,* 19.2: 216–40.

———. 1991. "The Paradigmatic Crisis in Chinese Studies: Paradoxes in Social and Economic History," *Modern China,* 17.3: 299–341.

————. 1990. *The Peasant Family and Rural Development in the Yangzi Delta, 1350-1988.* Stanford, Calif.: Stanford Univ. Press.

————. 1985. *The Peasant Economy and Social Change in North China.* Stanford, Calif.: Stanford Univ. Press.

Huang Xiaoxian. 1927. "Haimen nongmin zhuangkuang diaocha" (An investigation of the condition of peasants in Haimen), in Feng Hefa 1933, listed above, pp. 473-81.

"Huashang shachang lianhehui nianhui baogaoshu" (Report of the annual meeting of the Chinese Spinning Mill Owners' Association). 1934. *Zhonghang yuekan,* 9.1:189.

Ichiko Chuzo. 1968. "The Role of the Gentry: An Hypothesis," in Mary C. Wright, ed., *China in Revolution: The First Phase, 1900-1913,* pp. 297-317. New Haven, Conn.: Yale Univ. Press.

Institute of Pacific Relations, comp. 1939. *Agrarian China: Selected Source Materials from Chinese Authors.* Chicago: Univ. of Chicago Press.

Isaacman, Allen F. 1993. "Peasants and Rural Social Protest in Africa," in Cooper, Isaacman et al., listed above, pp. 205-317.

Isaacman, Allen F., Michael Stephen, Yussuf Adam, Maria João Homen, Eugenio Macamo, and Augustinho Pililao. 1980. "Cotton as the Mother of Poverty: Peasant Resistance to Forced Cotton Production in Mozambique, 1938-1961," *International Journal of African Historical Studies,* 13: 581-615.

Jessop, B. 1982. *The Capitalist State.* Oxford: Martin Robertson.

Jewsiewicki, B. 1980. "Political Consciousness Among African Peasants in the Belgian Congo," *Review of African Political Economy,* 19: 23-32.

Ji Bin, Wang Shiming, and Zheng Li. 1985. "Ershenzhen shihua" (A discussion of the history of Ershen town), in NT [6], vol. 7, pp. 1-4.

Jiangsu (JS) entries

[1] *Jiangsu nongmin yundong dangan shiliao xuanbian* (Collected archival materials on the Jiangsu peasant movement). 1983. Comp. Jiangsu sheng danganguan. Nanjing.

[2] *Jiangsu nongye dili* (Agricultural geography of Jiangsu province). 1979. Jiangsu kexu jishu chubanshe. n.p.

[3] *Jiangsu sheng fanzhiye zhuangkuang* (Situation of the textile industry in Jiangsu province). 1919. Ed. Jiangsu shiyeting. Wuxi.

[4] *Jiangsu sheng gexian gaikuang yilan* (A look at the general situation in each of the counties in Jiangsu province). 1931. 2 vols. n.p.

[5] *Jiangsu sheng nongcun diaocha* (Investigation of villages in Jiangsu province). 1933. Comp. Nongcun fuxing weiyuanhui. Shanghai.

[6] "Jiangsu sheng nongming yundong dashi nianbiao" (Yearly outline of major events in the Jiangsu peasant movement). 1983. In JS [1], pp. 429-47.

[7] "Jiangsu shengwei wei fadong liuji zhanzheng" (Jiangsu Provincial Party Committee: on mobilizing the guerrilla war). 1983. In JS [1], pp. 365-76.

[8] *Jiangsu shiye xingzheng baogaoshu* (Bureau of Industry report on industry in Jiangsu). 1913. Comp. Jiangsu sheng xingzheng gongshu shiyesi. Shanghai.

[9] *Jiangsu wenshi ziliao xuanji* (Collected source materials on the culture and history of Jiangsu province). 1981-87. 21 vols. Comp. Zhongguo renmin zhengzhi xieshang huiyi, Jiangsu sheng weiyuanhui wenshi ziliao yanjiu weiyuanhui. Nanjing.

Jin Zhihuai. 1984. "Jinsha shihua" (On the history of Jinsha), in NT [6], vol. 2, pp. 1–7.

Jing Su and Luo Lun. 1959. *Qingdai Shandong jingying dizhu de shehui xingzhi* (The social nature of Shandong managerial landlords during the Qing). Shandong: Renmin chubanshe.

Johnson, David, Andrew J. Nathan, and Evelyn S. Rawski, eds. 1985. *Popular Culture in Late Imperial China*. Berkeley: Univ. of California Press.

Johnson, Linda Cooke. 1993. "Shanghai: An Emerging Jiangnan Port, 1683–1840," in Johnson, ed., *Cities of Jiangnan in Late Imperial China*, pp. 151–82. Albany: State Univ. of New York Press.

Johnson, Michael, William Parish, and E. Lin. 1987. "Chinese Women, Rural Society, and External Markets," *Economic Development and Cultural Change*, 35.2: 257–77.

Jones, Susan Mann. 1978–79. "The Organization of Trade at the County Level: Brokerage and Tax Farming in the Republican Period," in Jones, ed., *Select Papers from the Center for Far Eastern Studies*, no. 3, pp. 70–99. Chicago: Univ. of Chicago Press.

———. 1974. "The Ningbo Bang and Financial Power at Shanghai," in Mark Elvin and G. William Skinner, eds., *The Chinese City Between Two Worlds*. Stanford, Calif.: Stanford Univ. Press.

Joseph, Gilbert. 1990. "On the Trail of Latin American Bandits: A Reexamination of Peasant Resistance," *Latin American Research Review*, 25.3: 7–53.

Joseph, Richard A. 1980. "Theories of the African Bourgeoisie: An Exploration." Paper presented at the Conference on the African Bourgeoisie, Dakar [as cited in Cooper, 1993, listed above].

JS citations, *see* Jiangsu

Kahn, Joel S. 1993. *Constituting the Minangkabau: Peasants, Culture and Modernity in Colonial Indonesia*. Providence, R.I.: Berg.

Kamachi Noriko. 1990. "Feudalism or Absolute Monarchism? Japanese Discourse on the Nature of the State and Society in Late Imperial China," *Modern China*, 16.3: 330–70.

Kang Zhongping. 1948–49. "Lun Zhongguo guanliao zibenzhuyi" (On bureaucratic capitalism), *Qunzhong*, 2 parts, 38: 14–16; 39: 14–15.

Kay, Geoffrey. 1975. *Development and Underdevelopment*. London: Macmillan.

Kearney, Michael. 1996. *Reconceptualizing the Peasantry: Anthropology in Global Perspective*. Boulder, Col.: Westview Press.

Keesing, Roger M. 1992. *Custom and Confrontation: The Kwaio Struggle for Cultural Autonomy*. Chicago: Univ. of Chicago Press.

Kincaid, Douglas. 1987. "Peasants into Rebels: Community and Class in Rural El Salvador," *Comparative Studies in Society and History*, 29.3: 466–94.

Kipnis, Andrew B. 1995. "Within and Against Peasantness: Backwardness and Filiality in Rural China," *Comparative Studies in Society and History*, 77.1: 110–35.

Kitching, Gavin. 1980. *Class and Economic Change in Kenya: The Making of an African Petite-Bourgeoisie*. New Haven, Conn.: Yale Univ. Press.

Kobayashi Kazumi. 1984. "The Other Side of Rent and Tax Resistance Struggles: Ideology and the Road to Rebellion," in Grove and Daniels, listed above, pp. 215–44.

Kojima Yoshio. 1978. "Kōsō tōsō: Kōnan deruta chitai o chūshin ni shite" (Rent resistance: with specific reference to the southern Yangzi delta), in Nozawa Yutaka and Tanaka Masatoshi, eds., *Kōza Chūgoku kin-gendaishi*, vol. 2, pp. 127–45. Tokyo: Tokyo Univ. Press.

———. 1973. "Dennō no zeiryō futan ni kan suru ichi kōsatsu" (An investigation of tenants' tax obligations), *Shicho*, 112: 64–75.

Kotani Hiroshi. 1977. "Han shokuminchi han hoken shakai kosei no gainen kitei" (A conceptual definition of a semicolonial semifeudal society), *Rekishigaku kenkyū*, 446: 68–76.

Kriedte, Peter, Hans Medick, and Jurgen Schlumbohm. 1981. *Industrialization Before Industrialization: Rural Industry in the Genesis of Capitalism*. Cambridge, Eng.: Cambridge Univ. Press.

Kuhn, Philip A. 1978–79. "Local Taxation and Finance in Republican China," in Susan Mann Jones and Philip Kuhn, eds., *Select Papers from the Center for Far Eastern Studies* no. 3, pp. 100–136. Chicago: Univ. of Chicago Press.

———. 1975. "Local Self-Government Under the Republic," in Frederic Wakeman Jr. and Carolyn Grant, eds., *Conflict and Control in Late Imperial China*, pp. 257–98. Berkeley: Univ. of California Press.

Kuhn, Philip, and Susan Mann Jones. 1979. "Introduction," in Jones, ed., *Select Papers from the Center for Far Eastern Studies*, no. 3, pp. v–xix. Chicago: Univ. of Chicago Press.

Kulinkoff, Alan. 1989. "The Transition to Capitalism in Rural America," *William and Mary Quarterly*, Jan.: 120–44.

Kusano Yasushi. 1977. "Kyū-Chūgoku no yazu kankō" (The practice of yazu in old China), *Shakaikeizai shigaku*, 43.4: 1–22.

———. 1975. "Kyū-Chūgoku no zenmen kankō" (The practice of topsoil rights in old China), *Tōyōshi kenkyū*, 34.2: 50–76.

———. 1970. "Sō-Gen jidai no suiriden kaihatsu to ichiden ryoshu kankō no hoga" (The development of rice paddies in the Song-Yuan period and the sprouts of the dual-ownership system), *Tōyō gakuho*, 2 parts 53.1: 42–77; 53.2: 46–79.

Leys, Colin. 1978. "Capital Accumulation, Class Formation, and Dependency—The Significance of the Kenyan Case," in Ralph Miliband and John Seville, eds., *The Socialist Register, 1978*, pp. 241–66. London: Monthly Review Press.

Li Lianjiang and Kevin J. O'Brien. 1996. "Villagers and Popular Resistance in Contemporary China," *Modern China*, 22.1: 28–61.

Li Shiyue. 1979. "1895–1898 nian Zhongguo minzu gongye de fazhan" (The development of Chinese national industry in 1895–98), in Huang Yiping, ed., *Zhongguo jindai jingjishi lunwen xuanji*, vol. 4, pp. 1295–1305. Shanghai: Shifan daxue lishixi.

Li Wenzhi. 1981. "China's Landlord Economy and the Sprouts of Capitalism," *Social Sciences in China*, March: 68–89.

———, ed. 1957. *Zhongguo jindai nongyeshi ziliao* (Source materials on the agricultural history of modern China), vol. 1: *1840–1911*. Beijing: Sanlian shudian.

Li Wenzhi, Wei Jinyu, and Jing Junqian. 1983. *Ming-Qing shidai de nongye zibenzhuyi mengya wenti* (The problem of capitalist sprouts in agriculture during the Ming-Qing period). Beijing: Zhongguo shehui kexue chubanshe.

Lin Jubai. 1984. *Jindai Nantong tubu shi* (History of the modern handwoven cloth industry in Nantong). Da Feng county.

Lin Zuobo. 1931. *Guanwai manyou ji* (Record of a trip to the northeast). Nantong.

Lippit, Victor. 1978. "The Development of Underdevelopment in China," *Modern China*, 4.3: 251–328.

Liu Dajun. 1940. *Shanghai gongyehua yanjiu* (A study of the industrialization of Shanghai). Changsha: Shangwu yinshuguan.

Liu Daosong. 1980. "Nantong zudian guanxi" (Rent relations in Nantong). Report and personal interview at round-table meeting, Nantong Library, Nantong, Dec. 19, 1980. [Liu is a library staff member.]

Liu Housheng. 1965. *Zhang Jian Zhuanji* (Biography of Zhang Jian). Hong Kong: Longmen shudian.

Liu Jiawang. 1920. "Nantong mianye qingxing" (The situation of the Nantong cotton industry), *Nongshang gongbao*, 6.12: 1–4.

Liu, Kwang-ching. 1981. "World View and Peasant Rebellion: Reflections on Post-Mao Historiography," *Journal of Asian Studies*, 40.2: 295–326.

————. 1978. "Limits of Regional Power in the Late Qing Period" and "The Qing Restoration," in John K. Fairbank, ed., *The Cambridge History of China*, vol. 10: *Late Qing, 1800–1911, part one*, pp. 609–90. Cambridge, Eng.: Cambridge Univ. Press.

Liu Ruilong. 1986. *Huiyi hong shisi jun* (Remembering the Fourteenth Red Army). n.p.: Jiangsu renmin chubanshe.

Liu Yan. 1957. "Minguo chengshi yongji fazhan xia de chuqi shimin yundong" (The early period of popular urban movements during the development of the urban economy at the end of the Ming), in *Zhongguo ziben zhuyi mengya wenti taolunji*, vol. 1. Beijing: Sanlian shudian.

Liu Yongcheng. 1980. "Lun Qingdai qianqi nongye guyong laodong de xingzhi" (On the nature of rural hired labor during the early Qing), in Zhongguo renmin daxue Qing shi yanjiusuo ed., *Qingshi yanjiuji*, pp. 91–112. Beijing: Zhongguo renmin daxue chubanshe.

London, Christopher E. 1997. "Class Relations and Capitalist Development: Subsumption in the Colombian Coffee Industry, 1928–92," *Journal of Peasant Studies*, 24.4: 269–95.

Lu, Hanchao. 1992. "Arrested Development: Cotton and Cotton Markets in Shanghai, 1350–1843," *Modern China*, 18.4: 468–99.

Lu Mei. 1985. "Rencai huicui tan Jinxi" (Jinxi: a galaxy of talent), in NT [6], listed below, vol. 5, pp. 5–6.

————. 1984. "Fangong hua jiu" (On Fan's Dike in former times), in NT [6], listed below, vol. 2, pp. 9–13.

Luo Qing. 1935. "Jiangsu beibu nongcun zhong de laodong funu" (Laboring women in the villages of northern Jiangsu), *Dongfang zizhi*, 32.14: 107–9.

MacKinnon, Stephen R. 1980. *Power and Politics in Late Imperial China: Yuan Shi-kai in Beijing and Tianjin, 1901–1908*. Berkeley: Univ. of California Press.

Mackintosh, Maureen. 1990. "Abstract Markets and Real Needs," in Bernstein et al., eds., *The Food Question: Profits Versus People?*, pp. 43–53. New York: Monthly Review Press.

Mallon, Florencia E. 1995. *Peasant and Nation: The Making of Postcolonial Mexico and Peru*. Berkeley: Univ. of California Press.

———. 1993. "Dialogues Among the Fragments: Retrospect and Prospect," in Cooper, Isaacman et al., listed above, pp. 371–401.

———. 1987a. "Patriarchy in the Transition to Capitalism: Central Peru, 1830–1950," *Feminist Studies*, 13.2: 379–407.

———. 1987b. "Nationalist and Anti-State Coalitions in the War of the Pacific: Junin and Cajamarca," in Steve J. Stern, ed., *Resistance, Rebellion, and Consciousness in the Andean Peasant World*, pp. 232–79. Madison: Univ. of Wisconsin Press.

Mann, Susan Archor. 1990. *Agrarian Capitalism in Theory and Practice*. Chapel Hill: Univ. of North Carolina Press.

Mann, Susan. 1987. *Local Merchants and the Chinese Bureaucracy, 1750–1950*. Stanford, Calif.: Stanford University Press.

Mao Daolai. 1980. "Rugao shihua" (On the history of Rugao), in RG, vol. 2, pp. 5–22.

Mao Jiaqi. 1979. "Jidu jiao Rujia sixing he Hong Xiuquan" (Christianity, Confucianism, and Hong Xiuquan), *Nanjing Daxue xuebao*, 2: 43–53.

Mao Zedong. 1990. *Report From Xunwu*. Tr. Roger R. Thompson. Stanford, Calif.: Stanford Univ. Press.

———. 1971. "Be Concerned with the Well-Being of the Masses," in *Selected Readings*, pp. 51–57. Beijing: Foreign Languages Press.

———. 1939. "Zhongguo geming yu Zhongguo gongchandang" (The Chinese Revolution and the Chinese Communist Party), in *Mao Zedongji*, 3: 97–136. Tokyo: Hokubosha, 1972.

Marks, Robert. 1985. "The State of the China Field, or the China Field and the State," *Modern China* 11.4: 461–509.

———. 1984. *Rural Revolution in South China*. Madison: Univ. of Wisconsin Press.

Marshall, Gordon. 1983. "Some Remarks on the Study of Working-Class Consciousness," *Politics and Society* 12.

Marx, Karl. 1977. *Capital, Volume One*. Tr. Ben Fowkes. New York: Vintage Books.

———. 1967. *Capital: A Critical Analysis of Capitalist Production*. 3 vols. New York: International Publishers.

McDermott, Joseph P. 1981. "Bondservants in the Taihu Basin During the Late Ming: A Case of Mistaken Identity," *Journal of Asian Studies*, 40.4: 675–701.

McElderry, Andrea. 1976. *Shanghai Old-Style Banks (Qianzhuang), 1800–1935*. Ann Arbor: Univ. of Michigan Papers in Chinese Studies, no. 25.

McGaffey, Janet. 1987. *Entrepreneurs and Parasites*. Cambridge, Eng.: Cambridge Univ. Press.

Medick, Hans. 1976. "The Proto-Industrial Family Economy: The Structural Function of Household and Family During the Transition from Peasant Society to Industrial Capitalism," *Social History*, 3: 219–315.

Meillassoux, Claude. 1981. *Maidens, Meal, and Money: Capitalism and the Domestic Community*. Cambridge, Eng.: Cambridge Univ. Press.

Memmi, Albert. 1991. *The Colonizer and the Colonized*. Boston: Beacon Press.

Mendels, Franklin. 1972. "Proto-industrialization: The First Phase of the Industrialization Process," *Journal of Economic History*, 32: 241–61.

Meskill, John. 1994. *Gentlemanly Interests and Wealth on the Yangzi Delta*. Ann Arbor, Mich.: Association for Asian Studies Monograph and Occasional Paper Series, no. 49.

Miao Qingping. 1935. "Nantong xian tubu shiye zhi gaijin" (Improvement of the cotton cloth industry in Nantong county), *Nonghang yuekan*, 2. 22: 15–17.

Midgal, Joel S. 1974. *Peasants, Politics, and Revolution: Pressures Toward Political and Social Change in the Third World*. Princeton, N.J.: Princeton Univ. Press.

Mies, Maria. 1986. *Indian Women in Subsistence and Agricultural Labour*. Geneva: International Labour Office.

Minami Manshū tetsudō kabushiki kaisha Shanhai jimusho. Chōsashitsu [MMT]. 1941. *Kōso-shō Nantsū ken nōson jittai chōsa hokokusho* (Report on an investigation of actual conditions in the countryside, Nantong county, Jiangsu province). n.p.

"Minguo banian mianchan diaocha baogao" (Report on an investigation of cotton production in 1919). 1920. *Nongshang gongbao*, 6.9: 24–25.

Mintz, Sidney. 1982. "Afterword: Peasantries and the Rural Sector—Notes on a Discovery," in Robert P. Weller and Scott E. Guggenheim, eds., *Power and Protest in the Countryside: Rural Unrest in Asia, Europe, and Latin America*. Durham, N.C.: Duke Univ. Press.

———. 1974. *Caribbean Transformations*. Chicago: Aldine.

Miyashita Tadao. 1942. *Shina ginkō seido ron* (The Chinese banking system). Tokyo: Ganshodo shoten.

Miyazaki Ichisada. 1954. "Mindai so-Shō chihō no shidaifu to minshū" (The local gentry and populace of Su-Song during the Ming), *Shirin*, 37: 1–33.

Mizoguchi Yūzō. 1978. "Iwayuru Tōrinha jinshi no shisō—zenkindaiki ni okeru Chūgoku shisō no tenkai" (The thought of the Donglin school—the development of Chinese thought in the premodern period), part 1, *Tōyō Bunka kenkyūjo kiyō*, 75: 111–41.

Moore, Barrington. 1966. *Social Origins of Dictatorship and Democracy*. Boston: Beacon Press.

Mori Masao. 1980. "The Gentry in the Ming: An Outline of the Relations Between the Shih-ta-fu and Local Society," *Acta Asiatica*, 38: 31–53.

———. 1977. "1645 ne Taisōshū Sakeichin ni okeru Uryūkai no hanran ni tsuite" (The rising of the Black Dragon Society in Shaqizhen, Taicangzhou, in 1645), in *Nakayama Hachirō kyōju shōju kinen minshinshi ronsō*, pp. 195–232. Tokyo: Ryogen shoten.

———. 1961. "Minsho Kōnan no kanden ni tsuite" (State land in the southern Yangzi delta in the early Ming), part 2, *Tōyōshi kenkyū* 19.4: 1–18.

Mu Xuan. 1980. "Nantong diqu tudi zutian guanxi qingkuang, ershi niandai dao sanshi niandai" (The general situation of land tenure relations in the Nantong area, 1920–30). Unpublished manuscript in Nantong Museum.

Muller, Viana. 1977. "The Formation of the State and the Oppression of Women: Some Theoretical Considerations and a Case Study in England and Wales," *Review of Radical Political Economics*, 9.Fall: 7–21.

Muramatsu Yuji. 1949. *Chūgoku keizai no shakai taisei* (The social structure of the Chinese economy). Tokyo: Tōyō keizai shimpōsha.

Nakai Hedeki. 1980. "Shin matsu no membōseki kigyō no keiei to shijō jōken" (Market conditions and management of the cotton-spinning industry at the end of the Qing), *Shakai keizai gaku*, 45.5: 55–83.

Nanjing daxue lishixi, Dasheng yichang changshi bianxie zuzhi [NJ]. 1959a. "Dasheng fangzhi gongsi: yichang jianshi, 1898–1958" (The Dasheng Textile Company: a brief history of the No. 1 mill, 1898–1958). Unpublished manuscript.

———. 1959b. "Dasheng ziben jituanshi" (A history of the Dasheng Capital Group). Unpublished manuscript.

Nantong [NT] entries.

[1] "Nantong Dasheng Shachang xingshuai guocheng (The rise and decline of the Dasheng Spinning Factory, Nantong). n.d. Unpublished manuscript.

[2] *Nantong difang zizhi shijiunian zhi chengji* (The accomplishments of 19 years of self-government in Nantong). n.d., n.p.

[3] Nantong fangzhi bowuguan. 1987. "Nantong fangzhi bowuguan fuguan shuomingpai neirong" (Contents of explanatory plates in the auxiliary exhibition of the Nantong Textile Museum). Unpublished document.

[4] "Nantong fangzhishi tulu" bianjizu. 1987. *Nantong fangzhishi tulu* (Pictorial record of the history of textiles in Nantong). Nanjing: Nanjing daxue chubanshe.

[5] "Nantong quanxian qiushou douzheng de zong jihua" (Plan for the autumn harvest struggle in Nantong county). 1983. In JS [1], listed above, pp. 201–7.

[6] *Nantong shihua* (Discussions of Nantong's history). 1983–85. 7 vols. Ed. Nantong xian renmin zhengfu. n.p.

[7] *Nantong: shiye jiaoyu sishan fengjing* (Nantong: industry, education, philanthropic enterprises, and scenery). 1920. n.p.

[8] "Nantong tubuye diaocha" (Investigation of the handwoven cloth industry in Nantong). 1930. *Gongshang banyuekan*, 2. 22: 1–14.

[9] *Nantong wenshi ziliao xuanji* (Collected source materials on the culture and history of Nantong). 1981–87. 7 vols. Comp. Zhongguo renmin zhengzhi xieshang huiyi, Jiangsu sheng Nantong shi weiyuanhui wenshi ziliao yanjiu weiyuanhui. n.p.

[10] *Nantong xian wenshi ziliao* (Source materials on the culture and history of Nantong county). 1987–92. 8 vols. Comp. Zhongguo renmin zhengzhi xieshang huiyi, Jiangsu sheng Nantong xian weiyuanhui wenshi ziliao yanjiu weiyuanhui. n.p.

Naquin, Susan. 1985. "The Transmission of White Lotus Sectarianism in Late Imperial China," in David Johnson et al., eds., *Popular Culture in Late Imperial China*. Berkeley: Univ. of Calif. Press, pp. 255–91.

———. 1982. "Connections Between Rebellions: Sect Family Networks in Qing China," *Modern China*, 8.3: 337–60.

———. 1976. *Millenarian Rebellion in China: The Eight Trigrams Uprising of 1813*. New Haven, Conn.: Yale Univ. Press.

Naquin, Susan, and Yu Chun-fang. 1992. *Pilgrims and Sacred Sites in China*. Berkeley: Univ. of California Press.

Nie Baozhang. 1979. *Zhongguo waiban zichan jieji de fasheng* (The rise of the comprador bourgeoisie in China). Beijing: Zhongguo shehui kexueyuan chubanshe.

Niida Noboru. 1962a. *Chūgoku hōseishi kenkyū: dorei nōdo hō kazoku sonraku hō* (Studies in the history of the Chinese legal system: laws on slaves and serfs and laws on the family and village). Tokyo: Tokyo Daigaku Shuppankai. 1981 reprint.

———. 1962b. *Chūgoku hōseishi kenkyū: keihō* (Studies in the history of the Chinese legal system: criminal law). Tokyo: Tokyo Daigaku Shuppankai. 1981 reprint.

———. 1962c. *Chūgoku hōseishi kenkyū: tochihō torikihō* (Studies in the history of the Chinese legal system: land law and contract law). Tokyo: Tokyo Daigaku Shuppankai. 1981 reprint.

Nishijima Sadao. 1984. "The Formation of the Early Chinese Cotton Industry," in Grove and Daniels, listed above, pp. 17–78.

———. 1966. *Chūgoku keizai shi kenkyū* (Studies in the economic history of China). Tokyo: Tokyo daigaku shuppankei.

———. 1948–49. "Mindai ni okeru momen no fukyū ni tsuite" (The spread of cotton cultivation during the Ming), *Shigaku zasshi*, 2 parts, 47.4: 1–22; 58.5–6: 19–47.

———. 1947. "Shina shoki mengyō shijō no kōsatsu" (An examination of the early Chinese cotton market), *Tōyō gakuhō*, 31.2: 122–48.

Nishimura Kazuyo. 1979. "Mindai no doboku" (Bondservantry in the Ming period), *Tōyōshi kenkyū*, 38.1: 24–50.

NT citations, *see* Nantong

Odell, Ralph M. 1916. *Cotton Goods in China.* Washington, D.C.: Government Printing Office.

Okuzaki Hiroshi. 1978. *Chūgoku kyoshin jinushi no kenkyū* (Studies of gentry-landlordism in China). Tokyo: Kyuko Shoin.

Ooms, Herman. 1985. *Tokugawa Ideology: Early Constructs, 1570-1680.* Princeton, N.J.: Princeton Univ. Press.

Overmyer, Daniel. 1976. *Folk Buddhist Religion.* Cambridge, Mass.: Harvard Univ. Press.

Ownby, David, and Mary S. Heidhues, eds. 1993. *"Secret Societies" Reconsidered: Perspectives on the Social History of Modern South China and Southeast Asia.* Armonk, N.Y.: M. E. Sharpe.

Oyama Masaaki. 1984. "Large Landownership in the Jiangnan Delta Region During the Late Ming-Early Qing Period," in Grove and Daniels, listed above, pp. 101–64.

———. 1974. "Mindai no daitochi shoyū to doboku" (Large landownership and slaves in the Ming), *Tōyō Bunka kenkyūjo kiyō*, 62: 77–131.

———. 1969. "Mindai no ryōchō ni tsuite: Tokuni zenhanki no Kōnan deruta chitai o chushin ni shite" (Tax captains in the Ming: with special reference to the southern Yangzi delta during the first half of the Ming), *Tōyōshi kenkyū* 27.4: 24–68.

———. 1960. "Shinmatsu Chūgoku ni okeru gaikoku menseihin no ryunyū" (The influx of foreign cotton goods into China in the late Qing period), *Kindai Chūgoku kenkyū*, 4: 1–108.

———. 1957–58. "Minmatsu Shinsho no dai tochi shoyū: toku ni Kōnan deruta chitai o chushin ni shite" (Large landownership in the Jiangnan delta region during the late Ming–early Qing period), *Shigaku zasshi*, 2 parts, 66.12: 1–30; 67.1: 50–72.

Patterson, Thomas C., and Christine W. Gailey. 1987. *Power Relations and State Formation.* Salem, Wis.: Sheffield Publishing Co.

Pearse, Arno S. 1929. *The Cotton Industry of Japan and China.* Manchester, Eng.

Peck, James. 1969. "The Roots of Rhetoric: The Professional Ideology of America's China Watchers," *Bulletin of Concerned Asian Scholars*, 2.1: 59–69.

Peng Zeyi et al., eds. 1957. *Zhongguo jindai shougongyeshi ziliao, 1840-1949* (Source materials on the history of the handicraft industry in modern China, 1840–1949). 4 vols. Beijing: Sanlian shudian.

Perlin, Frank. 1983. "Proto-Industrialization and Pre-Colonial South Asia," *Past and Present*, 98: 30–95.

Perry, Elizabeth. 1993. *Shanghai on Strike: The Politics of Chinese Labor*. Stanford, Calif.: Stanford Univ. Press.

——. 1980. *Rebels and Revolutionaries in North China, 1845–1945*. Stanford, Calif.: Stanford Univ. Press.

Pinchbeck, Ivy. 1930. *Women Workers and the Industrial Revolution, 1750–1850*. New York: A. M. Kelley.

Pomeranz, Kenneth. 1993. *The Making of a Hinterland: State, Society, and Economy in Inland North China, 1853–1937*. Berkeley: Univ. of California Press.

"Population Census of Jiangsu [Kiangsu], 1929." 1933. *Nankai Weekly Statistical Service* 5.16: 72; 74–75.

Post, Charles. 1982. "The American Road to Capitalism," *New Left Review*, 133: 30–51.

Postan, M. M. 1973. *Essays on Medieval Agriculture and General Problems of the Medieval Economy*. Cambridge, Eng.: Cambridge Univ. Press.

Potter, Sulamith H., and Jack M. Potter. 1990. *China's Peasants: The Anthropology of a Revolution*. Cambridge, Eng.: Cambridge Univ. Press.

Prazniak, Roxann. 1986. "Weavers and Sorceresses of Chuansha: The Social Origins of Political Activism Among Rural Chinese Women," *Modern China*, 12.2: 202–29.

Pred, Allan, and Michael John Watts. 1992. *Reworking Modernity: Capitalisms and Symbolic Discontent*. New Brunswick, N.J.: Rutgers Univ. Press.

Przeworsky, Adam. 1977. "Proletariat into a Class: The Process of Class Formation from Karl Kautsky's *The Class Struggle* to Recent Controversies," *Politics and Society*, 7: 343–401.

Qian Min. 1986. "Minchu Pingchao nongmin kangjuan baoyun jishi" (The true story of the Pingchao peasants' anti-tax struggle in the early Republic), in NT [9], listed above, vol. 6, pp. 10–25.

[Qianlong] Jiangnan tongzhi (Qianlong complete gazetteer of Jiangnan). 1737. 1967 Taibei reprint.

[Qianlong] Zhili Tongzhou zhi (Qianlong gazetteer of Tongzhou independent department). 1755. 16 juan. 1968 Taibei reprint.

Qiao Qiming. 1926. *Jiangsu Kunshan Nantong Anhui Suxian nongdian zhidu zhi bizhao yiji gailiang nongdian wenti zhi jianyi* (A comparison of tenancy in Kunshan and Nantong, Jiangsu, and Suxian, Anhui, and proposals for tenancy reform). Nanjing.

Qingdai dizu boxue xingtai (Patterns of land rent exploitation during the Qing dynasty). 1982. 2 vols. Comp. Zhongguo diyi lishi danganguan, Zhongguo shehui kexueyuan lishi yanjiusuo. Beijing: Zhonghua shuju.

Qingdai nongmin zhanzhengshi ziliao xuanbian (Collected source materials on the history of peasant wars in the Qing period). 1984. Ed. Zhongguo renmin daxue lishixi, Zhongguo diyi lishi danganguan. Beijing: Zhongguo renmin daxue chubanshe.

Ranger, Terence. 1987. "Peasant Consciousness: Culture and Conflict in Zimbabwe," in Teodor Shanin, ed., *Peasants and Peasant Societies*, pp. 311–27. London: Basil Blackwell.

———. 1985. *Peasant Consciousness and Guerrilla War in Zimbabwe.* Berkeley: Univ. of California Press.

Rankin, Mary Backus. 1986. *Elite Activism and Political Transformation in China.* Stanford, Calif. Stanford Univ. Press.

Rau, Bill. 1991. *From Feast to Famine.* London: Zed Books.

Rawski, Thomas. 1989. *Economic Growth in Prewar China.* Berkeley: Univ. of California Press.

Rohrlich, Ruby. 1980. "State Formation in Sumer and the Subjugation of Women," *Feminist Studies,* 6.Spring: 76–102.

Roseberry, William. 1993. "Beyond the Agrarian Question in Latin America," in Cooper, Isaacman et al., listed above, pp. 318–68.

———. 1982. "Peasants, Proletarians, and Politics in Venezuela, 1875–1975," in Robert Weller and Scott Guggenheim, eds. *Power and Protest in the Countryside,* pp. 106–31. Durham, N.C.: Duke Univ. Press.

Rowe, William T. 1993. "Introduction: City and Region in the Lower Yangzi," in Linda C. Johnson, ed., *Cities of Jiangnan in Late Imperial China,* pp. 1–16. Albany: State Univ. of New York Press.

———. 1985. "Approaches to Chinese Social History," in Oliver Zunz, ed., *Reliving the Past: The Worlds of Social History,* pp. 236–96. Chapel Hill: Univ. of North Carolina Press.

———. 1984. *Hankow: Commerce and Society in a Chinese City, 1796–1889.* Stanford, Calif.: Stanford Univ. Press.

"Rugao nongmin douzheng zhi jingguo" (The results of the peasant struggle in Rugao). 1983. In JS [1], listed above, pp. 136–40.

Rugao wenshi ziliao [RG] (Collected source materials on the literature and history of Rugao). 1980–83. 6 vols. Comp. Rugao xian xubian xianzhi bangongshi, n.p.

Sabean, David Warren. 1984. *Power in the Blood: Popular Culture and Village Discourse in Early Modern Germany.* Cambridge, Eng.: Cambridge Univ. Press.

Sacks, Karen. 1989. "Toward a Unified Theory of Class, Race, and Gender," *American Ethnologist,* 16.3: 534–50.

Sakai Tadao. 1960. *Chūgoku zenshu no kenkyū* (Studies on Chinese morality books). Tokyo: Kōbundō.

Scott, James C. 1976. *The Moral Economy of the Peasant: Rebellion and Subsistence in Southeast Asia.* New Haven, Conn.: Yale Univ. Press.

Seki Keizo. 1956. *The Cotton Industry of Japan.* Tokyo.

Sha Yangao. 1981. "Dui wo fuqin Sha Yuanbing de jidian huiyi" (Several points of remembrance about my father, Sha Yuanbing), in RG, vol. 4, pp. 66–69.

Shanghai qianzhuang shiliao (Historical materials on Shanghai native banks). 1960. Ed. Zhongguo renmin yinhang, Shanghai shifenhang. Shanghai: Zhongguo renmin yinhang.

Shanghai shi mianbu shangye (The cotton cloth commercial industry in Shanghai city). 1979. Ed. Zhongguo shehui kexueyuan jingji yanjiusuo. Beijing: Zhongguo shuju.

Shanin, Teodor. 1983. *Late Marx and the Russian Road: Marx and the Peripheries of Capitalism.* New York: Monthly Review Press.

Shao Qin. 1994. "Making Political Culture—The Case of Nantong, 1894–1930," Ph.D. diss., Michigan State Univ.

Shenbao (The Shanghai daily). Shanghai.

Shen Liangpan. 1980. "Shizhuang dequ de geming douzheng jian-shi" (A short history of the revolutionary struggle in Shizhuang district), in RG, vol. 2, pp. 78–84.

Shen Qixi. 1920a. "Chongming xian shiye guancha baogaoshu" (Report on an inspection of industry in Chongming county), *Nongshang gongbao*, 67: 2–3.

———. 1920b. "Haimen xian shiye guancha baogaoshu" (Report on an inspection of industry in Haimen county), *Nongshang gongbao*, 67: 3–4.

Shen Shike. 1934. *Haimen Qidong xian zhi tianzu zhidu* (The land tenure systems in Haimen and Qidong counties). Vol. 60 of Xiao Zheng, ed., *Minguo ershi niandai Zhongguo dalu tudi wenti ziliao*. Taibei: Taibei chengwen chuban youxian gongsi, 1977.

Sheng, Angela Yu-yin. 1990. "Textile Use, Technology, and Change in Rural Textile Production in Song China (960–1279)," Ph.D. diss., Univ. of Pennsylvania.

Shenshi nongshu (Mr. Shen's agricultural treatise). n.d. [ca. mid-17th century]. In *Congshu jicheng*, no. 1468. Shanghai: Shangwu yinshuguan, 1936.

Shenton, R. W., and Louise Lennihan. 1981. "Capital and Class: Peasant Differentiation in Northern Nigeria," *Journal of Peasant Studies*, 9.1: 47–70.

Shibao (Eastern Times). 1930. Shanghai.

Shigeta Atsushi. 1984. "The Origins and Structure of Gentry Rule," in Grove and Daniels, listed above, pp. 335–386.

Shih, Shu-mei. 1996. "Gender, Race, and Semicolonialism: Liu Na'ou's Urban Shanghai Landscape," *Journal of Asian Studies*, 33.4: 934–956.

Shina shōbetsu zenshi (Comprehensive gazetteer of China), 1920. Vol. 15: Jiangsu province. Tokyo: Toā Dōbunkai.

Shiraishi Hirō. 1960. "Shinmatsu Kōnan no nōson shakai: ōso kankō to kōso keikō" (Rural society in late Qing Jiangnan: the practice of rent deposits and the trend toward rent resistance), in *Chūgoku kindaika no shakai kōzō*, pp. 1–19. Ed. Tokyo kyoiku daigaku Ajia shi kenkyukai. Tokyo: Kyūko shoin.

Shiyebu. 1933. *Zhongguo shiye zhi: Jiangsu sheng* (China industrial handbooks: Jiangsu province). 4 juan. n.p.

Sider, Gerald M. 1976. "Lumbee Indian Cultural Nationalism and Ethnogenesis," *Dialectical Anthropology*, 1.2: 161–72.

Silverblatt, Irene. 1978. "Andean Women in the Inca Empire," *Feminist Studies*, 4.Oct.: 37–61.

Smith, Arthur H. 1899. *Village Life in China*. New York: Fleming H. Ravell.

Smith, Carol. 1987. "Culture and Community: The Language of Class in Guatemala," in Mike Davis, ed., *The Year Left*, vol. 2, pp. 197–217. London: Verso.

So, Alvin Y. 1986. *The South China Silk District: Local Historical Transformation and World System Theory*. Albany: State Univ. of New York Press.

Songjiang fuzhi (Gazetteer of Songjiang prefecture). 1631. n.p.

Srivastava, Ravi. 1989. "Interlinked Modes of Exploitation in Indian Agriculture During Transition: A Case Study," *Journal of Peasant Studies*, 16.4: 493–522.

Stacey, Judith. 1983. *Patriarchy and Socialist Revolution in China*. Berkeley: Univ. of California Press.

Stavrianos, L. S. 1981. *Global Rift: The Third World Comes of Age*. New York: Morrow.

Stern, Steve J. 1993. "Africa, Latin America, and the Splintering of Historical Knowledge: From Fragmentation to Reverberation," in Cooper, Isaacman et al., listed above, pp. 3–20.

————. 1988. "Feudalism, Capitalism, and the World-System in the Perspective of Latin America and the Caribbean," *American Historical Review*, 93.4: 829–72.

Stitcher, Sharon. 1985. *Migrant Labourers*. Cambridge, Eng.: Cambridge Univ. Press.

Stoler, Ann Laura, and Frederick Cooper. 1997. "Between Metropole and Colony: Rethinking a Research Agenda," in Cooper and Stoler, listed above, pp. 1–56.

Stone, Lawrence. 1975. "The Rise of the Nuclear Family in Early Modern England: The Patriarchal Stage," in Charles E. Rosenberg, ed., *The Family in History*, pp. 13–57. Philadelphia: Univ. of Pennsylvania Press.

Stover, Leon E. 1974. *The Cultural Ecology of Chinese Civilization: Peasants and Elites in the Last of the Agrarian States*. New York: Pica Press.

Sudō Yoshiyuki. 1954. *Chūgoku tochi seido shi kenkyū* (Studies in the history of China's land tenure system). Tokyo: Tokyo Daigaku Shuppankai. 1971 reprint.

Sun Jingzhi, ed. 1959. *Huadong diqu jingji dili* (Economic geography of the east China region). Beijing: Kexueyuan. English translation: U.S. Joint Publications Research Service, no. 11438. Washington, D.C., 1961.

Sun Xiaocun. 1935. "Jinnianlai Zhongguo tianfu zengjia de sulu" (The rising rate of land tax in China in recent years), *Zhongguo nongcun*, 1.7: 35–41.

Sun Yutang, ed. 1957. *Zhongguo jindai gongyeshi ziliao* (Source materials on the history of Chinese industry), vol. 2. Beijing.

Sweezy, Paul, et al. 1967. *The Transition from Feudalism to Capitalism*. New York: Science and Society.

Takahashi Kosuke. 1978a. "Shin-matsu jinushisei no saihen to nōmin" (Peasants and the reorganization of the landlord system in the late Qing), in Nozawa Yutaka and Tanaka Masatoshi, eds., *Koza Chūgoku kin-gendai shi*, vol. 1, pp. 265–96. Tokyo: Tokyo Univ. Press.

————. 1978b. "Sōron" (Introduction), in Nozawa Yutaka and Tanaka Masatoshi, eds., *Kōza Chūgoku kin-gendai shi*, vol. 2. Tokyo: Tokyo Univ. Press.

————. 1977. "Shinchō hōken kokka ron e no ichi shiten" (A view of the theory that the Qing was a feudal state), *Reikishi hyōron*, 324.

Takahashi Yoshiro. 1978. "Sodai denko no mibun mondai" (The problem of the status of tenants in the Song), *Toyoshi kenkyu*, 37.3: 64–91.

Tanaka Issei. 1974. "Jūgoroku seiki o chūshin to suru Kōnan no chihogeki no henshitsuni tsuite" (Change in Jiangnan local operas in the 15th and 16th centuries), *Tōyō Bunka kenkyūjo kiyō*, 63: 1–40.

Tanaka Masatoshi. 1984a. "Rural Handicraft in Jiangnan in the Sixteenth and Seventeenth Centuries," in Grove and Daniels, listed above, pp. 79–100.

————. 1984b. "Popular Uprisings, Rent Resistance, and Bondservant Rebellions in the Late Ming," in Grove and Daniels, listed above, pp. 165–214.

————. 1972. "Chūgoku no henkaku to hōkensei kenkyū no kadai" (Themes in the study of China's feudal system and transformation), *Rekishi hyōron*, 271: 51–77.

Tanigawa Machio and Mori Masao, eds. 1983. *Chūgoku Minshū hanranshi* (History of collective action in China). 4 vols. Tokyo: Heibonsha.

Taniguchi Kikuo. 1980. "Peasant Rebellions in the Late Ming," *Acta Asiatica*, 38: 54–68.

Ter Haar, B. J. 1992. *The White Lotus Teachings in Chinese Religious History*. Leiden: E. J. Brill.

Terada Takanobu. 1958. "So Shō chihō ni okeru toshi no mengyō shōnin ni tsuite" (Merchants in the urban cotton industry in Suzhou and Songjiang prefectures), *Shirin*, 41.6: 56–68.

Thompson, E. P. 1963. *The Making of the English Working Class*. New York: Vintage Books.

Tibebu, Teshale. 1990. "On the Question of Feudalism, Absolutism, and Bourgeois Revolution," *Review*, 13.1: 49–151.

Tilly, Charles. 1979. "Protoindustrialization, Deindustrialization, and Just Plain Industrialization in European Capitalism," Univ. of Michigan, Center for Research on Social Organization Working Paper Series no. 235.

———, ed. 1975. *The Formation of National States in Western Europe*. Princeton, N.J.: Princeton Univ. Press.

Tong, James W. 1991. *Disorder Under Heaven: Collective Violence in the Ming Dynasty*. Stanford, Calif.: Stanford Univ. Press.

Tongruhai mianye gonghui mianchan tongji baogaoshu (The Nantong, Rugao, and Haimen Cotton Association's statistical report of cotton production). 1923–25. Comp. Tongruhai mianye gonghui. n.p.

Tongruhai mianye nianbao (Cotton industry yearbook for Nantong, Rugao, and Haimen). 1923–24. Comp. Tongruhai mianye gonghui. n.p.

Tonghai xinbao (The new Tonghai newspaper). 1920–24. Nantong.

Tongji xuebao (Statistical journal). 1929. Nanjing: Guomin zhengfu, lifayuan, tongjiju.

Tongtong ribao (The Tongtong News). 1935. Nantong.

Tongzhou xingban shiye zhi lishi (History of the establishment of industries in Nantong). [TZ]. 1910. 2 vols. Nantong.

Tongzhou zhi (Gazetteer of Tongzhou). 1577. 8 juan. n.p.

Tongzhou Zhili zhouzhi (Gazetteer of Tongzhou independent department). 1754, 22 juan; 1875 [TZZ], 16 juan. n.p.

Tregear, Thomas R. 1970. *An Economic Geography of China*. London: Butterworth's.

Turner, Victor W. 1969. *The Ritual Process: Structure and Anti-Structure*. Chicago: Aldine.

Turton, Andrew. 1984. "Limits of Ideological Domination and the Formation of Social Consciousness," in Andrew Turton and Shigeharu Tanabe, eds., *History and Peasant Consciousness in Southeast Asia*, pp. 19–73. Senri Ethnological Studies, no. 13. Osaka.

Turton, Andrew, and Shigeharu Tanabe. 1984. "Introduction," in Turton and Tanabe, eds., *History and Peasant Consciousness in Southeast Asia*, pp. 1–8. Senri Ethnological Studies, no. 13. Osaka.

Vlastos, Stephen. 1986. *Peasant Protests and Risings in Tokugawa Japan*. Berkeley: Univ. of California Press.

von Glahn, Richard. 1991. "Municipal Reform and Urban Social Conflict in Late Ming Jiangnan," *Journal of Asian Studies*, 50.2: 280–307.

Wada Masahiro. 1978. "Yōeki yūmen jōrei no tenkai to Minmatsu kyojinno hōteki ichi" (Ordinances concerning degree-holders' exemption privileges from labor service and the legal status of *yuren* in the late Ming), *Tōyō gakuhō*, 60.1–2: 93–131.

Wakeman, Frederic, Jr. 1993. "The Civil Society and Public Sphere Debate: Western Reflections on Chinese Political Culture," *Modern China* 19.2: 108–38.

———. 1986. "China and the Seventeenth Century Crisis," *Late Imperial China*, 7.1: 1–26.

———. 1985. *The Great Enterprise: The Manchu Reconstruction of Imperial Order in Seventeenth-Century China*. 2 vols. Berkeley: Univ. of California Press.

———. 1975. "Introduction: The Evolution of Local Control in Late Imperial China," in Frederic Wakeman, Jr., and Carolyn Grant, eds., *Conflict and Control in Late Imperial China*, pp. 1–25. Berkeley: Univ. of California Press.

Walker, Kathy Le Mons. 1993a. "Economic Growth, Peasant Marginalization, and the Sexual Division of Labor in Early Twentieth-Century China: Women's Work in Nantong County," *Modern China*, 19.3: 354–86.

———. 1993b. "Peasant Insurrection in China Reconsidered: A Preliminary Examination of the Jun Mountain Peasant Rising, Nantong County, 1863," *Journal of Peasant Studies*, 20.4: 640–68.

———. 1986. "Merchants, Peasants, and Industry: The Political Economy of Cotton Textiles, Nantong County, 1895–1935," Ph.D. diss., Univ. of California, Los Angeles.

Wallerstein, Immanuel. 1974. *The Modern World-System: Capitalist Agriculture and the Origins of the European World Economy in the Sixteenth Century*. New York: Academic Press.

Walthall, Ann. 1986. *Social Protest and Popular Culture in Eighteenth-Century Japan*. Tucson, Ariz.: Association for Asian Studies Monograph 43.

Wang Jingyu and Sun Yutang, eds. 1957. *Zhongguo jindai gongye shi ziliao* (Source materials on the history of modern Chinese industry). 2 vols. Beijing.

Wang Nanping. 1936. "Jiangbei nongcun shikuang" (Rural conditions in northern Jiangsu), in Qian Jialu, ed., *Zhongguo nongcun jingji lunwenji*, pp. 612–20. Shanghai: Zhonghua shuju.

Wang Xiangwu. 1982. "Jiefang qian Nantong gongye chengzhang de guocheng ji tedian" (The process and special features of industrial growth in Nantong prior to liberation), in NT [9], listed above, vol. 2, pp. 1–25.

Wang Yeh-chien. 1973. *Land Taxation in Imperial China, 1750–1911*. Cambridge, Mass.: Harvard Univ. Press.

Wang Zhen. 1313. *Nongshu* (Book on agriculture). Beijing: Nongye chubanshe, 1981.

Wang Zunwu. 1980. Personal interview at round-table meeting, Nantong Library, Dec. 17, 1980. [Wang is a former manager of a Hangzhuang cloth firm.]

Warren, Bill. 1980. *Imperialism: Pioneer of Capitalism*. London: New Left Books.

Watson, James L. 1985. "Standardizing the Gods: The Promotion of T'ien Hou ('Empress of Heaven') Along the South China Coast, 960–1960," in David Johnson et al., eds., *Popular Culture in Late Imperial China*, pp. 292–324. Berkeley: Univ. of California Press.

Watson, James L., and Evelyn Rawski, eds. 1988. *Death Ritual in Late Imperial China*. Berkeley: Univ. of California Press.

Watson, Rubie S. 1991. "Afterword: Marriage and Gender Inequality," in Rubie S. Watson and Patricia B. Ebrey, eds., pp. 347–68. Berkeley: Univ. of California Press.

Watson, Rubie S., and Patricia B. Ebrey, eds. 1991. *Marriage and Inequality in Chinese Society*. Berkeley: Univ. of California Press.

Whelan, T. S. 1979. *The Pawnshop in China*. Ann Arbor: Univ. of Michigan Center for Chinese Studies.

White, Benjamin. 1989. "Problems in the Empirical Analysis of Agrarian Differentiation," in Gillian Hart, Andrew Turton, and Benjamin White, eds., *Agrarian Transformations: Local Processes and the State in Southeast Asia*, pp. 15-30. Berkeley: Univ. of California Press.

Wiens, Mi Chu. 1988. "Social Change and Fiscal Reform in the Fifteenth Century," *Ming Studies*, no. 26: 18-36.

———. 1980. "Lord and Peasant: The Sixteenth to the Eighteenth Century," *Modern China*, 6.1: 3-39.

———. 1979. "Masters and Bondservants: Peasant Rage in the Seventeenth Century," *Ming Studies*, no. 8: 57-64.

———. 1974. "Cotton Textile Production and Rural Social Transformation in Early Modern China," *Zhongguo wenxue yanjiu suo xuebao*, 7.2: 515-34.

Wiens, Thomas B. 1992. "Trends in the Late Qing and Republican Rural Economy: Reality or Illusion?" *Republican China*, 18.1: 63-76.

Winn, Peter. 1986. *Weavers of Revolution: The Yarur Workers and Chile's Road to Socialism*. Oxford: Oxford Univ. Press.

Wolf, Eric P. 1969. *Peasant Wars of the Twentieth Century*. New York: Harper & Row.

Wong, Young-Tsu. 1977. "Popular Unrest and the 1911 Revolution in Jiangsu," *Modern China*, 3.3: 321-44.

Wou, Odoric Y. K. 1994. *Mobilizing the Masses: Building Revolution in Henan*. Stanford, Calif.: Stanford Univ. Press.

Wu Chengming. 1985. *Zhongguo zibenzhuyi de mengya* (The sprouts of capitalism in China). Beijing: Renmin chubanshe.

———. 1983. "Lun Qingdai qianqi woguo guonei shichang" (On China's national market in the early Qing), *Lishi yanjiu*, 1: 98-106.

Wu Huisheng. 1980a. "Dasheng's Cotton Collection System." Paper presented at round-table meeting, No. 1 Textile Factory, Nantong, March 24, 1980.

———. 1980b. "Dasheng's Relations with Cloth and Cotton Firms." Paper presented at round-table meeting, No. 1 Textile Factory, Nantong, Dec. 19, 1980.

Wu, Leonard T. K. 1935. "China's Paradox: Prosperous Banks in National Crisis," *Far Eastern Survey*, 4.6: 41-46.

Wu Zhi. 1935. *Xiangcun zhibu gongye de yige yanjiu* (A study of rural textile industry). Shanghai: Shangwu yinshuguan.

Xi Jin shi xiaolu (Supplement to the Wuxi and Jingui gazetteers). 1753. n.p.

Xiao Zheng, ed. 1977. *Minguo ershi niandai Zhongguo dalu tudi wenti ziliao* (Materials on the land problem in mainland China during the 1930's). 200 vols. Taibei: Taibei chengwen chuban youxian gongsi.

Xu Chaoming. 1985. "Zhangzhishan shihua" (On the history of Zhangzhishan), in NT [6], listed above, vol. 5, pp. 1-4.

Xu Dixin. 1947. *Guanliao ziben lun* (On bureaucratic capitalism). Hong Kong.

Xu Guangqi. 1982. "Nantong jinrongye lishi ziliao" (Source materials on the history of the financial industry in Nantong), in NT [9], listed above, vol. 2, pp. 47-68.

Xu Xianzhong. 1564. *Wuxing zhangguji* (Historical materials on Wuxing). n.p.

Xu Xinwu. 1988. "The struggle of the handicraft cotton industry against machine textiles in China," *Modern China*, 14.1: 31–50.

———. 1981. *Yapin zhanzheng gian Zhongguo mian fangzhi shougongye de shangpin shengchan yu zibenzhuyi mengya wenti* (Commodity production in the cotton spinning and weaving industries in China before the Opium War and the problem of the sprouts of capitalism). n.p.: Jiangsu renmin chubanshe.

Xue Yunsheng. 1970. *Duli cunyi* (Concentration on doubtful matters while perusing the substatutes). Ed. Huang Jingjiu. 5 vols. Taibei: Chengwen chubanshe.

Yan Zhongping. 1963. *Zhongguo mianfangzhi shigao* (Draft history of cotton textiles in China). Beijing: Kexue chubanshe.

Yang Guozhen. 1988. *Ming-Qing tudi giyue wenshu yanjiu* (Studies in land contracts and documents of the Ming-Qing period). Beijing: Renmin chubanshe.

Yang, Phil Seung. 1988. "The Peasants of Suzhou, 1863–1945: Family Farms in Agrarian China." Ph.D. diss., Univ. of California, Los Angeles.

Yangzhou shifan xueyuan, comp. 1963. *Xinhai geming Jiangsu digu shiliao* (Historical materials on the 1911 revolution in the Jiangsu district). Nanjing: Jiangsu renmin chubanshe.

Yao Ruiguang. 1967. *Minfa wuguan lun* (On proprietorship in the civil codes). Taibei: Dazhongguo dushu gongsi.

Yazawa Kosuke. 1961. "Minkoku chūki no Chūgoku ni okeru nōminsō bunkai to sono seikaku" (The character of peasant differentiation in mid-Republican China), *Shakai keizai shigaku*, 27.3: 59–86.

Ye Mengzhu. 1936. *Yue shi bian* (Chapters based on the experience of life), in *Shanghai zhanggu congshu*, vol. 1. Ed. Shanghai tongshe. Shanghai: Zhonghua shuju.

Ye Xianen. 1981. "The Tenant-Servant System in Huizhou Prefecture, Anhui," *Social Sciences in China*, 1. March: 90–119.

———. 1979. "Ming-Qing Huizhou dianpu zhi shitan" (An inquiry into tenant-servants in Huizhou in the Ming-Qing), *Zhongshan daxue xuebao*, 2: 57–84.

Yin Yuepu. 1980. "The Bank of China and Nantong's Textile Industry," report and personal interview at round-table meeting, Nantong Library, Nantong, Dec. 18, 1980. [Yin is a former official of the Bank of China's Nantong branch.]

Yip Honming. 1988. "The Political Economy of Tobacco and Textiles, Weixian, Shandong." Ph.D. diss., Univ. of California, Los Angeles.

Yokohama Suguru. 1960–61. "Shindai ni okeru tambugyō no keiei ketai" (The structure of the cotton calendering industry in the Qing period), *Tōyō shi kenkyū*, 2 parts 19.3: 23–26; 19.4: 19–36.

You Qing. 1936. "Qidong nongcun jingji yu zudian zhidu" (The rural economy and land tenure system in Qidong), *Nonghang yuekan*, June: 57–81.

Yu Yikong. 1982. "Jiefang qian Nantong shangye fazhan jianshi" (A short history of commercial development in Nantong before liberation), in NT [9], listed above, vol. 2, pp. 28–47.

———. 1981. "Xinhai geming shi de Nantong shanghui" (The Nantong Chamber of Commerce at the time of the 1911 revolution), in NT [9], listed above, vol. 1, pp. 142–43.

Zhan Ran. [1934]. "Nantong de nongcun" (Rural villages of Nantong), in Feng Hefa, comp., *Zhongguo noncun jingji ziliao xubian*, pp. 24–26. Shanghai: Liming shuju, 1935.

Zhang Jian. 1931. *Zhang jizi jiulu* (Nine collections of Zhang Jian's essays). Ed. Zhang Xiaoruo. Shanghai: Zhonghua shuju.

Zhang Jintao. 1980. "Relations Between the Nantong Cloth Firms and Native Banks." Report and personal interview at round-table meeting, Nantong Library, Nantong, Dec. 18, 1980. [Zhang is a former manager of a Nantong cloth firm.]

Zhang Renren. 1915–16. "Nantong xian nongye gaikuang" (The general condition of agriculture in Nantong), *Nongshang gongbao*. 3 parts, 2.4: 1–12; 2.5: 9–20; 2.6: 7–22.

Zhang Xiaoruo. 1930. *Nantong Zhang jizhi xiansheng zhuanji* (Biography of Mr. Zhang Jian of Nantong). Shanghai: Zhonghua shuju.

Zhang Yiyong. 1935. "Jiangsu de tudi fenpei he zudian zhidu" (Land distribution and the tenure system in Jiangsu), *Zhongguo nongcun*, 1.8: 183–93.

Zhang Youyi, ed. 1957. *Zhongguo jindai nongyeshi ziliao* (Source materials on the agricultural history of modern China), vols. 2 and 3. Beijing: Sanlian shudian.

Zhang Yulan. 1957. *Zhongguo yinhangye fazhanshi* (A history of the development of the Chinese banking industry). Shanghai.

Zhang Zhiqing. 1980. "Native Banks and the Textile Industry in Nantong." Report and personal interview at round-table meeting, Nantong Library, Dec. 18, 1980. [Zhang is a former bank manager.]

"Zhongguo gongchandang lingdaoxia de Nantong diqu de kangri douzheng" (The struggle against Japan in the Nantong district under the leadership of the Chinese Communist Party). 1985. In NT [9], listed above, vol. 5, pp. 1–16.

"Zhongguo mianye yu Riben zhi guani" (The relationship between the Chinese cotton industry and Japan). 1917. *Nongshang gongbao* 3.10: 1–4.

Zhou Shengzi [ZSZ] (Annals of Tongzhou). [1645?] Comp. Shao Qian. 8 juan. n.p.

Zhu Fucheng. 1977. *Jiangsu Shatian zhi Yanjiu* (Research on the "sand fields" of Jiangsu), Vol. 69 of Xiao Zheng, ed., *Minguo ershi niandai Zhongguo dalu tudi wenti ziliao*. Taibei: Taibei chengwen chuban youxian gongsi.

Zhu Huchen. 1980. "Rugao diandangye qingkuang" (The situation of the pawnshop industry in Rugao), in RG, vol. 1, pp. 91–92.

Zhu Mingxia and Bian Xiaozhi. 1986. "Dongtai xian Beisanchang he Donghe liangchang nongmin fankang zhengshou kenmujuan de douzheng" (The peasant struggle against the collection of reclamation taxes in Beishanchang and Donghe reclaimed areas of Dongtai county), in JS [9], listed above, vol. 18, pp. 167–73.

Zhu Zhangmin and Cheng Yun. 1984. "Buji shengsheng chang Xingren" (The continuing sound of the loom in Xingren), in NT [6], listed above, vol. 2, pp. 7–9.

Zou Qiang. 1984. "Jiefang qian Nantong diqu de mianhua shengchan" (Cotton production in the Nantong district before liberation), in NT [6], listed above, vol. 2, pp. 31–37.

Zurndorfer, Harriet T. 1989. *Change and Continuity in Chinese Local History: The Development of Hui-chou Prefecture, 800–1800*. Leiden: E. J. Brill.

Character List

I have omitted all well-known place-names, personal names, and terms from this list.

Andongbang　安東幫

baidabu　白大布
Bailianjiao　白蓮敎
Bailian *jiaozhu*　白蓮敎主
Banjing (zhen)　搬經 (鎮)
banyu　半預
Baoanhui　保安會
Baochang　包場
baohuang　報荒
baojia　保申
Baotanhui　保坍會
Beishan　北山
benzhuang　本莊
Bi　畢
Bigongda　畢公大
buzhuang　布莊

Changzhou (fu/xian)　常州
chaisizhuang　差絲莊
chaozhuang　抄莊
Chen Ziyu　陳子迁
Cheng Yugang　程玉崗
chenghanchuan　承旱船
chepiao　折票
chitaobu　尺套布
Chongming (xian)　崇明 (縣)
Chuanggang　川港
chuanhaobang　船號幫
Chuansha (xian)　川沙 (縣)
Chuiwei　翠微
Chuiwei shishe　翠微詩社
cubu　粗布

da Ningbobang　大寧波幫
Dachang (zhichang)　大昌 (紙廠)
dachibu　大尺布
Dada (neihe lunchuan gongsi)　大達
　(內河輪船公司)
Dada (waijiang lunchuan gongsi)
　大達 (外江輪船公司)
Dadaohui　大刀會
Dafeng　大豐
Dafu　大阜
Dagang　大綱
daizhuang　帶莊
Dalai　大賚
Dalong (zaochang)　大隆 (皁廠)
Dasheng (shachang)　大生 (紗廠)
Dashengkui　大生魁
Datong (hangye zhuanyun gongsi)　大
　通 (航業轉公司)
Daxian (yan gongsi)　大顯 (鹽轉公司)
Daxing (mianchang)　大興 (面廠)
Dayou　大祐
Dayoujin　大有晉
Dayu　大豫
Dazhong (tongyun gonghang)　大中
　(通運公行)
Dazhonghua (shachang)　大中華 (沙
　廠)
Deji　得記
dianhu　佃戶
dianhuhui　佃戶會
dianpu　佃僕
diding yin　地頂銀
dingshou yin　頂首銀
dongbuzhou　東布州

Donglin　東林
Dongtai (xian)　東台 (縣)
Dongyang (xian)　東陽 (縣)
Du Jialu　杜家祿
dunzhuang　躉莊
duozhuang　掇莊

Fan di　範隄
Fan Ying　樊英
Fan Zhongyan　範仲淹
fenzhuang　分莊
Funing (xian)　阜甯 (縣)
Fusheng　阜生
Fuxin (mianfen gongsi)　复新 (面粉公司)
Fuyu　阜餘

Gao Anjiu　高安九
Gao Liqing　高笠卿
gong　公
Gong Shangwen　公尙文
Gongdachang　公大昌
gonghui　公會
Gu Baiyan　顧百言
guandu shangban　官督商辦
guanli　官利
Guangqin (shachang)　廣勤 (紗廠)
Guangsheng (youchang)　廣生 (油廠)
guanzhuang (*bu*)　關莊 (布)
Gulongchang　顧隆昌
gunu　雇奴

Haimen (ting/xian)　海門 (廳/縣)
Haiying　海營
hang　行
Hangzhuang　杭莊
Hanmulin (yinshuju)　翰墨林 (印書局)
haobang　號幫
haojia　豪家
He Liangjun　何良俊
He Tianlin　何天林
Hede　合德
Hengfenghe　恆丰和

Hengji　恆記
Hengshengfuji　恆生福記
Hengxiang　橫巷
Hongbang　紅幫
hou　侯
Huacheng　華成
Huafeng　華豐
huahang　花行
huahao　花號
Huainan　淮南
Huang Bichen　黃辟塵
huipiao　匯票
Huzhou (fu)　湖州 (府)

Jiading (xian)　嘉定 (縣)
jian　件
Jiang Chunping　江春平
Jiangbei　江北
Jiangnan　江南
Jiangyin (xian)　江陰 (縣)
Jiangzaogang　姜灶港
Jiaxing (fu)　嘉興 (府)
jie　界
jingzhuang　京莊
Jinsha (zhen)　金沙 (鎮)
jinshi　進士
Jiuda　久大
Jiulong　久隆
Junshan　軍山

kebang　客幫
Kobayashi Kazumi　小林一美

Langshan　狼山
Li Boyan　李伯言
Li Houyou　李厚祐
Li Jisheng　李計生
Li Shengbo　李昇伯
Li Yongchang　李泳裳
liangmin　良民
liangzhang　糧長
lijia　里甲
Lin Jubai　林舉百

Lin Men 林門
Lin Zuobo 林左波
Linji 林記
Liu Guixin 劉桂馨
Liu Housheng 劉厚生
Liu Kunyi 劉坤一
Liu Xuchu 劉旭初
Liu Yishan 劉一山
Liuhaisha 劉海沙
Liujia 六甲
Liuqiao 劉橋
Liuzhengda 劉正大
Liyong (shachang) 利用 (紗廠)
Lu Xisan 盧錫三
Lüsi 呂四
Luwanchang 陸完昌

Ma Yunxi 馬運溪
Ma Zhenting 馬振庭
Mao (zhen) 茅 (鎮)
maishen 賣身
Mao jia (zhen) 茅家 (鎮)
minbian 民變
Mingji 明記
minsheng 民生
Mori Masao 森正大

NanTongzhou zongshanghui 南通州
    總商會
nangong nuzhi 男工女織
naohuang 鬧荒
Nanshan 南山
Nantong 南通
Niida Noboru 仁井田陞
Ningbobang 寧波幫
Nishijima Sadao 西島定生
Nuan ge 暖閣
nupu 奴僕

Oyama Masaaki 小山正明

Pan Zhizhong 潘治中
pi 匹

Pingchao 平潮
Pudong 浦東

qianke 捐客
Qianrenhui 千人會
qianzhuang 錢莊
Qiao Qiming 喬啓明
Qidong (xian) 啓東 (縣)
qinglanbang 青籃幫
Qixinhui 齊心會
Quanchang 全長
quane yuzu 全額預租

Renyuanhao 仁元號
Renyuanxin 仁源新
Rugao (xian) 如皋 (縣)

sanbang 散幫
Santaihe 三泰和
Sanyutou 三圩頭
Shabu gongsuo 沙布公所
shanghui 商會
shanshu 善書
shatian 沙田
Shen Jingfu 瀋敬夫
Shen Shike 沈時可
Shen Xiejun 瀋諧均
shendaohui 神道會
shendong 紳董
Sheng Xuanhuai 盛宣懷
Shengkang (qianzhuang) 升康 (錢莊)
Shenji 慎記
shenpiao 申票
shenzhuang 申莊
Shian 石安
shidafu 士大夫
shiye jingweituan 實業警衛團
shouhua xitong 收花系統
Shunji 順記
Shunkang (qianzhuang) 順康 (錢莊)
Song Qi 宋乞
Songjiang (fu/xian) 松江 (府/縣)
Subei 蘇北

Suiji　遂濟
Suzhou (fu)　蘇州 (府)

Tai (xian)　泰 (縣)
Taicang (zhou)　太倉 (州)
Taiji　泰記
Tailong (qianzhuang)　泰隆 (錢莊)
Taixing (xian)　泰興 (縣)
Taizhou　泰州
Tanaka Masatoshi　田中正俊
Tang Shouqian　湯壽潛
Tangjia　唐家
Tangjiaza　唐家閘
Taoyuanchang　陶元昌
Tianhou Shengmu　天後聖母
Tian gangdang　天罡黨
tianye (lianhehui)　田業 (聯合會)
Tongbang　通幫
Tonghai kenmo gongsi　通海墾牧公司
Tonghaiyuan　通海源
Tongrentai (yanye gongsi)　通仁泰 (鹽業公司)
Tongsui　通遂
Tongyuanxin　通源信
Tongzhou (zhili zhou)　通州 (直隸州)
toukao　投靠
touxian　投獻
Touzongmiao　頭紙廟
tubu　土布
tuchan tuxiao　土產土銷

waisha　外沙
waituo　外托
Wang Shaolan　汪少蘭
Wang Yunchao　汪雲巢
Wang Ziqing　王子清
Wangzhengda　王正大
Wangzhengyuan　王正源
Wei Zhongxuan　魏中軒
Weigonghe　魏公和
Wu Didu　吳氏獨
Wu Dounan　吳斗南
wulai　無賴
wusheng laomu　無生老母

Wuqing (xian)　烏青 (縣)
Wuxi (xian)　無錫 (縣)

Xi Zhongping　習仲屏
xiang　鄉
xiangbang　鄉邦
Xiangji　翔記
Xiangshan (xian)　象山 (縣)
xiangshen　鄉紳
xiangping　鄉評
xianzhuang　縣莊
xianzu　現租
Xiaobu　小布
Xiaohai　小海
xiaonong jiazhangzhi　小農家長製
xibu　稀布
Xiehongqiao　斜洪橋
xindi　新地
Xing Yingchu　邢螾初
Xingjiayuan　邢家園
Xingren　興仁
Xingyongshu　邢永順
Xinji　新記
Xinnan　新南
Xintong　新通
xinzheng　新政
Xiting　西亭
Xixi　西溪
Xu Shulan　徐樹蘭
Xunwu　尋烏
Xuzhou　徐州

Yancheng (xian)　鹽城 (縣)
Yang Xiuqing　楊秀清
Yang Yi　楊逸
yangjing benwei　洋經本緯
Yangzhou　揚州
Yao Yongji　姚永濟
Yazawa Kosuke　安野省三
Yijiaohui　一角會
Yingkou　營口
Yisheng (niangzao gongsi)　頤生 (釀造公司)
yitian liangzhu　一田兩主

Yongan　永安
Yongchanglin　永昌林
Yu Dahua　余大花
Yu Xuexian　余學先
Yuansheng (qianzhuang)　源生 (錢莊)
Yuan Shikai　袁世凱
Yuandeji　源得記
Yuanguoji　遠國記
Yuanzaogang　遠灶港
Yudong　余東
Yuxi　余西
Yuyan　余鹽
yuzu　預租

Zesheng (shuili gongsi)　澤生水利公司
Zhang Cha　張詧
Zhang Jian　張謇
Zhang Jingpu　張靜甫
Zhang Jingxuan　章靜軒
Zhang Keqi　張克岐
Zhang Keqian　張克謙

Zhang Ren　張仁
Zhang Weishan　章維善
Zhang Xiaoruo　張孝若
Zhang Xuyan　張叔儼
Zhang Zhidong　張之洞
Zhangyuanda　章源大
Zhengdahe　正大和
Zhendong (shi)　震東市
Zhenjiang　鎮江
Zhongfu　中孚
Zhonghexing　中和興
Zhuizuju　追租局
Zisheng (tiechang)　資生 (鐵廠)
zhuangpiao　莊票
zhuangyuan　莊園
zhuanli　專利
ziqiang　自強
zizhi　自治
zizhi gongsuo　自治公所
zongshanghui　總商會
zuozhuang　坐莊

Index

In this index an "f" after a number indicates a separate reference on the next page, and an "ff" indicates separate references on the next two pages. A continuous discussion over two or more pages is indicated by a span of page numbers, e.g., "57-59." *Passim* is used for a cluster of references in close but not consecutive sequence.

Agrarian class relations, 11f, 39, 80–82, 170f, 174, 195f, 204, 239f, 246f. *See also* Landlord-tenant relations

Agrarian class struggles, 12, 32, 50, 65–84 *passim*, 160–70 *passim*, 185, 198–203 *passim*, 225–35 *passim*, 243–46 *passim*. *See also* Class conflict/struggle; Modern landlordism; Peasant struggles/resistance

Agrarian transitions, 4, 220f, 236, 245, 281n8. *See also* Capitalism

Agricultural laborers, 39, 48, 69, 161, 194, 205, 216

Agriculturally specialized districts, 22, 181, 186, 203–6 *passim*, 214, 221, 234

Agricultural wage labor, *see* Labor

Agricultural wages, 175, 189–93 *passim*, 216

Agriculture, 18, 33, 49, 73, 183, 188, 193, 205, 208, 213, 260n13; productivity in, 21, 220, 235, 239; and separation from household industry, 22, 74, 203, 236; history in China, 29–30, 53; cropping patterns, 31, 183, 211–13; and household industry, 40–41, 50–51, 74, 204–9; female labor, 70, 192–95, 211ff, 214–19 *passim*, 238, 276n7, 277n8; control by urban capital, 198, 237. *See also* Agriculturally specialized districts; Peasant family production/economy; Petty commodity production/economy; Subsistence farming/economy; *and specific crops by name*

Alternative histories, 4f, 79, 242, 247

Alternative nationalisms, 164, 169, 171, 229, 244–48 *passim*

Alternative visions of peasants, 9–10, 23, 44, 281

Amano Motonosuke, 278n15

Anhui Province, 54, 66, 179

"Anti-Western" Uprising (Chuansha, 1911), 166

Bandits, 65, 116, 150, 176, 218, 229, 273n10, 275n8, 280n10

Bank of China, 145–50 *passim*, 273nn6, 8, 10. *See also* Banks, modern

Bank of Communications, 146f

Bank of Jiangsu, 146f

Banks, modern, 145–50, 273nn6, 7

Banks, native, 55f, 90–93 *passim*, 133–39 *passim*, 146f, 272n1. *See also under* Dasheng Mills

Baohuang ("Reporting a poor harvest"), 184. *See also* Peasant struggles/resistance

Baran, Paul, 267n3

Barley, 211–13. *See also* Subsistence farming/economy

Bell, Lynda, 241, 268n10, 274n3

Bergère, Marie-Claire, 129, 131

Bernhardt, Kathryn, 10, 160f, 199

Bernstein, Henry, 250, 282n9

Bianco, Lucien, 274n4

Big Sword Society (Dadaohui), 168, 230, 275nn7, 8

Bondservants (*nupu*), 32–34, 61, 66–67, 258n6, 259nn8, 9, 263n8; history of, 32, 259n7; female, 37–39, 41; in twentieth century, 261n21, 277n10. *See also* Patriarchal landlordism; *under* Peasant struggles/resistance

Bourdieu, Pierre, 10, 257n14

Brandt, Loren, 162f, 202f, 257n17

Brass, Tom, 195

Brenner, Robert, 8, 257n13

Brokers, 35, 55, 89, 96ff, 121, 145. *See also* Ningbo clique

Bu, 207

Library of Congress Cataloging-in-Publication Data

Walker, Kathy Le Mons.
    Chinese modernity and the peasant path :
semicolonialism in the Northern Yangzi Delta /
Kathy Le Mons Walker.
        p.   cm.
    Includes bibliographical references and index.
    ISBN 0-8047-2932-8
    1. Peasantry—China—Yangtze River Delta—History.
2. Yangtze River Delta (China)—Social conditions.
3. Yangtze River Delta (China)—Economic conditions.
I. Title.
HD1537.C5W35   1999
305.5′633′09512—dc21
                                                        98-20035
                                                            CIP
                                                            Rev.

⊗   This book is printed on acid-free, recycled paper.

Original printing 1999
Last figure below indicates year of this printing:
08   07   06   05   04   03   02   01   00   99